Reporting at the Southern Borders

Undocumented immigration across the Mediterranean and the US-Mexican border is one of the most contested transatlantic public and political issues, raising fundamental questions about national identity, security, and multiculturalism—all in the glare of news media themselves undergoing dramatic transformations.

This interdisciplinary, international volume fills a major gap in political science and communication literature on the role of news media in public debates over immigration by providing unique insiders' perspectives on journalistic practices and bringing them into dialogue with scholars and immigrant-rights practitioners.

After providing original comparative research by established and emerging international affairs and media scholars as well as grounded reflections by UN and International Organization for Migration (IOM) practitioners, the book presents candid, in-depth assessments by nine leading European and North American journalists covering immigration from the frontlines, ranging from the *Guardian*'s Southern Europe editor to the immigration reporter for the *Arizona Republic*. Their comparative reflections on the professional, institutional, and technological constraints shaping news stories offer unprecedented insight into the challenges and opportunities for 21st-century journalism to affect public discourse and policymaking about issues critical to the future of the transatlantic space, making the book relevant across a wide range of scholarship on the media's impact on public affairs.

Giovanna Dell'Orto is an assistant professor at the School of Journalism and Mass Communication at the University of Minnesota and a former immigration reporter with The Associated Press (AP) in the United States and Italy. She received her PhD in mass communication from the University of Minnesota. Her AP articles have appeared in all major US newspapers, including the *New York Times*, and in the international press, including the *International Herald Tribune*. Her research and teaching interests focus on the role of the news media and of mediated discourses and national identity in international affairs, especially in transatlantic relations, historically and currently.

Vicki L. Birchfield is an associate professor in The Sam Nunn School of International Affairs at the Georgia Institute of Technology and director of the study-abroad program on the European Union and transatlantic relations. She served as director of the European Union Center of Excellence from 2008 to 2011 and currently codirects the Center for European and Transatlantic Studies. Birchfield received a DES from the Graduate Institute of International Studies from the University of Geneva, Switzerland, and a PhD in political science from the University of Georgia. Her research and teaching specializations are European politics, the European Union, comparative politics, and international political economy. Other research and intellectual interests include the interplay of capitalism and democracy, social movements and the politics of globalization, and transatlantic relations. She has been a visiting scholar at Sciences Po, Paris, and the University of Bordeaux and has been bestowed the honor of "Chevalier dans l'Ordre national du Mérite" (Knight in the National Order of Merit) by the French government.

Routledge Studies in Global Information, Politics and Society

**Edited by Kenneth Rogerson, Duke University and
Laura Roselle, Elon University**

International communication encompasses everything from one-to-one cross-cultural interactions to the global reach of a broad range of information and communications technologies and processes. *Routledge Studies in Global Information, Politics and Society* celebrates—and embraces—this depth and breadth. To completely understand communication, it must be studied in concert with many factors, since, most often, it is the foundational principle on which other subjects rest. This series provides a publishing space for scholarship in the expansive, yet intersecting, categories of communication and information processes and other disciplines.

Reporting at the Southern Borders

Journalism and Public Debates on
Immigration in the US and the EU

**Edited by Giovanna Dell'Orto
and Vicki L. Birchfield**

NEW YORK AND LONDON

First published 2014
by Routledge
711 Third Avenue, New York, NY 10017

Simultaneously published in the UK
by Routledge
2 Park Square, Milton Park, Abingdon, Oxon OX14 4RN

*Routledge is an imprint of the Taylor & Francis Group,
an informa business*

Library of Congress Cataloging-in-Publication Data

Reporting at the southern borders : journalism and public debates on
  immigration in the US and the EU / edited by Giovanna Dell'Orto and
  Vicki L. Birchfield.
    pages cm. — (Routledge studies in global information, politics and
society ; 2)
  1. United States—Emigration and immigration—Press coverage.
2. Immigrants—United States—Press coverage.   3. Mass media and
immigrants—United States.   4. European Union countries—Emigration
and immigration—Press coverage.   5. Immigrants—European
Union countries—Press coverage.   6. Mass media and immigrants—
European Union countries.   I. Dell'Orto, Giovanna, 1977– editor of
compilation.   II. Birchfield, Vicki L., 1965– editor of compilation.
  PN4888.I518R46 2013
  070.4'4930482—dc23
  2013013844

ISBN: 978-0-415-83588-6 (hbk)
ISBN: 978-0-203-49979-5 (ebk)

Typeset in Sabon
by Apex CoVantage, LLC

To all the courageous journalists on the border beat

Contents

PART III
Lampedusa and Schengen: Covering Immigration in
Today's Europe

PART IV
Fences and the Far West: Covering Immigration
in the United States

Tables and Figures

Acknowledgments

This project originated from a research collaborative grant from the University of Minnesota's Center for German and European Studies, directed by Sabine Engel, which led to an innovative graduate seminar team-taught by Birchfield and Dell'Orto, joining our students in Atlanta and Minneapolis via ITV. We are most grateful to CGES, the University of Minnesota's School of Journalism and Mass Communication (SJMC, particularly the generous support of director Al Tims) and the Georgia Institute of Technology's Sam Nunn School of International Affairs, for their encouragement.

In April 2012, we convened a workshop with all the contributors to this book at the University of Minnesota, which was sponsored, in addition to CGES and the SJMC, by the following programs at the University of Minnesota: Institute for Diversity, Equity and Advocacy; the Institute for Global Studies; the European Studies Consortium; and the following programs at the University of Minnesota: the department of political science; the department of French and Italian; Global Programs and Strategy Alliance; the Learning Abroad Center; and the Immigration History Research Center. SJMC graduate students provided essential support to the conference as well.

This book of course would not exist without our scholarly contributors had our professional contributors not taken time out of impossibly busy schedules to travel to Minneapolis and write exceptionally candid accounts of their practices. For their efforts and their refreshing insights, we want to thank all of them and recognize the support they received from their organizations: The Associated Press, the *Houston Chronicle, Corriere della Sera, Le Figaro, The Guardian,* the International Organization for Migration, *Le Monde, la Repubblica,* the *Arizona Republic,* the *El Paso Times,* and the United Nations Alliance of Civilizations. Dell'Orto also thanks The AP, where she worked as an immigration reporter in the Phoenix and Atlanta bureaus, especially Barry Bedlan, Steve Elliott, Ed Montes, and Maryann Mrowca.

Our contributors are among the dedicated, courageous journalists who brave dangers ranging from political controversy to cartel violence to report on a complex yet fundamental topic that affects us all. This book offers an objective analysis of their challenges and impacts. On this page, we want to also acknowledge their passion for work that greatly affects the public good. It is in recognition of that brave effort that we dedicate this book to border journalists.

Series Foreword

Communications studies holds a lure for scholars simply because it connects media processes, technological innovations, and people. This field of study can be applied to an infinite variety of topics and situations. One purpose of this series is to explore these interactions in innovative and inspiring ways.

Giovanna Dell'Orto and Vicki Birchfield have aggregated for us a sweeping example of how media studies can help us better understand the complex phenomenon of immigration. While there are a multitude of factors that have an impact on how immigration unfolds around the world, the media are assuredly among the most important.

This volume combines the perspectives of scholars, media professionals, and those who work directly with the immigrants themselves, producing a stimulating conversation that digs deeply into the intricacies and nuances of media control, diffusion, messaging, and interpretation. Academics, practitioners, policymakers, and individuals interested in both media and migration should find answers and steps forward in this work.

—Kenneth Rogerson and Laura Roselle, Series Editors

Contributors

Gervais Appave is the Special Policy Adviser to the Director General of the International Organization for Migration. He was the founding director of the Migration Policy, Research and Communication Department at the IOM between 2001 and 2006. Between 1997 and 2001 he was the head and coordinator of the Intergovernmental Consultations on Asylum, Refugee and Migration Policies in Europe, North America and Australia. He holds a BA degree (Hons) from the University of Sydney.

Stephen Bennett is a doctoral student in mass communication at the University of Minnesota, a former adjunct instructor of Middle East history at Illinois State University, and a former researcher and editorial intern at the Institute of Jerusalem Studies in Ramallah.

Rodney Benson is an associate professor in the Department of Media, Culture, and Communication at New York University and has been a visiting professor at universities in Denmark, France, Germany, and Norway. His research and critical essays have been published in the *American Sociological Review,* the *Journal of Communication, Le Monde Diplomatique,* and the *Christian Science Monitor.* Benson is the coeditor of *Bourdieu and the Journalistic Field* (Polity, 2005) and the author of *Shaping Immigration News: A French-American Comparison* (Cambridge, 2013).

Vicki L. Birchfield is an associate professor in The Sam Nunn School of International Affairs at the Georgia Institute of Technology. She is the author of *Income Inequality in Capitalist Democracies: The Interplay of Values and Institutions* (Penn State University Press, 2008) and *Toward a Common EU Energy Policy: Problems, Progress, and Prospects* (Palgrave Macmillan, 2011), coedited with John S. Duffield. She has published articles in *International Studies Quarterly,* the *European Journal of Political Research,* the *Review of International Studies, Globalizations,* the *Journal of European Public Policy,* and the *Review of International Political Economy.* She has been a visiting scholar at Sciences Po, Paris, and the University of Bordeaux and has been bestowed the honor of "Chevalier dans l'Ordre national du Mérite" (Knight in the National Order of Merit) by the French government.

Lourdes Cárdenas is a Mexican journalist with more than 20 years' experience working as an editor, producer, correspondent, and reporter for American and Mexican media in both print and television. Since June 2011, she has been at the *El Paso Times,* in charge of SomosFrontera, a Spanish-language electronic publication. Previously, she taught journalism at the University of Texas at El Paso. She has a master's degree in journalism from the University of Southern California and an MFA in creative writing from the University of Texas at El Paso, and she was a 2001 Nieman Fellow at Harvard University.

Jean-Philippe Chauzy was until early 2013 the spokesperson and the head of the Media and Communication Department at the International Organization for Migration. He led IOM's global media and communications strategy and advised the director general, deputy director general and senior staff, both at headquarters and in the field, on strategic communication matters, covering a wide range of often complex and sensitive migration issues. Prior to joining the Organization, Chauzy worked throughout the 1990s as a senior producer at Bush House, the home of the BBC World Service, and as a BBC regional correspondent in West Africa. He is now director of communications at the UN World Food Programme.

Jack Citrin is Heller Professor of Political Science and Director, Institute of Governmental Studies at the University of California, Berkeley. He received his BA and MA from McGill University and his PhD from UC Berkeley. His publications include *Tax Revolt, Something for Nothing in California* (coauthor, Harvard University Press, 1982); "American Identity and the Politics of Ethnic Change," *Journal of Politics,* 1990; and *American Identity and the Politics of Multiculturalism* (Cambridge, 2014).

Giovanna Dell'Orto is an assistant professor at the School of Journalism and Mass Communication at the University of Minnesota, where she received her PhD in 2004, and a former immigration reporter with The Associated Press in the United States and Italy. She is the author of *American Journalism and International Relations: Foreign Correspondence from the Early Republic to the Digital Era* (Cambridge University Press, 2013); *The Hidden Power of the American Dream: Why Europe's Shaken Confidence in the United States Threatens the Future of US Influence* (Praeger Security International, 2008); and *Giving Meanings to the World: The First US Foreign Correspondents, 1838–1859* (Greenwood Publishing Group, 2002).

Daniel González is the immigration reporter for the *Arizona Republic.* He has written about immigration, the border, and Latino affairs for the *Republic* since December 1999. He has received numerous local and national journalism awards and was named the 2010 Arizona journalist of the year for his immigration coverage. A graduate of the University of Iowa with a bachelor's degree in journalism, González also studied Spanish literature at the graduate level at Syracuse University. He has taught ethics/diversity and newswriting at Arizona State University's Walter Cronkite School of Journalism and Mass Communication.

Anne Grobet was until mid-2013 in charge of the Migration and Integration program of the United Nations Alliance of Civilizations (UNAOC). Seconded to the UN by the Swiss Department of Foreign Affairs as an expert for civilian peacebuilding, Grobet has studied international relations and Middle Eastern studies at the Graduate Institute of International and Development Studies of Geneva (IHEID). She is now Program Manager at the Cordoba Foundation in Geneva.

John Hooper became *The Guardian* and *The Observer*'s Southern Europe editor in October 2012, after more than a decade serving as the Rome-based Italy correspondent for both those newspapers and for *The Economist*. He began his career in journalism somewhat unconventionally when, as an 18-year-old Cambridge University freshman, he traveled to the breakaway state of Biafra to help make a network television documentary on the Nigerian civil war. Since then he has worked for the BBC, NBC, Reuters, and several other news organizations. In 1997, Hooper was part of the award-winning *Observer* team that uncovered the migrant trafficking disaster in which a Maltese vessel, the F174, sank with the loss of almost 300 lives.

Laure Mandeville has been the US chief of bureau for *Le Figaro* since January 2009. This is her second transatlantic experience since she first came to the United States 24 years ago, when she was a student of political science and the Russian sphere at Harvard University. In between, her passion for Russian culture and politics led her to tackle Eastern Europe, all the way to the Urals and beyond. After her language and political science studies, she joined the foreign news service of *Figaro* in May 1989 and for nearly 20 years covered the end of Communism and the post-Soviet world (Eastern Europe, Russia, the Baltic countries, the Caucasus, Ukraine, and Central Asia). She was *Figaro*'s correspondent in Russia from 1997 to 2000. She has also extensively covered the enlargement of the European Union, energy issues, Islam in Europe, and transatlantic relations. She is the author of *"L'Armée russe, la puissance en haillons"* (ed n° 1, 1994) and of *"La reconquête russe"* (Grasset, 2008), which received the "Louis Pauwels de la Société des gens de lettres" and "Ailleurs" awards in 2009.

Guido Olimpio is the Washington-based special correspondent for *Corriere della Sera,* where he has worked since 1987. He has been the paper's deputy foreign and news editor; from 1999 to 2003, he was correspondent in Israel, where he covered the Intifada and traveled frequently through the Middle

East. Since the 1980s, he has been researching and writing about international terrorism, eventually focusing on Islamist movements. In 1996, he testified before the task force on terrorism for the US Congress about Osama bin Laden, the Afghan mujaheddin, and Iranian activities in Europe.

Lise Olsen is investigative reporter at the *Houston Chronicle,* twice named Texas reporter of the year, and she served as a board member for Investigative Reporters and Editors from 2007 to 2011. During her time on the board, she served as the principal organizer of border workshops that supported a binational network of investigative reporters. In 1996, Olsen served as the director of the two-year IRE Mexico project, which subsequently became an independent nonprofit and later merged with the Mexican organization Centro de Periodismo y Etica Publica (CEPET).

Anna Popkova is a doctoral student at the School of Journalism and Mass Communication at the University of Minnesota. Popkova earned her MA degree from the University of Minnesota, a BA degree in mass communication with a minor in international studies from the University of North Dakota, and a five-year specialist degree in public relations from the Siberian State Aerospace University, Russia.

Martin A. Schain is a professor of politics at New York University. He is the author of *The Politics of Immigration in France, Britain and the United States: A Comparative Study* (Palgrave, 2012) and *French Communism and Local Power* (St. Martin's, 1985); coauthor of *Politics in France* (HarperCollins, 1992); coeditor and author of *Comparative Federalism: The US and EU in Comparative Perspective* (Oxford, 2006); *Shadows over Europe: The Development and Impact of the Extreme Right in Europe* (Palgrave, 2002); *Chirac's Challenge: Liberalization, Europeanization and Malaise in France* (St. Martin's Press, 1996), *The Politics of Immigration in Western Europe* (Cass, 1994); and editor of *The Marshall Plan: Fifty Years After* (Palgrave, 2001). Schain is the founder and former director of the Center for European Studies at NYU and former chair of the European Union Studies Association. He is coeditor of the transatlantic scholarly journal *Comparative European Politics.*

Riccardo Staglianò is a reporter at *la Repubblica,* writing feature articles and reportages for the weekly magazine *Il Venerdì,* covering national and international affairs. For 10 years (2000–2010), he taught new media courses at the Third University of Rome. In 2001, he won Premio Ischia di Giornalismo for journalists under the age of 35. He is the author of several books, including, most recently, *Grazie. Ecco perché senza immigrati saremmo perduti* (Chiarelettere, 2010), on immigration in Italy and *Toglietevelo dalla testa: Cellulari, tumori e tutto quello che le lobby non dicono* (Chiarelettere, 2012), on cellular phones and cancer.

Domenico Stinellis has directed The Associated Press photo coverage of Italy, the Vatican, and Malta since 2006. Stinellis joined the AP as a photographer and photo editor in Rome in 1994, after four years in the same capacity with Reuters. His pictures have appeared in several papers, magazines, and Web sites, including *Time, Newsweek, LIFE, Stern, National Geographic, New York Times, Washington Post, Los Angeles Times, Chicago Tribune, The Times* (London), and *The Economist*. In 2010, the Italian Television RAI History Channel dedicated an episode of its "Photosound" series to his work. He obtained a diploma in Japanese culture and language at the Italian Institute for Africa and the East (ISIAO) in Rome in 2003.

Elise Vincent has been a journalist for *Le Monde* since 2006, most recently in charge of covering immigration issues. Previously, she worked as a free-lancer for different French media, including *l'Express* and *L'Equipe*. She has a degree in history of international relations from the University of Paris-Sorbonne (Paris IV) and a degree in journalism from both the Centre de formation et de perfectionnement des journalistes (CFPJ) in Paris and the University Complutense in Madrid, Spain.

Rodrigo Zamith is a doctoral student in mass communication at the University of Minnesota. His primary research interest is the interplay of issue framing, public opinion, and policymaking, with a focus on foreign affairs. He has previously worked as reporter at the *Minneapolis Star-Tribune* and the *St. Paul Pioneer Press*. He holds a master's degree from Florida International University.

Introduction

Vicki L. Birchfield and Giovanna Dell'Orto

In 2010, one country stood out globally for how immigration was reshaping it—the vast majority of its workforce was foreign, many laboring illegally in perilous conditions and low-wage jobs, with virtually no civil society partici-pation. The country was Qatar; neither the United States nor any EU coun-try was among the top 10 countries with the highest share of migrants in their total population.[1] But Qatar is not making news, and neither are other immigration facts, such as that about half of undocumented immigrants in the United States are not running across deserts but overstaying their visas or that most migrant mobility in the European Union is internal, not driven by boatloads of North Africans landing on tiny islands.

And yet, in the news media, in the popular imagination, and in the political narratives of the two major Western powers, the United States and Europe, the image of immigration is one of fences and boats. We read of harrowing escapes and frenzied reactions, of chasing dreams and fearing invaders, of welcoming the world and securing the borders.

What we know about immigration processes and immigrants is shaped in part by news narratives, and therefore so are our opinions about policies on borders and integration. What neither academic discourse nor public debates tend to reveal or acknowledge, however, is how professional, institutional, and technology-driven practices shape coverage of immigration—which is the primary original contribution of this book.

Particularly in the wake of Arizona's controversial immigration law and the European Union's heated reaction to North African immigrants in the aftermath of the "Arab Spring"—not to mention presidential elections—immigration has grabbed headlines around the world. What is it like to cover these controversial issues for today's leading news orga-nizations at a time of crisis for journalism? How do journalistic practices generate the news frames that help shape public and political debates about one of the most poignant political, social, economic, and cultural dilemmas of our age?

This interdisciplinary, international book seeks to examine the intersec-tion of journalistic practices and public debates over immigration at the southern US and EU borders today from the perspective of a prominent group of North American and European journalists, as well as mass communication, international affairs, and comparative politics experts.

Unlike existing studies of media and migration, this book focuses on the different, yet convergent, practices of journalism across the Atlantic to understand news frames and their relationship to public discourse, therefore adding a vital dimension to the debates about media effects on policymaking. While empirical substantiation of causality is not our central aim, one critical premise is that the news media help negotiate and assign public meaning and understandings to social phenomena. News media discourses combine with other influences on public opinion formation and policy formulation to shape the essential deliberative space on matters of urgent public import.

Thus, the three central questions this book addresses are: How have North American and European journalists covered borders and immigrants? How have their jobs evolved in the new media environment and in a difficult time financially for elite news organizations? How is their immigration coverage shaped by their perceptions of public opinion and of the policymaking environment and by direct interactions with readers and political figures?

To help answer these questions, the book examines two broad comparative areas:

1. Journalistic practices for news coverage of third-country immigration and immigrants in France and Italy, reflecting both European and US perspectives; and
2. Journalistic practices for news coverage of immigration and immigrants in the United States, reflecting both domestic and European perspectives.

In addition, Parts I and II set the stage for the journalistic discussion by addressing these further questions: How have debates over national identity and multiculturalism shaped public understanding and political framing of immigration? How have the policies and politics of immigration and immigrant integration evolved in the United States, the European Union, and national and local environments? What are the broad patterns of news framing of immigration in the comparative transatlantic space?

Inherently torn between the human right to move freely in search of better conditions and the national right to control sovereign borders, immigration raises critical questions of security and integration that urgently call for public engagement. Today, few areas are more contested than south-to-north migrations into the United States, where state measures such as Arizona's SB1070 are under the microscope, and migration into the European Union, where managing migrant flows in the wake of the Arab revolutions is testing some of the Union's core policies related to integration and the free movement of people. And all of this is happening as many of today's news media struggle with the pressures of shrinking budgets and consumer-driven content that imperil public affairs reporting.

THE TRANSATLANTIC SPACE

While immigration is a global and multifaceted issue, the book focuses on a comparison among France and Italy and the southwestern United States, particularly Arizona and Texas—meeting spaces of some of the world's most advanced economies and desperately destitute populations. In all three cases, despite the European colonial heritage and the American "country of immigrants" mythology, current immigration trends represent a major historical change and sociological predictor, since demographic growth is stemming almost exclusively from immigrants. Furthermore, unlike in previous migration, the most debated immigrants in all three countries are racial and religious minorities, namely Latinos, Africans, and Muslims. In Europe especially, these minorities' workplace integration is weaker than in the United States, generating debates about welfare and social protections as a second frontier. With today's ease and growth of transnational ties through new communication technologies, immigrants can maintain social, political, and identity loyalties to their original countries at an unprecedented level, highlighting integration challenges.

This novelty is most starkly evident in southern Italy, where villages celebrate "sagra dell'emigrato"—a fair in memory of emigrants, millions of whom left for the Americas until the mid-20th century—while, just outside, thousands of Maghrebian workers tend to the tomato and fruit crops. Italy has become, in the mass media, the visible border of the European Union—the crossing point for thousands in desperate conditions arriving on its shores from North Africa via smugglers' boats. Findings in the German Marshall Fund's Transatlantic Trends 2010 report show that Italians have a distorted perception of the reality of immigration there—they estimate that one-quarter of Italy's population consists of immigrants, while in reality the share is 7 percent—and a majority of those whose perception remains uncorrected believes that figure represents too many immigrants. The report finds that Italians tend to view immigration more pessimistically than most other Europeans, and a majority of them believes that legal and illegal immigrants increase crime, even as they also acknowledge that immigrants fill jobs Italians no longer want to take.[2]

Many immigrants who land in Italy, however, have the goal of reaching France, where recent riots in immigrant neighborhoods reverberated through Europe. French public opinion toward immigrants, which number more than 5 million, has soured, with only 38 percent of French citizens arguing that immigration is an opportunity rather than a problem for the country, according to the Transatlantic Trends 2010 report.[3] Controversial government moves to ban face-covering veils in public spaces and to dismantle transient migrant camps in 2010 further enflamed public discourse, and the French public—albeit to a lesser degree than either American or Italian citizens—thought the government was doing a poor job of managing immigration and integrating immigrants. Interestingly, a large majority

(65%) of Italians strongly supported reinforcing border controls, while a majority of the French (54%) worried about the poor integration of immigrants, arguably reflecting the perceptions of Italy as a border country and of France as a settlement one.

US perceptions of immigration also focus unrealistically on undocumented and therefore "problematic" immigration, with a clear majority of Americans believing that most of the nearly 42 million immigrants in the United States are there illegally, while in fact those without papers account for less than one-third of all immigrants.[4] Beginning in the 1990s, an increase in border enforcement in California and Texas had the unintended consequence of funneling illegal immigrants, attracted in record numbers by the economic boom, into the rugged and desolate desert of southern Arizona. For more than a decade since, roughly half of all apprehensions of illegal border crossers by the US border patrol have taken place in Arizona. Simultaneously, annual migrant deaths along the border in Arizona have soared, resulting in intense public frustration and civil society efforts as well as controversial local enforcement attempts.[5] More recently, the Texas border, plagued by cartels, has become the scene of gruesome deathly violence, making it dangerous for reporters to cover on both sides.

Whether in the United States, France, or Italy, then, the perception of a critical inability to control the borders—"sealing" vast land and sea borders being itself an unrealistic option linked to exaggerated public perceptions of the actual number of immigrants and their alleged criminal activities—has led to a polarization of public debate and generated disputed legislative efforts. France and Italy openly discussed changing the Schengen agreement that guarantees borderless travel in the Union, while Arizona passed SB1070, a bill aimed at an attrition-through-enforcement strategy that raised issues of both potential civil rights violations and preemption of federal law. In June 2012, the US Supreme Court ruled some of its provisions unconstitutional but upheld its centerpiece, the requirement that state law enforcement officials verify immigration status if reasonable suspicion exists that a person stopped or arrested might be in the country illegally.[6] Despite continuing legal challenges, several other US states have replicated the law, including three southeastern ones—Alabama, Georgia, and South Carolina—where immigration has only recently become a source of major demographic movement and heated controversy. All of these ad hoc legislative strategies compound the confusion that reigns over what constitutes the appropriate authority to tackle immigration, with efforts at control generated in towns and islands, in state capitals and national parliaments, in the federal Congress and the supranational EU organs.

The 2012 US presidential election, with Latinos overwhelmingly preferring President Barack Obama, pushed the administration to promise immigration reform, which was moving through Congress as this book went to press, and the Republican Party to strategize how to reach Hispanic constituents, trends that will likely keep immigration debates high on the public and media agendas. Likewise, in Europe, the debt crisis and crushing austerity policies are fueling anti-immigrant attitudes that populist movements and right-wing parties eagerly exploit, rendering EU efforts at greater policy coordination on migration issues even more divisive and challenging.

Against this background, the conceptual and analytical strategy we pursue in this volume is comparative and interdisciplinary, bringing scholars and journalists with expertise on both sides of the Atlantic in dialogue to critically examine the apparent convergence in the overarching narratives surrounding immigration debates today despite the different media and political contexts within which they operate. No two regions in the world are as historically and politically interconnected and economically interdependent as Europe and the United States; in spite of the indisputable "rise of the rest," the transatlantic economy still commands 49 percent of global GDP.

Thus, even in the midst of relative decline and global power shifts from west to east and from north to south, both sides of the Atlantic seem to retain the lure of economic opportunity and political freedom for countless numbers of migrants each year. Yet as the post-9/11 era ushered in more restrictive visa policies and saw the increasing securitization of immigration, public discourse in Europe and the United States has shifted almost exclusively toward concern with undocumented or clandestine immigrants. Though the historical waves of immigration and the various approaches to integration have been starkly different in the two contexts over the course of the past century, the unifying trend presently is that the transatlantic space of immigration is widely perceived as inhospitable. The dimension of the immigration debates of primary interest here—chiefly the ways in which narratives of undocumented or unauthorized immigrants are being constructed by the news media and filtered through these distinct political environments—therefore delimits the scope of the inquiry. Such tightness of focus yields new insights into the complex interplay of news media, political discourse, and policy change by revealing and comparing how journalistic practices shape coverage of immigration.

THE JOURNALISTIC SPACE

If immigration in the 21st century is a battlefield of clashing ideologies, so is journalism, particularly in the Western news media environment. The convergence of sociopolitical and economic long-term trends with digital media technologies that emerged in the mid-1990s has radically transformed not only the practices of journalism, from production to reception, but also potentially its impact on the public sphere. American journalism, globally the most reliant on advertising for revenue, has been the most altered. This is especially true for newspapers and newswires, which still matter largely because of their outsized impact on newsgathering and in their role as record keepers.

Economic consolidation, the growing presence of media executives with roots and loyalties outside newsrooms, the increasing ability of political leaders to reach the public directly, bypassing the press corps and heightening public distrust of news media's accuracy and fairness, have all accelerated in the Internet era. Advertising revenues are down just as pressures to focus on the bottom line go up, which increases the vulnerability of hard-news reporting, already the least popular media content at a time when audience preferences become inescapable. The Internet became the leading source of news in late 2010, according to the Pew Research Center, depriving traditional media of both economic and social heft even though they still produce the vast majority of online news content.[7] It was perhaps emblematic of the challenges to sell public affairs news by even the elite press that, in May 2012, the *Los Angeles Times* received a $1 million grant from the Ford Foundation to hire reporters on several beats—including immigrant communities and the US-Mexican border. Audiences increasingly have the ability to choose only cognitively consonant information sources, following niche publications or personalized news streams that speak to their existing interests and perceptions. A recent study of the effects of selective exposure for Fox and CNN viewers in the United States on their attitudes toward Mexican immigrants, for example, found that, even when researchers controlled for demographic and ideological variables, the more viewers watched Fox, they more they supported restrictions on immigration.[8]

While these trends are exacerbated in the United States and while US professional journalistic practices are still different from French and Italian ones, the pervasiveness of US news and entertainment media worldwide and globalization per se are pushing some conformity, at least in the media systems most similar to American ones, such as those in Western Europe. Paradoxically, the homogenizing flow works in the other direction, too; as Starr has noted, "the American media system is moving in a European direction—toward a more ideological organization of both the public and the news media."[9] As Boczkowski illustrated, new practices of production and consumption of news, dominated by competition and speed, conspire both to encourage cursory treatment of public affairs and, most significant, to leave the press in a dangerous double bind regarding its political role.[10] The ability of news media to have an effect on public discourse stems from two interrelated factors—their importance to the mass public because they have privileged access to political actors and their importance to political actors because they are followed by the mass public on matters of public interest. But when practice and economic and technological pressures push journalistic content toward what the public is interested in—which is rarely what is considered in the public interest—then news media have a choice to either lose audience or stay away from public affairs, and in both cases they inevitably lose political relevance.

Such practices have led critics to reconsider the news media as a locus and facilitator of democratic deliberation. While non-news organizations—such as the widely popular entertainment programs *The Colbert Report* and *The Daily Show*—are successful in engaging the electorate and tend to provide a growing share of political information, they are unlikely to be able to substitute professional journalism.[11] All of these trends have an upside, too—the ability of ordinary citizens to commit to political action at almost no cost via social media, to have a larger say on traditional media coverage, to engage multiple sources of information for, plausibly, a broader perspective on world affairs. But the ambitions of informative and deliberative citizen journalism as an alternative to professional newsgathering are rarely realized, especially on issues such as immigration that, as stories that "ooze" instead of "break," as Roberto Suro puts it,[12] are particularly hard for even professional journalists to tackle. Furthermore, the proliferation of viewpoints online captures public attention on such controversial issues and, increasingly, unsubstantiated rumors can drive professional journalists' agenda, forcing them to spend already stretched resources disproving them.

Suro et al. have argued that both the news media and the social sciences have distorted our understanding of immigration, heightening the public's sense of fear, of borders as out of control, and of immigrant civic and political integration as threats to national identity. The consequence, they persuasively suggest, of the media's focus on immigrant-centered "human interest" stories is that the whole problematic is reduced to individual agency rather than systemic factors, making it ripe for partisan divides and less likely to inspire the kind of comprehensive, "grand bargain" policymaking that sweeping legislation requires. The surging advocacy by niche media—be they on the far right of the political spectrum or foreign-language immigrant sources—has proven remarkably effective at blocking legislation but not at building it.[13]

Benson, studying the different forms of journalism in the United States and in France, found that the French media tend to focus less on personal narratives and more on a multigenre format. Overall, however, his analysis showed that up to the mid-2000s, the increasing commercialization of some media on both sides of the Atlantic weakened their ability to function as a public sphere informed by diverse and broad voices, which has supported reasoned and critical discourse.[14] Like the French media, Italian news organizations are also influenced more by political than by market imperatives, but the tendencies discussed earlier—a privileging of entertainment content and the polarization of debate—are also growing in that country.

Previous research both in Europe and in the Americas has suggested that covering immigration has long been a challenge, not only in receiving countries but even in top sending countries such as Mexico, with a focus on the problems of illegal immigration.[15] From the 1970s to the mid-2000s, US news coverage focused on racism, humanitarian concerns, and, predominantly, immigration as a threat to public order, rather than on jobs and the broad economic factors driving the phenomenon. Throughout history, coverage has reflected the ambivalence of public opinion, divided on facts and perception about the numbers and kinds of immigrants that are "desirable." Mexican immigration—by far the largest since the 1970s—has been usually framed as outside the "nation of immigrants" image, as an "external threat" that sometimes degenerated in a dehumanizing discourse of Latino immigrants.[16] European news media also marginalize the labor market effect in driving illegal immigration and tend to focus instead on issues of "national culture," which is not constructed as having a narrative of immigration as part of its image. One study of coverage in Italy found evidence of folklorization and criminalization of immigrants,[17] along with "visible" stereotypes of the kind of the notorious Lega Nord campaign poster that featured a Native American above the slogan "They welcomed immigrants and ended up in reservations."

What distinguishes the analyses provided in this book from the studies cited, which examine news stories for images of immigrants, is the focus on remarkably candid, detailed accounts of journalistic practice, provided by the professionals themselves, and the comparative transatlantic perspective. There are presently no publications on journalism and immigration that engage both transatlantic audiences as this project seeks to do. Kerry Moore, Bernhard Gross, and Terry Threadgold's *Migrations and the Media* presents disparate cases from across the world, from Serbia to the Pacific, and topics, from human rights to media training, for a critical analysis of media texts as succumbing to a narrative of immigrant "threats and crises," with only one practitioner offering a reflection on broadcasting practices.[18] Marcelo M. Suárez-Orozco, Vivian Louie, and Roberto Suro's *Writing Immigration: Scholars and Journalists in Dialogue* provides both journalists' and scholars' perspectives but focuses mostly on immigration itself—the impact of enforcement on children, the dynamics of integration, the economic challenges. A few chapters are self-reflections on practices that echo some of our concerns (framing stories fairly and engagingly, journalism's own crisis),[19] but *Writing Immigration* is exclusively about US issues, by US authors, while a crucial strength of our book is the transatlantic juxtaposition of cases and contributors.

Our goal is to provide new insights and a deeper understanding of the role of journalism in the multidimensionality of immigration debates on both sides of the Atlantic. This is not a policy book that promotes specific partisan solutions to the problematic of either immigration or media coverage—in fact, our contributors represent organizations that espouse very different political choices. Rather, we aim to illuminate an urgent issue and propose it for public engagement in a transatlantic comparative dialogue, believing that objective scholarly and journalistic inquiry is the necessary starting point for informed public debate and policymaking. We bring three groups of experts, each of whose work is relevant to the others but very sporadically shared, in conversation with the goal of enlightening academic study of the role of the media in affecting understanding of controversial public issues. The unique value is the combination of new research on news content with insider reflection on just why, at the most intimate level, immigration is covered as it is.

The heartfelt questioning of journalistic work does not translate into a "how-to" book highlighting best practices or condemning worst ones.[20] Rather, we present a rare insider reflection on the practices that shape the very news stories that then become the object of scholarship, offering new in-depth capacity to analyze and assess their influence on public perception and discourse. By creating a dialogue among different parties in the discourse that engages a diverse set of expertise and a multiplicity of voices instead of privileging a single framework, we provide a groundbreaking resource for political science and communication scholars who study the role of the news media in policy and public debates. What allows these disparate voices to cohere is the common effort to deconstruct news narratives, from their production to their reception—practitioners and scholars work together to reflectively analyze the creation and negotiation of meaning in immigration news. Our ultimate goal is to provide scholars with a firsthand look at the realities on the ground and the details of journalistic routines; to offer journalists an insightful tool to explore different practices across not only regions but also media systems; and to present the general public with an international and comparative perspective on a topic of daily relevance.

CONTENT AND THEMATIC OVERVIEW

The book is organized into four sections, two presenting new academic research and two focusing on analysis of professional journalistic practices. Part I provides the broad sociopolitical context of the book with an overview of the policies, politics, and practices of immigration today in the European Union and the United States as well as the role of perceptions and communication practices that impact the everyday realities of changing societies. Jack Citrin opens Part I by focusing on the relationship between immigration and prevailing conceptions of national identity, revealing core attributes of political culture and the meaning of national identity as well as the impact of multiculturalism as an integration strategy. Next, Martin A. Schain evaluates the actual policies and general politics of immigration in Europe and the United States with a focus on three parameters—entry policy, integration policy, and border enforcement—showing approaches and impact to be quite different across the Atlantic. After these descriptions of both the philosophical groundwork of notions of national identity and their bearing on the immigration experience and then surveying the nuts and bolts of actual immigration policies, the following two chapters by human rights practitioners shift toward an exploration of how such practices are captured discursively in the public sphere. Anne Grobet's chapter elucidates the ways in which the United Nations Alliance of Civilizations focuses on changing media coverage of migration as an essential part of its aim to prevent conflict in polarized societies. Similarly, Jean-Philippe Chauzy and Gervais Appave discuss how distorted communication practices threaten the International Organization for Migration's efforts to humanely and justly manage migration worldwide.

The four chapters in Part II bring concrete empirical evidence to bear on the arguments, showing how and why news media discourse matters. Rodney Benson analyzes US and French mainstream national news coverage of immigration, finding a critical difference in news formats between the dominating personal narrative approach found in US newspapers and the multigenre, thematic approach taken in French ones. Benson argues that the multigenre format allows readers to go beyond the "human dimension" of individual immigrants to address the hows and whys of immigration as a social process. Focusing on the much less studied newswire services, Rodrigo Zamith's interpretative and computer-assisted textual analysis examines and compares English-language news stories on immigration by the leading newswire agencies in France and the United States, the Paris-based Agence France-Presse and the New York-based Associated Press. Zamith found distinct differences in the coverage of immigration in France and in the United States but remarkable similarities in the coverage of both contexts by the two newswire agencies. In particular, coverage in the United States was far more likely to focus on illegality and to emphasize law and order and border security than was coverage in France, which emphasized national identity.

Anna Popkova offers a compelling new look at the most immediate and direct impact of immigration news stories on public opinion by analyzing readers' comments on the articles published on the online platforms of the *New York Times* and *The Guardian*. Qualitative textual analysis of more than 1,000 comments reveals that even though the vast majority of comments in both newspapers were informed by the "politics of fear," there were also key differences in how the readers of the *New York Times* and *The Guardian* framed their worries, reflecting the differences highlighted in Zamith's essay. Closing Part II, Stephen Bennett and Zamith's chapter provides a useful foil to the focus on Western media by examining the differences in immigration coverage in Europe and the United States by a rising star in global journalism, Al Jazeera. Stories by both the Arabic- and the English-language networks suggest a more humanitarian advocacy practice than that embraced by mainstream European and US media.

The next two sections of the book engage the very agents who are actively shaping and producing the discursive context within which politicians and citizens are making sense (or not) of the complexities and challenges of immigration. Part III offers an insider's view of the journalistic practices that produce and refract the discursive landscape of immigration across Europe. Elise Vincent of *Le Monde* explains her strategies for enriching immigration coverage in France, with a particular focus on the era of President Nicolas Sarkozy, who made immigration a top priority of his political agenda. She argues that, lacking a distinct "southern border," France has focused the debate on immigrants' integration, making it a particularly treacherous field for journalists to cover without following the cues of extremists. The next chapter, by Associated Press photojournalist Domenico Stinellis, turns to a country with such a border, Italy. As a Rome-based international journalist, Stinellis masterfully details how border news photography has changed in practice and content over the past 20 years of the "digital revolution," from the first big wave of Albanian immigrants in 1991 to the Arab Spring. His analysis of AP photographs and the practices that created them documents the narrative implications of literally framing immigration.

John Hooper, *The Guardian*'s correspondent in Italy, similarly focuses on visibility, arguing that the tendency of Italian media to pay "scant attention to what cannot be seen and excessive attention to what can," a questionable journalistic practice per se, has distorted the public and political debate. Hooper concludes that visibility tends to drive coverage—where there is visible evidence, journalism can be compassionate if platitudinous, but most journalists tend to follow the agenda imposed by political actors and avoid pursuing the invisible stories that might shed more light. In the last chapter of this section, Riccardo Staglianò of *la Repubblica* goes even farther in his critiques and, in so doing, echoes concerns articulated by Grobet and Chauzy in Part I. He argues that media outlets have their share of responsibility for the misunderstanding and demonizing of immigrants, often amplifying instead of contextualizing or rebutting the fearmongering of politicians. Similarly to Vincent's strategies, Staglianò calls for doing more than "just holding a microphone to a politician."

Part IV turns back across the Atlantic. Daniel González, of the *Arizona Republic,* opens with a penetrating account of the diminution of resources with which immigration reporters have to work as they cover one of today's most important and challenging beats. Leaving day-to-day stories largely to the newswires—as noted in earlier chapters—González focuses on major immigration trend stories. After Arizona passed what was considered the toughest immigration law in the nation, González traveled to Germany, Italy, and Spain to put it in international perspective, finding numerous echoes of Arizona in Roman shantytowns and Andalucian border control centers.

The next two chilling chapters focus on the Texas border, providing perspectives by a US and a Mexican journalist who have both long investigated the rise in violence in literally binational cities such as El Paso/Ciudad Juárez. Lourdes Cárdenas of the *El Paso Times* reflects on the challenges of covering a new wave of middle- and upper-class Mexican refugees seeking to escape the cartels, while Lise Olsen of the *Houston Chronicle* portrays the sobering reality of a deadly border beat. Her alarm for border journalism sounds urgent, since investigative reporting on rapidly changing dynamics appears caught between deadly cartel violence striking Mexican journalists and ever-growing budget pressures pinning down US reporters. In contrast, the next chapter, by Guido Olimpio of *Corriere della Sera,* shows how a European correspondent "translates the American border for Italians," emphasizing the need to focus on individual dramatic stories of illegal immigrants or unusual topics in order to overcome an innate lack of interest. He candidly describes the massive research that underwrites his stories as well as the "Trojan horses" he has to use to hook readers—often playing with Italians' fascination with the "Old West."

Offering a closing reflection for Parts III and IV, Laure Mandeville, the US bureau chief of *Le Figaro,* emphasizes immigration as "a minefield for journalists" on both sides of the Atlantic. Voicing concerns echoed by her colleagues in the previous chapters, Mandeville suggests that the partisan and highly politicized approaches of the different parties involved make it hard to find sources who are not strident advocates; the existence of conflicting "truths" on the topic calls balance into question; and the temptation of political correctness can make it impossible to even address the troubling consequences of immigration without raising cries of racism.

The concluding chapter draws the connections between the various chapters, focusing on both the overarching parallels and the divergent perspectives proffered by this diverse group of scholars, practitioners and journalists. The unifying thread weaving different voices, methods, and observations together is the recognition that narratives, politics and public perceptions merge to shape one of the most consequential human crises of our time. Academic researchers and human rights practitioners critique the shortcomings of journalistic coverage of immigration and emphasize its role in exacerbating public and political debates. The uniqueness of this book is to juxtapose current multidisciplinary research with analyses from the frontlines—spotlighting the way journalists actually cover their beats, their understanding of their public and political role, and their own frustrations with a topic many call a minefield.

Critical divergences emerge in the roles and practices of national and international media—be they European newspapers covering Arizona or an American newswire reporting from Italy. More striking than the expected differences, however, are the similar challenges facing all journalists: the difficulty in breaking through the political agenda; the near impossibility of tackling the transformation of host societies without playing into the hands of extremist rhetoric; and the daily struggle to engage in investigative reporting with shrinking time and money resources. In Europe as in the United States, journalists feel straitjacketed by polarized public discourses that tend to cry over easily observable human dramas and ignore momentous sociopolitical shifts. Pressed for time and resources, news organizations increasingly publish snippets of breaking news that confirm the perception that immigration policies, at the border and beyond, and immigrants themselves are an out-of-control phenomenon.

Nevertheless, despite the many challenges and taboos on all ends of the political spectrum, these journalists strive to investigate, giving hope that the public conversation about immigration might continue to expand beyond "holding a microphone" to increasingly uncompromising politicians. Neither the stories and reports crafted by journalists nor the studies produced by academics can possibly capture the complexity of the micro and macro realities of immigration in the 21st century. We hope, however, that integrating the expertise and collective knowledge of the two may serve to enrich public discourse and facilitate deeper understanding and more productive policymaking on both sides of the Atlantic.

NOTES

1. "Top Ten Countries with the Highest Share of International Migrants in the Total Population," Migration Policy Institute, 2010, http://www.migrationinformation.org/datahub/charts/6.2.shtml.
2. German Marshall Fund of the United States, "Transatlantic Trends: Immigration," Key Findings (Washington, DC: GMF, 2010), 6, 12.
3. Ibid., 10.
4. Ibid., 25.
5. On Arizona civil society participation, see Cari Lee Skogberg Eastman, *Shaping the Immigration Debate: Contending Civil Societies on the US-Mexico Border* (Boulder, Colo., and London: FirstForumPress, 2012).
6. Adam Liptak, "Blocking Parts of Arizona Law, Justices Allow Its Centerpiece," *New York Times,* June 25, 2012.
7. "Internet Gains on Television as Public's Main News Source," Pew Research Center Publications, www.pewresearch.org. On survey data not reflecting the importance of print, see the testimony of Tom Rosenstiel, director of the Pew Research Center's Project for Excellence in Journalism: "Where the News Comes From—and Why It Matters," September 25, 2009, www.pewresearch.org.
8. Homero Gil de Zuniga, Teresa Correa, and Sebastian Valenzuela, "Effects of Selective Exposure to FOX and CNN Cable News on Attitudes toward Mexican Immigrants," unpublished paper presented to the International Communication Association meeting, Phoenix, AZ, May 2012.
9. Paul Starr, "An Unexpected Crisis: The News Media in Postindustrial Democracies," *International Journal of Press/Politics* 17, no. 2 (2012): 238.
10. Pablo J. Boczkowski, *News at Work: Imitation in an Age of Information Abundance* (Chicago: University of Chicago Press, 2010).
11. Bruce A. Williams and Michael X. Delli Carpini, *After Broadcast News: Media Regimes, Democracy, and the New Information Environment* (Cambridge: Cambridge University Press, 2011).
12. Banu Akdenizli, E. J. Dionne Jr., and Roberto Suro, "Democracy in the Age of New Media: A Report on the Media and the Immigration Debate," report by University of Southern California Annenberg School for Communication and Journalism and the Brookings Institution, September 25, 2008.
13. Ibid.; Roberto Suro, "Introduction," in Marcelo M. Suárez-Orozco, Vivian Louie, and Roberto Suro, eds., *Writing Immigration Scholars and Journalists in Dialogue* (Berkeley: University of California Press, 2011).
14. Rodney Benson, "What Makes for a Critical Press? A Case Study of French and US Immigration News Coverage," *International Journal of Press/Politics* 15, no. 1 (2010): 3–24.
15. Ibid.; Leo R. Chavez, *The Latino Threat: Constructing Immigrants, Citizens, and the Nation* (Stanford: Stanford University Press, 2008); Joel S. Fetzer,

Public Attitudes toward Immigration in the United States, France, and Germany (Cambridge: Cambridge University Press, 2000); Russell King and Nancy Wood, eds., *Media and Migration* (London and New York: Routledge, 2001); Summer Harlow and Ingrid Bachmann, "Going North: News Framing of Immigration in Mexico, Guatemala, and El Salvador," unpublished paper presented to the International Communication Association meeting, Phoenix, AZ, May 2012.

16. Otto Santa Ana, "'Like an Animal I Was Treated': Anti-immigrant Metaphor in US Public Discourse," *Discourse and Society* 10, no. 2 (1999): 191–224.

17. Giovanna Campani, "Migrants and Media: The Italian Case," in *Media and Migration,* ed. Russell King and Nancy Wood (London: Routledge, 2001), 38–52.

18. Kerry Moore, Bernhard Gross, and Terry Threadgold, eds., *Migrations and the Media* (New York: Peter Lang, 2012), especially the chapter by Janet Harris, "Reporting Migration: A Journalist's Reflection on Personal Experience and Academic Critique," 253–68.

19. Suárez-Orozco, Louie, and Suro, *Writing Immigration,* especially "Interlude I" by Patrick J. McDonnell and chapter 9, "Who Will Report the Next Chapter of America's Immigration Story?" by Tyche Hendricks.

20. Among many such texts, a particularly useful one for Europe is Jean-Paul Marthoz's *Couvrir les migrations* (Brussels: de Boeck, 2011). In the United States, university journalism programs are increasing their professional courses on border reporting as part of initiatives like Arizona State University's Southwest Borderlands.

Part I

EU and US Policies and Politics of Immigration Today

1 National Identity and the Challenge of Immigration

Jack Citrin

University of California, Berkeley[1]

Why does immigration roil the politics of so many countries, even aging societies that need people to help finance the welfare state benefits of their declining populations? Surely a large part of the answer is that immigration brings strangers into "our land," raising concerns about the erosion of a common national identity. The territorial nation-state remains the dominant political reality of our time; reports of its demise are vastly exaggerated. A nation is a set of people with a common "we-feeling" seeking a state of their own. The attributes giving rise to this sense of common identity may vary, but all nationalist doctrines insist that "the imagined community of the nation must be the primary focus of values, source of legitimacy, and object of loyalty and basis of identity,"[2] overriding the claims of minority communities within it.

By changing the ethnic composition of nation-states and increasing cultural diversity, immigration poses the problem of integration, of making newcomers members of the national "team." The greater the cultural similarity of immigrants to the native population, the less severe this problem may appear, and this has shaped attitudes and policies about who should be allowed to come, but even in the United States, often self-described as a nation of immigrants, public opinion surveys consistently show that Americans favor past immigration over more recent immigration, prefer legal to illegal immigrants, and overwhelmingly reject any conception of multiculturalism that challenges English as the country's common, unifying language.[3]

Assimilation, the gradual adoption of prevailing habits and beliefs by newcomers, is one political formula for sustaining social solidarity amid ethnic diversity. Multiculturalism, a policy, conceived in the 1970s, of encouraging the persistence of cultures distinct from the national mainstream, is the alternative embraced by many in both North America and Western Europe. Official support for multiculturalism peaked in the 1980s and 1990s, but there is widespread agreement that the political pendulum has swung toward the opposite pole.[4] In 1999, no European country had civic integration (assimilation) policies. By now, language training and civic education are widely adopted as tests not just for citizenship but also for immigration control.[5] The leaders of Germany, Britain, and France have publicly denounced multiculturalism as a disaster that threatens their nation's collective identity and echo the arguments of some academics that a strong overarching national identity is the better approach for integrating immigrants and building a sense of social solidarity in a diverse society.[6]

This chapter first reviews public opinion data from Europe and North America to show how conceptions of national identity are linked to preferences regarding immigration policy. Then it considers how the extent to which a country adopts multicultural policies is connected both to public attitudes toward immigrants and to trends in conceptions of nationhood. The evidence comes largely from International Social Survey Program (ISSP) data collected in 1995 and 2003 and the European Social Surveys (ESS) collected biennially between 2002 and 2010. Cross-national comparisons show that the contrasting histories of immigration in the United States and in Europe have resulted in different conceptions of where diversity fits into images of the nation. Yet the two forms of national identity often distinguished in the literature—the ethnic and the civic—are widely in evidence in the United States as well as in Europe, and these conceptions relate similarly to individuals' immigration attitudes in all countries.

MEANINGS OF NATIONAL IDENTITY

The construct of national identity has cognitive, affective, and normative dimensions. The cognitive facet refers to self-categorization, the answer to the question "who am I?" The affective dimension refers to the strength of one's identification with one's country. Patriotism, defined as pride in and love of one's country, is the standard referent here. Finally, national identities have normative content, by which is meant the criteria that define a nation's uniqueness. These are the attributes that distinguish "us" from them. In this chapter, I consider both the affective and the normative dimensions, paying particular attention to whether the subjective boundaries of the nation are defined in ethnic, "ascriptive" terms or in civic, "achievable" terms.

MEANINGS OF MULTICULTURALISM

In a descriptive sense, multiculturalism refers to the presence within a political society of many distinct religious, ethnic, or racial groups. Viewed this way, the United States, Canada, and virtually all European nation-states are and will remain multicultural societies. A second meaning of multiculturalism is ideological rather than demographic. In this incarnation, multiculturalism affirms the enduring moral and political significance of ethnic group consciousness and endorses policies designed to support minority ethnicities through special recognition and representation.

Proponents of multiculturalism assert that the welcoming stance adopted toward immigrants, distilled in the phrase "you can be yourselves and still belong here," will succeed in incorporating newcomers into the political community as loyal citizens. Once this is seen to happen, skeptical natives will no longer view immigrants as a threat to prevailing values and come to accept cultural heterogeneity as compatible with national cohesion. Advocates of assimilation regard these predictions as naïve at best and perverse at worst. In their view, multiculturalism elevates ethnic identification at the expense of commitment to a common democratic culture. Insistence on the value of "difference" provokes resentment that spills over into prejudice as well as an unwillingness to support redistribution measures because they might benefit those who are perceived as undeserving immigrant claimants. Only if immigrant minorities acculturate, advocates of assimilation argue, will they be accepted as full-fledged members of the national community and achieve both social integration and economic advancement.

In exploring the relationships between public opinion about immigration and the presence of multiculturalist policy regimes, I use the Multiculturalism Policy Index for Immigrant Minorities (MCP) developed by Banting and Kymlicka.[7] This measure assigns scores to countries by summing the number of the following policies of official recognition and representation for cultural minorities adopted:[8]

> Constitutional, legal or parliamentary affirmation of multiculturalism;
>
> The adoption of multiculturalism in the school curriculum;
>
> Inclusion of ethnic representation/sensitivity in the public media;[9]
>
> Exemptions from dress codes or Sunday closing legislation;
>
> Allowing dual citizenship;
>
> The funding of ethnic group organizations for cultural activities;
>
> Funding of bilingual education or mother-tongue instruction; and
>
> Affirmative action for disadvantaged immigrant groups.

Countries that adopt all these components of the MCP Index receive a total score of 8. Those adopting fewer than three of the eight policies are classified as having "weak" immigrant minority policies. Countries with scores between 3 and 5.5 are categorized as having a "modest" multicultural regime for immigrants, and those with scores between 6 and 8 are "strongly" multiculturalist.

Data from the Multiculturalism Policy Index show that, with the exception of the United States, the "settler" societies in North America and Australasia had more robust multicultural regimes than most European countries. Still, between 1980 and 2000, there was a decided shift toward the adoption of more multicultural policies. Five countries moved from the weak to the modest category and two from modest to strong. No country had a lower

MCP score in 2000 than in 1980. For the years between 2000 and 2010, the pattern of change is more mixed. Five countries actually moved in the direction of multiculturalism, as measured by the MCP Index, usually by changes in the content of media and school curricula. Prompted by electoral pressures, the Netherlands alone moved decisively to weaken its policies, which handle the administration of education and welfare policies separately for religious communities (Catholic, Protestant, and then Muslim). Yet, while many multiculturalist policies remained intact between the late 1990s and 2010, most Western European countries adopted civic integration requirements for naturalization, and several were imposing language requirements for new immigrants, policies that reflected a retreat from multiculturalism toward assimilationist views. And clearly the shift in rhetoric and policy was in part a response to the emerging electoral strength of radical-right political parties opposed to immigration.

THE CONTOURS OF PUBLIC OPINION

The United States and Europe approach the dilemmas of immigration policy from radically different historical perspectives, as spelled out by Schain's chapter in this volume. Despite ambivalent public views, immigration is a fundamental part of America's founding myth. Most Americans acknowledge that all of "us here now" or our ancestors—Native Americans aside—came from somewhere else. In Europe the story is quite different. Immigration does not figure in the construction of national identities of most nation-states in the ever-expanding European Union. Moreover, unlike the American case, immigrants came to Western Europe more recently, largely in reaction to a series of convulsions in Africa, Eastern Europe, and the Middle East. Against this background, the data from the 2002 ESS and a companion Citizenship, Involvment, Democracy (CID) American survey show more support for cultural diversity in the United States than in European countries.[10] This assertion derives from the level of agreement to these statements:

> "It is better for a country if almost everyone shares the same customs and traditions."

> "It is better for a country if there are a variety of religions among its people."

Figure 1.1[11] presents the country-level means for each item, coded so that high values equal support for homogeneity, along with the 95 percent confidence interval for each country's mean. The vertical line in each graph indicates the midpoint of the scale, so a country plotted to the left of the line is less committed to cultural homogeneity than a country to the right of the line.

Figure 1.1 shows that countries are relatively evenly distributed between a tendency to support *religious* homogeneity and a tendency to oppose it. But

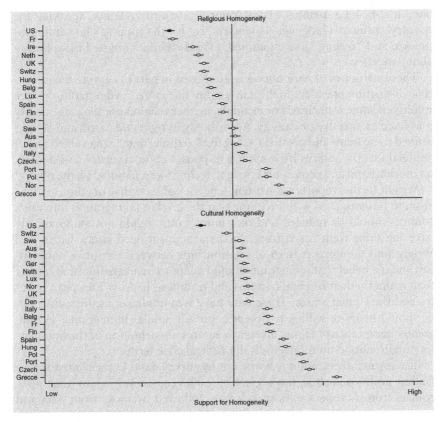

Figure 1.1   Beliefs about Societal Homogeneity

the majority in 19 of 21 countries agreed that a country would be better served if everyone shared the same customs and traditions. Only the United States and, to a lesser extent, Sweden fell on the accepting side of the mid-point. It appears that the long history of cultural and ethnic diversity in the United States has produced a distinctive and more favorable orientation toward cultural heterogeneity. This does not, however, extend to support for linguistic diversity. The American public is among the strongest in the conviction that speaking the host country's language should be a very important qualification for admitting immigrants, and those Americans who value cultural homogeneity are just like their European counterparts in opposing immigration.[12]

To explore how subjective conceptions of national identity influence immigration attitudes, I rely on questions embedded in the 1995 and 2003 ISSP programs. These surveys include a battery of questions asking respondents how important various criteria are in making someone a "true" national (American, Briton, German, and so forth). In the 2003 survey, the attributes included ancestry, nativity, having lived in the country most of one's life, being a member of the country's majority religion, speaking the country's principal language, having respect for the country's law and institutions, and "feeling" like a national. (The 1995 ISPP omitted the question about ancestry.)

These attributes of nationhood were chosen in part to capture the ethnic-civic distinction prevalent in the nationalism literature.[13] Admittedly, the face validity of some is unclear. For example, neither religion nor language ability is as fixed as ancestry or nativity. Accordingly, Wright and Citrin and Wright pruned these items and created "ascriptive" (ethnic) and "achievable" (civic) national identity indices by summing responses about ancestry and nativity on the one hand and respect for laws and feeling like a national on the other.[14]

Wright further reports a consistent tendency of ascriptive or ethnic nationalism to be associated with believing that the level of immigration into one's country should be reduced and that immigrants should not automatically have the same rights as citizens. In the aforementioned study, Citrin and Wright find the same pattern of relationships between ascriptive nationalism and the belief that immigrants should adapt to mainstream values rather than maintain their original customs and traditions in every European country and the United States. These data have two implications: first, the public should be more willing to accept culturally similar immigrants; second, greater acceptance of ethnic diversity requires a redefinition of the boundaries of nationhood on more ethnically neutral civic terms.

The former expectation is borne out by survey data. In the United States, Gallup polls conducted from 1984 to 2006 consistently show that newcomers from Europe are most welcome, followed by those from Asia and Latin America.[15] For example, in 2002, the proportion of Americans saying "too many immigrants are being admitted" was 27 percent for Europe, 32 percent for Africa, 43 percent for Asia, and 49 percent for Latin America. Instructively, opposition to immigration is centered on those groups that are providing most of the newcomers. Analysis of the 2008 American National Election Study shows that negative feelings about Hispanics are more strongly related to opposition to immigration than are similar feelings about Asians.

In the 2010 ESS, national samples from 26 European countries were asked about how many people should be allowed to be admitted from three different groups: people of the same race or ethnicity as the majority, people of a different race or ethnicity than the majority, and people from poorer countries outside Europe. (The latter two groups clearly overlap.) In the pooled sample of 48,620 respondents, the proportions saying "just a few" or none were 33 percent, 50 percent, and 55 percent, respectively. This opposition to culturally dissimilar immigrants prevailed in every country, ranging from highs of 86 percent in Greece and 88 percent in Cyprus to 29 percent in Poland and 11 percent in Sweden. Multiple regression analyses of the pooled 2002–2010 ESS surveys (not shown here but available on request) with controls for demographic variables, country, and year of survey show that opposition to admitting culturally dissimilar and poor immigrants had much

Table 1.1   The Effect of Pride on Anti-immigrant Sentiment, by Country

Country	Pride	Country	Pride	Country	Pride
DK	.133***	IE	.074**	ES	.037***
FI	.094***	AT	.071**	NL	.035**
DE	.093***	CH	.070***	PT	.004
US	.090**	SE	.058***	CA	.003
AU	.084***	GB	.050**	NZ	−.009
NO	.081***	FR	.046**		

stronger effects on beliefs about the negative consequences of immigration for a country's culture *and* economy than did feelings about newcomers with the same race or ethnicity.

In sum, in both the United States and Europe, immigration from the "southern border" is feared. Moreover, in both continents, as Table 1.1 shows, patriotism, measured as pride in one's country, is associated with *anti-immigrant* sentiment in every country except Portugal, Canada, and New Zealand. Affective as well as normative facets of national identity shape attitudes toward immigrants. The implication for policy may be that promoting a more accepting outlook could depend on a more selective policy or on a stronger commitment to programs of assimilation.

DO MULTICULTURAL POLICIES MAKE A DIFFERENCE?

Have trends in public attitudes varied in countries depending on the strength of their multicultural policies? Regarding conceptions of national identity, it is useful to compare the 1995 and 2003 ISPP surveys, given that this period saw the policy pendulum in Europe begin to swing toward assimilation and also that it was punctuated by 9/11. By insisting on the preservation of difference, multicultural policies can be perceived as threatening ideas of nationhood based on a common culture. So, to the extent that immigrants fail to assimilate, one might expect subjective definitions of national identity to become more "ascriptive" where there is stronger official support for multiculturalism.

Of the 11 countries surveyed in both ISSP studies, Australia and Canada fall into "strong" MCP category; the United States, New Zealand, the United Kingdom, and Sweden are in the "modest" group; and Austria, Germany, Ireland, Norway, and Spain are coded as having "weak" MCP regimes.

Figure 1.2, reproduced from Citrin,[16] tracks the change between 1995 and 2003 in the proportion of respondents naming nativity (being born in the country), religion (being a Christian), language (speaking the national language), respect for the country's laws and institutions, and psychological identification (feeling like a national) as "very important" for making someone a "true national."

Conceptions of national identity in Australia and Canada, the countries at the top of the multiculturalist heap, moved in an "ethnic" direction, with nativity, religion, and language being deemed more important, in the aggregate, than eight years previously. Overall, the middle MCP group also moved in the ascriptive direction. Disaggregating the results shows statistically significant increases in the proportions of the American public calling nativity, language, and religion very important. In New Zealand, opinion made a similar, if less pronounced, shift, but there was no such change in either the United Kingdom or Sweden. In the "weak" MCP countries, there was little noticeable change in outlook. One interpretation is that the movement toward more ascriptive definitions of nationality in the settler societies with growing immigrant populations indicated discontent with the purpose of multicultural policies. But one should not overlook the possible impact of 9/11, not just in the United States but in the other English-speaking countries with strong ties to America.

The ISPP data also show that between 1995 and 2003, concern about the cultural threat of immigrants grew concomitantly with stronger support for the assimilation of cultural minorities.[17] Agreement that immigrants posed a *cultural* threat rose regardless of a country's MCP score, but there was no corresponding increase in perceptions of immigrants as an *economic* threat whatever a country's MCP score. Wright confirms these shifts in outlook between 1995 and 2003 with a much more rigorous multilevel regression analysis.[18] He concludes that there is some evidence of an ethnocentric backlash against immigration in countries with stronger multicultural regimes.

The European Social Survey (ESS) conducted between 2002 and 2010 provides more recent data for a set of European countries. Using these data sets, I constructed an Immigrant Level Index by combining responses to questions about whether more immigrants with the same ethnic background as the host country, immigrants with ethnic backgrounds different from that of the host country, and those coming from poorer countries should be admitted and recoding them to give scores ranging from 0 to 1 (most anti-immigrant). Figure 1.3 presents the fluctuations in these attitudes between 2002 and 2010, with countries grouped by the strength of their multicultural policy regimes. The weak MCP countries are consistently more hostile to increased immigration. But the data also point to a sharp rise in anti-immigrant sentiment in the stronger MCP countries (Netherlands, Belgium, the United Kingdom, and Sweden) between 2008 and 2010. These were not the European countries where the economic downturn was most marked, so one can speculate that resentment of multiculturalism catalyzed by elite rhetoric and the rise of anti-immigrant parties helped produce the shift in public opinion, already predisposed to oppose immigration. The radical right, in a sense, is lighting already combustible material. Overall, though, aggregate attitudes toward immigration in most European countries changed very little between 2002 and 2012; reluctance to admit many more newcomers, regardless of their race, remained the dominant point of view.

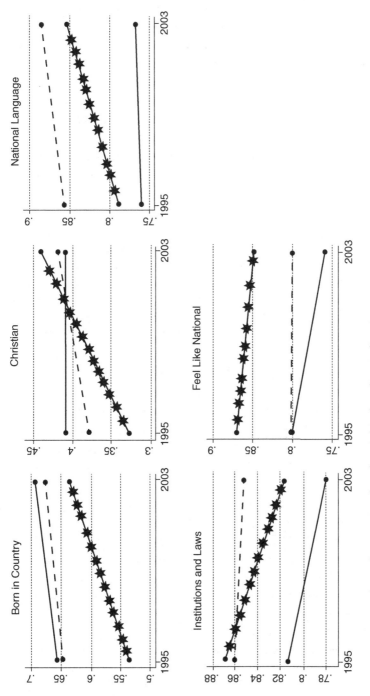

Figure 1.2 Trend in Ethnic Nationalism by Multiculturalism Policy Category

Indeed, Citrin and Wright find that there is a negative association between opposition to more immigration and political trust in all European countries sampled in the ESS and that this relationship is accentuated in countries with the strongest multicultural policy regimes (as measured by the MCP Index).[19] The implication is that multiculturalism can drive a wedge between those who are sympathetic to immigration and the larger group, which is hostile.

A SPECULATION ABOUT THE ROLE OF THE MEDIA

This chapter has emphasized the importance of subjective conceptions of national identity in undergirding opposition to immigration, which connects to the overall argument about the importance of media narratives of identity and immigration. Immigration policy focuses on who should be admitted, how many, and their rights and responsibilities. Research in social psychology has demonstrated a seemingly innate human tendency toward ethnocentrism.[20] Social identity theory based on the minimal group research paradigm has repeatedly shown that categorization of people as either "us" or "them" and in-group favoritism are ubiquitous, if not universal.[21] And, if this is true in the laboratory, how much more potent must the effects be when we consider ethnic groups deeply committed to their own way of life. So, when immigration brings people into impersonal contact with

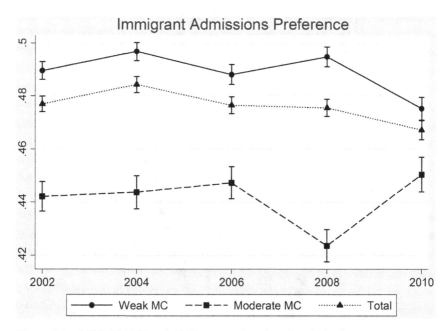

Figure 1.3   2002–2010 Trends in European Immigration Attitudes

others who are visibly different and when the latter demand cultural rights or receive government benefits that are viewed as unearned, negative political reactions are predictable.

And one factor that can exacerbate the natives' sense of threat is overestimation of the number of immigrants, as noted in the Introduction to this book. In a 2007 national survey of Americans, Sides and Citrin found that the median estimate for the number of immigrants in the country was 27 percent of the total population, more than double the census figure, and the median estimate for the number of illegal immigrants was 21 percent, almost seven times the official estimate.[22] The magnitude of these overestimates predictably was strongly related to beliefs that the level of immigration into the United States should be greatly decreased. More interesting perhaps is that correcting misinformation by telling respondents the official census data did not make attitudes significantly more favorable to immigrants. Since overestimation was correlated with living in areas with a recent influx of immigrants, one wonders whether the extent and nature of media coverage may have contributed to public misperceptions and in this way helped sustain restrictionist beliefs.

CONCLUSION

In this era of globalization, immigration cannot be willed out of existence even by those most opposed to it. Migration will continue to take different forms. In North America, liberal policy regimes remain intact, and the United States, in particular, will continue to grapple with the influx of illegal immigrants across its porous southern border. In Europe, EU citizenship provides the right of residential mobility, and this is one source of immigration, along with continuing pressure to admit refugees and a burgeoning problem of illegal entrants from Africa and the Middle East. So, despite the public's preference for restriction, with mass deportation probably off the table and the demise of the European Union a long shot, governments will have to continue to address the problem of integration.

The evidence of the surveys presented here does indicate a trend toward more support for assimilation and widespread belief in national identities founded on a common language and culture. In addition, a strong sense of national attachment linked to an ascriptive concept of nationality is associated with more negative opinions about immigration and less support for multiculturalist policies, particularly of the strong variety.

Assimilation can have coercive implications and take the form of a wholesale assault on the traditions of immigrants. But this need not be the case. If the United States can serve as an example, favoring individualism over group rights and assimilation over cultural separation has not excluded accepting the introduction of new streams into the common culture. Historically, the core of American assimilation encompasses learning English, venerating the country's political institutions, and national loyalty. If this is what Europe's new civic integration policies require, many multicultural policies can remain intact. Indeed, despite some concerns about the integration of Latino immigrants in the United States, the evidence is that their pattern of acculturation resembles that of their earlier European counterparts. By the third generation, most are monolingual in English, and patriotism is as high among the offspring of Latino immigrants as among white, native-born Americans.[23] So it may be that the swing toward assimilation in Europe contributed to stabilizing opinions about immigration between 2002 and 2012.

The task appears to be developing adequate programs to encourage linguistic and political assimilation of immigrants, and this may require a two-pronged approach. While evidence presented here suggests that multicultural policies can create an ethnocentric backlash among the native population, Wright and Bloemraad reach a tentative conclusion that countries with strong MCP regimes have somewhat greater success in raising the civic participation of immigrants.[24] So more research is needed to identity more precisely the potentially cross-cutting effects of these policies.

To the extent that multiculturalism enhances the place of ethnic identification as the fount of political identification and behavior, it creates obstacles for the inculcation of the inclusive conception of civic national identity that is open to immigration and to eroding some of the barriers between "us" and "them." In cross-sectional analyses, multiculturalist policies do not have a strong or consistent effect on anti-immigrant attitudes or political trust. Rather, they seem to function as latent predisposing factors that are triggered by situational factors—terrorist attacks, the demand for sharia law, the building of a giant mosque, debates about the burqa, debates about gender inequality—that evoke feelings of cultural threat and the sense that the politics of difference undermines national identity. Indeed, it is difficult to avoid the conclusion that the turmoil about immigration in Europe is at its core about the integration of Muslim migrants who fill low-skilled positions or the unemployed ranks—and these immigrants dominate a substantial segment of media coverage in France, as Zamith's study in this book found, supporting the argument made by several of the journalists' chapters that issues of visible difference tend to dominate media and public discourse.

To conclude, attitudes toward immigration are founded in large part on conceptions of nationhood and ethnocentric attitudes toward outsiders. These beliefs are entrenched but not immutable. How the immigration issue is framed may matter, and this is where an analysis of media choices can be important in either contributing to or narrowing the gap between elite attitudes and policies on the one hand and the preferences of publics that in a democracy constrain what governments do.

NOTES

1. This chapter represents a synthesis of research on immigration often conducted jointly by John Sides, Matthew Wright, Morris Levy, and me. I am grateful for their assistance and to Morris Levy for his special help in preparing this chapter.
2. Rogers Brubaker, "Religion and Nationalism: Four Approaches," *Nations and Nationalism* 18 (2012): 20.
3. Peter Schuck, "The Disconnect between Public Attitudes and Policy Outcomes in Immigration," in *Debating Immigration,* ed. Carol Swain (Cambridge: Cambridge University Press, 2007): 17–31.
4. Rogers Brubaker, "The Return of Assimilation?," in Brubaker, *Ethnicity without Groups* (Cambridge, MA: Harvard University Press, 2004), 116–31; Christian Joppke, *Selecting by Origin: Ethnic Migration in the Liberal State* (Cambridge, MA: Harvard University Press, 2005).
5. Sarah B. Goodman and M.M. Howard, "Evaluating and Explaining the Restrictive Backlash in Citizenship Policy in Europe," *Studies in Law, Politics, and Society* 60 (2013): 111–39; Christian Joppke, "Transformation of Immigrant Integration: Civic Integration and Antidiscrimination in the Netherlands, France, and Germany," *World Politics* 59 (2007): 243–73.
6. Samuel L. Gaertner and John F. Dovidio, *Reducing Intergroup Bias: The Common Ingroup Identity Model* (Philadelphia: Psychology Press, 2000); John E. Transue, "Identity Salience, Identity Acceptance, and Racial Policy Attitudes: American National Identity as a Uniting Force," *American Journal of Political Science* 51 (January 2007): 78–91.
7. Keith Banting, Richard Johnston, Will Kymlicka, and Stuart Soroka, "Do Multiculturalism Policies Erode the Welfare State?," in *Multiculturalism and the Welfare State: Recognition and Redistribution in Contemporary Democracies,* ed. Keith Banting and Will Kymlicka (Oxford: Oxford University Press, 2006), 49–91.
8. A related indicator not included in this measure is whether citizenship is based on jus soli or jus sanguinis, with the former policy clearly more open to a multiethnic polity.
9. This generally is implemented by rules allocating certain amounts of programming to minority groups, whether through foreign language programming or just control of content. One example, interestingly, is the representation of different kinds of music in the US Armed Forces Radio Network: a certain amount of R and B, soul, and rap, a certain amount of country music, and so forth.
10. Jack Citrin and John Sides, "Immigration and the Imagined Community in Europe and the United States," *Political Studies* 56 (2008): 33–56.
11. Reprinted from ibid.
12. Ibid.
13. Rogers Brubaker, *Citizenship and Nationhood in France and Germany* (Cambridge, MA: Harvard University Press, 1992); Liah Greenfeld, *Nationalism: Five Roads to Modernity* (Cambridge, MA: Harvard University Press, 1992).
14. Matthew Wright, "Policy Regimes and Normative Conceptions of Nationalism in Mass Public Opinion," *Comparative Political Studies* 43 (2011); Jack Citrin and Matthew Wright, "The Collision of National Identity and Multiculturalism among Mass Publics," paper presented at the annual meeting of the Midwest Political Science Association, April 4–7, 2008.
15. Jack Citrin and Matthew Wright, "The Politics of Immigration in a Nation of Immigrants," in *New Directions in American Politics,* ed. Raymond La Raja (New York: Routledge, 2013), 245.

16. Jack Citrin, "Are We All Now Multiculturalists, Assimilationists, Neither or Both?," paper presented at The Political Incorporation of Immigrants: Progress, Prospects and Pitfalls in Europe and North America, Berkeley, CA, March 5, 2009.
17. Ibid.
18. Wright, "Policy Regimes."
19. Jack Citrin, Morris Levy, and Matthew Wright, "Immigration, Multiculturalism, and Political Trust: A Janus-Faced Outcome?," paper presented at the 19th International Conference of Europeanists, Boston, March 24, 2012.
20. Donald R. Kinder and Cindy D. Kam, *Us against Them: Ethnocentric Foundations of American Opinion* (Chicago: University of Chicago Press, 2009).
21. Henri Tajfel, *Social Identity and Intergroup Relations* (Cambridge: Cambridge University Press, 1982).
22. John Sides and Jack Citrin, "European Opinion about Immigration: The Role of Identities, Interests and Information," *British Journal of Political Science* 37 (2007): 477–504.
23. Jack Citrin, Amy Lerman, Michael Murakami, and Kathryn Pearson, "Testing Huntington: Is Hispanic Immigration a Threat to American Identity?," *Perspectives on Politics* 5 (2007): 31–48.
24. Matthew Wright and Irene Bloemraad, "Is There a Trade-off between Multiculturalism and Robust Citizenship? Policy Regimes and Immigrant Incorporation in Comparative Perspective," *Political Perspectives* 10 (2012): 77–95.

REFERENCES

Banting, Keith, Richard Johnston, Will Kymlicka, and Stuart Soroka. "Do Multi-culturalism Policies Erode the Welfare State?" In *Multiculturalism and the Welfare State: Recognition and Redistribution in Contemporary Democracies*, ed. Keith Banting and Will Kymlicka. Oxford: Oxford University Press, 2006: 49–91.

Brubaker, Rogers. *Citizenship and Nationhood in France and Germany.* Cambridge, MA: Harvard University Press, 1992.

Brubaker, Rogers. "Religion and Nationalism: Four Approaches." *Nations and Nationalism* 18 (2012): 2–20.

Brubaker, Rogers. "The Return of Assimilation?" In *Ethnicity without Groups*, ed. Rogers Brubaker. Cambridge, MA: Harvard University Press, 2004: 116–31.

Citrin, Jack, "Are We All Now Multiculturalists, Assimilationists, Neither or Both?" Paper presented at The Political Incorporation of Immigrants: Progress, Prospects and Pitfalls in Europe and North America. Berkeley, CA, March 5, 2009.

Citrin, Jack, Amy Lerman, Michael Murakami, and Kathryn Pearson. "Testing Huntington: Is Hispanic Immigration a Threat to American Identity?" *Perspectives on Politics* 5 (2007): 31–48.

Citrin, Jack, Morris Levy, and Matthew Wright. "Immigration, Multiculturalism, and Political Trust: A Janus-faced Outcome?" Paper presented at the 19th International Conference of Europeanists. Boston, MA, March 24, 2012.

Citrin, Jack, and David O. Sears. "Balancing National and Ethnic Identities: The Psychology of E Pluribus Unum." In *Measuring Identity*, ed. Rawi Abdelal, Yoshiko Herrera, Alastair Johnston, and Rose McDermott. Cambridge: Cambridge University Press, 2009: 145–74.

Citrin, Jack, and John Sides. "Immigration and the Imagined Community in Europe and the United States." *Political Studies* 56 (2008): 33–56.

Citrin, Jack, and Matthew Wright. "The Collision of National Identity and Multiculturalism among Mass Publics." Paper presented at the annual meetings of the Midwest Political Science Association, April 4–7, 2008.

Citrin, Jack, and Matthew Wright. "The Politics of Immigration in a Nation of Immigrants." In *New Directions in American Politics,* ed. Raymond La Raja. New York: Routledge, 2013: 245.

Gaertner, Samuel L., and John F. Dovidio. *Reducing Intergroup Bias: The Common Ingroup Identity Model.* Philadelphia: Psychology Press, 2000.

Goodman, Sarah B., and M. M. Howard. "Evaluating and Explaining the Restrictive Backlash in Citizenship Policy in Europe." *Studies in Law, Politics, and Society* 60 (2013): 111–39.

Greenfeld, Liah. *Nationalism: Five Roads to Modernity.* Cambridge, MA: Harvard University Press, 1992.

Joppke, Christian. *Selecting by Origin: Ethnic Migration in the Liberal State.* Cambridge, MA: Harvard University Press, 2005.

Joppke, Christian. "Transformation of Immigrant Integration: Civic Integration and Antidiscrimination in the Netherlands, France, and Germany." *World Politics 59* (2007): 243–73.

Kinder, Donald R., and Cindy D. Kam. *Us against Them: Ethnocentric Foundations of American Opinion.* Chicago: University of Chicago Press, 2009.

Multiculturalism Policy Index. http://www.queensu.ca/mcp/ (accessed January 3, 2012).

Schuck, Peter, "The Disconnect between Public Attitudes and Policy Outcomes in Immigration." In *Debating Immigration,* ed. Carol Swain. Cambridge: Cambridge University Press, 2007: 17–31.

Sides, John, and Jack Citrin. "European Opinion about Immigration: The Role of Identities, Interests and Information." *British Journal of Political Science* 37 (2007): 477–504.

Tajfel, Henri. *Social Identity and Intergroup Relations.* Cambridge: Cambridge University Press, 1982.

Transue, John E. "Identity Salience, Identity Acceptance, and Racial Policy Attitudes: American National Identity as a Uniting Force." *American Journal of Political Science* 51 (2007): 78–91.

Wright, Matthew. "Policy Regimes and Normative Conceptions of Nationalism in Mass Public Opinion." *Comparative Political Studies* 43 (2011).

Wright, Matthew, and Irene Bloemraad, "Is There a Trade-off between Multi-culturalism and Robust Citizenship? Policy Regimes and Immigrant Incorporation in Comparative Perspective." *Political Perspectives* 10 (2012).

2   Policies and Politics of Immigration in the United States and the European Union

Martin A. Schain
New York University

INTRODUCTION: LESSONS FROM EUROPE?

In this chapter I evaluate immigration policy in the United States in comparative perspective. Although media on both sides of the Atlantic tend to report immigration in terms of crisis and failure, I argue that the differences in policy and policy impact have been stark. The European experience in confronting issues of immigration through public policy has been generally poor and badly managed, with unanticipated results that have been increasingly negative. Although the failures of American policy in dealing with illegal immigration and undocumented immigrants now residing in the United States have been politically front and center for most of the past decade, the considerable success of policies on legal entry and integration have generally gone unnoticed.

With few exceptions, policy on immigration has been poorly defined and often contradictory. The gap between policy outputs and outcomes has been considerable and appears to have nurtured the breakthrough and growth of radical-right political parties. Therefore, the lessons to be learned from Europe are generally negative—what not to do and how not to do it. I will examine three aspects of immigration policy in Europe and the United States: entry policy, integration policy, and border enforcement.

ENTRY POLICY

In many ways entry policy is the most difficult to analyze. Entry of immigrants for settlement into most European countries has been strictly limited for the past 40 years. For most of Europe, the postwar surge in immigration, related to recovery and economic growth, ended with the economic crisis of the early 1970s. The relatively open immigration policies of the previous 25 years rapidly drew to a close, through government decisions that ended the bilateral treaties of the German guest worker program, administrative decisions that ended more or less open immigration to France, and legislation that redefined citizenship in the UK. At the same time that countries in

Europe were developing more exclusionary policies, the United States began to implement more open policies, ending 40 years of exclusionary policy.[1]

Although the political framing of these policy decisions generally made it clear that immigration for settlement would be limited at best ("zero immigration" was the phrase often used in France), immigrants continued to arrive each year for several reasons: first, because court decisions limited restriction on entry, particularly for family members of resident immigrants; second, because European countries still needed workers in some service sectors, in construction and in some industries; finally, because of the spurt of asylum-seekers who were admitted during the 1990s. Thus, although the explicit rhetoric of immigration was and remains extremely restrictive, policies themselves remain, sometimes implicitly and sometimes explicitly, more nuanced. Since 2000, all major European countries have developed programs to attract "highly skilled" immigrants, although only the United Kingdom has been successful, and in 2007 the European Commission presented a plan for an EU "Blue Card" for these immigrants (the directive was enacted in 2009). The Blue Card directive was supposed to be the equivalent of the US green card. In fact, it is a relatively short-term work permit (two years, but renewable), and the United Kingdom, Ireland, and Denmark have opted out of its provisions. The advantage of the new permit is that it is applicable in all EU countries that have adopted it.[2]

Nevertheless, the real growth in immigration of third-country nationals has been among the less skilled and among those who enter for family unification.[3] Despite stated policies, inflow and populations of the foreign-born are higher in the European Union than in the United States, and resident stock is approaching the US levels (see Table 2.1).

A substantial part of this movement results from the fact that the number of citizens of EU member states migrating to member states other than their own has increased—by 10 percent a year since 2002—while immigration of non-EU nationals has remained stable since 2003. In 2006, EU nationals represented 40 percent of immigrants entering the (other) EU-27 countries. During the same period, the number of EU nationals returning to their country of origin declined by 20 percent.[4] This percentage has continued to grow (44 percent in 2008), contributing to the growing proportion of the resident foreign population in EU countries who come from other EU countries. More than a third of the foreign nationals in the EU-27 in 2009 were from other EU countries.[5] The general trend in Europe since 2002 has been for an increasing number of EU citizens to move to other EU countries for an extended period of time, indicating a relative success for free-movement policy.

Thus, there are decisions and some legislation throughout Europe that permit and, in the case of highly skilled immigrants, sometimes encourage continued immigration. Although most countries have some sort of residency laws that define legal residency of noncitizens, however, no country in Europe has passed or attempted to pass a comprehensive law on immigration

Table 2.1 Immigration and Immigrant Populations in France, Britain, and the United States, 1992–2009

A. Immigration Inflows for Permanent Settlement (th)				
	1992 total	Per thousand population	2009 total	Per thousand population
United Kingdom	175	3.0	471.3	7.1
France	116.6	2.0	126.2	2.0
United States a	974	3.8	1,130.8	3.7
European Union 15/25	1727.6	4.7	2,500	5.0

B. Immigrant Population (th)			
	Year	Thousands	% of population
United Kingdom (foreign-born)	2009	6,899	11.3
France (foreign-born)	2009	7,235	11.6
United States (foreign-born)	2009	38,948	12.7
EU 27 (foreign-born)	2010	47,348	9.4

C. Inflows by Entry Category (2009)			
	France	Britain	United States
Total	178,700	347,000	1,130,200
Family (%)	49	33.6	88.8
Work (%)	12.6	35.6	5.8

Note: a: Does not include those born of U.S. citizens.
Source: OECD, *International Migration Outlook, Annual Report 2011* (Paris: OECD Publications, 2011), pp. 281–283, 331, 331 341; *Trends in International Migration, Annual Report 2003* (Paris: OECD Publications, 2003), pp. 117–194, 286, 291, 305–310; Katya Vasileva, "Population and Social Conditions," *Eurostat, Statistics in Focus*, 34/2011, p. 2.

comparable to the US Immigration and Nationality Act, which defines in law both categories for entry and limits. Therefore, criteria for legal entry in Europe remain somewhat opaque and often poorly defined, contributing to what radical-right parties in Europe often call the gap between commitments to halt immigration and the realities of continuing immigration each year.

Moreover, the differences in entry requirements between Europe and the United States have been growing deeper over time. During the past decade,

major European countries have been moving toward linking entry with nar-
row concepts of integration that would tend to ensure cultural stability and
minimize challenges to the cultural status quo from immigration, perhaps
a rejection of multiculturalism in the broad US sense, as noted in Citrin's
chapter.[6] For example, requirements for entry in the Netherlands, France,
Germany, and (to a lesser extent) the United Kingdom have increasingly
demanded conformity with national social norms. Prime Minister David
Cameron of the United Kingdom (supported by France's then president
Nicolas Sarkozy and Germany's chancellor Angela Merkel) has called for
"muscular liberalism" to bar state aid to groups that do not share Britain's
liberal values, while France and the Netherlands have tightened admission
requirements even for those seemingly eligible for family unification.[7]

What appears to be a growing convergence in setting more demanding
entry requirements is related to growing collaboration among a key group
of EU immigrant receiving countries (the so-called G6). In 2006 the G6
agreed to create a committee of experts to investigate the procedures used
in all member states that linked entry to considerations of integration. They
then planned to propose such a policy to the other countries of the European
Union, as discussed later in this chapter.[8]

American policy on entry, by contrast, has moved decidedly in another
direction. Since 1965, US entry law has been strongly biased toward a
broad-based concept of family unification that effectively gives priority to
families of those residents born abroad. At the most basic level, immigration
law now favors and promotes diversity in other ways as well.

Between 1965 and 2000, the legal ceiling on immigration increased—
during good economic times and bad—by 50 percent. The Immigration
Act of 1990 included a program of "diversity visas," that would eventually
provide for the admission, on an annual basis, of 55,000 immigrants from
"underrepresented" countries. Entries from these countries are required to
have at least high school equivalency diplomas and/or work experience but
are then chosen by lottery. Thus, what began as an effort to relieve the
backlog of applications from Ireland—the initiative was taken by Senator
Edward Kennedy on behalf of his Irish constituents– ended as a mechanism
for increasing the diversity of the population of the United States.

Indeed, when the House/Senate conferees emerged with a final agreement on the 1990 legislation, they called their compromise agreement a
victory for cultural diversity, "for family unity, and for job creation."[9] What
makes this statement particularly striking is that, even as an afterthought,
American political leaders were seeking to promote what European leaders
either feared or sought to carefully manage—cultural diversity.

As we shall see, questions of cultural diversity are at the very core of
the problem of immigration in Europe and are the primary reasons that
entry has been increasingly linked to integration. Although diversity has
been critically debated in the United States (mostly around the time that the
diversity clause was passed), this question has faded from the immigration

debate since then.[10] The core political problem of immigration in the United States is illegal entry and undocumented immigrants in the country, as discussed later.

INTEGRATION POLICY AND INTEGRATION SUCCESS AND FAILURE

The gap in integration policy is also widening between Europe and the United States. Many European countries are beginning to develop explicit integration policies for immigrants that would be consistent with their more muscular entry requirements. In March 2006, the interior ministers of the six largest EU countries agreed to pursue the idea of a harmonized "integration contract" at the EU level, using the French and the Dutch models as a starting point.

Although this initiative was taken at the European level, it reflected a decidedly nationalistic movement in many EU countries, with a focus on national identity. The success of the List Pym Fortuyn in the Netherlands in 2002 (and Fortuyn's assassination) had substantially altered the dynamics of Dutch politics, while the debate over the *foulard* (the Islamic veil) in France in 2003 reflected a deep political strain supporting cultural unity.[11] These strains emerged in the United Kingdom after the attacks on the underground in 2005 and throughout the European Union during the discussions about the proposed "constitution" in 2005, rejected by referendum in both the Netherlands and France. By 2006, the French and the Dutch had already made evaluation of various cultural criteria of integration a condition for entry.

One of the first acts of the French presidency of the European Council in 2008 was to propose a comprehensive, compulsory EU integration program. The compulsory aspect was finally dropped in June, but a "European Pact on Immigration and Asylum" was passed by the European Council in October 2008 that emphasized three criteria for acceptance and integration in Europe: language mastery of the receiving country; knowledge of and commitment to the values of the receiving country; and access to employment.[12]

Much of this activity was generated by broad-based political perception that traditional—less interventionist—modes of integration had failed to produce desired results.[13] Although perceptions of policy failure on integration have been widespread and politically salient for the French, Germans, Dutch, and British, this issue has not been particularly salient for the Americans.

In the American case, the perception of failure (merged with analyses of race relations in the United States) was widespread among intellectuals during the decade of the 1990s but has faded since.[14] There is a considerable gap in public opinion between the general optimism of Americans about immigrant integration and the relative pessimism in key European countries.[15] According to the most recent comparative surveys that deal with questions of integration, Americans are generally more confident than Europeans that "immigrants in general are integrating well" and are far more confident in the pace of integration of Hispanic immigrants. By comparison, confidence in integration of Muslim immigrants (the rough comparison with Hispanics) is more than 70 percent lower than in the most confident country in Europe (France). These differences remain, even if we use a subsample of respondents for whom the question of immigration is their primary political concern. Indeed, by the 1990s, proposals to cut back on legal immigration could gain no congressional support, and there was durable support for multicultural model of America as a "nation of nations" (see Table 2.2).

In fact, integration, even without specific policies, *has* been generally more successful by most measures in the United States than in Europe, although in Europe integration policies have sometimes been more successful than the political rhetoric would indicate. In France, for example, civic value orientations of immigrants have generally been similar to those of the general population; so has their contention and anger. More than residents of most countries in Europe, French respondents tend to have confidence in the willingness of immigrants from Muslim countries, including devout Muslims, to adapt to French customs and French society. French respondents place a far higher value than their government on civic rather than cultural (or even linguistic) integration.

On the other hand, French policy has not been particularly strong in developing tools for combating discrimination, and France has failed to create either employment or educational opportunities for its minority populations. In addition, children from immigrant families in France have done

Table 2.2   Attitudes about Integration of Immigrant Populations

	US%	Fr%	UK%	Ger%	NL%	It%
"Immigrants in general are integrating well"	59	44	43	41	3	37
Among those for whom immigration first priority:	50	21	18	40	–	43
"Muslim immigrants are integrating well"		45	37	25	36	37
Among those for whom immigration first priority:		30	20	19	–	26
"Hispanic immigrants are integrating well"	78					
Among those for whom immigration first priority:	61					

Source: Data from German Marshall Fund of the United States, *Transatlantic Trends, Immigration* (Washington, DC, 2011), COUNTRY + Q 1a,29a, 29b, 29c.

comparatively poorly in the education system. On one hand, educational attainment among immigrant populations at the university level is as great as or greater than that of the native population in France, as it is in the United States and in Great Britain. On the other hand, the proportion of immigrants who drop out or who never get to upper secondary education is disastrously high in France, higher than in either Britain or the United States.

Moreover, there has been less improvement in France during the past decade than in Britain or the United States. These differences are confirmed by an analysis comparing achievement scores in reading, math, and science among immigrant children in 10 countries, including France and Britain, with scores for native children of the same age. The number of immigrant children with low achievement scores was almost 40 percent higher in France than in Britain. In fact, these differences persist at every level of the socioeconomic scale, from poor to more privileged children (see Table 2.4).[16]

This is important because educational attainment has a strong impact on unemployment rates for immigrants (for natives as well). However, educational achievement has a relatively small impact on unemployment rates, particularly for immigrants, as well as for native French, particularly when compared to comparable figures for Britain and the United States (see Table 2.3).

This reflects a long-term failure to address class inequalities in France. In France, a lycée student from a lower-class family has a chance of entering into higher education two times lower than that of a child growing up in comparable circumstances in Spain or in Ireland.

American integration policy has grown in scope and has become increasingly focused on antidiscrimination policy, which in turn has reinforced minority identity and legitimacy. An unintended consequence of this policy has been to open and reinforce political opportunities. Opportunities for both political expression and access to the political system have been far greater in the United States than in any country in Europe, including Britain and France.

The difference in political opportunities between the United States and Europe is partly explained by the difficulty new immigrant voters face in

Table 2.3   Unemployment Rates of Foreign-Born Populations, by Level of Educational Attainment, 2003–2004

	Lo Education	Med. Education	Hi Education	Diff lo/hi
France: For.-Bn.	18.4	14.4	11.8	−36%
Native	12.2	7.9	5.8	−52%
Britain: For.-Bn.	12.2	7.9	4.2	−66%
Native	8.8	4.7	2.3	−74%
US: For.-Bn.	9.1	5.7	4.3	−53%
Native	15.5	6.7	3.2	−79%

Source: OECD, *International Migration Outlook* (Washington, DC: OECD, 2007), p. 154.

Table 2.4   Educational Attainment of Immigrant Populations, 2004–2010

| | Less than upper-secondary education* | | | | University degree or higher | | | |
| | Native-born | | Foreign-born | | Native-born | | Foreign-born | |
	2004	2008–2010	2004	2008–2010	2004	2008–2010	2004	2008–2010
France 2010	35%	29.9%	56%**	51.1%	13%	14.2	12%	15.5
Britain	49	24.0#	45**	29.7	20	29.8	28	32.6
US	12.5	9.6	32.8	29.8	27	30.1	27	28.9

*UK = ISCED 2 level or below; France = BEPC (first cycle high school) or below, and US = no high school degree.

**no qualification: UK = 10% (2004); France = 50% (2004)

Sources: (France and Britain): *OECD in Figures*, 2005 (Washington, D.C.: OECD, 2006) p. 65; European Community Labour Force Surveys; INSEE, Enquête emploi, enseignement-éducation de 2005 et 2010, ages 15–65 working population; University College London, CreAm, Christian Dustmann and Nikolous Theordoropoulos, "Ethnic Minority Immigrants and Their Children in Britain," CDP 10/06, p. 20; Christian Dustmann, Tommaso Frattini, and Gianandrea Lanzara, "Educational Achievement of Second Generation Immigrants: An International Comparison," CDP No. 16/11, p. 27 (Washington, DC: US Bureau of the Census); US Congress, Congressional Budget Office, *A Description of the Immigrant Population* (November 2004); US Bureau of the Census, Current Population Survey, Table 40, Ages 25+, whole population with no high school diploma and BA+, released September 30, 2011.

penetrating the closed and better organized political party organizations in Europe, whereas in the United States the system is more open.[17] Of at least equal importance, however, has been the difference between the ways that European and US parties have tended to frame immigration issues. In Europe, immigration has often been framed in terms of identity politics, even among parties of the Left, and immigrant populations have been objectified as a challenge to cultural and/or political stability. In the United States, there has been a greater tendency to see immigrant populations as a potential political resource, capable of altering the *rapports de force* between the parties—something that was clearly evident in the 2012 presidential election.[18] Moreover, in Europe, even where immigrant representation has been relatively robust (the Netherlands, for example), immigrant groups have had relatively little influence on the outcomes of public policy.

BORDER ENFORCEMENT

Although there appear to be converging political concerns in Europe and the United States about the permeability of the border—the US border with Mexico, in particular, and the Schengen (external) border in Europe—in fact the US border has been far more permeable than its European counterpart. Nevertheless, the United States has devoted far more resources to border control than have the European countries involved. Therefore, has Europe developed a border control system that is more effective than that of the United States?

Estimating the number of undocumented migrants in any country is a formidable task, which always comes with political overtones. The task is complicated by a lack of any good way of knowing how many illegal immigrants have left the country. The difficulty is fully elaborated in the comparative report for the European Commission Clandestino Project.[19] These estimates vary between 1.9 and 3.8 million for the EU 27 in 2008, relatively close to the more political figures released by governments during the past decade.

Government estimates vary with the political climate and according to whether it is more politically advantageous to maximize the estimate (to support new budget allocations) or minimize the estimate (to demonstrate the effectiveness of border controls). What is striking about both the scholarly and the political estimates is that they are lower for Europe than for the United States, even if we consider variations by country. In France, 0.68 percent of the population (on the high side) is estimated to have entered the country illegally, a figure considerably lower than that for Britain (863,000, or 1.4 percent) and far lower than that for the United States (11–12 million, or 3.8 percent) (see Table 2.5).[20]

Table 2.5   Estimates of Undocumented Immigrant Populations, 2002–c.2008

Year	Population in millions		As % of population	
	minimum	maximum	minimum	maximum
EU				
2002 (EU-15)	3.1	5.3	0.8	1.4
2005	2.2	4.8	0.58	1.23
2008(EU-27)	1.9	3.8	0.39	0.77
France				
2006	0.18	0.4		0.68
US				
2002	9.0	9.9	2.9	3.2
2005	10.6	11.6	3.5	3.8
2008	11.1	12.1	3.6	3.9
2010	10.7	11.7	3.5	3.8

Sources: Clandestino Research Project, *Size and Development of Irregular Migration to the EU,* http://clandestino.eliamep.gr (accessed September 22, 2011); Pew Hispanic Center, *Unauthorized Immigrant Population: National and State Trends,* 2010, www.pewhispanic.org (accessed September 22, 2011).

The relatively low proportion of illegal immigrants in France has been attributed—in part—to the fact that illegal immigrants, until 2007, were able to claim legal residency after 10 years in the country. As a result, the number of illegal immigrants who have been legalized under periodic mass amnesties has been far lower in France than in other countries in Europe. It has also been attributed to the relatively small role that the informal labor market plays in France. "In general, the more a labor market is deregulated," argues François Héron, "the more it attracts irregular migration."[21] Moreover, during the past decade the number of undocumented immigrants in Europe has been declining (by at least 40 percent), both at the European level and among most of the member states. The most notable exception is the United Kingdom, where the clearing of backlogs of asylum seekers has resulted in a sharp increase caused by a change in status of the same people. In the United States, the undocumented immigrant population peaked about 2007 and has diminished slightly since.

However, it is not the border that is at issue in Europe, since it is widely conceded that the border was crossed legally in most cases (90%, according to the French Ministry of the Interior), but the ability of the state to keep track of immigrants once they are already in Europe. In the US case, the border is clearly at issue. The Pew Hispanic Center estimates that only 40–50 percent of those in the United States illegally entered legally through various ports of entry, and most of these are visa overstayers.[22] In both Europe and the United States, resources devoted to border control, as well internal control of immigrant populations, have increased during the past decade. While European authorities can claim some success, however (interestingly, they rarely do), the Americans can claim only modest success in return for the vast buildup of forces and equipment at the Mexican border.

In a similar way, Susan Martin has argued that most EU countries have focused on internal enforcement through the use of identity papers and controls in the labor market.[23] Martin compares this process to the Anglo-Saxon "island model" of enforcement, with its emphasis on frontier controls and weaker internal enforcement mechanisms. The difference can be seen in the pattern of expulsions, which are far higher by percentage in France and even in Britain than in the United States: roughly 3.6 percent of the estimated US undocumented population but 5 percent of undocumented persons in the United Kingdom and 7.5 percent of those in France in 2010 (see Figure 2.1).

Nevertheless, two trends of enforcement seem to be emerging. First, in small steps, the European Union appears to be moving toward elements of the "island model" of border control, driven by the unevenness of frontier controls among the member states, as well as by the mutual dependence that has always existed in the Schengen system. In the US case, there has been a stronger emphasis on internal controls of immigrant populations during the past decade, particularly through the use of high-profile raids and employer audits (see Table 2.6). Nevertheless, US internal efforts have tended to be more sporadic and focused on a series of short-lived "operations" since the

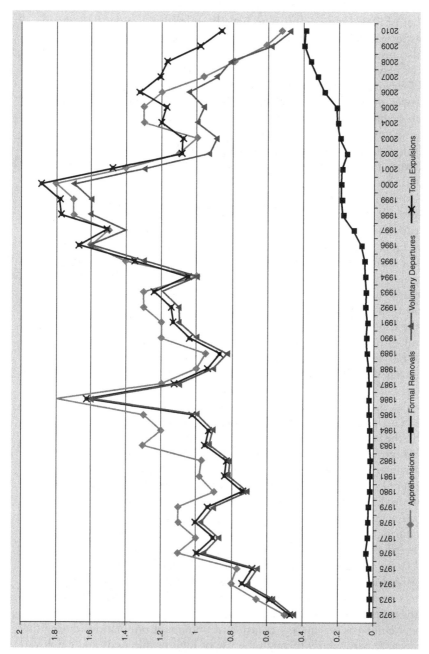

Figure 2.1   The Changing US Pattern: US Apprehensions and Expulsions, 1972–2010

Table 2.6   Employer Audits (I-9) in the United States

Year	Number of audits	Year	Number of audits
1990	10,000	2009	1,400
2003	2,200	2010	2,200
2008	503	2011 (est.)	2,496

Source: US Department of Homeland Security data; Peter Brownell, "The Declining Enforcement of Employer Sanctions," Migration Information Source, September 2011.

1990s. The bigger picture, however, is a trend toward the Europeanization of border control, through more frequent internal operations, a stronger emphasis on formal and recorded removals, and many fewer voluntary departures (that facilitate returns).

The number of formal removals of undocumented migrants from the United States has steadily grown since 2005 to about 400,000 in 2010, and stronger penalties have been imposed on employers, implying greater labor market controls. However, because "voluntary departures" have vastly diminished at the same time, the total number of expulsions since 2000 has steadily declined, from almost 2 million expulsions in 2000 to just over 800,000 in 2010. Of course, this does not mean that 11 million undocumented migrants in the United States are going to "self-deport."

CONCLUSIONS

In general, US immigration policy has been far better defined, more consistent, and more durable than that of Europe and has found greater political legitimacy. Neither mass opinion nor elite political opinion in America is deeply divided over entry and integration policies as elaborated in this chapter. For Europeans, ill-defined and inconsistent policies on entry and integration have poisoned the political dialogue on these issues and have fed and defined support for the radical right. A radical-right political party has become firmly established in France, has entered government in Austria and Switzerland, has become the firm support for a conservative government in Denmark over many years, and now challenges the established parties (at least in public opinion) in the United Kingdom. Therefore, it no longer makes sense to think about the radical right in Europe simply in terms of marginality and protest.[24]

On the other hand, Americans are deeply concerned and divided about the intractable problem of undocumented migration, which has festered for many years. The tools used in Europe—better-controlled labor markets, combined with periodic amnesties—are politically problematic in the United

States, while the militarization of the border appears to be of questionable effectiveness.

The United States has successfully avoided the pitfalls associated with the failed policies in Europe. The question is whether it can avoid the pitfalls associated with failed frontier policies in the United States. Ariane Chebel d'Appollonia notes that "Depicting immigration as the ultimate challenge to state sovereignty is a convenient way to explain the gap between stated objectives and actual outcomes."[25] In fact, the United States has dealt comparatively well with legal immigration. It has dealt less well with undocumented immigration and immigrants primarily because of the contradictions between stated policy on entry and vagaries of policy implementation. These differences in policies and outcomes are likely to contribute to the distorted public perceptions of the challenges of immigration in both the United States and Europe, which are discussed in the following chapters.

NOTES

1. For an account of the suspension of immigration in Europe, see Martin A. Schain, *The Politics of Immigration in France, Britain and the United States: A Comparative Study,* second edition (New York: Palgrave Macmillan, 2012), chs. 2, 5, and 8.
2. The directive is Council Directive 2009/50/EC. A "directive" is an EU law that requires each member state to pass legislation that transposes the directive into national law, with some latitude for national needs. The process had not yet been completed as of January 1, 2013.
3. In fact, the category of "family unification" is more complicated. In France, for example, most family migrants are admitted not under "family unification" rules but under the category of "private and family life." This category of admission was created in 1998. It usually involves temporary admission for foreign members of French families who do not easily fit the category of family unification. See insee, *Les immigrés en France* (Paris: insee, 2005), 70–72.
4. See Anne Herm, "Recent Migration Trends: Citizens of EU-27 Member States Become Ever More Mobile While EU Remains Attractive to Non-EU Citizens," *Eurostat, Statistics in Focus,* 98/2008, 1, 3.
5. Eurostat, *Migration and Migrant Population Statistics,* October 2010, http://epp.eurostat.ec.europa.eu/statistics_explained/index.phb/Migration, 3.
6. On this point, see Christopher Caldwell, *Reflections of the Revolution in Europe: Immigration, Islam and the West* (New York: Doubleday, 2009).
7. Peggy Hollinger, "Council of Europe Warns on Multiculturalism," *Financial Times,* February 16, 2011. The sharp movement toward consensus and away from multiculturalism is summarized and anlyzed in three articles in *Le Monde,* Febuary 26, 2011, under the rubric "Le multiculturalisme, entre modèle et crise." Two articles of particular interest are Eric Fassin, "Nicolas Sarkozy en marche vers le 'monoculturalisme,'" and Béatrice Durand, "En Allemagne, un mot d'ordre bien plus qu'une politique: l'idée de la nécessité d'une culture de référence l'emporte," 18–19.
8. Hugh Williamson, "EU Six Consider Introduction of 'Integration Contracts' for Immigrants," *Financial Times,* March 24, 2006.
9. Tichenor, Daniel J., *Dividing Lines: The Politics of Immigration Control in America* (Princeton: Princeton University Press, 2002), p. 274.

10. See Schain, *The Politics of Immigration*, 257.
11. See Paul Scheffer, *Immigrant Nations* (Cambridge: Polity Press, 2011), chs. 4 and 5.
12. See www.euractiv.com, July 2, 2008, "European Pact on Immigration and Asylum (13440/08), approved by the JHA Council on 25 Sept. and adopted by the European Council," statement issued by the French Council of Ministers, November 12, 2008. Accessed Feb. 2, 2009.
13. See Scheffer, *Immigrant Nations*, 325–33.
14. American multiculturalism was severely criticized by the 1990s. See in particular Peter Salins's approving account of the success of Americanization policies in *Assimilation American Style* (New York: HarperCollins, 1997), Part 3; Samuel P. Huntington, *Who Are We: The Challenges to America's National Identity* (New York: Simon and Schuster, 2005); and Arthur M. Schlessinger Jr., *The Disuniting of America: Reflections on a Multicultural Society* (New York: Norton, 1991, 1998).
15. There is also a striking difference between the priorities of mass publics for immigrant integration and the declared priorities of governments. Governments in Europe are far more insistent on sharing cultural values than are mass publics, and congruence is more evident in the United States than in Europe. See German Marshall Fund of the United States, *Transatlantic Trends: Immigration* (Washington, DC: GMF, 2010), 31.
16. Sylke Schnepf, "How Different Are Immigrants? A Cross-Country and Cross Survey Analysis of Educational Achievement," IZA (Institute for the Study of Labor)/Bonn, DP# 1398, November 2004, 12, 23, 33, 40, 34–36.
17. See Jennifer Hochschild and John Mollenkopf, eds., *Bringing Outsiders In: Transatlantic Perspectives on Immigrant Incorporation* (Ithaca, NY: Cornell University Press, 2009), in particular the article by Richard Alba and Nancy Foner, "Entering the Precincts of Power: Do National Differences Matter for Immigrant Minority Political Representation?" Also see Rahsaan Maxwell, *Ethnic Minority Migrants in Britain and France: Integration Trade-offs* (Cambridge: Cambridge University Press, 2012), for a different interpretation of differences.
18. See Schain, *The Politics of Immigration* (2012), 288–91; and Martin A. Schain, "Prospects for Political Integration," in *Immigrant Politics: Race and Representation in Western Europe*, ed. Terri E. Givens and Rahsaan Maxwell (Boulder, Colo.: Lynne Reinner, 2012), 130–40.
19. Henri Courau, *Undocumented Migration: Counting the Uncountable. Data and Trends across Europe: France Country Report* (January 2009), http://clandestino.eliamep.gr/wp-content/uploads/2009/10/clandestino_report_france_final_2.pdf , and Clandestino Project Overview, 5, http://clandestino.eliamep.gr.
20. The French estimate was given by the minister of the interior in an interview in *Le Figaro*, May 11, 2005; the British figures were quoted by Professor John Salt in *The Sunday Times* for April 17, 2005, as estimates that he did for the Home Office; and the American figure was cited by Thomas Friedman in the *International Herald Tribune* on April 6, 2006. In each case, the government has argued that there has been an increase; in the US case, the figure is double the numbers cited by Tapinos in 1999. In general, the comparison among France, Britain, and the United States—if not the exact figures—is confirmed in a massive report by the French Senate in April 2006. The report also deals with the complex problem of estimating the population of "irregular immigrants," which includes those who entered the country legally and whose situation evolved into illegality (the majority), as well as those who entered the country illegally (a relatively small number). See *Rapport de la commission d'enquête sur l'immigration clandestine, créée en vertu d'une résolution adoptée par le Sénat le 27 octobre 2005* (2 vols.), Journal Officiel

de la France, 2005, http://www.journal-officiel.gouv.fr/. In particular, see the testimony of François Héran in vol. 2, cited on p. 47 of vol. 1. He also cites the United States as one of the countries where the informal labor market is most important. The data cited by the report (vol. 1, 47) indicate that no country in Europe has a lower rate of irregular immigration than France.

21. See the testimony of François Héron, in vol. 2, *Rapport de la commission*.
22. See Pew Hispanic Center, "Modes of Entry for the Unauthorized Migrant Population," Fact Sheet, May 22, 2006, http://www.pewhispanic.org/.
23. Susan F. Martin, "Unauthorized Migration: US Policy Responses in Comparative perspective," paper presented to the International Studies Association meeting, March 2007.
24. See Cas Mudde, *Populist Radical Right Parties in Europe* (Cambridge: Cambridge University Press, 2007).
25. See Ariane Chebel d'Appollonia, *Frontiers of Fear: Immigration and Insecurity in the United States and Europe* (Ithaca, NY: Cornell University Press, 2012), ch. 4.

3 Responsible Reporting and Perceptions of Migrants in an Era of Unprecedented Mobility

Anne Grobet
United Nations Alliance of Civilizations

Since its inception in 2005 through the initiative of Turkey and Spain, the United Nations Alliance of Civilizations (UNAOC) has aimed to improve understanding and cooperative relations among nations and peoples across cultures and religions by building trust and bridging gaps. While its mandate addresses neither migration flows nor policies, the Migration program, one of UNAOC's four pillars (with Youth, Education, and Media), works to minimize negative stereotypes as well as the tendency to discriminate against migrants and minority groups with a view to improve management of diversity and to enhance social cohesion. It works every day to promote positive dialogue about migration and encourages the exchange of ideas and practices to further enhance the migrant experience, recognizing that diversity is a positive reality.

When addressing social cohesion, no one can ignore perceptions. As the manager of the Migration program, I am particularly interested in media coverage of migration, ranging from the representations of migrants to the impact on public perceptions. Because of my specialization in conflict transformation with a focus on the Middle East, I have been particularly attentive to the representations of Middle Eastern societies and Islam in the media and to their impact, whether positive or negative, true or false, accurate or inaccurate. The first step to more integrated societies is the relation of one to another. The essence of this relation lies in the experience and/or in the perceptions of the other. When these perceptions are built on experience, stereotyping is minimized, but when they are built on mediated perceptions, the relationship can be significantly impacted by misconceptions. In this regard, the social environment, public figures, and the media, among other factors, play an important role. Stereotyping is an easy path; it is popular, it is demagoguery, it helps sell stories. It does also, however, create serious damage and affects social cohesion in both the short term and the long term.

Our role at the UNAOC is to underline everyone's responsibility in creating more inclusive societies. As a citizen, as a politician, as a media outlet, as an organization, as the private sector, we all do have a responsibility in engaging in a dialogue based on respect, tolerance, and dignity and driven by an idea of justice. I believe that it is the essence of conflict prevention.

More concretely, the UNAOC is engaged in a dialogue with media professionals, conducting seminars to identify challenges and best practices but also opportunities when covering migration. Connecting migration experts with media professionals is also seen as a priority. The UNAOC believes that creating links and bridges between fields of expertise will lead to enriching each other's perspective and understanding—a dialogue such as this book. Providing further empirical evidence of the connection between migration and public perceptions, the UNAOC in partnership with the European Journalism Center (EJC) and five academic institutions has also just conducted a data journalism project to analyze and visualize online coverage of migration during periods of elections in France, the United States, and three other countries, looking qualitatively and quantitatively at the terminology and semantics used in online media in relation to migrants over a limited time period.[1] Through data collection and analysis and the use of new digital tools, the study focused on the main coverage trends to provide a comprehensive picture of the perceptions around migration to better address them.

It found that migration was covered primarily from the perspective of the host countries' politics, instead of as an international phenomenon. Following the release of the study, in February 2013, the UNAOC planned to follow up with governments, civil society organizations, and media, including those in the five countries, to raise awareness of the national media coverage of migration and to identify methods and opportunities to improve it. The UNAOC also provides content such as articles, photographs, reports, and good practices related to the inclusion of migrants to develop capacities, provide tools and information, and connect people to build more inclusive societies for the benefit of all. Finally, the UNAOC and others are advocating at the international policy level for the recognition of migrants' contribution to the development of communities and states.

This chapter seeks to capture some of the key challenges when addressing the migration and integration issue in the media from the UNAOC's perspective, which, acknowledging the media's responsibility in shaping public opinion, aims to promote responsible reporting for a more integrated future, and then to provide some of the solutions that we are working on to integrate among media.

SALIENCE OF MIGRATION DISCOURSES

In this era of unprecedented mobility, migration and the resulting growth in cultural and ethnic diversity often reinforce stereotyping. In today's societies, migration is often perceived as a threat to stability, prosperity, and/or identity. Many believe their countries are flooded by foreigners; several see migrants taking away jobs or think that migration represents downward pressures on salaries; others perceive migrants as a threat to national identity, values, and culture. Often migrants are used as scapegoats and are stigmatized and held responsible for existing problems.

These issues are especially prevalent in political discourses of far-right parties in Europe. For example, the Swiss People's Party (in German, Schweizerische Volkspartei, SVP), also known as the Democratic Union of the Center (in French, Union démocratique du centre, UDC), France's National Front (French: Front national, FN), and the Netherlands' Party for Freedom (Dutch: Partij voor de Vrijheid, PVV), among other right-wing populist political parties, emphasize migration as core to their policies and are constantly addressing national issues through the prism of migration. The 2011–2015 UDC program states that "migration brings enormous problems when looking at the labor market, social institutions, integration and security, education and public health, infrastructures, transports, town and country planning, environment protection."[2] The founder and leader of the Party for Freedom in the Netherlands, that country's third-largest party, Geert Wilders, stated in a speech in Rome in March 2011 that "multiculturalism is a culture of repudiation of Europe's heritage and freedoms. It weakens the West day by day. It leads to the self-censorship of the media and academia, the collapse of the education system, the emasculation of the churches, the subversion of the nation-state, the break-down of our free society."[3]

Such political statements on migration are made possible by the lack of accountability of politicians toward migrants, as described in Schain's chapter in this book. Indeed, in democracies based on public pressure, migrants who do not vote, who fear deportation, who generally do not mobilize—in a word, who do not represent a lobby—are not likely to affect electoral processes. Therefore, in contexts of economic downturn or during elections, the migration issue—and, by extension, the integration issue—becomes a subject of political dispute that is not counterbalanced by electoral purposes. Over the past years, we have witnessed how the migration and integration issues have taken on more and more importance at the national policy level, repeatedly becoming a key question in election processes and defining political landscapes, with political parties holding radical positions on migration and integration issues gaining support. In Greece, in May 2012, Golden Dawn (Greek: Chrysi Avgi)—an ultranationalist party, which ran on a virulent anti-immigration campaign and was referred to as a neo-Nazi party by CNN in 2010[4]—won 7 percent of the vote in the national elections, giving the party around 20 seats in the new parliament. Even more disturbing, those ideas have entered the mainstream discourse. Mainstream right-wing parties and politicians are now flirting with anti-immigrant rhetoric. In France, the Union for a Popular Movement (French: Union pour un mouvement populaire, UMP), a center-right political party, showed more and more similarities to the FN discourse on migration during the most recent presidential election. In the United Kingdom, under the influence of neoconservatives, David Cameron's recent speeches on multiculturalism (February 2011) and migration (April 2012) took a hard line.

In a world characterized by globalization and shaped by information, the media can spread mainstream and politicized stereotyping at an unparalleled pace and with extraordinary reach , as many chapters in the next section of this book discuss from theoretical, empirical, and professional perspectives. Contrary to the limited-effects theory (Klapper, 1960), and the cognitive dissonance theory (Festinger, 1957), which states that people are not inclined to change their opinions because that jeopardizes consistency and generates tension,[5] the power of media to focus the public's attention on specific issues and shape opinion is considerable, particularly through agenda-setting and framing. For example, Edward W. Said (1981) found that the media have played a significant role in determining what information should or should not be released about Islam and the Muslim worlds, denouncing their negative portrayal as capable of increasing social tensions and divisions. Cohabitation of people with different roots and viewpoints is challenging, as social, economic, and political divisions are numerous. However, the media can either provide today's pluralistic societies with a common sense of belonging or undermine social cohesion by stressing divides rather than commonalities and by perpetuating myths and prejudices. Over the past years, the migration issue has been extensively covered by media, regularly in negative terms. Today, with about 214 million international migrants worldwide, representing 1 out of every 33 persons,[6] shifting popular perceptions of migration—from threat to opportunity—is critical in improving social cohesion and building inclusive societies.

After a brief examination of the common myths and prejudices about migration and after exploring their potential origin, this chapter puts forward recommendations for reporting on migration that would foster the social and cultural norms of UNAOC. In conclusion, it discusses the issue of integration and presents a case study of media coverage that brings together the different elements discussed.

MYTHS AND PREJUDICES ABOUT MIGRATION: EXPLORING THEIR ORIGIN TO ADDRESS THEIR IMPACT

As emphasized by the International Organization for Migration (IOM) in its 2011 report "Communicating Effectively about Migration", which is discussed in the following chapter, "many remain poorly informed about the scale, scope and socio-economic context of migration."[7] In fact, at a time when migrants' positive contributions to societies are increasingly questioned, public perceptions of migration rely more on myths fueled by fears and misunderstandings than on facts.

This issue is well illustrated in the 2010 German Marshall Fund's report on Transatlantic Trends, also noted in the Introduction.[8] Survey respondents in the United States and in European countries generally overestimated how many migrants actually are in their countries. Also, majorities in all countries expressed their concern regarding the burden migrants are imposing on social services. However, as stated by the Urban Institute, in the United States, "when all levels of government are considered together, immigrants generate significantly more in taxes paid than they cost in services received."[9] In Italy, studies suggest that migrants contribute to taxes and are less likely to take advantage of welfare than are native-born Italians. Migrants' share of public expenditure is €10.5 million, while they contribute €12 million through taxes and other contributions, representing a profit for the Italian system[10]—a point elaborated by Stagliano's chapter in this book. Likewise, while survey findings suggest that 50 percent of European Union citizens believe migrants are abusing the noncontributory parts of the welfare system, a study on the social impact of globalization in the European Union stresses that there is no evidence of such abuse. Furthermore, the European Commission maintains that migration contributes to overall growth, greater productivity, and higher employment for everyone.[11]

Another of the most common myths around migration is related to the flow. Indeed, while migration is most often perceived as a south-to-north movement—the focus of media coverage, as this book argues—many do not know that a large part of human mobility is south-to-south or between developing countries. Despite an evident lack of data on migration in developing countries, the Migration Policy Institute stresses, "South-South migration may account for 47 percent of all migration originating in the South."[12]

As we look at these statistics, it is evident that misrepresentation of migration is commonplace. Resulting from a lack of information or from misinformation itself, it fosters prejudices that encourage mistrust and a social malaise between newcomers or second and third generations and host communities. It also increases divisions, leading to polarized societies, which, in turn, impact social, cultural, and economic aspects of everyday life. Feeding populations with misperceptions about migration negatively touches society as a whole.

In order to understand the impact of myths around migration, it is crucial to explore some of their potential causes. When addressing myths and perceptions, one refers to subjective and emotional mind-sets, and we can make no generalization or offer one theory sufficient to reflect on such complex processes. However, social psychology and sociological approaches, among others, are helpful and have been used by a number of scholars to address discrimination. For example, the minimal group paradigm developed in the early 1970s by Tajfel and colleagues as part of an attempt to understand the origins of prejudices and discrimination is of interest within the framework of migration. The minimal group paradigm argues that mere consciousness of the existence of another group can itself produce discrimination. This very act of categorization by itself produces prejudices that can be further expressed through its behavioral expression: discrimination.

When people are categorized as members of an out-group (them) or an in-group (us), members tend to favor their in-groups and discriminate against members of the other group even in most minimal group conditions.[13] While the minimal group methodology was applied and further developed to study discrimination and prejudices against migrants, Tajfel and Turner, conscious of the limits of the theory, shaped social identity theory (SIT).[14] On the basis of social categorization, social comparison and social identification, SIT argues that people tend to favor their own group because favoring the group they belong to increases their general esteem as people feel that they belong to the "best" group.[15] In other words, discrimination towards the out-group enhances the in-group's self-image.

In a study conducted by Bourhis and Sachdev (1991), results show that high- and equal-status group members tend to discriminate more against out-groups than low-status group members. Building on SIT, the authors explain such patterns by the tendency of high-status group members to report high levels of own-group identification, which turns into discrimination toward out-groups when people are trying to maintain their "positive social identities."[16] In the analysis of survey data from 11 countries, Staerklé, Sidanius, Green, and Molina take a deeper look at ethnic minority-majority asymmetry and attitudes toward migrants,[17] moving some distance from the minimal group paradigm that attachment to one's group necessarily entails hostility toward out-groups and building on Sachdev and Bourhis's approach. Their study, in line with research by scholars such as Herberg (1980), who stresses the "need for considering status, power and group factors as variable having independent and combined effects on the dynamic of intergroup relations,"[18] as well as Barth and Noel (1972), Marger (1985), and Schermerhom (1970), who "concur in considering differential power between ethnic groups as one of the more important determinants of discrimination and ethnic stratification in multiethnic societies,"[19] reflects on factors such as social status and level of identification and argues that "the minority or majority status of ethnic subgroups within nations shapes attitudes towards out-groups such as immigrants."[20]

The study suggests that in nation-states, ethnic majority groups discriminate against migrants on the basis of their ethnic and national identification and because of a "sense of ownership and entitlement to the nation, its institutions, rules and customs [that] make[s] them feel more inclined to 'protect the nation' against immigrants who are viewed as a threat to the ethnic group rather than to the nation as a whole."[21] Crisp, Paolini, and Rubin conducted a study in which participants were divided into two groups from which some random individuals were asked to join the other group, introducing a categorization of migrants and nonmigrants among individuals. As a result, participants rated migrants less positively than nonmigrants. Crisp et al. explain the migrant bias in terms of the difficulty people have in processing information about migrants and suggest that it is in part due to migrants' exclusion from their original group.[22] Reflecting on the various sociological approaches focusing on sociostructural variables such as status, power, and group numbers or on social psychology approaches focusing on cognitive and motivational aspects of intergroup behavior, one can stress the urgent need for building a common sense of belonging based on a comprehensive understanding of the migration phenomenon. It is crucial to address prejudices by providing people with realistic portrayals of migration, acknowledging both the challenges and the benefits of the issue while looking at commonalities.

As stated, the role of the media in shaping public opinions and behaviors is key. When playing agent of information and embracing the big picture, media can have a positive influence in enhancing pluralistic societies. On the other hand, when supporting stereotypes and prejudices, the media can reinforce a climate of tension. Better communication about migration becomes, then, a priority in the pursuit of intercultural understanding, and we have identified some positive steps toward this goal that guide our outreach mission at UNAOC.

IDENTIFYING PRIORITIES: FOUR STEPS FORWARDS

First, giving a "voice" to migrants is crucial, as giving exposure reduces misconceptions—and, as Zamith notes in this book, it is only rarely done in major news media. Representation of migrants in media as "subjects" who perceive, instead of focusing on migrants as "objects" who are perceived, can help shift understanding from the theoretical aspect to the human side of the story. Representation of migrants in the media should occur at two different levels: at the level of "content," or substance, and at the level of "frame," or structure. At the first level, social and political diversity should be better reflected in media content. When writing about migration issues, journalists should bear in mind the importance of providing the audience with a migrant perspective to widen the audience's viewpoint. At the structural level, one should insist on the need to better represent diversity in newsrooms. Indeed, how can media report accurately on diversity when most newsrooms are actually lacking diversity? Diversity in newsrooms ensures better understanding and consequently better reporting on issues that may be misunderstood or mistaken by homogeneous and standardized newsrooms.

Second, giving a "face" to migrants is essential to deconstruct the faceless mask of migration. The current discourse on migration erases all characteristics of individualization, which is the basis of human rights. It simplifies the complexity of migration and reduces the migrants to one single identity that compromises their rights as individuals. Moreover, public discourse is more inclined to condemn the group than to condemn individuals. Writing about migrants' stories as individuals as opposed to an undifferentiated entity of "migrants" acknowledges their rights as individuals and works against the construction of an anonymous, unnamed, and faceless phenomenon.

Third, highlighting the benefits of migration to help counter prejudices and polarizing speech is imperative. Given that migration remains a complex and challenging issue for today's societies, the media cannot lessen those challenges in their reporting. However, instead of pointing largely at failures, the media should put more emphasis on its numerous successes. Today's discourse on migration is very disconnected from evidence-based research. Migrants have played an essential role in the development of many modern states and of all societies. Migration has contributed and continues to contribute to a society's prosperity, measured in economic development, social dynamism, cultural richness, and diversity. This narrative is not sufficiently highlighted in the media, and when it is, it often does not embrace all aspects of migrants' contributions. Frequently, the positive discourse around migration focuses on the economic aspect of mobility. Promoting migrants as a driving force for the economy and development is not only true but important. However, one should not forget the social and cultural aspects of their contribution. Migrants cannot be portrayed only in terms of economic gain for destination countries (labor force) or in terms of economic gain for origin countries (remittances). Today, as migration is a global phenomenon, no country can argue that it is unaffected by migration. Maintaining population levels and age structures demographically, stimulating societies culturally and intellectually, bringing together talent for innovation—it is crucial that we engage countries and societies to look at these positive aspects of migration, and certainly time for such an examination.

Fourth, the media could reduce the impact of polarizing speeches by not providing them with as much space and by balancing the discourse with more moderate voices, a task many of the journalists in this book engage with on a daily basis, as discussed in later chapters. Polarized speeches tend to be prominent in some media. They allow some media to break through the constant massive flow of information with catchy headlines. In order not to amplify such discourse, the media may want to reconsider their assigned space. In addition, moderate voices should be consulted and highlighted when addressing sensitive issues such as migration and integration. By presenting balanced opinions, moderate voices allow media to provide the audience with comprehensive information to help enhance understanding that shapes our societies.

INTEGRATION: A RECIPROCAL PROCESS

In the immediate wake of any discussion of migration comes a corollary focus on integration. The two phenomena are intimately connected. Mobility fundamentally implies that one moves to a new environment, distant or close, of which he or she becomes a new component. Defining integration is complex. Integration is a comprehensive notion, and it may vary from place to place. In some places, it may refer to assimilation, meaning that one should give up one's social, cultural, and religious identity to become similar to those born in the new country or even invisible in order to be seen as "integrated." In other countries, integration means that differences are tolerated, accepted, and sometimes even encouraged: you can be who you are.

The UNAOC acknowledges diversity as a positive reality of today's societies. The UNAOC advocates for a type of integration that gives individuals the chance to enrich their identities with the inputs of their new environments and gives them the opportunity to enrich their environments with their own background, whether cultural or religious or both. Successful integration should mean that differences are accepted, not only in a conceptual way but also as a visible reality. Successful integration means that differences are respected and that the legal, social, and political framework is the same for everyone. Integration is about respect, visibility, dignity, justice, and equal rights.

In this regard, integration is a reciprocal process. Reciprocity implies that integration requires some obligations for the newly arrived. Learning the language and respecting the laws are nonnegotiable responsibilities, for example. Likewise, integration requires some obligations for the so-called host communities. They have to ensure that all people are equal in rights and opportunities and that they are entitled without any discrimination to *equal* protection of the law.

In the following section, to provide analysis, some of the ideas developed here are further elaborated through a concrete example of an event that received massive media coverage and that crystallized the discourse around migration in today's France. Both the questions of migration and integration are discussed, and we refer to media coverage and how at UNAOC we would suggest changes to it.

CASE: MEDIA COVERAGE OF THE TOULOUSE KILLINGS

On March 19, 2012, following two killings during which one French paratrooper and two French uniformed soldiers were found dead, Mohamed Merah, a French citizen, killed seven people, among them children outside a school in Toulouse, France. The majority of the media, while reporting on the killings, significantly highlighted Mohamed Merah's Algerian origin. Portraying Merah as French of Algerian origin was not incorrect, but the necessity and the relevance of such representation is questionable within the framework of working toward building more inclusive societies.

First of all, Merah's background could have nothing to do with his action, which appeared driven by psychological disorder, which of course is not related to any geographical, ethnical, religious, or cultural belonging. Pointing at Merah's background, however, implies giving it some meaning, possibly suggesting that in fact there is a connection, that the French citizen Merah acted not as such but as the son of a migrant, as a "foreigner" himself, as someone who does not belong "here." If that connection exists, one should go further into the explanation. Simply mentioning Merah's background and stigmatizing a community, whatever it is, serves to reinforce existing tensions and enhances the prejudice that migrants, specifically migrants of Arab origin, are at a minimum violent if not altogether terrorists. Thus, while condemning firmly the action and showing compassion to the families of the victims, one has to deepen one's thinking and question the causes of such action by analyzing how his origin might actually have impacted Merah's action. It is a common responsibility to understand how one individual can reach that point of violence if we are to prevent such action in the future.

By the focus on his name and his appearance, Merah was negatively reduced to his origin. While studying and looking for jobs, he apparently was constantly reduced to his migrant background, so that he was not formally recognized as a citizen equal in rights and opportunities to any other citizen.[23] Indeed, as stressed in a report of the European Union Agency for Fundamental Rights, "in the context of employment, minorities tend to have lower rates of participation in the employment market, higher rates of unemployment, be underrepresented among entrepreneurs, be highly concentrated in lower-skilled areas such as agriculture, industry and the service sector and have lower incomes by comparison to the majority population."[24] Likewise, in the context of housing, studies reveal that "members of certain minority groups appear more likely to experience *de facto* segregation,"[25] while in the area of education they "tend to enroll in schools with lower academic demands, have higher drop-out rates, and be over-represented in vocationally-oriented training and special education."[26] In such context, one can argue that Merah had been marginalized by French society and its system. As a second-generation migrant, Merah had not been provided with the fundamental rights he was entitled to as a French citizen. His fundamental rights as a citizen of a country and, moreover, as a human being were limited by his origin.

That said, it is important to underline that marginalization and discrimination cannot justify such action. Many people are victims of discrimination, and they do not choose violence as a response. Nevertheless, this analysis may present some elements of context and understanding. One can reasonably think discrimination has an impact. As verified in a study launched in 2010 by the European Union Agency for Fundamental Rights, "children between the ages of 12 and 18 (young people) who have experienced social marginalization and discrimination are highly likely to be more disposed to physical or emotional violence in comparison with those not experiencing marginalization."[27]

The coverage of Merah's case was extensive in the media, which significantly highlighted Merah's background in their reporting. There is no study yet that formally measures the impact of this specific coverage on people's perceptions around migrants and migration. However, stigmatizing a community, a culture, or a religion and holding it responsible encourages polarized speeches and stigmatization. Furthermore, polarized speeches and stigmatization increase the divide by reinforcing social categorization, identification, and comparison that can lead to discrimination. In opposition to an inclusive "us," media coverage strengthens a stigmatizing image of "them," which refers to the "other," reinforcing tension in society. All of these trends, exemplified in the Merah case, are areas where UNAOC actively works to promote change.

UNAOC ACTIVITIES RELATED TO IMMIGRATION COVERAGE

One concrete example of our activities in this field is the January 2013 high-level seminar "Covering Migration: Challenges Met and Unmet," which UNAOC organized with the Global Editors' Network, gathering four dozen editors in chief and migration experts from 27 countries across Europe and the Mediterranean. The participants created 17 concrete recommendations for better practices for media, governments, and nongovernmental organizations, such as honing journalists' knowledge on migration, including more migrants in the newsroom and as sources, and encouraging timely publication of accurate data and use of data. In particular, four areas were highlighted:

1. Expanding journalists' knowledge of the nuances of migration, including the creation of specialized training and guidelines as well as providing access to refugee camps and detention centers to facilitate understanding
2. Involving migrants in media coverage, in newsrooms, as sources (while allowing them to remain anonymous), and as ombudsmen through national press associations
3. Performing more checks on migration stories to ensure that the content reflects the most current factual data and conforms to ethical standards
4. Getting governments and NGOs to publicly recognize quality coverage of migration (e.g., through national awards) and to facilitate this coverage through giving journalists open access both to information and to migrant and expert sources.

CONCLUSIONS

Migration and its resulting diversity bring various challenges. Migration and diversity are demanding, making them complex issues to address. However, when looking at the big picture, one should recognize benefits as well as problems. In this era of the greatest human mobility ever recorded, communicating on the social, cultural, and economic benefits of migration helps counter the forces that fuel polarization and extremism. There is a real need to address the perceived risks of migration as a threat for stability, prosperity, and identity and to emphasize that the ever-increasing cultural diversity is, indeed, a driving force for development, innovation, and progress.

At UNAOC, in order to achieve our social justice aims, we encourage the media to be aware of their responsibility when engaging in dialogue around migration and integration. If some media are serving political purposes or even deliberately serving political discourse and consciously jeopardizing social cohesion with polarized speeches, others have to counterbalance such discourse and provide societies with responsible coverage of these issues. When addressing cultural, religious, or ethnic issues, the media cannot ignore their role in shaping public opinion, and we, through our media training, have worked to develop sensitivity and even a sense of duty.

On the other hand, migrants, civil society organizations, United Nations agencies, and international organizations have a responsibility in providing the media and public with a more comprehensive understanding of migration and integration issues. Giving more visibility to a responsible and comprehensive approach of these issues is crucial to enhance social cohesion.

In today's societies, there is an urgent need to build a common sense of belonging based on reciprocity, justice, dignity, and respect. For the benefit of the society as a whole, we should commit to these values. It is important to stress that such commitment cannot be seen as generous, magnanimous, or noble. It is simply a commitment based on a belief in human rights and social justice. Migration is a right recognized by international law, and diversity is a reality. Building inclusive societies is therefore not optional. People are migrating. People have always migrated. Our responsibility today is to ensure that this diversity is acknowledged as a positive reality, while still recognizing its challenges. Our responsibility is to reflect the complete picture of society.

In such an ever-changing society, institutions, the public, and, in turn, the media must become forward thinkers, learning to acknowledge and promote the benefits of migration and the diversity it brings to communities. In such a world, we can no longer afford to have a homogenized outlook; relying on the principles of justice, dignity, and respect, rights for migrants must be ensured.

NOTES

1. To access the study, including methodology and visualizations, see http://www.ejc.net/about/press_releases/data-based_pilot_study_looks_into_characteristics_of_migration_coverage/ (accessed May 22, 2012).
2. Democratic Union of the Center, *Programme du Parti*, 2011, http://www.udc.ch/display.cfm/id/101397 (accessed June 22, 2012).
3. Geert Wilders, *Speech in Rome, 25th of March 2011*, 2011, http://www.geertwilders.nl/index.php?option = com_content&task = view&id = 1740 (accessed June 20, 2012).

4. CNN World, *Explosion at Greek Neo-Nazi Office*, 2010, http://articles. cnn.com/2010–03–19/world/greece.explosion.neo.nazi_1_neo-nazi-greek-police-explosion?_s = PM:WORLD (accessed June 22, 2012).

5. Joseph T. Klapper, *The Effects of Mass Communication*. Free Press, 1960; Leon Festinger, *A Theory of Cognitive Dissonance*. Stanford University Press, 1962.

6. International Organization for Migration (IOM), 2012, http://www.iom.int/ jahia/Jahia/lang/en/pid/1 (accessed May 22, 2012).

7. IOM, *Communicating Effectively about Migration*, 2011, http://publications. iom.int/bookstore/free/WMR2011_English.pdf (accessed May 22, 2012).

8. German Marshall Fund of the United States, *Transatlantic Trends: Immigration 2011*, http://trends.gmfus.org/wp-content/uploads/2011/12/ TTImmigration_final_web.pdf (accessed May 22, 2012).

9. Michael E. Fix and Jeffrey S. Passel, *Immigration and Immigrants: Setting the Record Straight* (Washington, DC: Urban Institute, 1994), http://www. urban.org/publications/305184.html#V (accessed May 23, 2012).

10. IDOS Study and Research Centre, *Migration in Italy: Current Situation and Perspectives* (Rome: International Organization for Migration, 2011), http:// www.italy.iom.int/images/pdf/1951–2011EN.pdf (accessed May 23, 2012).

11. Iain Begg, Juraj Draxler, and Jørgen Mortensen, *Is Social Europe Fit for Globalization?* (Brussels: European Commission, Directorate-General, Employment, Social Affairs and Equal Opportunities, Unit E1—Social and Demographic Analysis, 2007), http://ec.europa.eu/employment_social/ social_situation/docs/simglobe_fin_rep.pdf (accessed June 5, 2012).

12. Migration Policy Institute, *South-South Migration and Remittances*, 2007, http://www.migrationinformation.org/Feature/display.cfm?ID = 641 (accessed May 23, 2012).

13. Henri Tajfel, *Experiments in Intergroup Discrimination*, 1970, http://war-dakhan.org/notes/Original%20Studies/Social%20Psychology/Henri-Tajfel. pdf (accessed June 13, 2012).

14. Henri Tajfel and J. C. Turner, "The Social Identity Theory of Inter-group Behavior." In *Psychology of Intergroup Relations,* ed. S. Worchel and L. W. Austin (Chicago: Nelson-Hall, 1986).

15. Henri Tajfel, *Social Identity and Intergroup Relations* (Cambridge: Cambridge University Press, 1982).

16. Richard Y. Bourhis and Itesh Sachdev, "Power and Status Differential in Minority and Majority Group Relations," *European Journal of Social Psychology* 21 (1991): 18.

17. Eva G. T. Green, Ludwin Molina, Jim Sidanius, and Christian Staerklé, *Ethnic Minority-Majority Asymmetry and Attitudes towards Immigrants across 11 Nations*, 2005, http://www.uv.es/garzon/psicologia%20politica/ N30–1.pdf (accessed June 15, 2012).

18. Bourhis and Sachdev, "Power and Status Differential in Minority and Majority Group Relations," 18.

19. Green et al., *Ethnic Minority-Majority Asymmetry.*

20. Ibid., 17.

21. Green et al., *Ethnic Minority-Majority Asymmetry.*

22. Richard J. Crisp, Stefania Paolini, and Mark Rubin, "A Processing Fluency Explanation of Bias against Migrants," *Journal of Experimental Social Psychology* 5 (2010).

23. European Agency for Fundamental Rights, *The Racial Equality Directive: Application and Challenges*, 2011, http://fra.europa.eu/fraWebsite/research/ publications/publications_per_year/pub_racial_equal_directive_synthesis_ en.htm (accessed June 5, 2012).

24. European Agency for Fundamental Rights, *The Racial Equality Directive.*
25. Ibid.
26. Ibid.
27. European Agency for Fundamental Rights, *Experience of Discrimination, Social Marginalisation and Violence: A Comparative Study of Muslim and Non-Muslim Youth in Three EU Member States,* 2010, http://fra.europa.eu/ fraWebsite/research/publications/publications_per_year/2010/pub-racism- marginalisation_en.htm (accessed June 10, 2012).

REFERENCES

Begg, Iain, Juraj Draxler, and Jørgen Mortensen. *Is Social Europe Fit for Globalization?* Brussels: European Commission, Directorate-General, Employment, Social Affairs and Equal Opportunities, Unit E1—Social and Demographic Analysis, 2007. http://ec.europa.eu/employment_social/social_situation/docs/simglobe_ fin_rep.pdf (accessed June 5, 2012).
Bourhis, Richard Y., and Itesh Sachdev. "Power and Status Differential in Minority and Majority Group Relations." *European Journal of Social Psychology* 21 (1991).
CNN World. *Explosion at Greek Neo-Nazi Office.* 2010. http://articles.cnn. com/2010–03–19/world/greece.explosion.neo.nazi_1_neo-nazi-greek-police- explosion?_s = PM:WORLD (accessed June 22, 2012).
Crisp, Richard J., Stefania Paolini, and Mark Rubin. "A Processing Fluency Explanation of Bias against Migrants." *Journal of Experimental Social Psychology* 11 (2010): 21–28.
Democratic Union of the Center. *Programme du Parti.* 2011. http://www.udc.ch/ display.cfm/id/101397 (accessed June 22, 2012).
European Agency for Fundamental Rights. *Experience of Discrimination, Social Marginalisation and Violence: A Comparative Study of Muslim and Non-Muslim Youth in Three EU Member States.* 2010. http://fra.europa.eu/fraWebsite/ research/publications/publications_per_year/2010/pub-racism-marginalisation_ en.htm (accessed June 10, 2012).
———. *The Racial Equality Directive: Application and Challenges.* 2011. http://fra. europa.eu/fraWebsite/research/publications/publications_per_year/pub_racial_ equal_directive_synthesis_en.htm (accessed June 5, 2012).
Fix, Michael E., and Jeffrey S. Passel. *Immigration and Immigrants: Setting the Record Straight.* Washington, DC: Urban Institute, 1994. http://www.urban.org/ publications/305184.html#V (accessed May 23, 2012).
German Marshall Fund of the United States. *Transatlantic Trends: Immigration 2011 Report.* 2011. http://trends.gmfus.org/wp-content/uploads/2011/12/ TTImmigration_final_web.pdf (accessed May 22, 2012).
Green, Eva G. T., Ludwin Molina, Jim Sidanius, and Christian Staerklé. *Ethnic Minority-Majority Asymmetry and Attitudes towards Immigrants across 11 Nations.* 2005. http://www.uv.es/garzon/psicologia%20politica/N30–1.pdf (accessed June 15, 2012).
IDOS Study and Research Centre. *Migration in Italy: Current Situation and Perspectives.* Rome: International Organization for Migration, 2011. http:// www.italy.iom.int/images/pdf/1951–2011EN.pdf [accessed May 23, 2012].
International Organization for Migration. *Communicating Effectively about Migration.* 2011. http://publications.iom.int/bookstore/free/WMR2011_English. pdf (accessed May 22, 2012).

Migration Policy Institute, 2007. *South-South Migration and Remittances*. 2007. http://www.migrationinformation.org/Feature/display.cfm?ID = 641 (accessed May 23, 2012).

Said, Edward W. *Covering Islam: How the Media and Experts Determine How We See the Rest of the World*. New York: Random House, 1981.

Tajfel, Henri. *Experiments in Intergroup Discrimination*. 1970. http://wardakhan. org/notes/Original%20Studies/Social%20Psychology/Henri-Tajfel.pdf (accessed June 13, 2012).

———. *Social Identity and Intergroup Relations*. Cambridge: Cambridge University Press, 1982.

———. and J. C. Turner, "The Social Identity Theory of Inter-group Behavior." In *Psychology of Intergroup Relations*. Edited by S. Worchel and L. W. Austin. Chicago: Nelson-Hall, 1986.

Wilders, Geert. *Speech in Rome, 25th of March 2011*. 2011. http://www.geertwilders.nl/index.php?option = com_content&task = view&id = 1740 (accessed June 20, 2012).

4 Communicating Effectively about Migration

Jean-Philippe Chauzy and Gervais Appave
International Organization for Migration

Few areas of public policy are subject to greater misrepresentation in public and political discourse yet are more influenced by public opinion than international migration. Despite the communications revolution, many remain poorly informed about the scale, scope, and socioeconomic context of migration. Communicating effectively about migration is critical, since managing migration also implies managing how migrants are perceived in society. From our perspective at the International Organization for Migration (IOM)—the world's leading intergovernmental organization for migration management and migrant rights—accurately informing relevant stakeholders and the wider public about migration may be the single most important policy tool in all societies faced with increasing diversity.

Societies with a rich diversity of skills and experiences are better placed to stimulate growth through their human resources, and migration is one of the ways in which the exchange of talent, services, and skills can be fostered. Yet migration remains highly politicized and often negatively perceived, despite the obvious need for diversification in today's rapidly evolving societies and economies. Nevertheless, international migration is likely to increase in scale and complexity due to growing demographic disparities, new global and political dynamics, and technological revolutions and social networks, with profound impacts on the socioeconomic and ethnic composition of societies. This will result in new policy challenges related to the successful integration of migrants into the host society, how they are perceived in their countries of origin, and, more broadly, the way migration is experienced by the community at large. These are all areas in which IOM has been active since it was founded, in 1951, to help displaced populations in Europe after World War II. With more than 7,800 staff working in more than 470 field locations, an annual operating budget of more than US$1.3 billion, and 151 member states, IOM is dedicated to promoting humane and orderly migration by providing services and advice to both governments and migrants. Our main goals are to help ensure the orderly and humane management of migration, to promote international cooperation on migration issues, to assist in the search for practical solutions to migration problems, and to provide humanitarian assistance to migrants in need, including refugees and internally displaced persons.

In all of these contexts, the image of migrants in their home and host societies acquires fundamental importance. The 2011 issue of IOM's flagship publication *World Migration Report: Communicating Effectively about Migration*[1] directly addresses the challenges faced in this era of globalization and unprecedented human mobility by calling for a fundamental shift in the way we communicate about migration. In order to benefit from the diversity that results from migration and to meet the challenges generated by such diversity, an informed and transparent political and public debate must take place. The risk of maintaining the status quo is threefold:

1. Continued politicized debate will serve only to foster sectarian agendas, rather than promoting broader national, regional, and international interests. One of the greatest challenges for those who seek to foster a rational debate is to prevent migration from being used as a political weapon to achieve electoral gains.
2. Negative attitudes and reactive approaches are likely to continue to dominate over positive attitudes and proactive approaches.
3. Both integration and reintegration efforts will inevitably be undermined unless migrants themselves become active participants in the migration debate, rather than being the subject of debate.

ADDRESSING PERCEPTIONS ABOUT MIGRANTS AND MIGRATION

While there is growing recognition that migrants can build cross-border social capital, that increasing cultural diversity can provide impetus for the stimulation of entrepreneurship, and that culturally diverse workforces are among the most profitable, the overall perception of migrants in many societies tends to be negative, and that can seriously hinder our work on the ground helping migrants and governments. Part of the reason for such negative perceptions is that migratory flows are more visible and more diverse than ever before, generating questions about the value of migration that, if left unanswered, result in misinformation and misperception.

This is particularly true in times of humanitarian crises, when scaremongering of "uncontrolled mass migration" tends to be rife. An example is the 2011 Libyan crisis, when the perceived threat of a so-called North African migration tsunami made headlines in many European media, as detailed in Stinellis's chapter. While there is no denying that Europe, specifically the Italian island of Lampedusa, witnessed an increase in the number of migrants, refugees, and asylum seekers arriving by boat, first from Tunisia following the fall of the Ben Ali regime and later from Libya, these numbers pale into insignificance in comparison with the total number of persons displaced by the crisis. By the end of 2011, some 52,000 people had arrived on Lampedusa at a time when neighboring countries had allowed almost

800,000 often traumatized and destitute migrants to cross their open borders in search of repatriation assistance, with some 260,000 receiving direct assistance from IOM.

Yet, these limited arrivals on European shores rekindled rampant anti-immigrant feelings among some segments of the European population, which in turn spurred some strong political responses. Those ranged from talk of increased protectionism to safeguarding national job markets to the reintroduction of limited internal border controls within the Schengen area. Similarly, there was very little recognition in the European press that it is because countries in North Africa kept their borders open and provided generous humanitarian assistance that a full-fledged humanitarian and migration crisis was averted.

UNDERSTANDING PUBLIC OPINION AND PERCEPTIONS

Public opinion and perceptions about migration vary between and within countries (as well as between subgroups within a community) and over time. Given such nuances, it is not possible to isolate a single public opinion; nonetheless, claims based on public opinion often gain saliency in political and public discourse, as noted in IOM's *World Migration Report*. The findings there, based on an extensive review of existing surveys and survey analyses globally, explore some of the more consistent factors influencing public opinion and what often lies at the core of prevailing negative sentiment.

One of the most consistent findings is the overestimation of the absolute numbers of migrants in a given country/region and of the proportion of the population that migrants represent—something that reflects Grobet's and Zamith's findings. Estimates tend to be even higher for irregular migrants. Research findings also show that when survey respondents are provided with more information about migrants/migration, rather than simply being asked if they think there are "too many migrants," their responses tend to be more favorable. Findings are therefore influenced by prevailing conventional wisdom, the way survey questions are worded (biased or not), and the respondents' understanding of what "migrant" means (labor migrant, refugee, asylum seeker, irregular migrant). Understanding who is a migrant can also influence the extent to which natives perceive migrants as contributing to a given place—and is a constant source of controversy within news organizations and their audiences.

The vast majority of research, however, focuses on opinions and perceptions in countries of destination, such as the United States or the nations of Western Europe. Considerably less empirical research has been done on the country-of-origin perspective with regard to emigration or return, although both factors are increasingly recognized at the policy level as being highly important issues. Findings of smaller-scale surveys and qualitative studies show that public opinion can vary greatly, with emigrants being considered by some to have abandoned the home country and by others to be national heroes. Opinions are also shaped by factors such as the length of time the migrant is abroad, the impact on the community or family left behind, and the economic situation in the home country.

More than 130,000 Chadians, for example, are estimated to have returned to their country from Libya during and after the Libyan crisis in 2011, many of them to food-insecure areas. The majority had lived in Libya for many years and had few if any connections to their places of origin. An IOM assessment carried out in March 2012 in the 14 regions of Chad with the highest number of returnees found that most are in urgent need of socioeconomic reintegration support to help them cope with the loss of income and the adaptation to a different lifestyle. The assessment found that the majority were unable to meet their basic needs of food, housing, health, and education and were struggling financially to provide for their families.

Perceptions and opinions are not static or formed in a vacuum. In both countries of origin and destination, they are sensitive to socioeconomic and demographic factors such as age, level of education, type of employment, and political inclinations. Although such factors are relatively constant in determining whether opinion is likely to be more positive or negative, findings show that opinion can and does change over time, particularly following increased levels of interaction with migrants and an increased understanding of what a migrant is and is not.

Attitudes are also often shaped by contextual factors. During periods of economic recession, when unemployment levels are high, or in times of political turmoil or conflict, doubts about the value of migration can and do arise. Additional findings show that such instances are typically followed by restrictionist political agendas or discourse and heightened negativity in the media—something clearly visible in Western Europe in the current recession. But these concerns, even when strongly felt, are also time sensitive, and they can recede when conditions improve. A closer look at public opinion reveals that, even in times of economic recession or crisis when negativity toward migrants may be higher, migration is not the issue of primary concern. It is, nonetheless, consistently present in opinion polls, which is not surprising, given its crosscutting nature and linkages to wider socioeconomic issues.

The populist nature of migration debates in many parts of the world today has created a climate in which it is all too easy to see migrants as responsible—directly or indirectly—for unemployment, security issues, or a lack of social cohesion, among others. These concerns, rooted in much more complex processes of change, will not be dispelled simply by making migration policies more restrictive. By unilaterally addressing migration, governments send the wrong message: that migration was indeed the cause of the perceived problem. What it does not do is address what is at the core of a population's concerns, which may or may not be migration per se. When we consider more carefully what is behind opinion poll results, it becomes clear that not all opinions are necessarily negative and that any deep-rooted concerns expressed often go beyond solely migration.

MEDIA, POLITICS, AND THE EVIDENCE BASE

Mobility is an accepted feature of contemporary society, and there is a certain level of understanding, recognition and even appreciation of the fact that migration brings added benefits to the economy. However, distorted communication about migration can trigger a vicious cycle that leads to misinformation being perpetuated through government policy, the mass media, the public at large, and vice versa, which can, in turn, skew discourse at all levels. Policies and political discourse can therefore play a major role in shaping the image of migrants in home and host societies. From our perspective, one of the biggest challenges in this regard is what and how governments communicate about migrants and migration policy to the wider public—because, as many of the journalists' chapters in this book illustrate, one of the major challenges in covering migration is in fact going beyond the repetition of political statements. IOM's High Level Dialogue on International Migration, which was established in 2000 and is held annually, is a platform for the debate of migration issues in the light of the best available research. IOM also strongly supports the many regional consultative processes that have emerged in many parts of the world to enable participating states to better understand the nature of contemporary migration.

IOM's engagement with the Alliance of Civilizations (UNAOC) and the Panos Institute Paris seeks to improve coverage of migration in the media by regularly bringing together top migration experts and media professionals from both countries of origin and countries of destination to share their ideas, experiences, and best practices. Those range from efforts to ensure that migration data are not published without adequate context to employing more migrants or individuals of migrant origin in newsrooms. Participants usually agree that migration is often the catch-all issue that masks the public's fears and uncertainties relating to unemployment, housing, or social cohesion in countries of destination or loss and waste of human capital and economic dependency in countries of origin.

Although direct causal links between media reporting and public opinion or policy cannot be made, the media do shape attitudes in significant ways. The 2011 report findings of media content analysis show that the media are often the public's primary source of information (statistics, trends, analysis) about migrants and migration. But the media's role goes further; by highlighting certain aspects of migration and not addressing others, they can "frame" the migration discourse and determine, to a significant extent, whether migration is viewed positively or negatively. Yet, an overwhelming majority of journalists who have taken part in IOM/UNAOC/Panos Institute Paris seminars say they do not have the necessary migration expertise to put this information in the public domain in an objective and informative manner. They also recognize that media reports rarely pay attention to or echo the voice of successful migrants or of employers, who remain key actors in today's global migration scene. Furthermore, the media can frame the debate by highlighting certain aspects of migration and not others (such as illegality) through episodic coverage or by exaggerating the facts, all of which reflect the increasing commercialization of media around the world.

Despite the growing body of evidence attesting to the benefits and costs of migration, there is a disconnect between the producers (academics, political analysts) and users (politicians, media, the wider public) of the evidence base. The IOM *World Migration Report* points to several reasons for this: discourse tends to focus more on politics than facts—for example, opinions of key stakeholders such as employers are often underreported; academic research has also only recently begun to take account of migration as an independent priority interest; policymakers face challenges in communicating migration facts and figures to the public, together with the related policies; a lack of migration policy evaluation prevents any firm conclusions being drawn about which policies are effective; and there is a lack of knowledge among the media on how to accurately report on migration issues. The limited use of evidence in migration policymaking (or the misuse of evidence for political purposes) and the lack of evaluation of the impact of migration policies can also mean that any policy failures are more easily attributed to the migrants themselves.

Finally, inaccurate representation of migrants and migration directly impacts migrants themselves. In host countries, the mass media often serve as a reference point for incoming migrants about the society they now live in. Evidence shows that migrants are very much aware of stereotyping and negative portrayals, especially in the media, which can lead to a sense of marginalization if left unchecked or if migrants' views are not given equal coverage.[2]

THE WAY FORWARD

The IOM *World Migration Report* highlights several examples of good practice among governments, civil society, international organizations, and media that have actively worked toward communicating effectively about migration. These initiatives do so by, for example, promoting a positive image of migrants and their contributions, dispelling migration myths through information or media campaigns, and giving migrants a voice in sharing their experiences. However, for such initiatives to have a lasting impact, they often need to be scaled up, adjusted to fit local contexts and, most important, be supported by strong political will as part of a long-term strategy. At IOM, we have been working to implement the following strategies:

1. *Building an open, balanced, and comprehensive migration discourse*

Here, the emphasis is on expanding the migration debate so that it does not simply revolve endlessly around the problems—real or imagined (both of which are generously aired)—but examines the broader picture. It is important that the new debate be proactive and not simply reactive to the dominant discourse. There are two areas of concern that are commonly used as starting points for discussions on migration, not to mention migration policy formulation: (1) how to deal with the migrant constituencies already in the country and (2) how to deal with those migrants who may be coming. A constructive, better-informed debate will begin with a broader consideration of the place that migration might realistically occupy in demographic, social, and economic planning. From this perspective, it may be possible to reframe the discourse so that it yields a more informed mainstream consensus, rather than a parochial view. The discourse should also extend beyond the national level to multilateral forums such as regional consultative processes on migration (RCPs), IOM's International Dialogue on Migration (IDM), and the Global Forum on Migration and Development (GFMD).

2. *Depoliticizing the debate and directly addressing issues of concern*

Many of the negative perceptions surrounding migration have their origins in partisan interpretations, rather than fact. There is, in any case, a need to openly discuss effects—both positive and negative—in an open and balanced way. The discourse should also address the broad national interest, rather than focusing on the interests of particular segments of society. Much of the research on the positive effects of migration relates to an entire society and economy. The force of these messages can be lost if the focus is placed upon impacts on particular subgroups in a given society or economy. On the other hand, discussion of local anxieties—for example, about what can be done to curb irregular migration or about local pressures on infrastructure caused by population growth—need not be avoided; the public should, instead, be informed about what has and has not worked, without placing blame for failed policy initiatives solely on migrants. A lack of readily available information for the public that directly addresses all of these issues is perhaps the greatest cause of continuing misunderstanding. The dissemination of information that addresses the concerns at hand, clearly explaining the rights of citizens and noncitizens, helps eliminate misunderstandings and ensures that policies are perceived as fair and respectful of everyone's rights.

3. *Working with the media to support balanced media reporting*

The media have significant influence over public discourse, shaping public opinion and thereby affecting all stakeholders, especially policymakers and politicians. At IOM, we increasingly ask a fundamental question: How can the media be engaged to present a more balanced picture of migration and its impacts? Balanced media reporting means avoiding single-issue headlines, over/underrepresentation of particular groups, and blanket labeling. It also implies recognition of the fact that migrants are not a homogenous group and that migration is often linked to many other public issues.

Governments play a crucial role in creating the social and political climate in which fair and accurate reporting can thrive and the evidence base is correctly used. Leadership is therefore important in delivering a more balanced picture about migration. This places significant responsibility on political opinion leaders, but they should not be the only source of leadership on this issue. Other stakeholders, such as civil society, the private sector, and the academic research community, also have an important role to play. Their role may involve working more closely with the media than has been the case in the past. While this may also be outside of the media's comfort zone to some extent, it is the responsibility of these actors to meet the media halfway to ensure that the media are better informed of the complexity of migration issues.

Providing guidance on how to report on migration is another key element, as noted in IOM's *World Migration Report*. Building the capacity of reporters and journalists, among others, either through trainings or informational materials, can help to create a core group of media specialists who are able to more accurately report on the topic. The provision of easily accessible guidelines on how to talk about migration provides a good starting point. Such guidance should ideally include the development of communication strategies on the part of researchers and the creation of partnerships within the media. The research community itself can play a key role in ensuring that its findings relate to the relevant policy and political context and that it actively engages in the debate, using the evidence and its own expertise without compromising its academic integrity.

Balanced media reporting also requires breaking down the barriers of diversity within the media. The removal of structural discrimination in mainstream media institutions to include a diverse group of people serves, in turn, to break down content discrimination by offering alternative points of view.

4. *Acknowledging migrants as active communication agents*

Clearly, one of the greatest challenges for all those wishing to promote accurate perceptions about migrants and migration is that of enabling the authentic voices of migrants to be heard. There is clear evidence that the more exposure nonmigrants have to migrants, on a person-to-person basis, the less negative they are inclined to be toward them.[3] However, migrants are too often viewed as passive agents in the migration debate, in both their countries of origin and their countries of destination. One significant way of reducing the level of misperception and its impact on migrants, whether as a result of political discourse or media reporting, is to ensure that migrants become active participants in the public debate. This can be done in many ways—for instance, by creating more space for ethnic media alongside mainstream media, integrating diversity into mainstream media, and encouraging the use of new social media tools to allow migrants to engage with a wide audience (migrants and nonmigrants) and to portray more accurate images of who they are and what they do.

Migratory flows can have profound impacts on the socioeconomic and ethnic composition of societies, resulting in new policy challenges related to the encounter between migrants and host societies. In this context, the image of migrants in their home and host societies is of fundamental importance, and all migration stakeholders have a vested interest in ensuring that it is not distorted through political or ideological considerations but is a fair reflection of their place in contemporary society.

NOTES

1. http://publications.iom.int/bookstore/free/WMR2011_English.pdf.
2. Henry Mainsah, "Cameroonians in Oslo: Diaspora and Uses of the Media," *Nordicom Review* 30, no. 1 (2009): 83–94; Nina Widyawati, "Representation of Migrant Workers in Malaysian Newspapers," in *Are We Up to the Challenge? Current Crises and the Asian Intellectual Community,* report by the 2005/2006 API Fellows (Tokyo: Nippon Foundation, 2008).
3. Oya S. Abah, German Public Opinion on Migration. In: *Migration, Public Opinion and Politics: The Transatlantic Council on Migration,* eds. Bertelsmann Stiftung and Migration Policy Institute (Gütersloh: Verlag Bertelsmann Stiftung, 2009), pp. 29–51.

Part II

Comparing Immigration News Frames in the United States and Europe

5 Why Narrative Is Not Enough
Immigration and the Genres of Journalism

Rodney Benson
New York University

Long-form narrative[1] has become the sacred totem of American journalism and, to judge from some of the chapters in this book, of many non-American journalists as well. It is held up as the best way to balance journalism's contradictory pressures. On the one hand, constructing dramatic tales infused with emotion provides a way to attract and keep the easily bored audience. On the other hand, narratives go beyond the politicians' sound bites to humanize issues, to show the concrete impact that policies have "on the ground." As *New York Times* immigration reporter Nina Bernstein once publicly remarked, "individual stories are a powerful way to convey larger forces."[2]

Against this US journalistic conventional wisdom, I argue in this chapter that personal narrative and structural context are not so easily reconciled. In its search for melodrama, personalized narrative journalism can give short shrift to structural complexities, power dynamics, and diverse perspectives—such as those characterizing immigration. Even when narrative connects the individual to larger trends (as with the classic "she is not alone" transition paragraph), its register tends to be descriptive rather than explanatory.

But if these critiques are accurate, what are the alternatives to narrative? This is where the kind of international dialogue fostered by this book can be helpful. Comparative research can help make us aware of other possibilities, other ways of doing things. Building on the comparative French-American research I conducted for my book *Shaping Immigration News,*[3] in this chapter I call attention to some differences in French and US journalistic practices, especially as they relate to newspapers. Despite their ongoing financial difficulties, newspapers continue to be leading providers of original news and commentary. My focus is on print versions of newspapers, but, as I will argue, similar questions of genre are highly relevant for the online versions as well.

Differing historical relations to political, market, and civic power have helped shape distinctive logics of practice—or forms of news—within the US and French journalistic fields. American newspapers are more dependent on advertising and more profit driven than French newspapers. On the other hand, French state press subsidies are second in Europe only to those in Italy[4] and have included "content-neutral" support to newspapers that add ideological diversity to the public debate. In the United States, narrative has emerged as American journalism's accommodation—and limited form of resistance—to overwhelming commercialization. In France, a multigenre "debate ensemble" format has developed as a means of coordinating—and critiquing—the debate of ideas among the major political parties and intellectual currents.

While it also has its shortcomings, this French multigenre approach suggests one way of overcoming the limitations of narrative. Bringing together news, background features, commentaries, and interviews with experts, the debate ensemble is well equipped to address structural complexity, ideological diversity, and historical context. It provides a way of going beyond the "human dimension" of individual immigrants to address the hows and whys of immigration as a social process. It incorporates narrative but is not limited to it. The format is most strongly developed in French newspapers but is also evident in public media in other countries (such as the US Public Broadcasting Service).

Before saying any more about the debate ensemble, however, let us first examine more closely the strengths and weaknesses of personalized narrative.

PERSONALIZED NARRATIVE JOURNALISM

Narrative is endorsed by American journalism's leading lights, from Harvard's Nieman Foundation to the top editors of the *New York Times* to the Pulitzer Prize committee, which increasingly honors feature articles that emphasize "emotional story-telling."[5] This is not a new development but rather the intensification of a long-standing mode of writing in American journalism. In his ethnographic study of international foreign correspondents in El Salvador during the 1980s, Mark Pedelty found that American journalists could be distinguished from their European counterparts by their emphasis on "dramatic narrative"; other comparative studies have called attention to the uniquely strong emphasis on narrative in American journalism.[6] Michele Weldon's detailed content analysis of multiple US newspapers showed that personalized narrative—marked by the anecdotal lead—has become even more common over the past decade.[7]

Is this a bad thing? Is not a solid narrative feature better than a sensationalistic crime story or a press conference report that reproduces only official sound bites? Compared to much of what we see online today— "snarky opinion pieces" and "top ten lists" being some of the favored genres—long-form narrative journalism can reasonably present itself as the quality alternative.[8] The question on the table is what journalism's "best practices" can or should offer to democratic public debate. It is important to candidly evaluate both the strengths and weaknesses of even the most prestigious genres.

Clearly, narrative provides a powerful technique to "humanize" the immigrant experience and to make the public aware of otherwise hidden social worlds. For instance, in "Two Jobs and a Sense of Hope,"[9] a *Washington Post* article captures the ironies of being an African immigrant in the American south. Presented as an example of a wave of sub-Saharan African immigration to the United States, this profile of Malian Adama Camara also provides a rare glimpse of the day-to-day experiences, feelings, and viewpoints of a janitorial worker, not the kind of individual who usually gets much opportunity to speak and be heard in the public sphere. In a far more daring approach to "get inside" the immigrant experience, the *New York Times* sponsored a reporter from the El Salvadoran newspaper *El Tiempo* to go undercover as a migrant on a smuggling ship (series title: "Dangerous Passage: From Ecuador by Sea").[10] In addition to gripping details about the voyage ("The rough waves and asphyxiating humidity quickly took their toll on passengers who have never seen the ocean before, much less ridden across it"), the story even includes lengthy conversations with the smugglers.

Perhaps the best-known example of a dramatic narrative approach to immigration is "Enrique's Journey," Sonia Nazario's Pulitzer Prize–winning six-part series for the *Los Angeles Times*. It may be a cliché to say so, but "Enrique's Journey" *is* truly heartbreaking. It is a story of a mother—one of many across Central America—who leaves her starving children behind in order to find work that will allow her to send money home to make their lives better. It is also a story of the child who sets out many years later in search of the mother, his harrowing journey, and the inevitable disappointments and difficulties of their reunion. In order to recreate this experience for readers, Nazario literally retraced Enrique's travels from Honduras to North Carolina, even risking her life riding on the tops of the same trains, and conducted dozens of interviews with Enrique and his relatives, other migrants, and immigration officials and aid workers. The story's ending is tragic. After having suffered so much because of his mother's departure, Enrique feels compelled to do the same to his new baby child. As Nazario concludes her series:[11]

One day [after arriving in the United States], Enrique phones Honduras. [His girlfriend] Maria Isabel is pregnant, as he suspected before he left. On Nov. 2, 2000, she gives birth to their daughter.

She and Enrique name the baby Katherine Jasmin.

The baby looks like him. She has his mouth, his nose, his eyes.

An aunt urges Maria Isabel to go to the United States, alone. The aunt promises to take care of the baby.

"If I have the opportunity, I'll go," Maria Isabel says. "I'll leave my baby behind."

Enrique agrees. "We'll have to leave the baby behind."

I do not mean to dispute the validity or importance of the emotional elements of Enrique's experience, powerfully conveyed by Nazario's writing. The question I want to raise is simply the extent to which this narrative—and narrative journalism in general—does what Nina Bernstein said it could do, that is, serve as a "powerful way to convey larger forces." In one of the many glowing reviews of the book version of *Enrique's Journey*, *Entertainment Weekly* wrote that "Nazario's impressive piece of reporting . . . turn[s] the current immigration controversy from a political story into a personal one." Yet something is lost in the translation. We experience in vivid detail what it would be like to live through Enrique's ordeal. We learn that he is one of many suffering the same fate. But we learn very little about why this is happening and what might be done to help him.

Despite Bernstein's insistence that the human dimension and social context can be interwoven, her reporting has also at times failed to make this connection. This is certainly the case in her profile of a Long Island immigration restrictionist activist.[12] In this article, the structural is doubly disadvantaged, both by the demands of narrative and by the failure of empathic understanding: from its opening paragraph, there is no doubt about the social distance between the reporter (and her likely elite urban audience) and the union member/restrictionist activist at the center of the story.

> ELMONT, N.Y.—The streets where Patrick Nicolosi sees America unraveling still have the look of the 1950's. Single-family homes sit side by side, their lawns weed-whacked into submission to the same suburban dream that Mr. Nicolosi's Italian-American parents embraced 40 years ago when they moved to this working-class community on Long Island.

Commenting on the article a few years later, Bernstein told me, "Certainly, the working-class perspective, the white working-class perspective can be quite different. . . . I like the fact that I have the freedom as a reporter to lay out those contradictions and give voice to someone like this who in fact was coming from a union perspective, from a, at least in some ways, a progressive perspective."[13] In the article, Bernstein gives Nicolosi his say, but always couched in relation to personal, even irrational emotions ("resentment," "worries," "working himself into a speech"), not to the kind of hard data that could either confirm or refute his arguments. The article continues:

> It is the economics of class, not the politics of culture or race, that fires Mr. Nicolosi's resentment about what he sees in Elmont, which is probably as diverse a suburb as exists in the United States. Like many working-class Americans who live close to illegal immigrants, he worries that they are yet another force undermining the way of life and the social contract that generations of workers strived so hard to achieve . . . "They're telling us Americans don't want to do these jobs,"

Mr. Nicolosi said. "That's a lie. The business owners don't want to pay. I know what my grandparents fought for: fair wages and days off. Now we're doing it in reverse." . . . "It's either a country of law and order and what my parents fought for, or we just turn it over to big business," he went on, working himself into a speech that connected many dots.

Instead of opening up a discussion about the validity of the "progressive" critiques offered by Nicolosi, a third-generation union member, the story's underlying thrust is intensely personal, a melodramatic "parable about being careful what you wish for." Nicolosi's campaign to stop homeowners from leasing unregulated basement apartments to illegal immigrants ultimately results in the eviction of a Mexican family with two children, one disabled, living across the street. Nicolosi is shunned, even by his neighbors who share his views on immigration. The reason, Bernstein writes (echoing her reporting creed): "People forget the human dimension." Bernstein closes with a lament from Nicolosi's next-door neighbor: "For every problem, there's a solution. For every solution, there's another problem." Narrative thus serves not to supplement structural analysis but effectively to silence it. The article's closing sentence could be read as a verdict that any government action is ultimately futile or counterproductive.[14]

Not all narrative articles are the same. Narrative techniques have a strong affinity with investigative reporting, at which Bernstein has excelled[15] and which is discussed by some of the journalists in this volume; narrative can also be more or less attuned to structural complexity and contradictions. With considerable effort, narrative journalism can weave together human agency and social context,[16] as do some novels, nonfiction books, documentaries, and multilayered television series such as *The Wire*. Still, there seems to be an underlying rhetorical tension between personalized narrative and the "deliberative exchange of ideas."[17] In the midst of telling a story, trying to inject "abstract political ideas" almost inevitably comes across as an inelegant, even tangential, disruption.[18]

Democracy's needs are multiple. Journalism, as its crucial handmaiden, also needs to be multiple. A central challenge for journalism is how to join narrative story telling with other approaches. It is a problem of the coordination of genres. I now turn to this question.

THE DEBATE ENSEMBLE FORMAT

When she transformed her newspaper series into a book, Sonia Nazario made one important change: she added an analytical "Afterword" in an attempt to answer the questions that her narrative did not.[19] Drawing on a careful reading of the available scholarship, Nazario accurately summarizes: "Any calculus of the benefits and burdens of immigration depends on who you are. People who own businesses and commercial interests that use cheap immigrant labor benefit the most from immigrants like Enrique and [his mother] Lourdes." These businesses "bitterly complain" whenever the government attempts to enforce laws prohibiting employment of illegal immigrants. On the other hand, Nazario adds, "those hardest hit by the influx of immigrants are disadvantaged native-born minorities who don't have a high school degree—namely, African Americans and previous waves of Latino immigrants. They must compete for the same low-end jobs immigrants take." For their part, "Most immigrants would rather stay in their home countries with their extended families. . . . What would ensure that more women can stay home—with their children, where they want to be? As [one] mother, says, simply . . .'There would have to be jobs. Jobs that pay okay. That's all.'"

The problem, in short, is economic and global. Nazario points to suggestions for ways to "bolster the economies of immigrant-sending countries," such as forgiving foreign debt of poor Central American countries, implementing more favorable terms of trade for immigrant-sending countries, and increasing US foreign aid donations. Whether Nazario's proposals are adequate is not the issue here (though in fact, they do represent a commendable effort to suggest international policy solutions rarely voiced in mainstream political debate). The issue is what it takes to fully represent a complex issue like immigration. As Nazario's analytical afterword illustrates, it takes more than personalized narrative.

Of course, European journalists use narrative techniques as well. In this volume, the Italian journalist Guido Olimpio explains how his detailed portraits of colorful individuals living near (or trying to cross) the US-Mexico border provide an essential means—a sort of Trojan Horse—to draw in Italian readers otherwise indifferent to happenings so far away. The difference, at least in France, is that features, profiles, or other types of personalized narratives rarely stand alone: in coverage of major events and trends, multiple genres are closely counterposed. In his comparative study of *Le Monde* and the *Washington Post* during the late 1970s, the French sociologist Jean Padioleau singled out *Le Monde* for its distinctive multigenre format: a "pluralist" assemblage of multiple discursive genres and perspectives, anchored by its twin commitments to thoroughly "document" (via publication of diverse original source materials) and "comment" upon the issues of the day.[20] The French newspaper *Libération* took this French multigenre approach to a new level beginning in 1981, with the launch of its *événement* format ["today's big news" or "topic of the day"]. In the words of its former long-time director, Serge July, "'*Événement*' is about putting the emphasis on what we judge to be the day's most important news. . . . All the newspaper's desks contribute, and the topic is approached and problematized from as many angles as possible: whether through investigation or analysis, news reports or interviews, the point is to show, decode, explain, confront, give sense to the news. . . giving rise to the newspaper's own editorial position."[21] Concretely, this means that the first two to five pages are a mix of genres—breaking news, analysis, background information, interviews, and editorial—all focused around a single topic. Virtually all of the major French national newspapers use some version of this format today.[22] I have termed this format a "debate ensemble" because it tends to bring together diverse social actors in a single space in order to facilitate a debate of ideas. Debate ensembles can be reactions to breaking events, such as when (then interior minister) Nicolas Sarkozy proposed new legislation to encourage immigration of high-skilled workers (*Libération*, May 18, 2006), or they can be explicitly thematic, as in an eight-page "dossier" on France's colonial history and its links to contemporary immigration politics (*Le Monde*, January 21, 2006).

Multiarticle, multigenre coverage exists in the United States, especially in response to major events, but it is far more common in France. About 73 percent of French page-one immigration "news packages" (lead article and any closely related inside articles) but only 20 percent of US news packages in my French-American comparative study consisted of multiarticle ensembles. Fifty-two percent of the sampled French news packages were multigenre, in that they incorporated genres beyond breaking news and features, such as guest commentaries, journalist-authored columns or analyses, official editorials, or interview transcripts; only 11 percent of the US sample was multigenre.

From a French perspective, it is not fair to critique an individual article's fairness or comprehensiveness; what matters is the entire "page" consisting of multiple articles and multiple genres of articles.[23] For example, in the wake of a recent party polemic about the "problem" of the replacement of traditional French butchers with Islamic halal butchers in the Paris region, *Le Monde*'s Elise Vincent sought to bring the debate down to earth with a feature about a local butcher shop that had recently made such a transition (see her chapter in this volume). In order to put this narrative in context, Vincent conducted an interview with the demographer Patrick Simon that ran alongside the feature. When *The Guardian* reprinted the feature—but not the interview—English-language readers were effectively deprived of the context provided by the original multigenre ensemble.[24]

The interview transcript can thus help provide the structural context too often underplayed in personalized narratives. Instead of reducing the views of a range of observers and actors in the immigration debate to short "sound bites," published interview transcripts allow them to articulate and defend their arguments at length. In contrast to the column or guest commentary, however, journalistic interrogation potentially forces the writer to directly engage with critiques and alternative framings (this can also be accomplished through comments on online articles or blogs, if the author is willing to respond, as discussed in Popkova's chapter). In my study of French newspaper coverage of immigration during the 2000s, interview transcripts appeared in 30 percent of news packages. Many interviews were of politicians, of course, but at *Libération, Le Monde,* and *Les Echos,* academics and other experts were the most frequently interviewed; at *L'Humanité* and *La Croix,* leaders of immigration associations and religious organizations were the most prominent.

At the same time, one finds a greater mixing of news and opinion on the same page in France than in the United States, with official editorials, columns, and guest commentaries often appearing alongside news articles in the front portion of the newspaper. News analyses or commentaries can potentially explore issues and perspectives not already in the mainstream. In their event news reports or features, reporters often feel constrained to represent the range of opinion expressed by authoritative and powerful sources. Guest commentators and columnists have the autonomy to go beyond official accounts in order to broaden and deepen the public debate.[25]

In-depth, multiperspectival coverage is facilitated by professional practices that break down barriers between news and opinion as well as between different types of news. At the *New York Times,* news and opinion editors work on different floors and conduct their own separate meetings to choose the day's top news stories and editorials; at *Le Monde,* however, the topic and position of the day's editorial are decided at the same meeting where page-one decisions are made.[26] At US newspapers, immigration reporters are generally part of the general information "metropolitan" or "national" news desks. In France, most immigration reporters are part of the "social problems" (*société*) desks. In contrast to political reporters focused on the days' events, the social problems desk editors and reporters have "a more magazine-like conception of information . . . understanding events as illustration of broader problems."[27] As a result, the pages allotted to this desk consist of "thematic dossiers, mixing analyses, reportages and testimonies, less strictly tied to breaking news."

At a macro level, the multigenre debate ensemble format seems to be closely linked to public or other noncommercial funding and ownership, whereas the narrative approach is more dominant among commercial media. In part because the French journalistic field is less commercialized than the US field, French newspapers are more likely to use the multigenre approach. However, even in the United States, noncommercial media such as the PBS *Newshour* also tend to organize news as a debate ensemble.[28] Thus, while shaped by distinctive national histories, journalistic practices can and do cross national boundaries (with or without overt attempts to export them). What works "elsewhere" may in fact work "here" as well, with all due adaptations to local circumstances.

THE CIVIC BENEFITS OF MULTIGENRE NEWS

Fair enough, some American journalists might say. But does the public really want this kind of journalism? Isn't it boring? Multigenre journalism does not have to be. French newspapers rely mostly on newsstand sales, so they use dramatic headlines and images to entice buyers. The debate ensemble is a kind of "daily magazine" that tries to both "reflect upon" and "convey the emotion" of the news.[29] The French format is not without its own types of sensationalism. It is simply another way of accommodating journalism's competing needs to attract audiences and serve civic functions.

On the basis of my research, I can only concur with the British media scholar Simon Cottle that news formats "play a critical role in either enabling or disabling the range of viewpoints and discourses sustained by vying social interests."[30] I find that narrative articles with classic "anecdotal" leads present fewer substantive critical statements than other types of news articles. On the other hand, in both France and the United States, I find that multigenre news provides a wider range of voices (speakers) and viewpoints (issue frames) than narrative news, even when word length is held constant. Because a much higher proportion of its coverage is multigenre, French news tends to be significantly more pluralist and critical.[31] Whereas American immigration coverage has increasingly focused on the dramatic humanitarian and public order frames, French coverage continues to make substantial room for complex conceptual aspects of immigration, such as its links to the global economy. What effect does this kind of multiperspectival news have on public knowledge or civic empowerment? Recent audience research suggests: "When people are exposed to several competing interpretations [or frames] they are able to think about the political situation in more complex and original ways," and this translates into citizens who are better able to "perform their civic duties."[32]

Journalists should not underestimate their audiences. Even if they are enticed by melodramatic story telling, many readers clearly want more than that. In the days and weeks following the publication of "Enrique's Journey," the *Los Angeles Times* published 17 letters to the editor. It is almost certain that many more letters were submitted; it is likely that the *LA Times* opinion page editors made some attempt to print a representative sample. Thus, the series clearly caught people's attention and opened up a space for public debate. But what did the readers—or at least this small sample of readers— want to talk about? Only two letter writers focused on the compassionate humanitarian elements emphasized in Nazario's account. All the other letter writers raised structural and policy questions: Why are the immigrants coming? Who or what is causing this mass exodus? What are the social costs and benefits? What are the best policy solutions? About half of these letters were strongly against illegal immigration, though in many cases the writers put the blame less on the immigrants than on ineffective border control or news media who failed to focus on the larger problems. The other half either sought to defend undocumented immigration's economic benefits or to redefine the problem in terms of Central American poverty and economic underdevelopment.

And what did the *LA Times* do with this emerging debate? Almost nothing. In the weeks that followed, the newspaper published only one op-ed article—by the University of Southern California sociologist Pierrette Hondagneu-Sotelo—that provided any additional social context. As far as I can determine from database searches, the newspaper never published an official editorial taking a position on the causes and consequences of and the solutions to the problems identified by the series. It declined to try to shed light as well as heat on the issue.

And yet the public *is* interested: this hunger for explanations rather than just stories is surely part of what is driving the growing audiences for openly partisan news outlets like Fox and MSNBC. But they deserve better than the partial truths that these outlets often provide. In my interviews, some American journalists have told me they are hesitant to enter into the debate about causes, consequences, and solutions because the research itself is so conflicted. In fact, as Nazario showed in her book's afterword, immigration scholars agree on most of the crucial issues. The links between immigration and neoliberal economic policymaking are especially strong: these are "inconvenient truths" that need to be heard by the public and policymakers.

Journalists who are not afraid to cover the dangerous stories on the border need not be afraid to wade into the academic research thicket and work with scholars to make these findings accessible and interesting to the public. Instead of succumbing to a cynical relativism, journalists should pay closer attention to the social conditions underlying the production of expertise: there is a crucial difference between the packaged sound bites (often with hidden agendas) mass-produced by many think tanks and the critical knowledge produced by careful academic scholarship subject to rigorous peer review.[33]

People want to connect the dots. Journalists ought to help them. There are signs that journalists in the United States as well as in France are beginning to realize this. Interview transcripts are increasingly appearing in the *Los Angeles Times,* in both the opinion and news pages. The *New York Times'* long-standing Week in Review has been transformed into a "Sunday Review" that makes ample room for the voices of writers, artists, and scholars alongside journalists.[34] In the online versions of the *New York Times* and other leading newspapers, opinion is no longer relegated to the back pages but is featured at the top of the homepage. The Internet has become a laboratory for experimentation and mixing of genres and formats. In-depth articles about immigration are easily retrievable years after their first publication and can also be linked to databases, maps, interactive graphics, expert debates, and other genres and types of information, analysis, and commentary. NYTimes.com also now has a regular feature called "Room for Debate" in which various experts and activists discuss topics of the day and readers submit comments. On the Web, at least some of the format differences between French and US newspapers are decreasing rather than increasing, as news, opinion, and other genres mix more freely online.[35]

Over the course of several weeks or months, any good newspaper is likely to cover immigration from a variety of angles. The multigenre format's extra contribution is clear: in a single day's edition, it helps its readers break out of the endless news cycles of seemingly unrelated events, factoids, and dramas in order to see how the many moving parts might just fit together. If one civic purpose of journalism is to help the public understand issues such as immigration in all their multiplicity, then journalism must also become more multifaceted. In the long run, this will require resources, as several journalist contributors to this book rightly emphasize; it will also require improving journalistic working conditions in ways that allow for the production of intellectually autonomous knowledge. But the first step is to see that there are in fact alternatives to the dominant narrative-based practices. The challenge for journalists—as well as scholars, policymakers, and activists—is to find new ways to work together to enrich and expand the public debate.

NOTES

1. At a metaphoric level, much if not all of human knowledge can be characterized as narrative; even structural accounts can be analyzed in relation to classical narrative forms such as tragedy, comedy, romance, and irony. See, e.g., Ronald Jacobs, *Race, Media, and the Crisis of Civil Society* (Cambridge: Cambridge University Press, 2000), 11–12. My use of the term narrative is narrower: I call attention to personalized dramatic narrative articles aimed at telling the "stories" of nonelite individuals.
2. Nina Bernstein, remarks to French-American Foundation conference "Covering Immigration," Paris, November 2009.
3. See Rodney Benson, *Shaping Immigration News: A French-American Comparison* (Cambridge: Cambridge University Press, 2013). The book draws on more than 70 interviews with French and American journalists, historical/archival research on media institutions and policies, and discourse and image analysis of more than 2,000 newspaper and television "news packages" about immigration from 1973 to 2006.
4. Rasmus Kleis Nielsen and Geert Linnebank, *Public Support for the Media: A Six-Country Overview of Direct and Indirect Subsidies* (Oxford: Reuters Institute for the Study of Journalism, 2011).
5. Karin Wahl-Jorgensen, "The Strategic Ritual of Emotionality: A Case Study of Pulitzer Prize–winning Articles," *Journalism* 14 (2012): 6. While emotional storytelling is especially prevalent in US journalism, it is certainly used by journalists in other countries as well. See, e.g., Mervi Pantti's study of Finnish and Dutch television journalists, "The Value of Emotion: An Examination of Television Journalists' Notions on Emotionality," *European Journal of Communication* 25 (2010): 168–81.
6. Mark Pedelty, *War Stories* (London: Routledge, 1995). See also Daniel Hallin and Paolo Mancini, "Speaking of the President: Political Structure and Representational Form in US and Italian Television News," *Theory and Society* 13 (1984): 829–50; Jean Padioleau, *Le Monde et le Washington Post* (Paris: Presses Universitaires de France, 1985); and Myra Marx Ferree, William Anthony Gamson, Jürgen Gerhards, and Dieter Rucht, *Shaping Abortion Discourse: Democracy and the Public Sphere in Germany and the United States* (Cambridge: Cambridge University Press, 2002).
7. Michele Weldon, *Everyman News* (Columbia: University of Missouri Press, 2008).

8. See, e.g., Mallory Jean Tenore, "What Do We Mean by 'Longform Journalism' and How Can We Get It 'to Go'?," Poynter.org, March 1, 2012, http://www.poynter.org/latest-news/top-stories/165132/what-do-we-mean-by-longform-journalism-how-can-we-get-it-to-go/ (accessed February 26, 2013).

9. Anne Hull, "Two Jobs and a Sense of Hope: A Young Man from Mali Discovers a Tough Life on a Time Clock," *Washington Post*, December 11, 2002, A-1.

10. Ginger Thompson and Sandra Ochoa, "By a Back Door to the US: A Migrant's Grim Sea Voyage," *New York Times*, June 13, 2004, 1.

11. Sonia Nazario, "Enrique's Journey/Chapter 6; At Journey's End, A Dark River, Perhaps a New Life," *Los Angeles Times*, October 7, 2002, A-1. The complete series was published in slightly adapted form as Sonia Nazario, *Enrique's Journey* (New York: Random House, 2007).

12. Nina Bernstein, "On Lucille Avenue, the Immigration Debate," *New York Times*, June 26, 2006, 1.

13. Author telephone interview with Nina Bernstein, June 14, 2008.

14. For Bernstein's own interpretation of this article, see Nina Bernstein, "The Making of an Outlaw Generation," in *Writing Immigration*, ed. M. M. Suárez-Orozco, V. Louie, and R. Suro (Berkeley: University of California Press), 31–34. See also Yale law professor Peter Schuck's chapter in the same volume ("Some Observations about Immigration Journalism," 82–88), for a listing of the "structural" stories and "invisible victims" generally ignored by US immigration journalists, whom he sees as primarily driven by a "passion for narrating the drama of individual lives."

15. See, e.g., Nina Bernstein, "Few Details on Immigrants Who Died in Custody," *New York Times*, May 5, 2008, 1, the first of a series of reports that was awarded the Hillman Prize for outstanding "social justice" journalism. Regarding the links between personalized narrative and investigative reporting, see James Ettema and Theodore L. Glasser, *Custodians of Conscience: Investigative Journalism and Public Virtue* (New York: Columbia University Press, 1998).

16. See, for instance, the *New York Times* series "Remade in America" (March–April 2009), which makes links between the "newest immigrants and their impact on American institutions" (the family, social services, businesses, politics, hospitals, workplaces, and schools). Notably, however, the series' structural analysis is substantially bolstered online through links to other genres, especially expert debates and interactive databases (http://projects.nytimes.com/immigration/, accessed May 29, 2013).

17. See Hartmut Wessler, "Investigating Deliberativeness Comparatively," *Political Communication* 25 (2008): 8.

18. Hallin and Mancini, "Speaking of the President," 845.

19. Nazario, *Enrique's Journey*, 255–60.

20. Padioleau, *Le Monde et le Washington Post*, 92–98.

21. Serge July, "*Libération* encore plus *Libé*," *Libération*, October 11–12, 2003. Over the years, *Libération* has modified its *événement* formula in various ways, but the basic elements remain the same.

22. This claim is based on my own periodic observations and conversations with journalists across a range of French newspapers, including not only the French contributors to this volume but also, among many others, Philippe Bernard of *Le Monde*, Jean-François Fogel of *Libération* (who subsequently served as a page one "design" consultant for *Le Monde*), Pascale Egré of *Le Parisien* (and formerly of *L'Humanité*), and Jean-Jacques Rouche of *La Dépêche du Midi* in Toulouse.

23. See Sandrine Boudana, "Journalistic Objectivity as a Performance: Construction of a Model of Evaluation and Application to the Case of the

French Press Coverage of the Second Intifada" (PhD diss., Humanities and Social Sciences, Hebrew University, Jerusalem, 2010), Appendix I, viii. On the basis of her interviews with French newspaper journalists, Boudana summarizes the French approach as follows: "Each article only represents a piece of the puzzle . . . no article can pretend to completeness, each one offers an angle. Completeness should emerge from a corpus of texts considered as a whole."

24. See Elise Vincent, "Yves Béguin et Lahcen Hakki, un passage de témoin en douceur dans la boucherie: A Pantin, le dernier boucher 'traditionnel' a cédé son pas de porte à un artisan 'halal'" and "Une forme d'intégration locale assez réussie," transcript of interview with Patrick Simon by Elise Vincent, both in *Le Monde*, March 6, 2012, 12. An English-language translation of Vincent's article appeared online in *The Guardian* on March 13, 2012, http://www.guardian.co.uk/world/2012/mar/06/le-medi-bospolder-housing-multiculturalism, accessed May 29, 2013.

25. For example, *New York Times* columnist (and Nobel Prize–winning economist) Paul Krugman has raised insightful critiques of US immigration policies that are uncomfortable for the left as well as the right. See, e.g., Paul Krugman, "North of the Border," *New York Times*, March 27, 2006, 19. On the important and often overlooked civic contributions of opinion journalism, see Ronald Jacobs and Eleanor Townsley, *The Space of Opinion* (Oxford: Oxford University Press, 2011).

26. These conclusions are based on my own observations and interviews at these newspapers. Former *Times* executive editor Bill Keller said at a Columbia Journalism school event held on February 3, 2011: "The editorial page is not my domain. The editorial page answers to a different boss. I'm not aware of what they're doing" (author notes). See also Eugénie Saïtta, "*Le Monde*, vingt ans après," *Réseaux* 131 (2005): 191–225.

27. Nicolas Hubé and Nicolas Kaciaf, "Les pages 'société' ou les pages 'politique' en creux: Retour sur des conflits de bon voisinage," in *Les frontières journalistiques*, ed. I. Chupin and J. Nollet (Paris: L'Harmattan, 2006), 192–204. Consistent with this thematic understanding of the beat, it should not be surprising that when leading French immigration journalists write books they are often not narrative epics (as in *Enrique's Journey*) but rather short and snappy compendiums of the scholarly literature. See, e.g., two such books by *Le Monde* journalists: Philippe Bernard, *L'immigration: Le défi mondial* (Paris: Gallimard, 2002), and Laetitia Van Eeckhout, *L'immigration* (Paris: La Documentation française, 2007).

28. See Benson, *Shaping Immigration News*, chap. 8.

29. Jean-Claude Perrier, *Le roman vrai de Libération* (Paris: Juilliard, 1994), 123–24, 202.

30. Simon Cottle, "The Production of News Formats: Determinants of Mediated Public Contestation," *Media, Culture and Society* 17 (1995): 279.

31. While my emphasis is on genre in this chapter, obviously other factors are important in explaining French-American differences, notably France's multiparty political system and the contingent historical legacies of relations among journalism, political parties, civil society associations, and the academy. Even if US newspapers fully adopted French-style news formats, these historical and structural differences would ensure that news content in the two countries would continue to differ at least in some ways.

32. Mauro Porto, "Frame Diversity and Citizen Competence," *Critical Studies in Media Communication* 24 (2007): 312–18; see also Dennis Chong and James N. Druckman, "Framing Theory," *Annual Review of Political Science* 10 (2007): 110.

33. See Thomas Medvetz, *Think Tanks in America* (Chicago: University of Chicago Press, 2011).
34. See Arthur S. Brisbane, "Surrounded by Opinion, The Times Raises Its Voices," *New York Times*, July 3, 2011, Sunday Review, 10.
35. Rodney Benson, Mark Blach-Orsten, Matthew Powers, Ida Willig, and Sandra Vera Zambrano, "Media Systems Online and Off: The Form of Print and Online News in the United States, France, and Denmark." *Journal of Communication* 62, no. 1(2012): 21–38.

BIBLIOGRAPHY

Benson, Rodney. *Shaping Immigration News: A French-American Comparison.* Cambridge: Cambridge University Press, 2013.
———, Mark Blach-Orsten, Matthew Powers, Ida Willig, and Sandra Vera Zambrano. "Media Systems Online and Off: The Form of Print and Online News in the United States, France, and Denmark." *Journal of Communication* 62, no. 1 (2012): 21–38.
Bernard, Philippe. *Immigration: Le défi mondial.* Paris: Gallimard, 2002.
Bernstein, Nina. "The Making of an Outlaw Generation." In *Writing Immigration*, ed. M. M. Suárez-Orozco, V. Louie, and R. Suro. Berkeley: University of California Press, 2011: 23–43.
Boudana, Sandrine. "Journalistic Objectivity as a Performance: Construction of a Model of Evaluation and Application to the Case of the French Press Coverage of the Second Intifada." PhD diss., Humanities and Social Sciences, Hebrew University, Jerusalem, 2010.
Chong, Dennis, and James N. Druckman. "Framing Theory." *Annual Review of Political Science* 10 (2007): 103–26.
Cottle, Simon. "The Production of News Formats: Determinants of Mediated Public Contestation." *Media, Culture and Society* 17 (1995): 275–91.
Ettema, James S., and Theodore L. Glasser. *Custodians of Conscience: Investigative Journalism and Public Virtue.* New York: Columbia University Press, 1998.
Ferree, Myra Marx, William Anthony Gamson, Jürgen Gerhards, and Dieter Rucht. *Shaping Abortion Discourse: Democracy and the Public Sphere in Germany and the United States.* Cambridge: Cambridge University Press. 2002.
Hallin, Daniel, and Paolo Mancini. "Speaking of the President: Political Structure and Representational Form in US and Italian Television News." *Theory and Society* 13 (1984): 829–50.
Hubé, Nicolas, and Nicolas Kaciaf. "Les pages 'société' ou les pages 'politiques' en creux: Retour sur des conflits de bon voisinage." In *Les frontières journalistiques*, ed. I. Chupin and J. Nollet. Paris: L'Harmattan, 2006: 189–212.
Jacobs, Ronald. *Race, Media, and the Crisis of Civil Society.* Cambridge: Cambridge University Press, 2000.
———, and Eleanor Townsley. *The Space of Opinion.* Oxford: Oxford University Press, 2011.
Medvetz, Thomas. *Think Tanks in America.* Chicago: University of Chicago Press, 2011.
Nazario, Sonia. *Enrique's Journey.* New York: Random House, 2007.
Nielsen, Rasmus Kleis, and Geert Linnebank. *Public Support for the Media: A Six-Country Overview of Direct and Indirect Subsidies.* Oxford: Reuters Institute for the Study of Journalism, 2011.
Padioleau. Jean. *Le Monde et le Washington Post.* Paris: Presses Universitaires de France, 1985.

Pantti, Mervi. "The Value of Emotion: An Examination of Television Journalists' Notions on Emotionality." *European Journal of Communication* 25 (2010): 168–81.

Pedelty, Mark. *War Stories*. London: Routledge, 1995.

Perrier, Jean-Claude. *Le roman vrai de Libération*. Paris: Juilliard, 1994.

Porto, Mauro. "Frame Diversity and Citizen Competence." *Critical Studies in Media Communication* 24 (2007): 303–21.

Saïtta, Eugénie. "*Le Monde*, vingt ans après." *Réseaux* 131 (2005): 191–225.

Schuck, Peter H. "Some Observations about Immigration Journalism." In *Writing Immigration*, ed. M. M. Suárez-Orozco, V. Louie, and R. Suro. Berkeley: University of California Press, 2011: 73–89.

Van Eeckhout, Laetitia. *L'Immigration*. Paris: La Documentation française, 2007.

Wahl-Jorgensen, Karin. "The Strategic Ritual of Emotionality: A Case Study of Pulitzer Prize–winning Articles." *Journalism* 14 (2012): 1–17.

Weldon, Michele. *Everyman News*. Columbia: University of Missouri Press, 2008.

Wessler, Hartmut. "Investigating Deliberativeness Comparatively," *Political Communication* 25 (2008): 1–22.

6 Just off the Wire
AP's and AFP's Coverage of Immigration in France and the United States

Rodrigo Zamith
University of Minnesota

One of the core premises of this book is that a central site for the debate over immigration, especially in its border security and integration parameters, has been the mass media, which play an important role in how publics come to understand controversial issues.[1] This is particularly true for newswire services, whose stories are reproduced in thousands of newspapers every day.[2] Furthermore, newswire stories often serve as a starting point for original work, thereby setting initial boundaries for reporting.[3] Newswire services are therefore important locales in which the construction of meaning occurs, yet they remain largely unstudied in academic literature. The purpose of this chapter is to provide the first systematic analysis and comparison of the social realities of immigration constructed and disseminated nationally by the leading newswire agencies in France and the United States—Agence France-Presse and The Associated Press—between 2007 and 2011.

WIRES, FRAMES AND STRUCTURAL CONSTRAINTS

Media scholars have long contended that mass media play a significant role in the formation of knowledge[4] and that media depictions influence the construction of meaning by individuals.[5] A useful framework for conceptualizing the power of communicating texts may be drawn from framing theory, which posits that the manner in which media present issues affects receivers' understanding of those issues.[6] This study relies primarily on the conceptualization of media frames offered by William Gamson and Andre Modigliani, who define them as "a central organizing idea or story line that provides meaning to an unfolding strip of events."[7]

Because the purpose is to analyze the reality constructed through news content, this study focuses on occurrence of media frames at the textual level.[8] In order to assess this coverage, I performed a frame analysis, which systematically examines texts for the selection of framing devices (e.g., metaphors, keywords, and appeals to principle) and reasoning devices (defining problems, interpreting causes, making moral evaluations, prescribing solutions) in order to promote a particular understanding of an issue.[9] As several scholars have noted, differences in the selection of words, phrases, and images can exert appreciable influences on citizens' perceptions of and attitudes toward issues in several ways, including issue interpretation and attitudes,[10] cynicism and negative associations,[11] and support for policies.[12] More specifically, in the context of immigration, Juan-José Igartua and Lifen Cheng found that the type of frame stressed in a news story affected individuals' perceptions of the extent to which immigration is a problem, as well as their attitudes toward immigration and beliefs about the consequences of immigration for the country.[13] This is particularly important, as attitudes toward immigration are grounded more in individuals' perceptions—largely shaped by messages from politicians and the media—than in objective economic or demographic conditions at the national level.[14]

News media—both in print and online—in the United States and Europe have become increasingly reliant on newswire services in recent years, due to economic pressures and the increased workload faced by journalists.[15] However, despite this trend, studies of newswire services remain scarce and are almost nonexistent in the context of immigration. As the use of newswires becomes more prevalent, it becomes increasingly important to study them and the messages they disseminate.

According to Pamela Shoemaker and Stephen Reese, there are four key macro-level factors that influence media content: journalistic routines and norms, the structure of the media organization, contextual factors like the political environment, and ideology.[16] The little existent scholarly literature on newswire agencies suggests that there are limited differences between The Associated Press and Agence France-Presse across two of these factors: journalistic norms and ideology. Both AP and AFP consider objectivity to be a key goal and employ similar routines.[17] Furthermore, both newswire services focus on episodic spot news, with speed and competition characterizing their modus operandi, leading them to "speak in the language of breaking stories."[18] The two agencies also strive to be nonideological and have a shared understanding of the nature and definition of news.[19] Indeed, as noted by Chris Paterson, "because news agencies must please all news editors, everywhere, they must work harder than their client journalists to create the appearance of objectivity and neutrality."[20]

In terms of structure and external factors, the two agencies show marked differences, although some similarities remain. Both AP and AFP have their main headquarters in the United States and France, respectively, as well as regional bureaus in major economic capitals around the world and a number of correspondents elsewhere.[21] However, the two have distinct sources of funding and very different relationships with their national governments. According to Rodney Benson, the French press receives fewer legal protections and is more likely to be subject to overt interference by the government than the US press.[22] Furthermore, in contrast to its US counterpart, the French press receives considerable subsidies,[23] which Benson notes may be used to induce a form of covert pressure. AFP, in particular, is a government-chartered public corporation that, although officially independent of the French government and operating with a mandate of independence and neutrality, nonetheless includes government representatives on its executive board and receives indirect subsidies from the French government in the form of subscriptions for its various services.[24] AP, meanwhile, operates as a not-for-profit cooperative that is entirely independent of the US government.

Furthermore, the two countries share some similarities in the composition of their populations and in the nature of the debate over immigration but have employed distinct policies to address it. Both France and the United States have a history of being immigrant-receiving countries, and foreign-born individuals now account for 12.7 percent and 11.6 percent of their overall population, respectively, percentages largely made up of immigrants coming through the host country's southern borders.[25] Indeed, the two largest immigrant groups in France are Algerians and Moroccans, which together account for roughly one-quarter of the country's foreign-born population.[26] In the United States, Mexicans constitute the largest immigrant group, accounting for 30.4 percent of the country's foreign-born population.[27] Additionally, immigration policy has been hotly contested in both countries by similar social actors, including political parties, interest groups, and academics, and the debates are dominated by similar themes, including illegal immigration, economic benefits and threats, and the impact on the domestic culture.[28]

However, as Martin Schain notes, over the past 40 years, the immigration policy objectives of France and the United States have been quite distinct, with French policy seeking to drastically reduce immigration and American policy seeking to permit immigration on the basis of criteria of family unification, labor needs, and diversity.[29] He adds that political parties in France have largely framed the issue in terms of identity, emphasizing restriction, rather than openness. In particular, the growing influence of the extreme right in France in recent years has led to greater marginalization of immigrants. This is contrasted by the political parties in the United States, which have tended to view immigrant voters as a political resource, thus promoting more open policies.[30] However, a recent wave of anti-immigrant sentiment in the United States has also led to anti-immigrant proposals by several US legislators, at both the national and the state levels.

Structural and political factors therefore suggest that there may be differences in the coverage of immigration in the United States and in France by Agence France-Presse and The Associated Press, despite the similarities in ideology and journalistic routines. This study thus sought to explore such potential differences by asking: Where is the coverage of immigration by AFP and AP coming from? How does AP's coverage of immigration in the United States compare to its coverage of immigration in France? How does AFP's coverage of immigration in France compare to its coverage of immigration in the United States? And, finally, how does the coverage of immigration in the United States by AP compare with that of AFP, and how does the coverage of immigration in France by AFP compare with that of AP?

A NOTE ON METHOD

According to Roberto Suro, although the influx of foreign-born individuals to the United States has remained fairly steady in recent years, media coverage of and public interest in the issue of immigration has been marked by sharp ups and downs.[31] In light of this, I adopted a longitudinal design in order to mitigate the risk of a short-term spike in the salience of the issue. News stories were obtained through a search in the LexisNexis database for articles in which the words "immigrant*" or "immigration" appeared in either the headline or the lead of articles dated between January 1, 2007, and December 31, 2011. These dates were selected to generate a substantial amount of recent coverage and to negate the risk of event-driven bias. Last, articles had to appear in the English-language feeds of either The Associated Press or Agence France-Presse. After I removed briefs and duplicate stories, the sample consisted of 6,286 news stories (2,312 from AFP and 3,974 from AP).[32]

In order to comprehensively and reliably assess a substantial amount of coverage, I adopted a mixed-method, exploratory design.[33] I first performed an inductive reading of 20 random news stories each for AP and AFP in both France and the United States ($n = 80$). The purpose of this part of the analysis was to identify the recurring frames in the coverage, evaluate narratives in a holistic manner, and assess the depictions of immigrants. I also identified key words that were used repeatedly in association with frames and themes, which I later used in the computer-assisted analysis. Frames were noted only if they included a combination of framing devices (e.g., metaphors, keywords, and appeals to principle) and reasoning devices (defining problems, interpreting causes, making moral evaluations, prescribing solutions) and were salient in the coverage.[34] A total of nine frames, shown in Table 6.1, and 42 associated themes were identified during this analysis.

In order to assess the depiction of immigrants, I focused on the language used to describe them (e.g., positive or negative adjectives), the extent to which they were factored into the article (e.g., central focus or peripheral focus), the depth in which they were discussed (e.g., treated as individuals or as a distant mass), and the frames and contexts that were associated with them in the news text. Thus, stories that associated immigrants with lawlessness and crime or painted them as thieves of natives' jobs would be categorized as containing unfavorable depictions. Conversely, stories that associated immigrants with social or economic benefits or painted them as hardworking individuals diligently pursuing a better life would be categorized as containing favorable depictions. Whenever stories contained both positive and negative depictions, I paid attention to which type of depiction was most salient in the news story as well as the placement of the depictions,

Table 6.1   Frame Definitions

Frame Name	Description
Border Security	The need to secure or police borders, including the building of fences or the expansion of border patrols
Driving Factors	The reasons why immigrants migrate, including a search for the American Dream or an escape from violence or other turmoil
Law and Order	Associations with law enforcement, including depictions of lawless immigrants, enforcement of employment verification, and matters of deportation and detention
Legal	Legal challenges to or rulings about the lawfulness of legislation and ordinances or criminal trials and asylum pleas
Morality	Evaluations of the morality of the issue, including discussions about immigrants' civil rights, the exploitation of immigrants, and the separation of families
National Identity	The threats posed by immigration to national identity, including the dimensions of integration, language, and values
Policy	Legislative responses to the issue of immigration, including amnesty, definitions of citizenship, and immigration reform
Politics	The political effects of addressing the issue, including the impact on candidates' election prospects
Social Movement	Collective action by activist actors in support of or opposition to particular issue-relevant aims, including rallies and demonstrations

with depictions occurring close to the beginning of the article being assessed as having greater prominence and therefore given more weight.

After the interpretive analysis was completed, I created a custom computer program to analyze each news article in the final sample.[35] This program systematically assessed whether themes were present in an article on the basis of the use of combinations of keywords, with the expectation that certain themes would likely, though not necessarily, suggest the presence of specific frames.[36] While lexical choice is certainly an important component of frames, it is worth noting that frames often manifest themselves in latent manners, which the computer program used in this study would be unable to pick up. Findings from the interpretive and computer-assisted analyses, which were conducted separately, were largely consistent.

FRAMING IMMIGRATION ON THE WIRES

Origin of Stories

In the United States—where 75.3 percent (*n* = 2,991) of AP's global coverage originated—articles were derived from 418 unique locations, with 52.8

percent of the articles coming from the top 10 cities. AFP's coverage of immigration in the United States—which accounted for 22.6 percent (n = 523) of its global coverage—originated in 51 unique locations, with 88.3 percent of the articles coming from the top 10 cities. Although there are distinct differences in the long tail, the bulk of the coverage still originated from the same few cities for both AP and AFP. Indeed, nine of the top 10 cities were the same for AP and AFP, and Washington, DC, accounted for a disproportionate amount of the coverage in both samples, although significantly more so in AFP's case.

In France—where 2.5 percent (n = 100) of AP's global coverage originated—articles were derived from 21 unique locations, with 89.0 percent of the articles coming from the top 10 cities. AFP's coverage of immigration in France—which accounted for 8.7 percent (n = 201) of its global coverage—originated in 30 unique locations, with 90.5 percent of the articles coming from the top 10 cities. As with the US coverage, there was a substantial amount of overlap among the top 10 cities, with six of them appearing on both lists; additionally, a vast amount of coverage originated from Paris for both AP and AFP (see Table 6.2).

In terms of the US coverage, this indicates that, although AP reported from far more locations and had a notably lower degree of concentration than AFP, the bulk of the coverage still originated in the same few cities. In France, there was also considerable overlap between AP and AFP in the bulk of the coverage, though less than in the United States; additionally, there was far less geographical diversity and a very high degree of concentration of stories by both outlets. These findings suggest that there was significant geographic overlap among the bulk of the stories—certainly in France and to a lesser extent in the United States—thus minimizing the added geographic diversity in the long tail offered by AP in the United States and AFP in France. Also noteworthy was that AFP devoted more coverage to immigration in the United States than in France, although this may have been influenced by the sample, which included only stories from the English-language newswire.

Immigration in the United States

AP's coverage of immigration in the United States was most likely to invoke the policy and law-and-order frames, with the politics frame also receiving substantial attention (see Table 6.3). The interpretive analysis indicated that AP focused on federal-level policies, which were frequently depicted neutrally and in terms of procedural actions in legislative bodies, although particularly controversial state legislation also received some attention. There was also a substantial amount of coverage devoted to the enforcement of existing laws, especially in terms of raids on immigrants and issues relating to employment verification. Last, electoral politics loomed large, with the issue of immigration often raised either in terms of how it would affect a candidate's chances or as part of the candidate's platform.

Table 6.2 Top 10 Cities in France and US Coverage by AP and AFP

	US Coverage				France Coverage			
	Associated Press		Agence France-Presse		Associated Press		Agence France-Presse	
Rank	City	%	City	%	City	%	City	%
1	Washington, DC	21.9	Washington, DC	54.3	Paris	69.0	Paris	71.6
2	Phoenix	7.0	New York	9.6	Cannes	4.0	Strasbourg	5.5
3	New York	6.9	Los Angeles	7.1	Villiers-le-Bel	4.0	Calais	5.0
4	Los Angeles	4.8	Phoenix	5.4	Strasbourg	3.0	Tours	3.5
5	Miami	2.4	Miami	4.4	Calais	2.0	Argenteuil	1.0
6	Boston	2.3	Chicago	3.8	Clichy-sous-Bois	2.0	Vaulx-en-Velin	1.0
7	San Francisco	2.0	El Paso	1.1	Tours	2.0	Cannes	1.0
8	El Paso	1.9	San Francisco	1.0	Argenteuil	1.0	Marseille	1.0
9	Chicago	1.7	Wichita	1.0	Douai	1.0	Henin Beaumont	0.5
10	Atlanta	1.7	Atlanta	0.8	Evian	1.0	Lille	0.5

Note: The percent column refers to the amount of coverage within the respective region and by the respective outlet. For US coverage, The Associated Press figures add up to 52.8% ($n = 1,578$); Agence France-Presse figures add up to 88.3% ($n = 462$). For France coverage, The Associated Press figures add up to 89.0% ($n = 89$); Agence France-Presse figures add up to 90.5% ($n = 182$). Article origin is derived from its dateline.

Table 6.3 Frame Salience in France and US Coverage by AP and AFP

	US Coverage		France Coverage	
Frame	Associated Press	Agence France-Presse	Associated Press	Agence France-Presse
Border Security	13.3%	21.4%	4.0%	6.5%
Driving Factors	6.9%	5.9%	7.0%	3.5%
Law and Order	33.1%	19.1%	7.0%	11.4%
Legal	19.5%	14.0%	6.0%	6.0%
Morality	12.0%	15.1%	10.0%	11.4%
National Identity	4.1%	6.7%	29.0%	25.4%
Policy	38.1%	41.7%	33.0%	25.4%
Politics	29.0%	41.5%	58.0%	55.2%
Social Movement	14.6%	16.8%	16.0%	19.9%

Note: Individual articles may contain more than one frame and columns thus do not add up to 100%.

AFP's coverage of immigration in the United States was most likely to invoke the policy and politics frames (see Table 6.3). The interpretive analysis indicated that AFP also focused on federal-level policies and on controversial state legislation and similarly employed a script of conflict, both within and between parties and in terms of how it would impact candidates' standing and electoral chances. Last, substantial attention was devoted to the importance of securing the border with Mexico by highlighting statements by officials to that effect as well as by explicitly noting how legislative acts would achieve it.

As shown in Table 6.3, there were considerable differences between AP's and AFP's US coverage among four of the frames: AFP was more likely to emphasize the politics and border-security frames, while AP was more likely to emphasize the law-and-order and legal frames. Lesser differences were found among the remaining five frames, with AFP being more likely to emphasize the policy, morality, national-identity, and social-movement frames, while AP was more likely to emphasize the driving-factors frame.

Regarding the depiction of immigrants in the news articles, both AP and AFP tended to follow similar schemas. The majority of the stories failed to either quote immigrants or devote significant attention to individual immigrants, instead treating them abstractly. Indeed, the issue of immigration was largely discussed in a manner that was detached from the actual immigrants. As a result, the majority of the coverage treated immigrants neutrally, although there was a notable amount of unfavorable portrayals as a result of associations of immigrants with lawlessness—especially in AP coverage—and the juxtaposition of their cheap labor with the economic hardship faced by Americans. When immigrants were described at length, they were more likely to be depicted favorably, with narratives generally characterizing them as hardworking individuals and highlighting their plight or calling attention to the negative effects that state and federal policies had on them. Notably, the majority of stories treated immigration predominantly as a Latino issue; for example, stories including the politics frame often referenced the impact candidates' positions would have on their ability to secure the Latino vote. Furthermore, the majority of immigrants featured in news stories were Latino, often identified explicitly through references to their country of origin or implicitly through their surnames.

Last, a framework of illegality was present in more than half of the coverage of immigration in the United States by both AP and AFP. AP used this schema in 57.8 percent of its articles, while AFP used it in 52.2 percent of its articles.

Immigration in France

AP's coverage of immigration in France was most likely to invoke the politics frame, with the policy and national-identity frames also receiving substantial attention (see Table 6.3). The interpretive analysis indicated that AP focused on electoral politics, with a substantial amount of the coverage discussing candidates' positions in relation to those of Front National, the third-largest political party in France, which has adopted a hardline stance against immigration as a centerpiece of its platform. AP also devoted attention to immigration policies, particularly at the national level, which were frequently associated with individual political leaders, such as the president and the minister of the interior. Last, the impact of immigration and of immigrants on French identity was very salient in the coverage, especially in political statements by both candidates and incumbents remarking on the inability of immigrants to integrate into society.

AFP's coverage of immigration in France was also most likely to invoke the politics frame, with the policy and national-identity frames similarly receiving substantial attention (see Table 6.3). The interpretive analysis indicated that AFP also focused on electoral politics, with a substantial amount of the coverage discussing candidates' positions in relation to those of the Front National. National immigration policies also received some attention and were frequently associated with particular political leaders rather than large legislative bodies. Last, the impact of immigration and of immigrants on French identity was also salient in the coverage, manifesting itself most often in political statements by political actors.

As shown in Table 6.3, there was only one frame that exhibited a notable difference in AP's and AFP's France coverage: the policy frame, which AP was more likely than AFP to emphasize. Lesser differences were found among the remaining eight frames, with AFP being more likely to emphasize the law-and-order, social-movement, border-security, and morality frames, while AP was more likely to emphasize the national-identity, driving-factors, and politics frames; the legal frame was equally emphasized by both outlets. Both the interpretive and the computer-assisted analyses suggested that there was greater congruity between AP and AFP in the coverage of immigration in France than in their coverage of immigration in the United States.

Regarding the depiction of immigrants in the news articles, again both AP and AFP tended to follow similar schemas. The majority of the stories failed either to quote immigrants or to devote significant attention to individual immigrants, and both organizations tended to depict immigrants in a neutral manner, although negative depictions appeared in several articles quoting institutional actors' remarks about the threat that immigrants posed to French values and norms. The majority of articles using such quotes offered limited context; additionally, if a rebuttal by another source was made, it was generally placed below the negative depiction. When immigrants were described at length, depictions were only slightly more often favorable than unfavorable. Favorable depictions generally manifested themselves in references to the inadequate social conditions and institutional challenges faced by immigrants in France, as well as to their efforts to deal with these difficulties. Notably, the majority of stories treated immigration predominantly as a Muslim and North African issue, with a large number of immigrants featured in news stories being first- or second-generation immigrants from the Maghreb.

Last, a framework of illegality was present in less than one-third of the coverage of immigration in France by both AP and AFP. AP used this schema in 32.0 percent of its articles, while AFP used it in 28.4 percent of its articles.

Differences Between Nations

As shown in Table 6.3, there were considerable differences between AP's coverage of immigration in the United States and in France in five of the frames: the US-based coverage was more likely to emphasize the law-and-order, legal, and border-security frames, while the France-based coverage was more likely to emphasize the politics and national frames. Lesser differences were found among the remaining four frames, with the US-based coverage emphasizing the policy and morality frames and the France-based coverage emphasizing the social-movement and driving-factors frames.

Similarly, there were considerable differences between AFP's coverage of immigration in the United States and in France on five of the frames: the US-based coverage was more likely to emphasize the policy, border-security, and legal frames, while the France-based coverage was more likely to emphasize the national-identity and politics frames (see Table 6.3). Lesser differences were found among the remaining four frames, with the US-based coverage emphasizing the law-and-order, morality, and driving-factors frames and the France-based coverage emphasizing the social-movement frame.

Regarding the depiction of immigrants in the news articles, both AP and AFP generally failed either to quote immigrants or to devote significant attention to individual immigrants, although immigrants were more likely to be quoted in stories about immigration in France than they were in stories about immigration in the United States. The majority of the coverage by both outlets depicted immigrants in a neutral manner, although the US-based coverage was more likely to include favorable depictions. Favorable depictions of immigrants in the United States were more likely to emphasize their hardworking nature, while those in France were more likely to emphasize immigrants' efforts to overcome social challenges like poverty. Negative depictions of immigrants in the United States were more likely to highlight their lawlessness, while those of immigrants in France were more likely to highlight their threat to French values and norms. Additionally, both organizations tended to associate the issue of immigration with Latinos in the United States and with Muslims and North Africans in France.

Last, both AP and AFP were more likely to use a framework of illegality in their news stories about immigration in the United States (57.8% and 52.2%, respectively) than they were about immigration in France (32.0% and 28.4%, respectively).

Frames of Immigration on International Wires

This chapter argues that there were significant differences in the coverage of immigration in the United States and France by The Associated Press and Agence France-Presse in terms of frame selection, depiction of immigrants, and the use of a framework of illegality. However, while the differences were pronounced between the two countries, they were far more limited between the two newswire agencies.

In particular, coverage about immigration in the United States was far more likely to emphasize law and order and border security, whereas coverage about immigration in France was far more likely to emphasize national identity. News coverage of immigration in France was thus arguably more likely to associate immigrants with a threat to native values and norms, whereas coverage about immigration in the United States was more likely to associate immigrants with a threat to native livelihood and security. The "other," therefore, became hazardous to social cohesion in one context and to individual safety in the other.

Additionally, the issue of immigration was treated almost exclusively by both newswire agencies as a Latino matter in the United States and as a Muslim or North African matter in France. In promoting these associations, both organizations appear not only to oversimplify the issue but also to misinform their audience. Indeed, more than 45 percent of the United States' foreign-born population immigrated from places outside Latin America,[37] and more than 57 percent of France's foreign-born population immigrated from places outside Africa.[38]

Furthermore, there were distinct differences in the use of a framework of illegality, with both AP's and AFP's coverage about immigration in the United States being far more likely to employ such a schema than their coverage of immigration in France. The finding that immigration in the United States was more often discussed in terms of illegal than legal immigration, which is consistent with the work of Banu Akdenizli and colleagues,[39] has serious implications for public understanding of the issue and for policymaking. Indeed, through this distortion—undocumented immigrants make up less than one-third of both the inflow of immigrants and the country's foreign-born population[40]—both AP and AFP arguably perpetuated the notion of an out-of-control problem that must be resolved through drastic measures. Consequent to such framing is a perceived necessity for any policy attempting to address any aspect of immigration to include a component that addresses illegal immigration, which, given the loaded nature of that debate, often results in the polarization of actors, thereby hindering legislators' ability to compromise. This has serious implications for critical immigration matters like foreign worker visas, refugee protection, and reform of the naturalization process. The finding that immigration in France was more often discussed outside these bounds arguably suggests that it might be easier for readers of AP and AFP copy to distinguish between legal and illegal immigration there. However, the disproportionate use of the politics frame suggests that the issue may be just as politicized in France as in the United States, if not more so. This, too, poses serious challenges to developing rational policies about immigration.

These differences may in many ways be byproducts of the distinct political contexts surrounding immigration in these two nations, and they are worthy of further study. Indeed, the findings in this chapter in many ways reflect the policies and the political discourse surrounding the issue in those two countries, with French political parties largely framing immigration in terms of identity and French policies emphasizing restriction in order to protect French culture, while US policy has been comparatively more inclusive as political parties increasingly view immigrant voters as a valuable political resource. It is thus unsurprising that the difference in the use of the national-identity frame in the coverage of immigration in the United States and in France was the greatest among all frames and that its use was more prevalent in France. Similarly, it is perhaps not unexpected that immigrants in the United States were more likely to be depicted in a positive manner than those in France, although this difference was not as marked.

However, despite these distinct differences between the two contexts, this study also found a remarkable amount of congruity in the coverage. Indeed, the bulk of the coverage originated in the same few cities, although it is worth noting that in the United States AP had a notably lower degree of concentration than AFP. Furthermore, both newswires largely relied on the same frames in covering immigration in France and had some notable overlaps in their coverage of immigration in the United States. They also focused overwhelmingly on specific immigrant groups within the two different countries and largely depicted them abstractly and in a neutral manner. Last, their use of a framework of illegality was quite similar.

While it was expected that differences in the structures of AP and AFP would yield some distinctiveness in their reporting, it is possible that such differences were minimized by the relative harmony of their journalistic norms and their nonideological nature. Furthermore, these similarities may perhaps offer further evidence of the increasing homogenization of news.[41] According to Pablo Boczkowski, the coupling of journalistic practices and norms, such as monitoring, with the instant access afforded by modern technologies results in news that looks more and more alike in competing news media. In an effort to match each other's work, these two agencies may be, in effect, replicating each other's material. Unfortunately, this analysis cannot indicate the extent to which these similarities are actually a by-product of replication, nor can it provide insight into the potential leader-follower relationship. Nonetheless, these similarities raise some concerns about the ability of these two newswire agencies to bring distinct and diverse viewpoints to the public sphere.

CONCLUSION

This study provides the first systematic comparative analysis of the coverage of immigration by the leading newswire agencies in the United States and France. The study found distinct differences in the coverage of immigration in the two countries between 2007 and 2011 but remarkable similarities in the coverage by the two newswire agencies. In particular, coverage of immigration in the United States was far more likely to emphasize law and order and border security than the coverage in France, whereas the coverage in France was far more likely to emphasize national identity than the coverage in the United States. More than half of the coverage of immigration in the United States by both newswire agencies used a framework of illegality, which was present in less than one-third of the coverage of immigration in France. Additionally, the issue of immigration was treated almost exclusively by both newswire agencies as a Latino matter in the United States and as a Muslim or North African matter in France. Last, the bulk of the coverage in both countries originated in the same few locations, although the concentration was notably higher in France.

Given how fundamental newswires are to the shaping of overall media coverage, these findings have important practical and theoretical implications. First and foremost, the difference in the repeated characterization of immigrant "otherness" may facilitate efforts by anti-immigrant advocates to depict immigration as hazardous to social cohesion in France and to individual and national safety in the United States. Second, by associating immigration with specific groups, the newswire agencies may be priming readers to link immigration with Latinos in the United States and with Muslims and North Africans in France, possibly lending further legitimacy to efforts to "control" immigration through racial and ethnic profiling or through quota systems. Third, the difference in the use of a framework of illegality arguably makes it easier for policymakers in France to address legal immigration separately from illegal immigration than in the United States, though the issue remains highly politicized in France as well.

Theoretically, the substantial congruity in several aspects of AP's and AFP's coverage may be interpreted as support for the idea that news products are becoming increasingly homogenized or that journalistic norms and ideology may be more important determinants of the journalistic product than the structure of media organizations or certain extramedia factors, at least as far as global news agencies are concerned. Additionally, the finding that distinctive differences existed between the coverage of immigration in the United States and in France and that these differences in many ways reflected the policies and political discourse surrounding the issue in these two countries suggests that, in the context of immigration, there may indeed be a close, interconnected, and interdependent relationship between policymaking and the construction of media narratives.

NOTES

1. Banu Akdenizli et al., *A Report on the Media and the Immigration Debate* (Washington, DC: Brookings Institution, 2008), http://www.brookings.edu/~/media/Files/rc/reports/2008/0925_immigration_dionne/0925_immigration_dionne.pdf; Denis McQuail, *Mass Communication Theory: An Introduction*, 3rd ed. (London: Sage, 1994); Gaye Tuchman, *Making News: A Study in the Construction of Reality* (New York: Free Press, 1978).
2. Oliver Boyd-Barrett, "Globalizing the National News Agency," *Journalism Studies* 4, no. 3 (2003): 371–85; Chris Paterson, "News Agency Dominance in International News on the Internet," in *Converging Media, Diverging Politics: A Political Economy of News Media in the United States and Canada*, ed. David Skinner, James R. Compton, and Michael Gasher (Lanham, MD: Lexington Books, 2005), 145–64.
3. Justin Lewis, Andrew Williams, and Bob Franklin, "Four Rumours and an Explanation," *Journalism Practice* 2, no. 1 (January 2008): 27–45, doi:10.1080/17512780701768493.
4. Maxwell E. McCombs and Donald L. Shaw, "The Agenda-setting Function of Mass Media," *Public Opinion Quarterly* 36, no. 2 (July 1, 1972): 176–87; McQuail, *Mass Communication Theory*.
5. James W. Carey, *Communication as Culture: Essays on Media and Society* (Boston: Unwin Hyman, 1989); Baldwin Van Gorp, "The Constructionist Approach to Framing: Bringing Culture Back In," *Journal of Communication* 57, no. 1 (March 1, 2007): 60–78, doi:10.1111/j.0021–9916.2007.00329.x.
6. Robert M. Entman, "Framing: Toward Clarification of a Fractured Paradigm," *Journal of Communication* 43, no. 4 (December 1, 1993): 51–58, doi:10.1111/j.1460–2466.1993.tb01304.x.
7. William A. Gamson and Andre Modigliani, "The Changing Culture of Affirmative Action," in *Research in Political Sociology*, eds. R. G. Braungart and M. M. Braungart (Greenwich, CT: JAI Press, 1987), 143.
8. Bertram T. Scheufele and Dietram A. Scheufele, "Of Spreading Activation, Applicability, and Schemas: Conceptual Distinctions and Their Operational

Implications for Measuring Frames and Framing Effects," in *Doing News Framing Analysis: Empirical and Theoretical Perspectives*, ed. Paul D'Angelo and Jim A. Kuypers (New York: Routledge, 2010), 110–34.

9. Entman, "Framing"; Stephen D. Reese, "Finding Frames in a Web of Culture: The Case of the War on Terror," in *Doing News Framing Analysis: Empirical and Theoretical Perspectives*, ed. Paul D'Angelo and Jim A. Kuypers (New York: Routledge, 2010), 17–42.

10. Sean Aday, "The Framesetting Effects of News: An Experimental Test of Advocacy Versus Objectivist Frames," *Journalism and Mass Communication Quarterly* 83, no. 4 (December 1, 2006): 767–84, doi:10.1177/107769900608300403; June W. Rhee, "Strategy and Issue Frames in Election Campaign Coverage: A Social Cognitive Account of Framing Effects," *Journal of Communication* 47, no. 3 (September 1, 1997): 26–48, doi:10.1111/j.1460-2466.1997.tb02715.x; Fuyuan Shen, "Effects of News Frames and Schemas on Individuals' Issue Interpretations and Attitudes," *Journalism and Mass Communication Quarterly* 81, no. 2 (June 1, 2004): 400–16, doi:10.1177/107769900408100211.

11. Claes H. de Vreese, "The Effects of Strategic News on Political Cynicism, Issue Evaluations, and Policy Support: A Two-wave Experiment," *Mass Communication and Society* 7, no. 2 (2004): 191–214, doi:10.1207/s15327825mcs0702_4.

12. Frauke Schnell and Karen Callaghan, "Terrorism, Media Frames, and Framing Effects: A Macro- and Microlevel Analysis," in *Framing American Politics*, ed. Karen Callaghan and Frauke Schnell (Pittsburg: University of Pittsburg Press, 2005), 123–47.

13. "Moderating Effect of Group Cue While Processing News on Immigration: Is the Framing Effect a Heuristic Process?," *Journal of Communication* 59, no. 4 (December 1, 2009): 726–49, doi:10.1111/j.1460-2466.2009.01454.x.

14. John Sides and Jack Citrin, "European Opinion about Immigration: The Role of Identities, Interests and Information," *British Journal of Political Science* 37, no. 3 (2007): 477–504, doi:10.1017/S0007123407000257.

15. Lewis, Williams, and Franklin, "Four Rumours and an Explanation"; Paterson, "News Agency Dominance in International News on the Internet"; H. Denis Wu, "A Brave News World for International News?," *International Communication Gazette* 69, no. 6 (December 2007): 539–51, doi:10.1177/1748048507082841.

16. Pamela J. Shoemaker and Stephen D. Reese, *Mediating the Message: Theories of Influences on Mass Media Content*, 2nd ed. (White Plains, NY: Longman, 1996).

17. Beverly Horvit, "International News Agencies and the War Debate of 2003," *International Communication Gazette* 68, no. 5/6 (December 2006): 427–47, doi:10.1177/1748048506068722.

18. Nilanjana Bardhan, "Transnational AIDS-HIV News Narratives: A Critical Exploration of Overarching Frames," *Mass Communication and Society* 4, no. 3 (Summer 2001): 294–95.

19. Jonathan Fenby, *The International News Services* (New York: Schocken, 1986); Paterson, "News Agency Dominance in International News on the Internet."

20. "News Agency Dominance in International News on the Internet," Papers in International and Global Communicaton (Leeds, UK: Centre for International Communications Research, May 2006), 6.

21. Bardhan, "Transnational AIDS-HIV News Narratives."

22. Rodney Benson, "What Makes for a Critical Press? A Case Study of French and US Immigration News Coverage," *International Journal of Press/Politics* 15, no. 1 (January 1, 2010): 3–24.

23. Pierre Albert, *La presse française* (Paris: Documentation Française, 1998); Michel Mathien, *Économie générale des médias* (Paris: Ellipses, 2003).
24. Deborah Baldwin, "No Bad News, We're French," *American Journalism Review* 18, no. 3 (April 1996): 15; Boyd-Barrett, "Globalizing the National News Agency"; Legifrance, "Loi N° 57–32 Du 10 Janvier 1957 Portant Statut de L'Agence France-Presse," March 24, 2012, http://www.legifrance. gouv.fr/affichTexte.do;?cidTexte = LEGITEXT000006068171.
25. Joel S. Fetzer, *Public Attitudes toward Immigration in the United States, France, and Germany* (Cambridge: Cambridge University Press, 2000); Organisation for Economic Co-operation and Development, *OECD Factbook 2011: Economic, Environmental and Social Statistics* (Paris: Organisation for Economic Co-operation and Development, 2011).
26. Jennifer L. Hochschild and John H. Mollenkopf, *Bringing Outsiders In: Transatlantic Perspectives on Immigrant Political Incorporation* (Ithaca, NY: Cornell University Press, 2009).
27. Ibid.
28. Benson, "What Makes for a Critical Press?"
29. Martin Schain, *The Politics of Immigration in France, Britain, and the United States: A Comparative Study* (New York: Palgrave Macmillan, 2008).
30. Ibid.
31. Roberto Suro, "America's Views of Immigration: The Evidence from Public Opinion Surveys," in *Migration, Public Opinion and Politics: The Transatlantic Council on Migration*, ed. Bertelsmann Stiftung and the Migration Policy Institute (Gütersloh, Germany: Verlag Bertelsmann Stiftung, 2009).
32. The original search yielded 4,077 articles from AFP and 5,417 from AP. Briefs were defined as articles that consisted of 250 or fewer words. Duplicates were removed through the use of a custom program that systematically identified and removed duplicate items. This program used "fuzzy string" searching, a technique for identifying strings based on approximate, rather than exact, matches, to identify and remove duplicate stories appearing within the same outlet. I used a conservative approach that removed exact duplicates and only articles that both were similar and appeared in proximity to each other. When duplicates were identified, the most recent article was retained because it is assumed that the most recent article represents the final version of that article.
33. See John W. Creswell and Vicki L. Plano Clark, *Designing and Conducting Mixed Methods Research* (Thousand Oaks, CA: Sage, 2007).
34. Entman, "Framing"; Reese, "Finding Frames in a Web of Culture: The Case of the War on Terror"; Baldwin Van Gorp, "Strategies to Take Subjectivity Out of Framing Analysis," in *Doing News Framing Analysis: Empirical and Theoretical Perspectives*, ed. Paul D'Angelo and Jim A. Kuypers (New York: Routledge, 2010), 84–109.
35. Because I analyzed all stories within the given parameters (e.g., keywords, length, and nonduplicate), I consider this to be a census of the relevant reports disseminated by the two agencies within the five-year period 2007–2011 and not a random sample of a larger hypothetical population. I thus opted not to report the results of any inferential statistical tests in the main text of this chapter. However, because some readers may nonetheless be interested in these results, I report them here. For the frame salience in news articles about immigration, I performed separate chi-square analyses for each frame. In the US-based coverage ($n = 3,494$), there was a statistically significant difference between AP and AFP among five frames: border security ($\chi^2 = 23.636$, $p < .01$), law and order ($\chi^2 = 40.730$, $p < .01$), legal ($\chi^2 = 8.863$, $p < .01$), morality ($\chi^2 = 3.978$, $p < .05$), national identity ($\chi^2 = 6.929$, $p < .01$),

and politics (χ^2 = 32.246, p < .01). In the France-based coverage (n = 301), there were no statistically significant differences between AP and AFP. There were statistically significant differences among five frames between AP's US- and France-based coverage (n = 3,071): border security (χ^2 = 7.394, p < .01), law and order (χ^2 = 30.199, p < .01), legal (χ^2 = 11.372, p < .01), national identity (χ^2 = 128.233, p < .01), and politics (χ^2 = 38.624, p < .01). There were statistically significant differences among six frames between AFP's US- and France-based coverage (n = 724): border security (χ^2 = 22.710, p < .01), law and order (χ^2 = 6.069, p < .05), legal (χ^2 = 8.941, p < .01), national identity (χ^2 = 48.408, p < .01), policy (χ^2 = 16.541, p < .01), and politics (χ^2 = 11.050, p < .01). In terms of the use of a framework of illegality, there was a statistically significant difference in the US-based coverage between AP and AFP (χ^2 (1, n = 3,494) = 5.675, p < .05). There was no such difference in the France-based coverage (n = 301). Last, there were statistically significant differences in the use of a framework of illegality by both outlets between US and France (χ^2 (1, n = 3,071) = 26.250, p < .001 for AP and χ^2 (1, n = 724) = 33.271, p < .001 for AFP).

36. Specifically, the program opened individual news articles and ran a series of Boolean queries on each sentence using a predefined set of rules. These rules were developed through a combination of a study of the lexical choices during the interpretive analysis and an analysis of the most commonly used words in the entire sample, obtained through the use of another computer program I developed. In total, there were 57 distinct rules to account for the 42 themes previously identified. Rules could include 'AND', 'OR', and 'NOT' operators. Sample rule: (humane OR humanely OR lenient) AND (immigrant OR immigrants OR migrant OR migrants OR alien OR aliens OR undocumented) NOT (sentence OR sentencing OR crime OR ruling OR judgment). These rules were refined several times and pretested on a random sample of 200 news stories to improve instrument validity. Articles were additionally coded for the presence of the terms of 'illegal' or 'undocumented' in conjunction with 'alien*', 'immigrant*', 'immigration', or 'worker*' to assess whether the article discussed the issue within a framework of illegality.

37. US Census Bureau, "Foreign-born Population by Sex, Age, and Year of Entry: 2010," 2011, http://www.census.gov/population/foreign/files/cps2010/T2.1.csv.

38. Institut national de la statistique et des études économiques, "Répartition des immigrés par pays de naissance," 2008, http://www.insee.fr/fr/themes/tableau.asp?reg_id = 0&ref_id = immigrespaysnais.

39. Akdenizli et al., *A Report on the Media and the Immigration Debate*.

40. Paul Taylor et al., *Unauthorized Immigrants: Length of Residency, Patterns of Parenthood* (Washington, DC: Pew Hispanic Center, December 1, 2011), http://www.pewhispanic.org/files/2011/12/Unauthorized-Characteristics.pdf.

41. Pablo J. Boczkowski, *News at Work: Imitation in an Age of Information Abundance* (Chicago: University of Chicago Press, 2010).

7 Liking Stories

Readers' Comments on Online Immigration Articles for the *New York Times* and *The Guardian*

Anna Popkova

University of Minnesota

As European countries that used to be the countries of emigration transform into countries of immigration, their policymakers, mass media, and general public increasingly turn their attention to the experience of the United States—historically a country of immigration. The United States, in turn, pays more attention to the immigration debate in modern Europe, as it recognizes the similarities between its own and European immigration issues. Transatlantic perspectives on immigration are becoming a highlight of the contemporary immigration debate—a trend reflected both in scholarly literature[1] and in media narratives.[2]

The notion of the immigration *debate* implies that the ways of thinking, writing, and talking about immigration issues are as important as the issues themselves. The discourse of immigration constructed and reproduced by three actors—policymakers, the mass media, and the public—receives a great deal of attention on both sides of the Atlantic. While all three actors are interconnected, two—policymakers and the mass media—depend on the public as the electorate for the former and the audience for whom to produce content for the latter. Since, as noted in Schain's and Citrin's chapters, the immigration debate has been closely tied to electoral politics both in the United States and in Europe,[3] there have been continuous efforts to assess public opinion on issues of immigration. Researchers have mostly used surveys and polls. However, scholars also noted that one of the biggest challenges of using surveys for gauging public opinion on immigration issues is that many questions in those surveys address racial and ethnic prejudice. The growing power of political correctness in Western democracies "trains" people to give answers that are socially desirable or at least socially acceptable,[4] posing a challenge for researchers seeking to "elicit respondents' true level of prejudice."[5] As Elizabeth Bird put it, "[survey studies] showed that by the end of the late twentieth century, [people] knew how to give an appropriate response to a survey on racial attitudes."[6] Political pollster Jeremy Rosner also notes that "polls . . . often obscure the contours of intensity in attitudes that can be even more important to electoral leaders than the aggregate balance of opinion."[7] Rosner adds that "this is particularly important on [immigration] issue, where passions run high."[8] John Durham Peters, in his discussion of the historical tensions in the nature of public opinion, argues that public opinion research "takes the public out of the public opinion."[9] In other words, the "machinery of polling" takes away the power of opinion production from the citizens and transfers it to the experts (the pollsters), who produce polls that become "symbols of public opinion."[10] Thus, public opinion research overlooks such elements of public opinion formation as discussion and deliberation, which, at least according to Jurgen Habermas and his theory of the public sphere, are crucial for a democratic process of decision making where the public, the media, and the policymakers are involved, át least in theory, on equal terms.

Public opinion research, however, was developed when media and communication technologies functioned in ways that did not present many opportunities for citizens' direct involvement. The changing media environment, with increasing number and diversity of interactive communication technologies, presents such opportunities.[11] Moreover, it challenges the traditional media, calling on them to make adjustments in order to survive. Particularly, as the print media develop their online platforms, more of them, both in the United States and in Europe, introduce and popularize the "reader comment" feature—a tool that allows readers to comment on the articles and to respond to other comments. While many scholars ponder whether reader comment sections serve as spaces for democratic deliberation,[12] this study looks at the reader comment sections as spaces that allow a focus on *discursive* aspects of public opinion that get overlooked in traditional public opinion research based on polling techniques.

This project analyzes the immigration debates that unfolded among the readers of two national newspapers—the *New York Times* in the United States and *The Guardian* in Great Britain—through an analysis of readers' comments on articles published and open for readers' feedback in spring and summer of 2011. The articles in the *New York Times* discussed the implementation of the "Secure Communities" program in the United States in summer 2011. This federal program required all state or local police to send the fingerprints of booked people to the Department of Homeland Security databases to be checked for immigration status and violations. The articles in *The Guardian* addressed the "influx" of North African migrants into Western European countries in the aftermath of the spring 2011 revolutions in North African states.

By examining the reader comment sections in the *New York Times* and *The Guardian*, this chapter seeks to identify the themes emerging in readers' discussions of immigration issues on both sides of the Atlantic and to compare and identify similarities and differences between them. By accomplishing these two goals, this project also explores the potential of studying reader comment section as an approach that allows a focus on the discursive aspects of public opinion.

THE MEDIA, POLICY, AND PUBLIC OPINION RESEARCH

Researchers have examined very extensively the links among policymaking, the mass media, and public opinion. As Baum and Potter note in their comprehensive summary of the literature on the topic, "in short, scholars have investigated every conceivable causal link between the public, decision makers (foreign and domestic), and the media."[13] Two general approaches have dominated the field: establishing causal links among the three elements of the triangle and synthesizing the three into a single framework based on the notion of the inherent interconnectedness and interdependence of the three.

Scholars who examined causal relationships among the three elements tended to focus on the explicit links between the selected two, while usually implying the presence and potential influence of the third one. For example, such theories as the CNN effect, the manufacturing consent, the indexing hypothesis, and the media-policy interaction model examine the relationship between the mass media and foreign policy, focusing on the direction of influence and only implying the role of the public and public opinion in this relationship.[14] Similarly, such concepts as rally-round-the-flag and casualty aversion analyze the links between public opinion and policymakers, while only implying the influence of the mass media as a potential "third element" in this interaction process.[15]

In contrast, the authors and proponents of synthetic theories and models of the relationships among the public, policymakers, and the media operate under the assumption that the three actors are interdependent and that "exclusive attention to one or two of the three may distort theoretical predictions and empirical findings."[16] For example, a model of "cascading activation" proposed by Robert Entman as part of his theory of framing illustrates the process of information flow from policymakers to the media and finally to the public.[17] Even though the model is hierarchical, with the public being placed on the bottom of the cascade (as an actor having the most limited access to information), Entman emphasizes the interconnectedness and interdependence of the three actors by highlighting the importance of the "feedback loops"—processes through which "news feeds information about citizens back to officials."[18]

The "cascading model" resonates with other conceptualizations of the interdependent relationships among the media, policymakers, and the public. Journalists depend on policymakers as main sources for stories; Michael Schudson calls them parajournalists and argues that they strongly influence media narratives because parajournalists function as key figures— "authoritative sources"—that possess important and credible information and also "make information available on a regular basis in a form that the media can easily digest."[19] At the same time, journalists depend on the audience/public and its interests, so stories have to be tied to local or domestic issues.[20] This is typically done using culturally congruent frames[21] that organize and structure the ideas[22] and function as "schemata of interpretation"[23] or as "interpretive packages"[24] that help both journalists and audiences make sense of the information.[25] Policymakers, in turn, pay close attention to mass media content, which they often use, in addition to the public opinion polls, to assess public attitudes toward various issues.[26] Scholars who examine news production as a sociocultural process of meaning-making that involves multiple influences by multiple actors[27] emphasize that the process is "multi-faceted" and that "influences travel in different directions."[28] Some scholars, for example Pan and Kosicki, focus on the role of the public in this process and argue that citizens take part in it by participating in public deliberation.[29] This idea resonates with the theory of the public sphere and the potential of the space created through the use of the reader comment feature to become a site where public discourse is shaped and reflected.

By focusing on the discursive aspects of public opinion that is part of a larger process of meaning-making where the media, the policymakers, and the public are interdependent and interconnected, this chapter seeks to answer the following questions: What themes emerge from the readers' comments on the *New York Times* articles covering the Secure Communities program in the summer of 2011? What themes emerge from the readers' comments on *The Guardian* articles covering immigration to Europe in the aftermath of the Arab revolutions of spring 2011? What are the similarities and the differences between the public narratives on immigration found in the *New York Times* and in *The Guardian*? What do these similarities and differences tell us about the current discourses of immigration in the United States and Great Britain?

Immigration to Europe in the Wake of the Revolutions in North Africa

The revolutions in North African countries in the winter and spring of 2011 produced a dual controversial effect in European countries. On the one hand, democratic Europe cheered the revolutions, supporting "emerging democracies." On the other hand, scores of North Africans—for the most part, Tunisians and Libyans—crossed the Mediterranean, fleeing the political unrest and the economic crisis caused by the revolutions. This migratory movement—perhaps bigger in the popular imagination than in reality, as discussed in Stinellis's chapter—caused anxiety, resentment, and controversy among European policymakers and the public and in the mass media. Italian policymakers called the situation "a humanitarian crisis" and fumbled for administrative and policy solutions. One of these solutions involved granting some migrants temporary Schengen visas, which enabled many francophone Tunisians to go to France; however, France stopped them at the border. This event sparked a debate all over Europe, including Great Britain, which is not part of the Schengen zone, about the possibility of the Schengen dissolution, which evolved into a larger "open versus closed borders" and "who gets to come in and who doesn't" discussion. The articles in *The*

Guardian that served as a basis for the readers' comments analyzed in this project addressed different aspects of this debate.

Debate over Implementation of the Secure Communities Program in the United States

Immigration was a highly debated topic in the summer of 2011 in the United States as well. One of the debates addressed the implementation of the Secure Communities federal program. As the US Immigration and Customs Enforcement website states, Secure Communities "prioritizes the removal of criminal aliens, those who pose a threat to public safety, and repeat immigration violators."[30] However, opponents of Secure Communities claimed that it encouraged racial profiling and hurt some citizens and legal residents because of glitches in the electronic verification system. Additional debate unfolded after many undocumented immigrants were caught through the program and sentenced to deportation.

This chapter compares these two events for three main reasons. First, both dealt with questions of exclusion and inclusion of "the other." Second, both dealt with the inclusion and exclusion of the "illegal" other—a point that links the social identity aspect of immigration to the immigration policy one. Third, both debates revolved around specific policies and received a great deal of attention from the media and the public—aspects that are important given the theoretical framework of interconnectedness and interaction between the actors of the media-policy-public triangle.

"Reader Comment" Sections in the *New York Times* and *The Guardian*

There are similarities and differences in ways *The Guardian* and the *New York Times* manage the comments on their websites. *The Guardian* actively promotes "*The Guardian* community" and tries to use the reader comment feature to connect with its readers and encourage dialogues among them. The website has a section with elaborate rules about "community standards" and "participation guidelines,"[31] as well as an FAQ section, addressing questions of comment moderation. All rules and answers to the FAQs are written in a personal, friendly tone. The comments are postmoderated by members of the moderation team, and readers are encouraged to report content that does not adhere to the standards, such as "personal attacks (on authors, other users or any individual), persistent trolling and mindless abuse," "posts that are obviously commercial or otherwise spam-like," or "content that might put [*The Guardian*] in legal jeopardy, such as libelous or defamatory postings."[32] Free registration is required to post comments. *The Guardian* requires that the readers provide their real names when they register but not in the display names that correspond to the comments.

The *New York Times,* in contrast to *The Guardian,* does not make similar efforts to create a community of readers. While there is a set of rules and FAQs about posting comments, those rules are written in a more formal style. However, the comments in the *New York Times* are premoderated: a comment goes to the team of moderators before being posted, in a process lasting less than 24 hours. Another important aspect that differentiates the *New York Times'* reader comment feature from *The Guardian's* is that a *New York Times* reader must be a subscriber, not only a registered user, to be able to post a comment. The price of the *New York Times* subscription (the cheapest version includes the privilege of posting comments) is about \$35 per month.[33] Just like *The Guardian,* the *New York Times* asks for a real name and location of every poster (a reader who posts a comment) but does not require it with the comment. Both the *New York Times* and *The Guardian* have a "recommend" feature that allows readers to show support for specific comments.

METHODOLOGY

This study is based on a qualitative textual analysis of the reader comments posted in response to the articles on immigration published on the *New York Times'* and *The Guardian's* online platforms in the spring and summer of 2011. Both newspapers allow comments on only a few selected articles and, *The Guardian* more so than the *New York Times,* tend to open up editorials and op-ed pieces for reader comments more often than the news stories. Thus, this analysis did not distinguish between the comments posted in response to different types of stories (e.g., news versus editorials).[34] For *The Guardian,* 603 comments were analyzed—a sum total of the comments posted in response to five articles opened for public comment from April 6, 2011, to June 14, 2011. All articles open for comments were opinion pieces that were critical of the European policies and administrative actions discussed and implemented in response to migration from North Africa. The topics ranged from addressing the poor conditions in the "migrant processing" facilities, to pointing out the hypocrisy in cheering for the emerging democracies on one hand and providing a "military-security" response on the other, to questions of integrity and diversity as important elements of a "progressive vision" of European future.

For the *New York Times,* 468 comments were analyzed—a total of the comments posted in response to one news story and three editorials on Secure Communities published and opened for public comment from June 3, 2011, to August 16, 2011. The news story discussed the protests that took place in six US cities as a response to a wave of deportations resulting from the implementation of the Secure Communities program. The story addressed the arguments supporting the program and the arguments opposing the program. Two editorials critiqued President Obama's inability to stop the program's implementation. One of these editorials also supported the decision by Massachusetts, Illinois, and New York to withdraw from participating in the program. In contrast, the last article—an op-ed piece—critiqued the decision of the three states to withdraw from the program and supported the implementation of Secure Communities.

The comments to the nine articles were analyzed according to the grounded theory approach.[35] In the initial stage of open coding—"a process of unrestricted coding . . . during which an analyst goes through the texts line by line and marks those chunks of text that suggest a category"[36]—15 categories were identified for the comments in *The Guardian* and 18 for the comments in the *New York Times*. The categories were then integrated during the axial coding—a stage during which "the codes are used to make connections between categories. . . thus [resulting] in the creation of either new categories or a theme that spans many categories."[37] As a result, 15 categories from *The Guardian's* comments were "collapsed" into 4 "notional categories,"[38] and 18 categories from the *New York Times* were integrated into 4 "notional categories" as well. At the third stage, the categories were "dimensionalized." According to Spiggle, "dimensionalization involves identifying properties of categories and constructs. . . . Once a category has been defined, the analyst may explore its attributes or characteristics along the continua or dimensions."[39] In addition to analyzing the comments themselves, I noted the amount of support comments received through the "recommend" feature during the analysis of the findings and indicated this in the footnotes for each comment quotation.[40]

ANALYSIS AND FINDINGS

The textual analysis of the readers' comments in *The Guardian* and the *New York Times* revealed the similarities and the differences in themes that were most prevalent among the readers of the two newspapers. This section first discusses the similarities, though pointing out some variations within each common theme. It then describes the themes that were unique for the comments in either the *New York Times* or in *The Guardian* but not found in both. It is important to note at the outset that the number of comments reflecting readers' support for restricting immigration was overwhelmingly high for both newspapers. While the opinions and ideas of the readers were wide ranging and diverse, it was, for the most part, a diversity of "anti-immigration and anti-immigrant" views. In the vast majority of cases, anti-immigration comments received much stronger support through the "recommend" feature than the pro-immigration comments.

Opposition to Unwanted/Illegal Immigration

Readers of both newspapers insisted in their comments that "European people don't want a large influx, no matter what the reasons are"[41] and, similarly, "The MAJORITY of Americans, regardless of affiliation, want immigration laws enforced and those in this country illegally removed"[42] (caps in the original).[43] This idea was expressed by the readers in a variety of ways. For example, readers of *The Guardian,* when responding to the journalists' criticism of Italy's restrictive immigration policies, asserted that "many in the UK would like to see our government take a similar stance on the problem of unwanted immigrants arriving here too"[44] and raised the question of "what about the voice of the majority of people in this and, indeed, all countries across Europe who would very much like an immigration policy that is fair on **them**?"[45] The *New York Times* readers, in turn, asserted that "the vast majority of Americans are fed up with illegal aliens"[46] and that "most of the country wants them out of here."[47] Some even supported their arguments with "data" ("surveys repeatedly show that 65% to 85% of American citizens want ALL illegals deported")[48] and with references to other sites that support user-generated content: "Survey the various blogs on our countries newspapers and you will see that Americans are increasingly vocal in their opposition to illegal immigration."[49]

Readers of *The Guardian* connected the idea that a majority of citizens oppose unwanted immigration to electoral politics, urging policymakers to "listen to what European people have to say. . . . Or would you rather start sending ballot papers to North Africa and Middle East when we have elections next time?"[50] *New York Times* readers often connected the idea of "anti-illegal immigration majority" to accusations that the *New York Times* had a "pro-illegal immigration bias":

> The Times' opposition to this totally sensible approach to identifying and deporting illegal aliens with extensive criminal histories shows just how far out of touch it is with the average American.[51]

> Contrary to constant editorials by the New York Times, most Americans do indeed want enforcement of our immigration laws.[52]

While the readers of both newspapers shared the belief that the majority of Europeans and Americans oppose unwanted (a term used more often by readers of *The Guardian*) and illegal (a term used by an overwhelming majority of the *New York Times* readers) immigration, they were similarly convinced that unwanted/illegal immigration poses a threat to their countries. Readers emphasized different aspects of the perceived threat, however, with comments in *The Guardian* highlighting the "threat to culture and values" and the *New York Times* readers focusing on economic risks and crime—a finding that recalls Zamith's comparison of AP and AFP coverage in the previous chapter.

Unwanted/Illegal Immigration as a Threat

Immigrants as a Threat to European Culture and Values

A great majority of comments in *The Guardian* emphasized that "too many recent arrivals to Europe . . . have cultural beliefs completely at odds with the concept of democracy and the respect of human rights, especially if you are female, gay, or secular."[53] While some readers' comments reflected doubts—"there is no guarantee that all of the people who are leaving these nations will necessarily fit in with Western Liberal attitudes"[54]—others were quite straightforward in stating that "we'd probably be more open to immigrants from North Africa if they liked our culture."[55]

Illegal Immigrants as "Criminals Who Steal Our Jobs and Lower Wages"

The *New York Times'* readers shared a fear of immigrants and immigration but primarily focused on threats posed by the immigrants' "taking over" the job market and on equating illegality with criminality. One of the most prominent ideas expressed was that "breaking country's law is a crime and therefore all illegal aliens are criminals."[56] Most comments were very assertive—"People who are here illegally are criminals. Don't you get it?"[57] Some readers seemed to be both puzzled and irritated by the fact that other people would not accept such claims: "Illegal entry into the Unites States or remaining here with an expired visa is a crime. How can anyone state or believe otherwise?"[58] Some compared "illegal immigration" to a robbery and to other types of crime:

> "Illegal" means they've already broken the law, just as certainly as would be the case if they'd committed a robbery.[59]

> It is common to read of some illegal alien who has killed one or more victims in a traffic accident while driving drunk, and it is rare that this is a first offence. Why not deport them before they kill somebody?[60]

In addition to equating illegality with criminality, a great majority of comments pointed to the threat posed by "illegals" to the US job market. Comments expressed readers' confidence that "illegal immigrants [are taking] jobs from Americans"[61] and "flooding the economy and driving wage levels for those jobs down to the point where legal Americans can't afford to take them."[62] Some asserted that "when we enforce immigration law we protect the economic rights of our most vulnerable citizens,"[63] disputing the idea that "immigrants do the jobs Americans won't do" and calling for action:

> If Obama really wants to create more jobs, he could deport the millions of illegal aliens who are stealing US jobs in construction, fast food,

retail, restaurant and janitorial work, etc. Americans WILL do these jobs, just not for the slave wages that illegals will accept! Send these invaders back where they belong! We don't need them or their families taking our jobs or absorbing our resources.[64]

Rights and Fairness

Another overarching and common theme in reader comments on both sides of the Atlantic addressed the question of who gets to come in (and stay) and who does not. In other words, readers of both newspapers felt that questions of rights and fairness were extremely important to consider in the immigration debate.

Citizens' Rights First

Readers of both newspapers uniformly argued that citizens' rights should come first.[65] Readers of *The Guardian* stated that "the principles of democracy oblige European governments to listen to their *citizens.*"[66] *New York Times* readers expressed similar views: "We need elected officials that will put the interests of US citizens before illegal aliens!"[67] A comment in *The Guardian* stated that "The British have done enough to help the rest of the world, it's about time our politicians **PUT THE BRITISH PEOPLE FIRST.**"[68] The statement was echoed by a comment in the *New York Times:* "The purpose of our immigration laws is to help Americans. And that's it. Americans should not be asked to meet the economic desires of the entire world."[69]

Interestingly, the readers of both newspapers called those who expressed a concern about "unwanted/illegal" immigrants "traitors":

> If you don't believe me that many of our EU leaders are traitors, then consider why so many in our establishment put the rights of these refugees and minorities in general before their own people.[70]

> What I don't understand are people who want to ignore the law and harbor illegal aliens. They are traitors to the working class and to their countries. Shame on them for choosing others over their own countrymen.[71]

While readers of both newspapers gave similar attention to the "citizens' rights first" dimension of the "rights and fairness" theme, there were also dimensions within this theme that were unique in *The Guardian*'s and the *New York Times*' comments.

Refugees versus Economic Migrants

A great majority of comments in *The Guardian* raised questions about why "all the refugees seem to be young fit men between the ages of the late teens and early thirties."[72] One reader, responding to a comment by *The Guardian*'s staff about migrants being pushed out of their countries, asked: "Ever seen real refugees flee? Old men, women, children, pregnant women, the sick, the injured, horses and carts if they are lucky, a suitcase at most,"[73] and provided an answer as well: "These men are economic chancers who know that we are a soft touch. Which is why they have so much cheek to demand we look after them. They aren't even grateful as proper refugees are. . . . They are just a bunch of chancers."[74] Most readers were convinced that the migrants were "not fleeing any particular danger":[75] "When people are genuinely in fear, as in Darfur, women and children *have* to try to escape. I think in this case we are seeing a lot of economic migrants. They should just be put on a boat and sent back."[76] The emerging consensus among the readers seemed to be that "these people are economic migrants using the unrest as a plausible excuse to settle in Europe."[77] Some readers pointed to the difference between refugees and economic migrants—a crucial perspective difference, as *The Guardian*'s John Hooper writes in his chapter—as a justification for their opposition to "unwanted immigration":

> I don't doubt that there are genuine refugees and I have a lot of sympathy for them. In part my anger towards bogus refugees, which the vast majority are, is because it precludes us from helping genuine ones. . . . I don't believe 99% of these men currently fleeing this "Arab spring" are genuine.[78]

The juxtaposition of refugees and economic migrants in the context of the "rights and fairness" theme resembled the juxtaposition of legal immigrants and illegal ones in the comments by the *New York Times* readers.

Legal versus Illegal Immigration

"Illegal immigration and immigration are two totally different things and the [former] is wrong"[79]—asserted a *New York Times* reader. Readers drew a sharp line between legal immigrants, who "bring massive things to the table . . . [and] should be encouraged,"[80] and "the illegal border crossers [who] bring with [them] far less good and quite a bit more bad."[81] In their comments, readers acknowledged that "virtually all Americans are legal immigrants or descendants of them"[82] but emphasized that their "ancestors got here through whatever legal channels were in effect at the time they arrived."[83] Moreover, readers insisted that "giving illegal immigrants a free pass"[84] was not only "unfair to immigrants who came here LEGALLY and followed all the laws of the land,"[85] "jumping through hoops"[86] and waiting in lines, but "would be an insult,"[87] a "slap in the face to those who went through the correct process to become citizens."[88] Comments overwhelmingly supported what one of the readers called a "legal melting pot":[89]

Immigrants who respect our laws and honor our nation by obeying them enrich this country with their skills, talents, traditions, and cultures. Those who disregard our laws are a blight that needs to be removed at any cost.[90]

The notion of legality takes us to the next overarching theme—"the power of law"—that was much more prevalent in the comments of the *New York Times* readers.

The Power of Law

This theme had an overwhelming presence in almost all comments posted by readers of the *New York Times* in response to the articles, especially the ones that questioned current immigration law. Readers stated that "the law is the law"[91] and "must be enforced,"[92] "regardless of how we feel about it."[93] Readers insisted that "this is a nation of laws"[94] and that "as long as we want to consider us to be a nation of law and justice we all have to obey our laws."[95] Undocumented immigrants, according to majority of readers, "are breaking the law, and that should not be permitted."[96] Hence, readers asserted, anyone should be ready to face the consequences of breaking the law:

You are breaking the law and as such you must endure the consequences of your actions should you get caught.[97]

It's maddening when people break the law, and then protest when it is being enforced.[98]

"Without enforcement of our laws, we will drift to anarchy,"[99] stated one reader. Another comment echoed this idea: "Either laws are enforced and must be obeyed or law becomes meaningless."[100] The power of the law seemed the most popular weapon in hands of the readers whose comments supported the idea of "pushing the other out." Similarly, most readers of *The Guardian* who argued against "letting the other in" used a tactic of taking the debate outside Europe.

Taking the Debate Outside

Many readers of *The Guardian* raised the following questions: "Why try to escape to Europe?"[101] "Is EU the only place to seek asylum rather than another Arab or African state?"[102] "Africa is a huge continent, why don't these people seek asylum in Chad, Niger, Algeria?"[103] (One reader provided an answer: "Oh that's right . . . no free money.")[104] Other readers questioned the necessity of leaving, saying that "North Africa must sort itself out, establish democracy and the rule of law at home," and it is "hard to understand how you 'make bold steps' in the direction of democracy by leaving the country where a revolution is taking place to achieve this."[105] One comment even stated: "If these people are too chicken to stay and fight, then they're not the type of people I want here in the first place."[106]

Some readers took a rather interesting position, suggesting that "the most humane response is one that deters people from risking their lives in boats. Enticing more to come by the promise of welfare and citizenship is not a kindness."[107] Another comment echoed this idea: "A firm EU policy affirming that it will no longer accept asylum claims will stop all those young men from making an attempt—and stop all that death that no one can put a number to. And then the families back home no longer have to swallow a bitter reality that its child is no longer living."[108] Last, many readers explicitly stated that they are "all for providing aid to developing countries [but are not in favor] of letting people into Europe who have no right to be here."[109]

The "Positive Minority"

While the overwhelming majority of comments in both newspapers expressed anti-immigration views, a small portion of comments expressed opinions challenging the negative ones. Here too, there were differences and similarities in how positive views were conceptualized by the readers of *The Guardian* and the *New York Times*.

Showing Humanity and Understanding the Complexity

Authors of positive comments in both newspapers shared a call for "showing humanity."[110] As one of the *New York Times* posters wrote, "if we make it our business to go to far away countries to fight wars to bring people freedom, why can't we look at our next door neighbor and show some sympathy? Show some HUMANITY!!"[111] Others also called for "humane immigration reform."[112] Among the posters who expressed this view, several also pointed that immigration is a complex matter, and attention must be paid to the nuances: "It's all so simple, isn't it? Deport all the illegals!! Without one moment's pause to consider how complicated our immigration laws are, and how easy it is to get tripped up by them."[113] The idea resonates with one expressed by *The Guardian*'s poster who responded to two anti-immigration comments posted earlier: "the debate is far more nuanced than the reductions you both appear to be making."[114] It is important to note that, while this poster elaborated on the idea when responding to each negative post, the comment received 15 support clicks, far fewer than the 240 and 87 the two negative posts received.

Making a United Effort to Help Those in Need

A common theme in the positive comments of *The Guardian*'s readers called for a united effort of all European states, including Great Britain, to help those in need, "embrace a common asylum policy,"[115] and "[take] an even share of responsibility for refugees."[116] One reader connected the idea specifically to the British context: "I'm proud to be British, and, in the same way I like to walk down my street thinking that I've shouldered some of the burden for maintaining the community I live in, I'd like to be a proud traveler thinking that I've shouldered some of the burden of helping those in dire circumstances."[117]

Acting as a Nation of Immigrants

The positive comments in the *New York Times* also resonated with a theme of commonness and solidarity by drawing on the idea of America as "nation of immigrants." Posters accused those who expressed anti-immigrant views of "forgetting their history":

> YOUR ancestors came here for a better life. Why now do you want to exclude the latest wave of people coming here hoping to have a better life for themselves and their children?[118]
>
> Good thing Grandma snuck in from Ireland before there were any laws forbidding her to do so. Yes—we like our "illegals" to be white, ASP, and English-speaking. Of course, my comment is in the minority. But that doesn't make it wrong.[119]

It is remarkable how the author of the last comment observed that the comment was "in the minority." While this was clearly a trend in the comment threads for both newspapers, it is also important to note that the op-ed piece in the *New York Times* that was supportive of the Secure Communities program generated more pro-immigration comments than did the threads generated in response to articles that critiqued the program. This raises an interesting question of whether the readers felt the need to post comments mostly when they disagreed with the arguments made in the article.

DISCUSSION AND CONCLUSIONS

At least two points are important when interpreting this chapter's findings. First, a textual analysis of the readers' comments reveals that the vast majority of readers on both sides of the Atlantic expressed views informed by what Brian Massumi called "the politics of fear."[120] This finding is fairly consistent with some of the conclusions of previous research on public opinion on immigration. As Rosner's summary suggests, "although attitudes toward migration are complex, and although publics in the United States, United Kingdom and most other countries bring conflicting perceptions and attitudes to the topic, publics virtually everywhere in the world prefer more rather than less control of migration."[121] This summary is also supported by recent polls. For example, a 2011 Transatlantic Trends report on immigration attitudes in the United States and Europe states that 53 percent of Americans and 68 percent of respondents from the United Kingdom viewed immigration as more of a problem than an opportunity, 58 percent of Americans and 71 percent of respondents from the United Kingdom were "highly worried" about illegal immigration, and 47 percent of respondents in the United States and 57 percent of those in the United Kingdom perceived that there are "too many immigrants."[122]

This chapter, however, focused on exploring the discursive aspects of reader comments posted by specific audiences of specific media outlets. Both the *New York Times* and *The Guardian* are considered to be fairly liberal media, and some examples in the analysis illustrated readers' awareness and critique of the newspapers' liberal stances toward immigration. In case of the *New York Times* especially, where readers must be subscribers in order to be able to post, the number and the language of the anti-immigration comments raises a question about whether the "liberal readers" are "passing the immigration issue test." The immigration debate on both sides of the Atlantic is often conceptualized along the lines of "conservative versus liberal" politics, with the general assumption that liberals tend to hold pro-immigration views. However, the findings of this project challenge this assumption and call attention to a closer and a more critical examination of the discourse of immigration reflected in spaces that attract—at least in theory—liberal audiences.

While this chapter did not compare the findings derived from analysis of the readers' comments to opinion polls, it seems important to discuss how these two approaches could inform and complement each other. For example, analysis of reader comments provides important insights into the question of "*how* people talk about immigration"—something that surveys do not often capture, partially because they are question driven and "often define the boundaries and meaning of an issue too narrowly."[123] While surveys capture general attitudes, analysis of comments makes identifiable and observable the discourse that readers shape and reflect. A big caveat of studying public opinion by analyzing readers' comments is that it is virtually impossible (at least at this time) to connect the findings to readers' demographic information—most people provide very limited personal data, which is likely what allows them to express their genuine opinions. However, a mixed-method study combining survey methodology with the qualitative analysis of the readers' comments might produce important and robust results.

Second, the findings of this project, put in a framework that emphasizes the interdependence of the actors in the triangle linking media, policy, and public opinion, have important implications for all three sets of actors. While researchers have examined the connections and interactions among policies, public opinion, and media texts and their readers, does the growing popularity of the reader comment feature call for an exploration of the relationships between the "passive" readers (who read but do not comment) and the content posted by the "active" readers (posters)? Do the comments and posts, together with or aside from the articles that they accompany, have an impact on public opinion about immigration?

The growing popularity of different types of user-generated content gives strong reason to believe that the reader comment feature in the newspapers' online platforms will grow and develop. Given the findings of this project, how will the media, journalists, and editors continue to manage the comment function on highly charged topics like immigration? What implications might the growing quantity of user-generated content on online platforms have on journalism as a profession and as a practice? For example, if a journalist sees that the debate is being dominated by comments informed by "the politics of fear," should she stay faithful to the standards of objective journalism and maintain neutrality, or should she intervene and try to introduce alternative ways of thinking about an issue? Will the comments influence journalists' approach to reporting and writing? It seems fair to argue that the literal *visibility* that the public discourse gains through the comment feature gives an old debate a new twist.

The implications for the policymakers are similar. The use of the reader comment feature by media consumers plays an important role in the democratic process not only by enabling public deliberation and debate but also by allowing policymakers to hear the voices of their constituents. At the same time, given the findings of this project, certain issues present a complicated dilemma for policymakers. If the opinion of the majority is informed by "the politics of fear," should it lead to the policies based on this type of politics? Or, returning again to the idea of interconnectedness among the actors and placing it in the historical perspective, could it be that the immigration policies have been for the most part (and a long time) informed by the politics of fear and that we observe the results in the reader comment section of the large national newspapers on both sides of the Atlantic?

NOTES

1. See, for example, *Migration, Public Opinion and Politics: The Transatlantic Council on Migration,* ed. Bertelsmann Stiftung and the Migration Policy Institute (Gütersloh, Germany: Verlag Bertelsmann Stiftung, 2009); Terri Givens, Gary P. Freeman, and David L. Leal, *Immigration Policy and Security: US, European, and Commonwealth Perspectives* (New York: Routledge, 2008); Ana Maria Manzanas Calvo, "Contested Passages: Migrants Crossing the Rio Grande and the Mediterranean Sea," *South Atlantic Quaterly* 105, no. 4 (2006): 759–75; Martin Schain, *The Politics of Immigration in France, Britain, and the United States: A Comparative Study* (New York: Palgrave Macmillan, 2008).
2. See, for example, Cristopher Caldwell, "Europe's Arizona Problem," *New York Times,* June 11, 2011; Daniel González, "Arizona Law Inspires Italian Politician," *The Arizona Republic,* special edition "Crossings: A Planet on the Move," December 12, 2010, SP10.

3. Schain, *The Politics of Immigration in France, Britain, and the United States.*
4. Mary Jackman and Michael Muha, "Education and Intergroup Attitudes: Moral Enlightenment, Superficial Democratic Commitment or Ideological Refinement?," *American Sociological Review* 49, n. 6 (1984): 751–69.
5. Peter Burns and James Gimpel, "Economic Security, Prejudicial Stereotypes, and Public Opinion on Immigration Policy," *Political Science Quarterly* 115, 2 (2000): 201–225.
6. Elizabeth Bird, *The Audience in Everyday Life: Living in a Media World* (New York: Routledge, 2003), 88.
7. Jeremy Rosner, "The Politics of Immigration and the (Limited) Case for New Optimism: Perspectives from a Political Pollster," in *Migration, Public Opinion and Politics: The Transatlantic Council on Migration,* ed. Bertelsmann Stiftung and the Migration Policy Institute (Gütersloh, Germany: Verlag Bertelsmann Stiftung, 2009).
8. Ibid.
9. John Durham Peters, "Historical Tensions in the Concept of Public Opinion," in *Public Opinion and the Communication of Consent,* ed. Theodore L. Glasser and Charles T. Salmon (New York: Guilford Press, 1995), 3–32.
10. Ibid.
11. See, for example, Henry Jenkins, *Convergence Culture: Where Old and New Media Collide* (New York: New York University Press, 2006).
12. See, for example, Anthony G. Wilhelm, "Virtual Sounding Boards: How Deliberative Is On-line Political Discussion," *Information, Communication and Society* 1, no. 3 (1998): 313–38; Lincoln Dahlberg, "The Internet, Deliberative Democracy and Power: Radicalizing the Public Sphere," *International Journal of Media and Cultural Politics* 3, no. 1 (2007): 47–64; Greg Goldberg, "Rethinking the Public/Virtual Sphere: The Problem with Participation," *New Media and Society* 13, no. 5 (2011): 739–54.
13. Matthew A. Baum and Philip B. K. Potter, "The Relationship between Mass Media, Public Opinion, and Foreign Policy: Toward a Theoretical Synthesis," *Annual Review of Political Science* 11 (2008): 39–65, 41.
14. For a comprehensive overview of these theories and concepts see, for example, Derek Miller, *Media Pressure on Foreign Policy: The Evolving Theoretical Framework* (New York: Palgrave Macmillan, 2007); Piers Robinson, *The CNN Effect: The Myth of News, Foreign Policy and Intervention* (London and New York: Routledge, 2002); Eytan Gilboa, "The CNN Effect: The Search for a Communication Theory of International Relations," *Political Communication* 22, no. 1 (January 2005): 27–44; Piers Robinson, "The CNN Effect: Can the News Media Drive Foreign Policy?," *Review of International Studies* 25 (1999): 301–9; Steven Livingston and Todd Eachus, "Human Crises and US Foreign Policy: Somalia and the CNN Effect Reconsidered," *Political Communication* 12 (1995): 413–29; Lance Bennett, "Towards a Theory of Press-State Relations in the United States," *Journal of Communication* 40 (June 1990): 103–27.
15. See, for example, William D. Baker and John R. Oneal, "Patriotism or Opinion Leadership?: The Nature and Origins of the 'Rally 'Round the Flag' Effect," *Journal of Conflict Resolution* 44, no. 5 (2001): 661–87; James Patrick and John R. Oneal, "The Influence of Domestic and International Politics on the President's Use of Force," *Journal of Conflict Resolution.* 35 (1991): 307–32; John R. Oneal and Anna Lillian Bryan, "The Rally 'Round the Flag Effect in U.S. Foreign Policy Crises, 1950–1985," *Political Behavior* 17, no. 4 (1995): 379–401; Terrence L. Chapman and Dan Reiter, "The United Nations Security Council and the Rally 'Round the Flag Effect," *Journal of Conflict Resolution* 48 (2004): 886–909; Richard A. Brody, *Assessing the President: The Media, Elite Opinion, and Public Support*

(Stanford, CA: Stanford Univ. Press. 1991); Tim Groeling and Matthew A. Baum, "Crossing the Water's Edge: Elite Rhetoric, Media Coverage, and the Rally-Round-the-Flag Phenomenon." *The Journal of Politics* 70, no. 4 (2008): 1065–85; Scott Sigmund Gartner and Gary M. Segura, "War, Casualties and Public Opinion," *Journal of Conflict Resolution* 42, no.3 (2000): 278–300; and Peter D. Feaver and Christopher Gelpi, *Choosing Your Battles: American Civil-Military Relations and the Use of Force* (Princeton, NJ: Princeton University Press, 2004).

16. Baum and Potter, "The Relationship between Mass Media, Public Opinion, and Foreign Policy."

17. Robert M. Entman, "Cascading Activation: Contesting the White House's Frame after 9/11," *Political Communication* 20 (2003): 415–32; Entman, *Projections of Power in the News: Framing News, Public Opinion and US Foreign Policy* (Chicago: University of Chicago Press, 2003).

18. Entman, *Projections of Power in the News*, 13.

19. Michael Schudson, *The Sociology of News* (New York and London: Norton, 2003).

20. Michael Gurevitch, Mark R. Levy and Itzhak Roeh, "The Global Newsroom: Convergences and Diversities in the Globalization of Television News," in *Communications and Citizenship: Journalism and the Public Sphere in the New Media Age* eds. Peter Dahlgren and Colin Sparks (London: Routledge, 1991), 195–217.

21. Entman, *Projections of Power in the News*.

22. Stephen D. Reese, "The Framing Project: A Bridging Model for Media Research Revisited," *Journal of Communication* 57, no. 1 (2007): 148–54.

23. Erving Goffman, *Frame Analysis: An Essay on the Organization of Experience* (Harper & Row, 1974).

24. William A. Gamson and Andre Modigliani, "Media Discourse and Public Opinion on Nuclear Power: A Constructionist Approach," *American Journal of Sociology* 95 (1989): 1–37.

25. Todd Gitlin, *The Whole World is Watching: Mass Media in the Making & Unmaking of the New Left* (Berkeley: University of California Press.1980).

26. Entman, *Projections of Power in the News*.

27. See, for example, Herbert Gans, *Democracy and the News* (Oxford University Press, 2003); Schudson, *The Sociology of News* (1983); Pamela J Shoemaker and Stephen D. Reese, *Mediating the Message: Theories of Influences on Mass Media Content* (Longman, 1996); Charlotte Ryan, *Prime Time Activism: Media Strategies for Grassroots Organizing* (South End Press, 1991); and Gitlin, *The Whole World is Watching*.

28. Z. Pan and G. M. Kosicki, "Framing as a Strategic Action in Public Deliberation," in *Framing Public Life: Perspectives on Media and Our Understanding of the Social World*, ed. S. D. Reese, O. H. Gandy, and A. E. Grant (Mahwah, NJ: Erlbaum, 2001), 47.

29. Ibid.

30. US Immigration and Customs Enforcement, Secure Communities, http://www.ice.gov/secure_communities/.

31. "Community Standards and Participation Guidelines," *The Guardian*, http://www.guardian.co.uk/community-standards.

32. For a full list of community standards and a detailed explanation of each rule, see "Community Standards and Participation Guidelines," *The Guardian*, http://www.guardian.co.uk/community-standards.

33. *New York Times*, http://www.nytimes.com/subscriptions/Multiproduct/lp0418.html?campaignId = 38F9Y&scp = 1-spot&sq = subscribe&st = cse. The price of $35 per month was accurate for the dates of this study (2011).

34. This methodological choice in fact raises an interesting conceptual question of whether the readers themselves distinguish among the different story types when they respond to them in the comment section. While the distinction is tremendously important for journalists and journalism scholars, how important is it for the readers? How much does it influence their perception of the article content and the resulting feedback? Even though this study did not aim to answer this question, the textual analysis of the comments did not reveal any notable differences in ways the readers responded to different types of articles.

35. Barney Glaser and Anselm Strauss, *The Discovery of Grounded Theory: Strategies for Qualitative Research* (Chicago: Aldine, 1967).

36. Thomas R. Lindlof and Bryan C. Taylor, *Qualitative Communication Research Methods*, 2nd ed. (Thousand Oaks, CA: Sage, 2002).

37. Ibid.

38. Ibid.

39. Spiggle (1994), cited in Lindlof and Taylor, *Qualitative Communication Research Methods*, 222.

40. When looking at the number of "recommend" clicks corresponding to the quotations from specific posts later in the chapter, it is important to pay attention to the post number (e.g., #6 or #130). The general tendency for both newspapers is that the readers seem to be paying greater attention to the first few dozens of posts, and then their attention wanes. In other words, it is more typical, in general, for the earlier posts to get a higher number of clicks. Thus, for example, 11 "recommend" clicks for a post #130—one most likely surrounded by posts receiving no or 2–6 clicks on average—can be as powerful in terms of the amount of support as 110 "recommend" clicks for post #6.

41. Post #22, Cian Murphy, "Europe's Asylum System Is in Crisis," *The Guardian*, May 11, 2011. This post received 56 "recommend" clicks.

42. Post #16, Julia Preston, "Federal Policy Resulting in a Wave of Deportations Draws Protests," *New York Times*, August 16, 2011 (118 "recommend")

43. The spelling, punctuation, use of capital letters, italics, special symbols, and so on in all quoted comments are original, unless noted otherwise by the author of this chapter.

44. Post #1, Simon McMahon, "Italy Is Failing North African Refugees," *The Guardian*, April 6, 2011 (393 "recommend").

45. Post #7, Les Back, "Fortress Europe? There Is a Better Way," *The Guardian*, April 27, 2011 (199 "recommend").

46. Post #57, Julia Preston, "Federal Policy Resulting in a Wave of Deportations Draws Protests," *New York Times*, August 16, 2011 (41 "recommend").

47. Post #124, Julia Preston, "Federal Policy Resulting in a Wave of Deportations Draws Protests," *New York Times*, August 16, 2011 (15 "recommend").

48. Post #82, Julia Preston, "Federal Policy Resulting in a Wave of Deportations Draws Protests," *New York Times*, August 16, 2011 (9 "recommend").

49. Post #20, *New York Times*, "How a Democracy Works," June 3, 2011 (30 "recommend").

50. Post #1, Cian Murphy, "Europe's Asylum System Is in Crisis," *The Guardian*, May 11, 2011 (251 "recommend").

51. Post #130, *New York Times*, "Resistance Grows," June 7, 2011 (11 "recommend").

52. Post #6, *New York Times*, "Resistance Grows," June 7, 2011 (106 "recommend").

53. Post #43, Cian Murphy, "Europe's Asylum System Is in Crisis," *The Guardian*, May 11, 2011 (36 "recommend").

54. Post #44, Les Back, "Fortress Europe? There Is a Better Way," *The Guardian*, April 27, 2011. 27 ("recommend").

55. Post #12, Daniel Korski, "Europe's North Africa Policy Drowns in a Flood of Migrants," *The Guardian*, May 10, 2011 (260 "recommend").
56. Post #11, Julia Preston, "Federal Policy Resulting in a Wave of Deportations Draws Protests," *New York Times*, August 16, 2011 (58 "recommend").
57. Post #5, *New York Times*, "Resistance Grows," June 7, 2011 (77 "recommend").
58. Post #9, *New York Times*, "Resistance Grows," June 7, 2011 (123 "recommend").
59. Post #25, Julia Preston, "Federal Policy Resulting in a Wave of Deportations Draws Protests," *New York Times*, August 16, 2011 (63 "recommend").
60. Post #56, Peter H. Schuck, "Three States Short of a Secure Community," *New York Times*, June 22, 2011 (6 "recommend").
61. Ibid.
62. Post #89, Julia Preston, "Federal Policy Resulting in a Wave of Deportations Draws Protests," *New York Times*, August 16, 2011 (17 "recommend").
63. Ibid.
64. Post #72, Julia Preston, "Federal Policy Resulting in a Wave of Deportations Draws Protests," *New York Times*, August 16, 2011 (14 "recommend").
65. Post #19, Daniel Korski, "Europe's North Africa Policy Drowns in a Flood of Migrants," *The Guardian*, May 10, 2011 (93 "recommend").
66. Post #1, Cian Murphy, "Europe's Asylum System Is in Crisis," *The Guardian*, May 11, 2011 (251 "recommend").
67. Post #20, *New York Times*, "How a Democracy Works," June 3, 2011 (30 "recommend").
68. Post #45, Daniel Korski, "Europe's North Africa Policy Drowns in a Flood of Migrants," *The Guardian*, May 10, 2011 (140 "recommend").
69. Post #50, Peter H. Schuck, "Three States Short of a Secure Community," *New York Times*, June 22, 2011 (8 "recommend").
70. Post #21, Simon McMahon, "Italy Is Failing North African Refugees," *The Guardian*, April 6, 2011 (126 "recommend").
71. Post #64, Peter H. Schuck, "Three States Short of a Secure Community," *New York Times*, June 22, 2011 (2 "recommend").
72. Post #1, "Daniel Korski, "Europe's North Africa Policy Drowns in a Flood of Migrants," *The Guardian*, May 10, 2011 (413 "recommend").
73. Post #19, Les Back, "Fortress Europe? There Is a Better Way," *The Guardian*, April 27, 2011 (240 "recommend").
74. Ibid.
75. Post #2, Simon McMahon, "Italy Is Failing North African Refugees," *The Guardian*, April 6, 2011 (328 "recommend").
76. Post #47, Simon McMahon, "Italy Is Failing North African Refugees," *The Guardian*, April 6, 2011 (115 "recommend").
77. Post #1, Daniel Korski, "Europe's North Africa Policy Drowns in a Flood of Migrants," *The Guardian*, May 10, 2011 (413 "recommend").
78. Post #45, Daniel Korski, "Europe's North Africa Policy Drowns in a Flood of Migrants," *The Guardian*, May 10, 2011 (79 "recommend").
79. Post #104, *New York Times*, "Resistance Grows," June 7, 2011 (10 "recommend").
80. Post #82, *New York Times*, "Resistance Grows," June 7, 2011 (10 "recommend").
81. Ibid.
82. Post #22, Peter H. Schuck, "Three States Short of a Secure Community," *New York Times*, June 22, 2011 (46 "recommend").
83. Post #121, *New York Times*, "Resistance Grows," June 7, 2011 (11 "recommend").

84. Post #84, *New York Times,* "How a Democracy Works," June 3, 2011 (26 "recommend").
85. Post #53, Peter H. Schuck, "Three States Short of a Secure Community," *New York Times,* June 22, 2011 (24 "recommend").
86. Post #64, *New York Times,* "How a Democracy Works," June 3, 2011 (31 "recommend"); Post #25, "Federal Policy Resulting in a Wave of Deportations Draws Protests," *New York Times,* August 16, 2011 (63 "recommend").
87. Post #71, *New York Times,* "How a Democracy Works," June 3, 2011 (26 "recommend").
88. Post #16, Julia Preston, "Federal Policy Resulting in a Wave of Deportations Draws Protests," *New York Times,* August 16, 2011 (118 "recommend").
89. Post #81, Julia Preston, "Federal Policy Resulting in a Wave of Deportations Draws Protests," *New York Times,* August 16, 2011 (8 "recommend").
90. Post #11, *New York Times,* "Resistance Grows," June 7, 2011 (69 "recommend").
91. Post #66, Julia Preston, "Federal Policy Resulting in a Wave of Deportations Draws Protests," *New York Times,* August 16, 2011 (12 "recommend").
92. Post #69, *New York Times,* "How a Democracy Works," June 3, 2011 (19 "recommend").
93. Post #60, Peter Schuck, "Three States Short of a Secure Community," *New York Times,* June 22, 2011 (2 "recommend").
94. Post #47, *New York Times,* "How a Democracy Works," June 3, 2011 (29 "recommend").
95. Post #48, Julia Preston, "Federal Policy Resulting in a Wave of Deportations Draws Protests," *New York Times,* August 16, 20111(7 "recommend").
96. Post #17, Peter H. Schuck, "Three States Short of a Secure Community," *New York Times,* June 22, 2011 (16 "recommend").
97. Post #59, Peter H. Schuck, "Three States Short of a Secure Community," *New York Times,* June 22, 2011 (40 "recommend").
98. Post #49, Peter H. Schuck, "Three States Short of a Secure Community," *New York Times,* June 22, 2011 (23 "recommend").
99. Post #20, *New York Times,* "How a Democracy Works," June 3, 2011 (30 "recommend").
100. Post #9, *New York Times,* "Resistance Grows," June 7, 2011 (123 "recommend").
101. Post #12, Simon McMahon, "Italy Is Failing North African Refugees," *The Guardian,* April 6, 2011 (225 "recommend").
102. Post #45, Simon McMahon, "Italy Is Failing North African Refugees," *The Guardian,* April 6, 2011 (145 "recommend").
103. Post #22, Les Back, "Fortress Europe? There Is a Better Way," *The Guardian,* April 27, 2011 (218 "recommend").
104. Post #22, Les Back, "Fortress Europe? There Is a Better Way," *The Guardian,* April 27, 2011 (218 "recommend").
105. Post #15, Cian Murphy, "Europe's Asylum System Is in Crisis," *The Guardian,* May 11, 2011 (112 "recommend").
106. Post #20, Cian Murphy, "Europe's Asylum System Is in Crisis," *The Guardian,* May 11, 2011 (99 "recommend").
107. Post #2, Simon McMahon, "Italy Is Failing North African Refugees," *The Guardian,* April 6, 2011 (328 "recommend").
108. Post #47, Bill Frelick, "Treating Refugees as Refuse," *The Guardian,* June 14 (17 "recommend").
109. Post #24, Cian Murphy, "Europe's Asylum System Is in Crisis," *The Guardian,* May 11, 2011 (137 "recommend").

110. Post # 40, Simon McMahon, "Italy Is Failing North African Refugees," *The Guardian*, April 6, 2011 (37 "recommend").
111. Post # 96, Julia Preston, "Federal Policy Resulting in a Wave of Deportations Draws Protests," *New York Times*, August 16, 2011 (5 "recommend").
112. Post # 98, Ibid.,4 "recommend."
113. Post # 102, Julia Preston, "Federal Policy Resulting in a Wave of Deportations Draws Protests," *New York Times*, August 16, 2011 (9 "recommend").
114. Post # 41, Simon McMahon, "Italy Is Failing North African Refugees," *The Guardian*, April 6, 2011 (15 "recommend").
115. Post # 12, Cian Murphy, "Europe's Asylum System Is in Crisis," *The Guardian*, May 11, 2011 (6 "recommend").
116. Post #22, Bill Frelick, "Treating Refugees as Refuse," *The Guardian*, June 14 (0 "recommend").
117. Post # 2, Cian Murphy, "Europe's Asylum System Is in Crisis," *The Guardian*, May 11, 2011 (18 "recommend").
118. Post # 97, Julia Preston, "Federal Policy Resulting in a Wave of Deportations Draws Protests," *New York Times*, August 16, 2011 (4 "recommend").
119. Post #118, Julia Preston, "Federal Policy Resulting in a Wave of Deportations Draws Protests," *New York Times*, August 16, 2011 (9 "recommend").
120. Brian Massumi, "Everywhere You Want to Be: Introduction to Fear," in *The Politics of Everyday Fear*, ed. Brian Massumi (Minneapolis and London: University of Minnesota Press, 1993).
121. Rosner, 79.
122. German Marshall Fund of the United States, "Transatlantic Trends: Immigration 2011," http://trends.gmfus.org/files/2011/12/TTImmigration_final_web1.pdf.
123. Ibid., 83.

BIBLIOGRAPHY

Primary Sources

Back, Les. "Fortress Europe? There Is a Better Way." *The Guardian*, April 27, 2011. http://www.guardian.co.uk/commentisfree/2011/apr/27/sarkozy-berlusconi-schengen-europe?INTCMP = SRCH.
Frelick, Bill. "Treating Refugees as Refuse." *The Guardian*, June 14, 2011. http://www.guardian.co.uk/commentisfree/2009/jun/14/gaddafi-berlusconi-refugees-human-rights?INTCMP = SRCH.
"How a Democracy Works." *New York Times*, June 3, 2011. http://www.nytimes.com/2011/06/04/opinion/04sat1.html?scp = 1&sq = How%20a%20Democracy%20Works&st = Search.
Korski, Daniel. "Europe's North Africa Policy Drowns in a Flood of Migrants." *The Guardian*, May 10, 2011. http://www.guardian.co.uk/commentisfree/2011/may/10/europe-north-africa-unrest?INTCMP = SRCH.
McMahon, Simon. "Italy Is Failing North Africa's Refugees." *The Guardian*, April 6, 2011. http://www.guardian.co.uk/commentisfree/2011/apr/06/italy-north-africa-refugees-lampedusa?INTCMP = SRCH.
Murphy, Cian. "Europe's Asylum System Is in Crisis." *The Guardian*, May 11, 2011. http://www.guardian.co.uk/commentisfree/libertycentral/2011/may/11/europe-asylum-system-crisis?INTCMP = SRCH.
Preston, Julia. "Federal Policy Resulting in a Wave of Deportations Draws Protests." *New York Times*, August 16, 2011. http://www.nytimes.com/2011/08/17/us/

politics/17immig.html?_r = 1&scp = 1&sq = Federal%20Policy%20Resulting%20 in%20a%20Wave%20of%20Deportations%20Draws%20Protests&st = cse.

"Resistance Grows." *New York Times,* June 7, 2011. http://www.nytimes. com/2011/06/08/opinion/08wed1.html?scp = 1&sq = Resistance%20Grows&st = Search.

Schuck, Peter H. "Three States Short of a Secure Community." *New York Times,* June 22, 2011. http://www.nytimes.com/2011/06/23/opinion/23Schuck.html?scp = 1&sq = Three%20States%20Short%20of%20a%20Secure%20Community&st = cse.

Secondary Sources

Althaus, Scott L., and Jill A. Edy. "Revising the Indexing Hypothesis: Officials, Media, and the Libya Crisis." *Political Communication* 13, no. 4 (October 1996): 407.

Baker, William D. and John R. Oneal. "Patriotism or Opinion Leadership?: The Nature and Origins of the 'Rally 'Round the Flag' Effect." *Journal of Conflict Resolution* 44, no. 5 (2001): 661–87.

Baum, Matthew A. and Philip B. K. Potter. "The Relationship between Mass Media, Public Opinion, and Foreign Policy: Toward a Theoretical Synthesis." *Annual Review of Political Science* 11 (2008): 39–65.

Bennett, W. L. "An Introduction to Journalism Norms and Representations of Politics." *Political Communication* 13, no. 4 (October 1996): 373.

Bennett, Lance. "Towards a Theory of Press-State Relations in the United States." *Journal of Communication* 40 (June 1990): 103–27.

Bird, S. Elizabeth. *The Audience in Everyday Life: Living in a Media World.* New York: Routledge, 2003.

Brody, Richard A. *Assessing the President: The Media, Elite Opinion, and Public Support.* Stanford, CA: Stanford University Press, 1991.

Bryant, Antony, and Kathy Charmaz. *The SAGE Handbook of Grounded Theory.* London: Sage, 2007.

Burns, Peter and James Gimpel. "Economic Security, Prejudicial Stereotypes, and Public Opinion on Immigration Policy." *Political Science Quarterly* 115, 2 (2000): 201–25.

Calvo, Ana Maria Manzanas. "Contested Passages: Migrants Crossing the Rio Grande and the Mediterranean Sea." *South Atlantic Quaterly* 105, no. 4 (2006): 759–75.

Chapman, Terrence L. and Dan Reiter. "The United Nations Security Council and The Rally 'Round the Flag Effect." *Journal of Conflict Resolution* 48 (2004): 886–909.

Entman, Robert M. "Cascading Activation: Contesting the White House's Frame after 9/11." *Political Communication* 20 (2003): 415–32.

———. *Projections of Power in the News: Framing News, Public Opinion and US Foreign Policy.* Chicago: University of Chicago Press, 2003.

Feaver, Peter D. and Christopher Gelpi, *Choosing Your Battles: American Civil-Military Relations and the Use of Force.* Princeton, NJ: Princeton University Press, 2004.

Gamson, William A. and Andre Modigliani. "Media Discourse and Public Opinion on Nuclear Power: A Constructionist Approach." *American Journal of Sociology* 95 (1989): 1–37.

Gans, Herbert. *Democracy and the News.* Oxford University Press, 2003.

Gartner, Scott Sigmund and Gary M. Segura. "War, Casualties and Public Opinion." *Journal of Conflict Resolution* 42, no.3 (2000): 278–300.

German Marshall Fund of the United States. "Transatlantic Trends: Immigration 2011." http://trends.gmfus.org/files/2011/12/TTImmigration_final_web1.pdf.

Gilboa, Eytan. "The CNN Effect: The Search for a Communication Theory of International Relations." *Political Communication* 22, no. 1 (January 2005): 27–44.

Gitlin, Todd. *The Whole World is Watching: Mass Media in the Making & Unmaking of the New Left*. Berkeley: University of California Press,1980.

Givens, Terri E., Gary P. Freeman, and David L. Leal. *Immigration Policy and Security: US, European, and Commonwealth Perspectives*. New York: Routledge, 2009.

Glaser, Barney G., and Anselm L. Strauss. *The Discovery of Grounded Theory: Strategies for Qualitative Research*. Chicago: Aldine, 1967.

Goffman, Erving. *Frame Analysis: An Essay on the Organization of Experience*. Harper & Row, 1974.

Groeling, Tim and Matthew A. Baum. "Crossing the Water's Edge: Elite Rhetoric, Media Coverage, and the Rally-Round-the-Flag Phenomenon." *The Journal of Politics* 70, no. 04 (2008): 1065–85.

Gurevitch, Michael, Mark R. Levy and Itzhak Roeh. "The Global Newsroom: Convergences and Diversities in the Globalization of Television News." In *Communications and Citizenship: Journalism and the Public Sphere in the New Media Age*. Edited by Peter Dahlgren and Colin Sparks, 195-217. London: Routledge, 1991.

Jackman, Mary R., and Michael J. Muha. "Education and Intergroup Attitudes: Moral Enlightenment, Superficial Democratic Commitment, or Ideological Refinement?" *American Sociological Review* 49, no. 6 (December 1984): 751–69.

Lindloff, Thomas R., and Bryan C. Taylor. *Qualitative Communication Research Methods*. 2nd ed. Thousand Oaks, CA: Sage, 2002.

Livingston, Steven, and Todd Eachus. "Humanitarian Crises and US Foreign Policy: Somalia and the CNN Effect Reconsidered." *Political Communication* 12, no. 4 (October 1995): 413–29.

Massumi, Brian. "Everywhere You Want to Be: Introduction to Fear." In *The Politics of Everyday Fear*, ed. Brian Massumi. Minneapolis and London: University of Minnesota Press, 1993.

Migration, Public Opinion and Politics: The Transatlantic Council on Migration. Edited by Christal Morehouse. Gütersloh, Germany: Verlag Bertelsmann Stiftung, 2009.

Miller, Derek. *Media Pressure on Foreign Policy: The Evolving Theoretical Framework*. New York: Palgrave Macmillan, 2007.

Nord, David Paul. *Communities of Journalism: A History of American Newspapers and Their Readers*. History of Communication. Urbana: University of Illinois Press, 2001.

Oneal, John R. and Anna Lillian Bryan. "The Rally 'Round the Flag Effect in U.S. Foreign Policy Crises, 1950–1985." *Political Behavior* 17, no. 4 (1995): 379–401.

Patrick, James and John R. Oneal. "The Influence of Domestic and International Politics on the President's Use of Force." *Journal of Conflict Resolution*. 35 (1991): 307–32.

Peters, John Durham. "Historical Tensions in the Concept of Public Opinion." In *Public Opinion and the Communication of Consent*. Edited by Theodore L. Glasser and Charles T. Salmon, 3-32. New York: Guilford Press, 1995.

Reese, Stephen D. "The Framing Project: A Bridging Model for Media Research Revisited." *Journal of Communication* 57, no. 1 (2007): 148–54.

Robinson, Piers. "The CNN Effect: Can the News Media Drive Foreign Policy?" *Review of International Studies* 25 (1999): 301–9.

———. *The CNN Effect: The Myth of News, Foreign Policy and Intervention*. London and New York: Routledge, 2002.

Rosner, Jeremy D. "The Politics of Immigration and the (Limited) Case for New Optimism: Perspectives from a Political Pollster." In *Migration, Public Opinion and Politics: The Transatlantic Council on Migration*. Edited by Christal Morehouse, 77–87. Gütersloh, Germany: Verlag Bertelsmann Stiftung, 2009.

Ryan, Charlotte. *Prime Time Activism: Media Strategies for Grassroots Organizing*. South End Press, 1991.

Schain, Martin. *The Politics of Immigration in France, Britain, and the United States: A Comparative Study.* 1st ed. Perspectives in Comparative Politics. New York: Palgrave Macmillan, 2008.

Shoemaker, Pamela J. and Stephen D. Reese. *Mediating the Message: Theories of Influences on Mass Media Content.* Longman, 1996.

Schudson, Michael. *The Sociology of News.* 1st ed. Contemporary Societies. New York: Norton, 2003.

Suro, Roberto. "America's Views on Immigration: The Evidence from Public Opinion Surveys." In *Migration, Public Opinion and Politics: The Transatlantic Council on Migration.* Edited by Christal Morehouse. Gütersloh, Germany: Verlag Bertelsmann Stiftung, 2009.

Villa, Dana R. "Postmodernism and the Public Sphere." *American Political Science Review* 86, no. 3 (1992): 712–21.

Zaller, John, and Dennis Chiu. "Government's Little Helper: US Press Coverage of Foreign Policy Crises, 1945–1991." *Political Communication* 13, no. 4 (October 1996): 385.

8   A (More) Humanitarian Take
Al Jazeera English and Arabic Coverage of Immigration in the West

Stephen Bennett and Rodrigo Zamith
University of Minnesota

With negative attitudes toward immigration rising in nearly all segments of the population in both the United States and the European Union,[1] it is perhaps not surprising that numerous studies, including new research in the previous chapters, indicate that the news media in these countries can play an important role in making immigration a more salient issue and, often, in fomenting and perpetuating anti-immigrant attitude by emphasizing the illegal elements of immigration, engaging in the use of stereotypes, and focusing on individual cases while ignoring the larger structural forces at work.[2] The international media landscape of the 21st century, however, is being reshaped by a rise of the rest—the Doha-based Al Jazeera networks, both Arabic and English, are an increasingly crucial player in the global flow of news.

In addition to its rising prominence and legitimacy, Al Jazeera lends considerable attention to immigration in both Europe and the United States, especially from the perspective of "sending" countries in North Africa, making it an important voice in the debate. This chapter examines coverage of immigration in Italy and the United States by Al Jazeera Arabic (AJA) and Al Jazeera English (AJE), with a particular emphasis on discursive differences across the Atlantic and between the channels. Relative to the Western news media discussed in previous chapters, this study also highlights Al Jazeera's unique spin on immigration as an alternative model of journalistic practice.

A NEW INTERNATIONAL VOICE

Both AJA and AJE are becoming increasingly influential international news sources,[3] especially among Middle Eastern opinion leaders,[4] and are seen as more credible than comparable organizations like CNN and the BBC by their millions of viewers in both the East and the West.[5] Al Jazeera was created in 1996 as an Arabic-language independent news network that communicated issues relevant to the Arab world to a pan-Arab audience; 10 years later, the editorially independent AJE was launched

to reach worldwide audiences.[6] Through the adoption of Western journalistic norms and techniques,[7] stressing values such as fairness, balance,
and the presentation of multiple points of view,[8] Al Jazeera has gained
substantial credibility both in the Middle East and abroad.[9] According to
Nisbet et al., Al Jazeera and other emerging pan-Arab television news stations are becoming increasingly powerful communication channels within
the Muslim world.[10] Indeed, in their study of media influences on perceptions of the United States, Nisbet et al. found that individuals turning
to pan-Arab regional networks like Al Jazeera were more likely to hold
more negative perceptions of the United States than those who turned to
Western networks like CNN or the BBC, though others found that political identification may serve as a moderator of Al Jazeera's influence on
public opinion.[11] Furthermore, these effects may be even more powerful in
light of two-step theories of opinion formation, with Al Jazeera serving as
a key source of information for opinion leaders.[12]

While researchers and media analysts often fail to distinguish between Al
Jazeera's English- and Arabic-language channels,[13] we argue that important
distinctions exist in their coverage, especially given the distinct audiences.
Studies suggest that the vast majority of visitors to AJE's website come from
Western countries, while AJA's Arabic website is visited almost exclusively
by individuals in Arab countries, and that these individuals have different
reasons and motivations for turning to the network.[14]

ISSUE COVERAGE BY AL JAZEERA ENGLISH
AND AL JAZEERA ARABIC

According to el-Nawawy and Powers, AJE viewers view the broadcaster as
more "conciliatory" than CNN International and the BBC, covering contentious issues in a manner that creates an environment more conducive
to cooperation and negotiation. They also found that the more viewers
watched AJE, the less dogmatic their thinking became, leading to greater
tolerance of conflicting antagonists in contentious issues.[15] AJE has been
found to be more likely than comparable global outlets to treat groups with
unequal power equally in discourse, to place historic elements of stories in
new contexts that are easier to understand for modern-day viewers, and to
refrain from using scare quotes in its headlines or to overplay the social and
discursive context of conflicts.[16] In contrast, Cherribi found that AJA used
the conflict over women's wearing of the *niqab* (veil) in France to build a
global Muslim identity, mobilize a shared public opinion, and construct
a transnational Muslim community, leading him to characterize Al Jazeera
as a religious channel with news programming rather than a neutral news
channel.[17]

Further, in a study of the representation of different countries and regions
in AJE and AJA news broadcasts, al-Najjar found that both channels

devoted roughly one-third of their coverage to select countries but that, in the remainder of the coverage, AJA was more likely to feature other Arab nations than AJE, which was more likely to feature European nations and to focus on human rights and protests rather than internal politics.[18] Similarly, Fahmy and Emad found that the online coverage by AJE and AJA of the conflict between the United States and Al Qaeda was very similar but that AJE gave its stories greater emphasis.[19]

A NOTE ON METHODOLOGY

In this study, we focused on a set of comparative questions: Is there any difference between how AJA and AJE covered immigration in the United States? Is there any difference between how AJA and AJE covered immigration in Italy? Is there any difference between how AJA covered immigration in Italy and in the United States? Is there any difference between how AJE covered immigration issues unfolding in Italy and in the United States?

The first author examined all video clips and articles more than two paragraphs in length that were posted on AJA and AJE's websites from January 2010 to April 2012 and that contained the following terms: immigrant OR immigration OR refugee OR refugees AND Italy OR Arizona; اللاجئون لاجئ المهاجر هجرة إيطاليا أريزونا. The date range allowed for the sample to include coverage of immigration in the post-9/11 security context, as well before and after the 2011 "Arab Spring." The date range of this sample also includes coverage of immigration in the United States during the recent political debates over Arizona's controversial bill, SB-1070. The search returned a total of 14 video clips and 11 news stories specifically relevant to the issue of immigration. The primary discursive elements sought in sample were depictions of immigrants, political debates and their context, plight/situation of immigrants, push/pull factors, and the responses of receiving countries.

In order to study those discourses and any differences between the two Al Jazeera channels, we relied on the methodology of critical discourse analysis (CDA), which has been used across disciplines to address structural relationships of power created by language, specifically in immigration coverage studies.[20] For example, Buonfino found that media discourse on immigration in the European Union was made into a political issue at the nation-state level, with inherent contradictions between the shared ideals of equality and the presentation of immigration as a security threat.[21] Similarly, Triandafyllidou observed a distinct ingroup-outgroup "othering" of immigrants by citizens of Greece, Italy, and Spain and found that national identity was redefined by citizens when immigration was interpreted as a security concern.[22] In our analysis, we focused on Fairclough's third aspect of CDA, centering on power and class relationships as observed through discourse.[23]

AN ALTERNATIVE VOICE ON IMMIGRATION:
AL JAZEERA ENGLISH'S COVERAGE
OF IMMIGRATION IN ITALY

AJE provided in-depth coverage of immigration in Italy for several months before the outbreak of the Arab Spring, which resulted in the massive influx of North African and sub-Saharan African immigrants into Italy after December 2010, airing several two-minute news segments and featuring print stories online. In a 2010 feature piece titled "The Enemy Within," direct connections were drawn among immigration, Islamophobia, and debates over multiculturalism in Italy: "Some accuse the [Italian] government of racism and Islamophobia, others believe that immigrants are an enemy within."[24] Here the coverage openly advocates for immigrants by focusing on structural and economic factors such as job shortages, lack of resources in home countries, and conflict, such as the "plight of the immigrants," as push-pull factors. The attacks of September 11, 2001, are marked as a turning point in Italian views of Islam and Muslims. After 9/11, immigrants were deemed a "security issue" by the state, although the North Africans referenced in the story are specifically described as economic migrants, thereby drawing a contrast between state discourse and the "reality" of immigrants and immigration. The article targets Italian media, focusing on their antagonistic discourse toward Muslim immigrants and their spreading of anxieties about the erosion of Italian culture. As a result, "many Italians are opposed to having mosques in their neighborhoods because they fear extremism, crime, and violence" and because some feel that the presence of mosques "prevents immigrants from integrating fully." AJE coverage in general appeared to exhibit great anxiety itself over the culture debate taking place in Europe, with immigration serving as a central issue.

AJE stories on immigration in Italy after the outbreak of the Arab Spring continue this trend of being deeply humanistic and focusing on individual immigrants' stories, while highlighting larger systemic and structural factors. For example, one televised feature shows footage of exhausted-looking sub-Saharan immigrants who were abused in Libya and are scared to return home. In another story aired on AJE a month later that follows the situation of a young Cameroonian worker named Calvin, the reporter states, "These young men are not here by choice. One could say they are casualties of war" ("Future Uncertain for Libyan Refugees in Italy," 2011). As the story of Calvin's experience in the refugee camp unfolds, the reporter continues: "Calvin just wants to work and get his life back on track. But his legal status is unclear, so for now he just waits and ponders a future he can't control." The camera then cuts to Calvin smoking a cigarette, looking on as refugees are assisted in the camp.

The journey undertaken by immigrants is regularly and repeatedly described as "dangerous" and their sea vessels described in several stories as "rickety." In the February 2011 piece "Italy Alarm over Tunisian

Migrants," the reader is told of "hundreds of migrants" who "slept under open skies at Lampedusa's port, wrapped in space blankets." In the televised story "Italy Struggles with Tunisia Influx," boats that are "open to the elements" are "lining up" to land in Lampedusa. Both televised and print stories regularly note the presence of any women and children on such journeys, as the boats that arrive are often carrying only men. Pictures and video footage follow these themes by showing incoming immigrants packed tightly and precariously into boats of various sizes. The worried-looking men and women shown are dressed for cold weather on their journey across the Mediterranean and eager to get on shore.

European governments are regularly and openly criticized, most heavily by sources but also by journalists, for their lack of preparedness and for their resistance to "accepting responsibility" for the immigrants themselves. Trifling politicians are discussed in virtually all of the reporting, very often by critical nongovernmental aid workers. One woman described only as an "aid worker" states, "People have regained their democracy [in Tunisia] with much hardship and difficulty. There are probably many political refugees" ("Italy Struggles with Tunisia Influx," 2011). One emotional African refugee states that he "worked in Libya for four good years . . . if [the Italian government] can intervene in Libya, then they can take care of me. They can do this for me" ("Libyan Workers Stranded in Italy," 2011). Italian political leaders' comments often reflect a defensive posture, touting their efforts while complaining about the "burden" they bear from the influx of North African immigrants and looking to other European and North African governments for help. In keeping with the themes of "The Enemy Within," one official discussing the influx of Tunisian refugees says that the Italian authorities are concerned that escaped convicts are "hiding among the refugees" ("Italy Struggles with Tunisia Influx," 2011). When sub-Saharan Africans began arriving on Italian shores in May 2011, one reporter stated that, unlike the Tunisian immigrants, "they'll be likely to claim asylum, *a new headache for Italy who would rather they hadn't come in the first place*" ("Hundreds of Immigrants Reach Italian Island," 2011, emphasis ours).

AL JAZEERA ARABIC'S COVERAGE OF IMMIGRATION IN ITALY

AJA has fewer stories covering immigration in Italy, but its coverage shares similar themes with AJE coverage overall in providing the perspective and plight of immigrants themselves. This appears to match Al Jazeera's agenda to act as counterweight to Western-dominated news systems, counteracting Western coverage that marginalizes the situation of illegal immigrants. Human rights and international law are often invoked in Arabic-language coverage, unlike AJE coverage—the search function on AJA's website actually features a "Freedom and Rights" category. This most likely reflects the great emphasis placed on human rights and international law in Arabic media within the context of the Arab-Israeli conflict and Israeli presence in the Occupied Territories.

AJA uses immigrants' arrival in Italy to criticize the Libyan leader Muammar Gaddafi, which provides further evidence for the current geopolitics of Al Jazeera as a whole. As Al Jazeera's coverage was largely viewed as pivotal and indispensable within the wider media coverage of the Arab Spring, its spotlight quickly turned to Gaddafi after the fall of dictators in Egypt and in Tunisia. After the NATO intervention in the Libyan uprising, Gaddafi turned on Italian prime minister Silvio Berlusconi and Italian authorities, with whom he had re-established diplomatic relations in 2009, threatening to create "a sea of chaos" on the Mediterranean by sending waves of migrants to Italy's shores. While there was no actual evidence of Gaddafi's role, Italian authorities are quoted in a 2011 AJA story titled "The Continuing Flow of Refugees to Italy," speculating on his involvement in sending a recent ship full of migrants to Italy. Also noteworthy is that the ship was clearly noted in the story as being full of sub-Saharan immigrants, appearing to strike a slightly more negative tone about this group's arrival. But, just as in AJE coverage, AJA stories mention the miserable journey undertaken by immigrants across the Mediterranean and the presence of children and women, some of whom are noted as being pregnant.

However, the criticism of the Italian government is more detailed and more pointed in AJA reporting than in AJE coverage. In a 2011 story titled "Italy Passes Law against Immigrants," AJA discusses the Italian legislature's approval of a law governing migrants waiting in "detention and expulsion centers" and the extension of their processing time up to 18 months. Only briefly mentioning one statement from the nativist and anti-immigrant Northern League political party, the story gives substantial voice to the political opposition to the law in Italy for the entire second half of the story. One leftist Italian politician notably describes the detention centers as "Guantanamo Bay." While the coverage is sparser in AJA than the regular coverage provided by AJE, there are many discursive parallels, with much harsher criticism of European and Arab governments.

AL JAZEERA ENGLISH ON IMMIGRATION IN THE UNITED STATES

AJE coverage of immigration in the United States, almost exclusively focused on Arizona, is particularly fascinating. AJE aired at least four half-hour specials on different feature programs investigating the "climate of fear" faced by Mexican immigrants living in the United States illegally. One surprising aspect is the sheer amount of focus given to the challenges faced by illegal immigrants and the harsh toll that new laws like Arizona's SB1070 take on families portrayed in these televised specials. One show, *Activate*, which documents the political activism of young people around the world, features a Latina teenager living illegally in the United States as she leads political action in hope of reforming US law. Josh Rushing's *Faultlines* provided a look at SB1070 from multiple perspectives, highlighting viewpoints from Mexican immigrants, law enforcement, and American political figures.

AJE is quite critical of US government positions and policy on illegal immigration. In particular, it lends substantial attention to Republican political figures, especially Jan Brewer, the governor of Arizona who championed the passage of SB1070. Her portrayal is especially unflattering, with her proud comments supporting the bill always met with a reporting angle that draws attention to its "chilling effect" on hardworking Mexican immigrants. Her exploitation of the immigration issue is specifically and repeatedly presented as cheap political maneuvering. Some of the stories seem to carry an "only in America" tone or to suggest surprise and disbelief at the actual harshness of US border enforcement. The harshness of the laws on people who compose such a necessary part of the American economy is described as raw political gain combined with a bit of the absurdist theater that is American politics, with the coverage of Brewer serving as a prime example.

In an interesting link to US military action in the Middle East, a 2010 opinion piece for *In Focus* titled "US Drones Prowl Mexico Bicentennial" discusses the American use of a fleet of drones to patrol the US-Mexico border 24 hours a day. The use of drones is labeled a "disturbing development" in "growing tensions with the country's biggest trading partner and fiercest historical adversary." The characterization of Mexico as the "fiercest historical adversary" of the United States is historically questionable, at best. The article uses elements of US-Middle East policy and warfare as a model for observing US actions to control immigration and to label Mexican migrants as security threats.

In the sheer breadth of coverage, it is clear that AJE has its finger on the pulse on American politics as a whole. From the Democratic support for the DREAM Act to the use of immigration as a wedge issue in Republican presidential primary debates, as well as in the Arizona gubernatorial race, AJE's reporting is comprehensive and accurately conveys differing political positions on these issues. However, a number of op-eds by writers like Mark LeVine and Roza Kazan launched relentless attacks against Republicans on immigration policies. In the 2012 article "Republicans Change Tune for Hispanic Votes", the Republican candidates for the 2012 presidential nomination are labeled as "two-faced politicians," yet the article does accurately track their vacillating statements on illegal immigration, which change depending simply on the demographics of the state holding the next primary election for the nomination. One 2011 piece titled "Global Capitalism and the 21st Century Fascism" is an articulate but polemical attack on reactionary politics and the economic exploitation of the downtrodden but stands out as a piece that would hardly see the light of day in the American media.

Much of the reporting focuses on the stories of immigrants themselves and their dangerous travels across the border. Some interviews with illegal immigrant workers show their dismay at how they are being treated as pawns within the US political system and criminalized after years of hard work. In a 2011 segment titled "US State to Enforce Tough Immigration Bill," one immigrant states, "We're not here to do any harm; we came here to do good. We do hard work. Most people—Americans—won't do it. I have worked in grease up to my knees, in terrible heat." The report then cuts to a scene of Alabama governor Robert Bentley standing with three other white men, congratulating one another on the signing of their harsh anti-illegal immigrant law. A similar scene was aired about SB1070, depicting Brewer signing the Arizona law and shaking hands with several white men afterward. The local political organizing undertaken by Latino immigrants in Arizona constitutes much of the televised coverage, lending them substantial political agency in the eyes of AJE viewers. The professional tone of the reporting, excluding the written op-ed pieces, is playing to and addressing both an American and a global audience. Much attention is also given to the apparent dysfunction, extreme partisanship, and gridlock that were the reality of US legislative politics in 2012. As a result, the plights of immigrants in limbo are juxtaposed with the political wrangling evidenced in AJA's and AJE's reporting on Italy.

AL JAZEERA ARABIC ON IMMIGRATION IN THE UNITED STATES

The coverage of AJA on immigration and immigrants in the United States is also notable, if only for the fact that it is essentially nonexistent. Where there is coverage, it is intended for an Arabic audience and placed in the context of wider global issues. The search on AJA, even with an expanded set of search terms, resulted in no in-depth televised specials, op-eds, or usable published articles that fell within the scope of this study. Simply put, the issue of illegal immigrants and US policy toward them is not seen as important to a regional Arabic audience.

THE IMPORTANCE OF CONTEXT

The most striking differences between AJA and AJE found in this research are in the coverage of immigration in the United States. AJE, as a news organization, appears exceptionally interested in and in touch with US politics, and it lends highly sympathetic coverage to immigrants and the challenges they face as a result of recent anti-immigrant legislation. It is remarkable that AJA has no meaningful coverage of the issue as a regional Arabic news source. AJA's lack of coverage of illegal immigrants in the United States may be a result of the Arab world's own history of violating the human rights of its own illegal workers. These problems are especially pronounced in the treatment of foreign domestic workers in Lebanon and Saudi Arabia and in the conditions faced by construction workers in the United Arab Emirates and other wealthy Persian Gulf states. Our findings suggest that AJA may not wish to raise a debate on human rights violations associated with illegal immigration in the United States, perhaps in order to avoid the risk that viewers will push for a wider investigation into similar problems within the Arab world, thereby upsetting its viewership across the region.

Conversely, there are numerous parallels in the coverage by AJA and AJE of immigration in Italy. Both channels and electronic news sites run stories that attack politicians in North Africa and Europe, especially Gaddafi and Berlusconi, and they do well in providing insight into what African—especially North African—immigrants face after their arrival in Italy. The living situations are well documented in AJE, but this study found no such corresponding coverage on AJA. Notably, both AJA and AJE centered their coverage on the island of Lampedusa, with AJE covering an immigrant processing center in Genoa, in northern Italy, only once. In the coverage by both sources, immigrants are portrayed as being caught in limbo because of European politicians shirking their duty to face up to the refugee/immigrant problem and the consequences of their intervention in Libya.

In regard to differences in AJA coverage of immigration in Italy and the United States, it appears that AJA believes that its Arabic audience is interested in the situations of North African immigrants and refugees and not at all interested in the situation facing immigrants, primarily Latinos, to the United States. This may very well be true.

We argue that the only differences in AJE's coverage of immigration in the United States and in Italy are situational and contextual. In both cases, the politicians that led the decision making on immigration are portrayed as dysfunctional, self-interested, and completely unsympathetic to the plight of immigrants. The humanity of these North African and Latino immigrants is absent from the political discourse highlighted in politicians' statements and emerges only in AJE's brand of humanitarian reporting within the news story. The immigrants in both regions are portrayed by AJE as political pawns, exploited for short-term political gain by white politicians competing for power. Meanwhile, the immigrants and refugees given a voice in the stories stress their respectable work histories and express dismay at their treatment, thus creating an image of governments on two different continents that are unwilling to take responsibility for a massive structural social problem. Taking this into account, Al Jazeera clearly emphasizes a humanitarian perspective on the issue of immigration in their reporting, which sets its coverage apart from its Western counterparts.

CONCLUSIONS

Our study found appreciable differences in coverage by AJA and AJE on the subject of immigration, reflective of the fact that Al Jazeera, as a news organization, is very mindful of its regional viewing audiences, which in turn is perhaps a reflection of its remarkable rise in popularity and legitimacy as a news source throughout the world. However, it also raises questions as to how Al Jazeera views its role as a news outlet both regionally and globally. Al Jazeera has surely come to understand and appreciate its role in perpetuating the Arab Spring (though this deserves additional study). Although it is inadvisable to generalize in light of this study's focus on a relatively small corpus of the coverage, this chapter contributes to research on immigration reporting and adds to literature observing Al Jazeera's coverage of contentious political and social issues. The growing global popularity of Al Jazeera and the nature of its stories on immigration might prod Western news outlets to offer more thorough coverage of humanitarian issues surrounding immigration in both Europe and the United States, more adequately engaging the reality and hardships so often faced by immigrants across the world, as Al Jazeera has seemingly striven to do.

NOTES

1. Roberto Suro, "America's Views of Immigration: The Evidence from Public Opinion Surveys," in *Migration, Public Opinion and Politics: The Transatlantic Council on Migration*, ed. Bertelsmann Stiftung and the Migration Policy Institute (Gütersloh, Germany: Verlag Bertelsmann Stiftung, 2009); Bart Meuleman, Eldad Davidov, and Jaak Billiet, "Changing Attitudes toward Immigration in Europe, 2002–2007: A Dynamic Group Theory Approach," *Social Science Research* 38 (2009): 352–65; Christian Dustmann and Ian Preston, "Racial and Economic Factors in Attitudes to Immigration," *B.E. Journal of Economic Policy and Analysis* 7, no. 1 (2007): 1–39.
2. Chareton Thibault and Chrissa LaPorte, "Media and Immigration: An International Dialogue Organized by the French-American Foundation-United States." Maya Press, 2011, http://equality.frenchamerican.org/sites/default/files/media_immigration_report_2011.pdf.
3. Philip Seib, "Hegemonic No More: Western Media, the Rise of Al-Jazeera, and the Influence of Diverse Voices," *International Studies Review* 7, no. 4 (2005): 601–15.
4. Nashat A. Aqtash, "Credibility of Palestinian Media as a Source of Information for Opinion Leaders," *Journal of Arab and Muslim Media Research*, 3, no. 1–2 (2010): 121–36.
5. Thomas J. Johnson and Shahira S. Fahmy, "See No Evil, Hear No Evil, Judge as Evil? Examining Whether Al-Jazeera English-language Website Users Transfer Credibility to Its Satellite Network," in *International Media in a Global Age*, ed. Guy Golan, Thomas J. Johnson, and W. Wanta (New York: Routledge, 2010), 241–60.
6. Mohammed el-Nawawy and Shawn Powers, *Mediating Conflict: Al-Jazeera English and the Possibilityof a Conciliatory Media* (Los Angeles: Figueroa Press, 2008).
7. Muhammad I. Ayish, "Political Communication on Arab World Television: Evolving Patterns." *Political Communication* 19, no. 2 (2002): 137–54.
8. Shahira Fahmy and Thomas J. Johnson, "Show the Truth and Let the Audience Decide: A Web-based Survey Showing Support among Viewers of Al-Jazeera for Use of Graphic Imagery," *Journal of Broadcasting and Electronic Media* 51, no. 2 (2007): 245–64.

9. Aqtash, "Credibility of Palestinian Media"; see also Johnson and Fahmy, "Show the Truth."
10. Erik C. Nisbet, Matthew C. Nisbet, Dietram A. Scheufele, and James E. Shanahan, "Public Diplomacy, Television News, and Muslim Opinion." *Harvard International Journal of Press/Politics* 9, no. 2 (2004):11–37.
11. Erik C. Nisbet and Teresa A. Meyers, "Anti-American Sentiment as a Media Effect? Arab Media, Political Identity, and Public Opinion in the Middle East," *Communication Research* 38, no. 5 (2011): 684–709.
12. Elihu Katz and Paul F. Lazarsfeld, *Personal Influence* (New York: Free Press, 1955).
13. Sam Cherribi, "From Baghdad to Paris," *Harvard International Journal of Press/Politics* 11, no. 2 (2006): 121–38. See also Noureddine Miladi, "Satellite TV News and the Arab Diaspora in Britain: Comparing Al-Jazeera, the BBC and CNN," *Journal of Ethnic and Migration Studies* 32, no. 6 (2006): 947–60; Erik C. Nisbet, "Media, Identity, and the Salience of Democracy in the Arab Public Sphere," paper presented at the annual meeting of the American Political Science Association, Chicago, 2007.
14. Fahmy and Johnson, "Show the Truth"; see also Johnson and Fahmy, "See No Evil, Hear No Evil."
15. El-Nawawy and Powers, *Mediating Conflict*.
16. Leon Barkho, "The Discursive and Social Paradigm of Al-Jazeera English in Comparison and Parallel with the BBC," *Communication Studies* 62, no. 1 (2011): 23–40.
17. Cherribi, "From Baghdad to Paris."
18. A. I. al-Najjar, "How Arab Is Al-Jazeera English? Comparative Study of Al-Jazeera Arabic and Al-Jazeera English News Channels," *Global Media Journal: American Edition* 8, no. 14 (2009): 1–35.
19. Shahira S. Fahmy and Mohammed Al Emad, "Al-Jazeera vs. Al-Jazeera: A Comparison of the Network's English and Arabic Online Coverage of the US/Al Qaeda Conflict," *International Communication Gazette* 73, no.3 (2011): 216–32.
20. Jan Blommaert and Chris Bulcaen, "Critical Discourse Analysis," *Annual Review of Anthropology* 29 (2000): 447–66; Harald Bauder, "Media Discourse and the New German Immigration Law," *Journal of Ethnic and Migration Studies* 34, no. 1 (2007): 95–112.
21. Alessandra Buonfino, "Between Unity and Plurality: The Politicization and Securitization of the Discourse of Immigration in Europe," *New Political Science* 26, no. 1 (2004): 23–49.
22. Anna Triandafyllidou, "The Political Discourse on Immigration in Southern Europe: A Critical Analysis," *Journal of Communication and Applied Social Psychology* 10 (2000): 373–89.
23. Norman Fairclough, "Discourse and Text: Linguistic and Intertextual Analysis within Discourse Analysis," *Discourse and Society* 3, no. 193 (1992): 193–217.
24. Frederico Ferrone, Michelle Manzolini, and Akram Adouani, "The Enemy Within," Al Jazeera, 2010, http://www.aljazeera.com/focus/2010/06/201062 3101433585493.html.

REFERENCES

Al-Najjar, A. I. "How Arab Is Al Jazeera English? Comparative Study of Al Jazeera Arabic and Al Jazeera English News Channels." *Global Media Journal: American Edition* 8, no. 14 (2009): 1–35.

Aqtash, Nashat A. "Credibility of Palestinian Media as a Source of Information for Opinion Leaders." *Journal of Arab and Muslim Media Research* 3, no. 1–2 (2010): 121–36.

Ayish, Muhammad I. "Political Communication on Arab World Television: Evolving Patterns." *Political Communication* 19, no. 2 (2002): 137–54.

Barkho, Leon. "The Discursive and Social Paradigm of Al Jazeera English in Comparison and Parallel With the BBC." *Communication Studies* 62, no. 1 (2011): 23–40.

Bauder, Harald. "Media Discourse and the New German Immigration Law." *Journal of Ethnic and Migration Studies* 34, no. 1 (2007): 95–112.

Blommaert, Jan, and Chris Bulcaen. "Critical Discourse Analysis." *Annual Review of Anthropology* 29 (2000): 447–66.

Buonfino, Alessandra. "Between Unity and Plurality: The Politicization and Securitization of the Discourse of Immigration in Europe." *New Political Science* 26, no. 1 (2004): 23–49.

Campani, Giovanna. "Migration and Integration in Italy: A Complex and Moving Landscape" (2007), http://migrationeducation.de/38.1.html?&rid = 81&cHash = e5c8e1d629b6234d84577d1805d9a67b.

Cherribi, Sam. "From Baghdad to Paris." *Harvard International Journal of Press/Politics* 11, no. 2 (2006): 121–38.

Dustmann, Christian, and Ian Preston. "Racial and Economic Factors in Attitudes to Immigration." *B.E. Journal of Economic Policy and Analysis* 7, no. 1 (2007): 1–39.

El-Nawawy, Mohammed, and Shawn Powers. *Mediating Conflict: Al Jazeera English and the Possibility of a Conciliatory Media.* Los Angeles: Figueroa Press, 2008.

Fahmy, Shahira, and Thomas J. Johnson. "Show the Truth and Let the Audience Decide: A Web-based Survey Showing Support among Viewers of Al Jazeera for Use of Graphic Imagery." *Journal of Broadcasting and Electronic Media* 51, no. 2 (2007): 245–64.

Fahmy, Shahira S., and Mohammed Al Emad. "Al Jazeera vs Al Jazeera: A Comparison of the Network's English and Arabic Online Coverage of the US/Al Qaeda Conflict." *International Communication Gazette* 73, no. 3 (2011): 216–32.

Fairclough, Norman. "Discourse and Text: Linguistic and Intertextual Analysis within Discourse Analysis." *Discourse and Society* 3, no. 193 (1992): 193–217.

Ferrone, Frederico, Michelle Manzolini, and Akram Adouani. "The Enemy Within." Al Jazeera, 2010, http://www.aljazeera.com/focus/2010/06/2010623101433585 493.html.

Golan, Guy. "Inter-media Agenda Setting and Global News Coverage." *Journalism Studies* 7, no. 2 (2007): 37–41.

Johnson, Thomas J., and Fahmy, Shahira S. "See No Evil, Hear No Evil, Judge as Evil? Examining Whether Al Jazeera English-language Website Users Transfer Credibility to Its Satellite Network," in *International Media in a Global Age,* ed. Guy Golan, Thomas J. Johnson, and W. Wanta. New York: Routledge 2010: 241–60.

Katz, Eliha, and Paul F. Lazarsfeld. *Personal Influence.* New York: Free Press, 1955.

Miladi, Noureddine. "Satellite TV News and the Arab Diaspora in Britain: Comparing Al Jazeera, the BBC and CNN." *Journal of Ethnic and Migration Studies* 32, no. 6 (2006): 947–60.

King, Russell, and Nancy Wood. *Media and Migration.* New York: Routeledge, 2001.

Meuleman, Bart, Eldad Davidov, and Jaak Billiet. "Changing Attitudes toward Immigration in Europe, 2002–2007: A Dynamic Group Theory Approach." *Social Science Research* 38 (2009): 352–65.

Nisbet, Erik C. "Media, Identity, and the Salience of Democracy in the Arab Public Sphere." Paper presented at the annual meeting of the American Political Science Association, Chicago, 2007, http://www.allacademic.com/meta/p209273_index.html.

Nisbet, Erik C., and Teresa A. Myers. "Anti-American Sentiment as a Media Effect? Arab Media, Political Identity, and Public Opinion in the Middle East." *Communication Research* 38, no. 5 (2011): 684–709.

Nisbet, Erik C., Matthew C. Nisbet, Dietram A. Scheufele, and James E. Shanahan. "Public Diplomacy, Television News, and Muslim Opinion." *Harvard International Journal of Press/Politics* 9, no. 2 (2004): 11–37.

Seib, Philip. "Hegemonic No More: Western Media, the Rise of Al-Jazeera, and the Influence of Diverse Voices." *International Studies Review* 7, no. 4 (2005): 601–15.

Suro, Roberto. "America's Views of Immigration: The Evidence from Public Opinion Surveys." In *Migration , Public Opinion and Politics: The Transatlantic Council on Migration.* Edited by Bertelsmann Stiftung and the Migration Policy Institute. Gütersloh, Germany: Verlag Bertelsmann Stiftung, 2009.

Thibault, Chareton, and Chrissa LaPorte. "Media and Immigration: An International Dialogue Organized by the French-American Foundation-United States." Maya Press, 2011, http://equality.frenchamerican.org/sites/default/files/media_immigration_report_2011.pdf

Triandafyllidou, Anna. "The Political Discourse on Immigration in Southern Europe: A Critical Analysis." *Journal of Communication and Applied Social Psychology* 10 (2000): 373–89.

Vliegenthart, Rens, and Conny Roggeband. "Framing Immigration and Integration: Relationships between Press and Parliament in the Netherlands." *International Communication Gazette* 69, no. 3 (2007): 295–319.

Part III

Lampedusa and Schengen: Covering Immigration in Today's Europe

9 Journalistic Strategies to Write about Immigration under Nicolas Sarkozy's Presidency

Elise Vincent
Le Monde

Since April 2010, I have been covering immigration issues as a reporter for *Le Monde,* France's newspaper of record, based in Paris. This has coincided with a momentous time for understanding immigrants and immigration processes because, from May 2007 to May 2012, France had a president, Nicolas Sarkozy, who put immigration at the top of his political agenda. For those five years, immigration was one of the main topics of political debate in France, to a degree that had never been reached before. So, as a journalist, immigration was also a very specific—daily—exercise.

In this chapter, after introducing the principal dimensions of the French debate over immigration in the 21st century, I illustrate how, as a journalist, I alternate among three strategies when on this beat: covering the relentless flow of daily political statements, which is a necessary but hardly independent form of news; writing long educational *"contre-enquête"* features focused on dismantling popular myths; and, most difficult but rewarding of all, seeking to influence the political debate by uncovering what powerful interests want to keep hidden.

MAIN ASPECTS OF THE FRENCH DEBATE ABOUT IMMIGRATION

Demographics

First, a brief review of the main statistics concerning immigration in France. Overall, there are about 8 million immigrants in France, according to the 2008 census, which corresponds to around 9 percent of the population. It is a significant number, but it is a much smaller percentage than, for instance, in Germany, where immigrants represent around 13 percent of the population, or Spain (14 %), the United States (14%), or even Switzerland (23%). In terms of entries, France grants around 200,000 residence permits per year; 45 percent of them are granted to family members of immigrants already in France. Between 10 percent and 15 percent of residence permits are reserved for labor immigration. The rest are for asylum seekers and European citizens traveling inside the Schengen free-trade area.

It is also important to keep in mind that around 100,000 immigrants get French nationality each year, even though this number has recently started to decrease because of legislation imposing stricter rules. The figure that has constantly increased concerns deportations; 30,000 undocumented migrants are deported each year, although one-third of them are ethnic Roma, coming mainly from Romania and Bulgaria, who, most of the time, eventually return to France. Another 30,000 illegal immigrants are instead regularized each year, which means they can get an official residence permit (for 1 year or for 10 years). This works generally if you can prove your presence in France for a minimum of 5 years (more frequently after 10 years) and also that you have a job and "family connections" in France. This number includes people who entered France as asylum seekers and get refugee status.

From an ethnic point of view, the largest group of immigrants in France, about 2 million people, comes from Europe. Most of them were born in Portugal (580,000), Italy (310,000), or Spain (250,000). The second largest community of immigrants comes from North Africa: Algerians are the most numerous (around 700,000), followed by Moroccans (around 650,000) and Tunisians (230,000). Immigrants from Asia number around 750,000. Most of them were born in China; a certain number of people come from Vietnam, Laos, Cambodia, or, recently, Bangladesh or Sri Lanka. There are also about 660,000 migrants from sub-Saharan Africa, a large percentage from Mali, Senegal, Cameroun, or Ivory Coast.

Chronology

In order to understand how intense the debate was during Nicolas Sarkozy's presidency, here is a short "chronology" of his statements and actions regarding immigration during his 2007–2012 term in office—note the multiple references to "national identity," which suggest its importance in this debate, as many chapters in this book suggest:

2007

May:　　　　Creation of a ministry of immigration and "national identity."

September:　Sarkozy tries to impose DNA tests on families applying to join immigrant relatives already in France. That measure is very controversial, because human rights activists consider it stigmatizing of immigrants and a way to imply that they are all cheaters. Sarkozy and his minister of home affairs, Eric Besson at that time, later give up because they realize it will be difficult to implement and very expensive, too.

2008

April:　　　　Beginning of a two-year conflict between the government and undocumented workers. Hundreds of them demonstrate to claim their regularization. Very few will finally obtain their papers.

September: Destruction of the "Calais Jungle," a place where immigrants from mainly Afghanistan and eastern Africa are waiting in tents, in very poor conditions, before trying to cross the English Channel (La Manche) illegally on boats to reach the United Kingdom.

2009

July: Start of discussions to ban the "burqa" (full veil) in public spaces.

December: Start of the official debate on "national identity."

2010

March: Proposal of a new bill on immigration, containing many measures, the most important of which is the attempt to reinforce the deportation system.

July: Sarkozy's Grenoble speech: Sarkozy proposes to withdraw French nationality from all immigrants who commit a crime against a policeman and forced evacuations of all the places illegally occupied by Roma and "Tsiganes." In his speech, Sarkozy formally links immigration and the crime rate, the first president to do so officially.

September: Debate in Parliament about the new immigration bill.

November: Beginning of discussions to restrict access to French nationality. To become a French citizen, immigrants must prove that they have lived in France for a minimum of 5 years (most immigrants ask for citizenship after 10 years) or that they have been married to a French citizen for a minimum of 4 years. They must also prove that they speak a minimum of French words and that they have a job.

2011

March: Senate passes the new law on immigration.

April: Decision to reduce labor immigration and controversy over Muslims who pray in the streets because they do not have enough mosques.

May: Decision to reduce the options for foreign students who want to stay in France to work after their studies.

June: The new law on immigration goes into effect.

Fall: Reduction of 30 percent in the number of naturalizations (a higher level of French-language fluency and higher income are now required). A new database is introduced to control foreigners and their social security benefits in order to ensure they do not defraud welfare.

As the chronology illustrates, the radicalization of Sarkozy's attitude occurred in 2010, particularly during the summer, with what is now considered, politically, for many reasons, the turning point of his presidency: the Grenoble speech, which centered on immigration as a problem for France.

Geography

As the outline also indicates, the debate about immigration in France is less focused on the question of the "borders" than it is in the United States, partly because there are no "direct" borders with any source country that is a source of emigration. The Mediterranean Sea separates France from Africa. And even if thousands of migrants from Africa cross the sea by boats every year and reach Italy, Spain, or Malta, very few of them actually reach France that way. The important number of arrivals of Tunisian immigrants after Ben Ali lost power in January 2011 was an exception.

In France, most immigrants simply come by plane, with tourist visas and student cards (50,000 per year). Some of them (mainly from Asia, including China, Bangladesh, and Afghanistan, but also from Somalia and Kosovo) enter France illegally through its eastern borders. But the "control" of these borders does not really depend on French authorities, because France is part of the Schengen agreement. It depends on how countries such as Greece and Poland are controlling their own borders. So, for French public opinion, the result of this "borderless" situation is that attention is not totally focused on one point of entry. Rather, for those who fear immigration, it is much more a global threat. It comes from everywhere, but they do not really know how. And they are just counting the number of "colored people"—as they put it—who, according to them, keep increasing in the streets. That makes the debate on immigration issues a very broad topic for a journalist to report on.

A Polymorphous Debate

If I tried to summarize it, I would say that the debate regarding immigration issues in France has four main aspects. The first one concerns all the questions about "controlling" the inflows, from deportation to immigrants' rights. It concerns also family immigration (should these immigrants get an automatic right to come?), and it may also include asylum seekers (do they really come because they are threatened in their home country?). The second main aspect of the debate concerns the question of the "cost" of immigration, with questions like: Are immigrants overrepresented among those living on public welfare? Or are immigrants cheating to get more social benefits? The third aspect of the debate concerns the security aspects, such as the classic one: Do immigrants account for the largest numbers of criminals?

But what is very specific to France—and to many other European countries, as well, and in contrast to the United States—is that we have a very sharp and permanent debate that links immigration to a question of "identity." This debate includes all the questions about religion, particularly Islam: Do women have the right to wear the veil? Where? Do Muslims have the right to build their own mosques? With whose money? If they do not have this right, do they have the right to pray outside, directly in the streets? Is France a Christian country? This debate about identity also includes all the questions about what we call integration of the immigrants, as Schain's chapter illustrates: Do they succeed at school as well as the natives? If not, why? Why do they suffer so much from unemployment (more than twice the average national rate)?

Thus, during this period, news on immigration issues has been a permanent feature in French media. Almost every day there were political statements on the radio and controversies, big or small. Every day the debate was cleaved and Manichean. Of course, that was what Sarkozy wanted, part of his political strategy. But, for me as a journalist, it was often a very delicate exercise.

DIFFERENT JOURNALISTIC METHODS TO TRY TO GET AROUND THIS PROBLEMATIC SITUATION

First Approach: "Facts, Just Facts"

When you find yourself covering a public official's statements on immigration, even if you do not agree with some of them, you do not have a lot of choice. Your first job is to tell the facts to the readers. A journalist has to be as neutral as she can. So, generally, one statement equals one article. It is also always the first step before going further, with writing a news analysis for instance.

In June 2011, for example, I covered the proposal by several right-wing legislators to limit the possibility of obtaining two citizenships at the same time. It was a short article. So I explained factually the position of these legislators and then, in order to give another opinion on their proposal, I quoted the Socialist Party, which was criticizing it. I proceeded exactly the same way, in November 2011, when I had to cover an announcement by the minister of the interior, who said he wanted to create a new database to know whether or not immigrants who get social benefits cheat. The article was short. This time, the Socialist Party had not said anything. So I mentioned studies that were explaining how it is difficult to prove the percentage of "cheaters" among immigrants, even if cheating does exist. I could multiply that kind of example. They form one of the most important portions of all the articles I published each year (Figure 9.1).

Le Monde
Mardi 29 novembre 2011

Lutte contre la fraude sociale : Claude Guéant cible les étrangers

Le ministre veut connecter le fichier des étrangers résidant en France avec celui de la Sécurité sociale

Après avoir annoncé, vendredi 25 novembre, vouloir s'attaquer aux « faux » demandeurs d'asile (*Le Monde* du 26 novembre), le ministre de l'intérieur, Claude Guéant, a déclaré, dimanche, vouloir s'attaquer aux *« fraudes sociales »* imputables aux étrangers.

Interrogé sur Europe 1 lors de l'émission « Le Grand rendez-vous », en partenariat avec iTélé et *Le Parisien*, M. Guéant a annoncé son intention de *« connecter »*, dès le 1er janvier 2012, *« les fichiers des étrangers résidant en France et les fichiers de Sécurité sociale »*. Une façon d'avoir *« des moyens plus efficaces pour lutter contre ces fraudes spécifiques »*, a-t-il plaidé.

Le ministre doit se rendre à Créteil, la préfecture du Val-de-Marne, mardi 29 novembre, pour examiner un dispositif *« pilote »* de coopération entre la police et la Caisse d'allocations familiales (CAF). Un dispositif qui, selon son entourage, aurait permis depuis sa mise en œuvre, en avril, de recouvrir *« 175 000 euros d'indus »*. La volonté de M. Guéant de s'attaquer aux *« fraudes sociales des étrangers »* est le résultat d'un décret paru il y a bientôt six mois – le 8 juin – qui réforme l'Application de gestion des dossiers des ressortissants étrangers en France (Agdref). Ce *« fichier des étrangers »*, comme l'appelle le ministre, existe depuis 1993 et enregistre toutes les demandes de titres de séjour et de voyage.

Mais, depuis juin, Agdref a été fusionné avec un autre fichier, dit « ELOI », qui recense, lui, toutes les mesures d'éloignement. Et parmi un certain nombre d'innovations, Agdref – rebaptisé Agdref 2 – peut désormais être consulté par les agents des organismes chargés de la gestion d'un régime obligatoire de Sécurité sociale.

Ces derniers peuvent ainsi vérifier la régularité du séjour des étrangers et identifier notamment les « faux-papiers ». Cette réforme, en gestation depuis longtemps, a été rendue possible par le vote, en mars, de la loi d'orientation et de programmation pour la performance de la sécurité intérieure (Loppsi 2). La possibilité de consulter Agdref était aussi l'une des recommandations, en juin, du rapport sur la fraude de la Mission parlementaire d'évaluation et de contrôle des lois de financement de la protection sociale (Mecss).

Sur Europe 1, dimanche, M. Guéant a dit vouloir cibler les étrangers qui *« résident régulièrement sur le sol* [français], *touchent des allocations pour des enfants qui ne vivent pas en France »*, ainsi que ceux qui font *« des allers et retours entre la France et leur pays d'origine »*. Pour bénéficier de droits en France, il faut en effet ne pas résider hors du territoire plus de trois à six mois (selon les allocations).

« Vieux migrants »

Cette dernière remarque visait particulièrement les *« vieux migrants »*, précise-t-on Place Beauvau. Ces immigrés, souvent originaires du Maghreb ou d'Afrique subsaharienne, venus travailler en France pendant les « trente glorieuses » et qui vivent aujourd'hui en foyer. Un contentieux juridique existe toutefois sur le sort de ces derniers, un certain nombre d'associations et de parlementaires défendant leur droit à profiter sans conditions de leur retraite.

Le chiffrage des fraudes imputables aux étrangers reste toutefois un exercice difficile. En mars 2010, une enquête publiée par *Politiques sociales et familiales*, le magazine de la Caisse nationale des allocations familiales (CNAF), avait pointé la surreprésentation des immigrés et de leurs descendants dans les minima sociaux. Mais dans son rapport, la Mecss n'avait donné qu'un montant global de la fraude aux prestations sociales : soit 2 à 3 milliards d'euros par an.

L'annonce de M. Guéant s'inscrit dans la droite ligne des thèmes de campagne de l'UMP. Elle reprend aussi un sujet défendu par la candidate du FN à l'élection présidentielle, Marine Le Pen. Interrogée sur LCP le 23 novembre dans « Question d'info », en partenariat avec *Le Monde*, AFP et Dailymotion, Mme Le Pen avait détaillé comment elle souhaitait lutter contre la *« fraude sociale »* – qu'elle impute en grande partie à l'immigration. *« Il faut développer la transmission à l'intérieur de l'administration des documents qui fondent la délivrance de papiers »*, avait-elle plaidé. ■

ELISE VINCENT ET JEAN-BAPTISTE CHASTAND

Election présidentielle

Dominique de Villepin propose une « équipe de France des meilleurs »

A l'occasion d'une récente entrevue avec le chef de l'Etat, Dominique de Villepin a proposé à Nicolas Sarkozy d'avoir un gouvernement resserré à une dizaine de *« grands talents »*. Selon l'ancien premier ministre, interrogé dimanche 27 novembre sur BFMTV2012/*Le Point*/RMC, ceux qui peuvent faire partie de cette *« équipe de France des meilleurs »* sont le secrétaire national de l'UMP, Jean-François Copé – *« bon dans l'action »*, – le ministre des finances, François Baroin, le président du Parti radical, Jean-Louis Borloo, l'ex-ministre Thierry Breton, ou encore les socialistes Gérard Collomb et François Rebsamen. Egalement questionné sur ses relations avec le président de la République, M. de Villepin a affirmé avoir *« tourné la page »* de l'affaire Clearstream et entretenir désormais des relations *« républicaines, apaisées »* avec le locataire de l'Elysée. Il a encore affirmé n'avoir pas *« dealé »* avec Nicolas Sarkozy, en précisant qu'il n'aurait pas accepté de *« responsabilités dans un gouvernement quelconque dans cette mandature »*. Sans toutefois exclure une participation au prochain quinquennat. – *(AFP.)* ■

UMP Claude Guéant et Jean-François Copé nient tout complot contre Dominique Strauss-Kahn

Le ministre de l'intérieur, Claude Guéant, et le secrétaire général de l'UMP, Jean-François Copé, ont vivement dénoncé, dimanche 27 novembre, la *« thèse du complot »* exposée par le journaliste américain Edward Epstein dans la *New York Review of Books* et nié toute implication de l'UMP dans cette affaire. L'enquêteur conclut qu'on a voulu nuire à DSK pour *« faire capoter »* sa candidature à l'élection présidentielle. *« Grotesque »*, a commenté M. Copé. *« S'il y a quelqu'un qui estime qu'il y a complot, il n'a qu'à déposer une plainte »*, a conseillé M. Guéant.

Droit de veto à l'ONU : le Parti socialiste nuance l'accord avec les écologistes

M. Hollande a assuré que la place de la France aux Nations unies ne sera pas modifiée s'il est élu

François Hollande a dû trancher et désavouer un nouveau point de l'accord entre Verts et socialistes, lundi 28 novembre, en promettant au micro de BFM-TV et RMC qu'il n'y aurait pas de remise en cause du veto français à l'ONU s'il était président, *« Tant que je serai dans la situation d'exercer la responsabilité de mon pays si les Français me la confient, il n'y aura pas de remise en cause du droit de veto, de remise en cause unilatérale du droit de veto »*, a précisé le candidat socialiste, en ajoutant : *« Les Nations unies doivent évoluer, il y a une réflexion qui peut être engagée, une gouvernance mondiale. »*

L'UMP, rejointe par le centre et une partie de la gauche, pilonne le PS sur ce sujet depuis une semaine. C'est le ministre de l'intérieur, Claude Guéant, qui a déniché, mercredi 23 novembre, ce point passé inaperçu de l'accord entre le PS et Europe-Ecologie Les Verts (EELV).

Selon le texte, *« la France fera des propositions précises pour réformer et démocratiser l'ONU afin qu'elle structure un ordre juridique et normatif global : siège européen, suppression du droit de veto, meilleure représentativité des pays du Sud au sein du Conseil de sécurité, renforcement du rôle des organisations non-gouvernementales »*. Il n'en fallait pas plus pour que Claude Guéant juge que *« les deux partis, donc M. Hollande, proposent qu'au Conseil de sécurité* [de l'ONU], *ce soit désormais un représentant de l'Union européenne qui siège et que, par conséquent, la France n'y siège plus »*.

> « François Hollande s'apprête à brader l'un des fondamentaux de notre indépendance »
> **Jean-François Copé**
> secrétaire général de l'UMP

Une attaque relayée par Jean-François Copé, pour qui *« François Hollande s'apprête à brader l'un des fondamentaux de notre indépendance »*. Et d'ajouter : *« Imagine-t-on François Mitterrand engager la France dans une abdication de son statut de membre permanent du Conseil de sécurité ? »*. Une attaque, là encore, de la stature présidentielle de M. Hollande.

L'accord n'évoque pourtant pas, comme l'interprète l'UMP, la perte d'un siège français mais la mise en place d'un siège européen, même si un cumul semble improbable.

François Hollande (ici lors d'une conférence de presse à Paris, dimanche 27 novembre), a déclaré, lundi, sur BFM-TV, qu'il ne remettrait pas en cause le veto français à l'ONU s'il était président. FRED DUFOUR/AFP

Plus lapidaire, le passage sur le droit de veto posait question : cinq pays, membres permanents du Conseil de sécurité, possèdent ce droit : Etats-Unis, Russie, Chine, Grande-Bretagne et France. Et aucun ne compte se priver d'un tel avantage, même si, depuis une trentaine d'années, Paris plaide, avec Londres, pour un élargissement du cercle des membres permanents à d'autres nations : Allemagne, Brésil ou Inde.

En matière de relations internationales, l'accord prend des positions plus idéalistes que concrètes qui rappellent une résolution votée par le Parlement européen en 2004. Le Parti populaire européen (PPE), dans lequel siège l'UMP, avait alors voté, avec la gauche, un texte prônant un élargissement du conseil de sécurité et une modification du droit de veto, qui aurait nécessité deux pays et non plus un seul.

L'UMP n'a pas été la seule à s'inquiéter du contenu de l'accord Verts-PS. François Bayrou a également jugé *« infiniment troublant »* que l'on veuille gommer *« la seule arme qui permette encore à la France d'être au rang des puissances majeures »*. A gauche, Jean-Pierre Chevènement a lui aussi fait part de son inquiétude devant un texte qui *« ne tient pas debout »*.

Convoqué à la défense de l'accord, Pierre Moscovici, directeur de campagne de M. Hollande, avait déjà fait, vendredi, la distinction entre grands principes et réalités : *« Il n'est pas question de remettre en cause le statut de membre permanent de la France au Conseil de sécurité de l'ONU, ni le droit de veto »*, avait-il assuré, ajoutant qu'il n'y avait rien d'anormal à vouloir, *« avec les Verts, poursuivre des idéaux et souhaiter des changements de long terme »*.

Les écologistes, eux, défendent une interprétation plus formelle du texte. Cécile Duflot jugeait vendredi que *« des positions européennes portées sur la politique internationale »* seraient *« plus utiles que cet anachronique droit de veto de la France »*. Pour la candidate d'EELV Eva Joly, le droit de veto de la France à l'ONU est *« un privilège dépassé, réservé à quelques pays »*.

Cette nouvelle différence de lecture entre partenaires à gauche inquiète, au sein du PS, après l'épisode du nucléaire. Le PS se débat toujours sur cette question face à l'UMP, qui accuse, Nicolas Sarkozy en tête, socialistes et écologistes de vouloir *« brader »* l'indépendance énergétique du pays en mettant fin au nucléaire. Une vision caricaturale de la position médiane du candidat socialiste, mais qui permet là aussi à la droite d'attaquer M. Hollande sur les thématiques plus régaliennes et internationales dans lesquelles M. Sarkozy est jugé le plus positivement dans les enquêtes d'opinion.

L'accord avec EELV, qui devait permettre à François Hollande de relancer sa campagne, apparaît de plus en plus, aux yeux de certains socialistes, comme un *« énorme cafouillage »*, selon les termes Michel Vauzelle, président PS de la région PACA. ■

SAMUEL LAURENT

Certains points de l'accord divergent du projet du PS

Le nucléaire ou le siège français à l'ONU ne sont pas les seuls points de l'accord entre les Verts et le PS qui pourraient faire polémique. Le texte évoque ainsi la reconnaissance de l'Etat palestinien, qui ne figure pas en tant que tel dans le projet socialiste, même si François Hollande y est favorable. Il propose aussi la mise en place d'une *« contribution climat énergie »* similaire à la taxe carbone retoquée en 2009, mais qui serait deux fois plus chère (36 euros par tonne de CO_2 en 2012 contre 14 euros dans la loi de 2009), ou un encadrement des prix dans la grande distribution qui ne figurait pas non plus dans le projet socialiste. Un passage précise par ailleurs la mise en place de la proportionnelle aux législatives : *« entre 15 % et 20 % des députés, au moins 100 sièges en fonction du redécoupage sur la base d'une analyse partagée »*. Le PS parlait jusqu'ici d'une *« dose »*, sans plus de détails.

Hélie Denoix de Saint Marc décoré par Nicolas Sarkozy

Le chef de l'Etat élève à la dignité de grand-croix l'ancien résistant et ex-putschiste de 1961

Nicolas Sarkozy devait remettre, lundi 28 novembre, aux Invalides, lors de la traditionnelle prise d'armes d'automne, les insignes de grand-croix de la Légion d'honneur à l'ancien commandant Hélie Denoix de Saint Marc, 89 ans.

Résistant, survivant de la déportation, auteur de nombreux livres, le chef de bataillon de Saint Marc commandait par intérim le 1er régiment étranger de parachutistes de la Légion, à qui le général Maurice Challe avait fait appel pour conduire le putsch d'avril 1961 en Algérie. Le 1er REP a été dissous. Le commandant Denoix de Saint Marc, condamné à dix ans de réclusion, a été libéré après cinq ans.

« C'est un personnage emblématique des hauts et des bas de notre armée », souligne le ministre de la défense, Gérard Longuet. *« Monsieur le Président, on peut demander beaucoup à un soldat, en particulier de mourir, c'est son métier*, avait déclaré le commandant lors de son procès devant le tribunal militaire le 5 juin 1961. *Mais on ne peut lui demander de tricher, de se dédire, de se contredire, de mentir, de se renier, de se parjurer. »* Le geste de M. Sarkozy *« n'est pas un acte politique »*, explique Franck Louvrier, conseiller en communication de l'Elysée. *« C'est un acte militaire, c'est en tant que chef des armées que le président de la République remet cette décoration. »*

Rassembler les droites

Les putschistes d'Alger ont été amnistiés et réintégrés dans les cadres de l'armée par six décrets et lois successifs, de 1963 à 1982. Le texte du gouvernement Mauroy avait ainsi réintégré les deux derniers généraux vivants, Raoul Salan et Edmond Jouhaud, à l'issue d'un vif débat et en dépit de l'opposition de Pierre Joxe. *« Il appartient à la nation, au bout de vingt ans, de pardonner »*, avait justifié François Mitterrand.

La décoration de M. de Saint Marc s'inscrit dans la continuité, justifie M. Louvrier. *« De Gaulle l'a amnistié en 1968. Il fut rétabli dans ses droits civils et militaires par Valéry Giscard d'Estaing et élevé à la dignité de grand officier de la Légion d'honneur le 29 mars 2003 par Jacques Chirac »*.

Il n'empêche. M. Sarkozy tente, à cinq mois de la présidentielle, de rassembler toutes les droites françaises. *« Par petites touches, c'est le président rassembleur qui se confirme »*, commente l'ancien ministre de l'intérieur Brice Hortefeux.

Promu par le même décret que M. de Saint Marc, Hocine Chieb-Bouares, 70 ans, harki et président d'associations d'anciens combattants, devrait être décoré lors d'une future prise d'armes.

Le ministre des transports et leader de la Droite populaire, Thierry Mariani se réjouit d'un *« signe »* vis-à-vis des harkis. *« Il y a une demande de reconnaissance : 2012 ne sera pas seulement l'élection présidentielle, ce seront les 50 ans de la fin de la guerre d'Algérie, et un certain nombre de Français attendent un signe. »* Dans ce contexte, le député UMP Jacques Myard, souverainiste gaulliste, estime qu'il faut *« saluer un grand soldat »* en M. Denoix de Saint Marc. Et il poursuit, à propos des harkis : *« L'histoire des harkis n'est pas une page glorieuse de la France. Nous les défendons, mais nous leur disons aussi qu'il faut savoir tourner la page. »*

Selon le ministre de la défense, parler de cette période *« de manière apaisée semble un devoir absolu »*. M. Longuet ajoute : *« On peut se tromper d'orientation, moi-même je me suis beaucoup trompé. »* ■

ARNAUD LEPARMENTIER ET NATHALIE GUIBERT

Figure 9.1 First Approach: Facts, Just Facts (courtesy of *Le Monde*)

The major editorial difficulty I had to experience during that period was that the statements were always coming from the same side: the right wing (or the far right). The left wing in France, particularly the socialist party (PS), has been divided for years on the topic of immigration. So the PS never—or very rarely and with vague cases—answered Sarkozy's or his officials' statements. The PS defends human rights but does not have real proposals on immigration. It is not a critic. For a journalist, that poses a problem, because it means that it was always the most "conservative" positions that were dominating the terms of the debate—in a straight news story, without another political source to quote, it becomes impossible to strongly "balance" the statements. This observation is not unique to immigration issues, but the problem with immigration is that it affects widely people's passions, angers, hopes and . . . their votes. And that is how, on April 22, 2012, in the first round of the presidential election, the far-right, anti-immigrant National Front (FN) reached one of its best results ever, with almost 20 percent of the votes—even if, of course, its success was not only a response to the fear of immigrants among the public.

Second Approach: Writing Pedagogical Articles

Until a few months ago, in *Le Monde,* we had a special type of article that was especially shaped to answer readers' questions on important breaking news or controversies. These articles were called *"contre-enquête."* You had one or two full pages to explain things in detail, with shades. I used it every time a controversy about immigration was happening. It was a way for me to try to write about what were the real stakes of the debate. Then, this type of article disappeared because a new editor in chief was nominated. *Le Monde* has maintained its tradition of investigation, but the form was different.

For example, during the summer of 2010, I published several *"contre-enquête"* articles when Sarkozy announced he wanted to deport to their home country "all people" who illegally occupied public property. At that time, his proposal was quite controversial, and everybody (politicians, journalists, the public) was confusing "Roma" and "gens du voyage," or what the English call "travelers." So, to clarify the debate, I wrote a long article to explain the difference between what we call "Roms" (who are immigrants from Romania and Bulgaria who may live in camps) and "gens du voyage" (who are French people who live in caravans and sometimes illegally occupy places but whom you cannot deport). I described the problems these communities are effectively causing for many reasons (e.g., delinquency and the fact that they do not always send their children to school). But, at the same time, I wrote about all the widely documented solutions that could be implemented.

During winter 2011, I also decided to write several *"contre-enquête"* stories when a large number of immigrants from Tunisia and Libya were crossing the Mediterranean Sea to reach Europe. In one article, I thus tried

Figure 9.2   Second Approach: *Contre-enquête* (courtesy of *Le Monde*)

to evaluate whether there was a real a risk of "invasion" in the aftermath of the "Arab Spring." The answer, as Stinellis's chapter also argues, was clearly "no"—even if there were in fact all of a sudden an important number of people crossing by sea. Still in the aftermath of the Arab Spring, referring particularly to the debates over Schengen and between Italy, where many immigrants landed, and France, I did an investigation to know what part of immigration you can "control" and what part you cannot—which is by far the largest part, given the difficulties in enforcing border controls both within and outside the European Union and the ultimate "inexorable" regularization of undocumented workers. The headline on the full page asked two questions: "Is It Possible to Control Migratory Flows?" and "Are the Schengen Accords a Thing of the Past?" (Figure 9.2).

In a different manner, when the government announced, in April 2010, that it wanted to reduce "labor immigration," I wrote an analysis summarizing all the economic theories known about immigration. Thus, I tried to give a balanced answer to this question: Do immigrants take natives' jobs or not?

As with the "*contre-enquêtes*" I have previously described, my aim was to write articles that could answer the questions of any readers, whether pro-immigration or anti-immigration. Doing it that way—which means being as balanced as possible—was, I believe, the only way to help the debate to move forward. As shown in the examples, with these kinds of articles I have tried to explain all that it is possible to explain about immigration to a general public. But even these articles, in the (supposedly) most influential daily newspaper in France, have not changed the debate a lot. Having a look at the letters to the editor, I noticed that my articles reached either people—pro- or anti-immigration—who did not want to be convinced by any kind of explanation or they were preaching to the choir. The only things that help to improve the debate seem to be things that are not already known or not visible—as many of my colleagues argue in this volume. And it is up to the journalist to find time and ways to write about them.

Therefore, a Third Approach

This third approach cannot be used all the time. It does not replace the first two but rather completes them. The general idea is that even if breaking news and controversies on immigration are permanent, it is essential to preserve time to investigate subjects that are not right in the middle of the controversy, such as how immigrants are organizing their community, in which kind of businesses they work, what kinds of networks they establish, their political weight, and so on. This may not seem not original to US readers, but in France it is not an easy job. There are no official statistics on ethnicity. It is not a good strategy to present yourself as a "community leader"—you may be accused of being against the Republic. So it takes a lot of time to find the right people to talk to, people who can offer a counterweight to the well-oiled media machines of usually anti-immigrant politicians.

The Risk of Being Trapped in Sarkozy's Media Strategy

What confirmed for me the necessity of such third approach was precisely Sarkozy's intelligent media strategy, in which I ran a big risk of being trapped if I was not paying attention. In fact, since he was elected in 2007 with an important part of the Front National's votes, Sarkozy had to appear "severe" with the immigrants. In reality, until June 2011 (his rhetoric changed after that date), all his statements were most of the time just words. Deportations of the Romas, for instance, increased for only two or three months; after that, their situation was not good, but there were no more deportations than there were before 2010. (The initiative, during summer 2012, of the new socialist minister of the interior, Manuel Valls, who also decided to evacuate Romas' camps, did not change anything.) Until June 2011, also, deportation centers were almost empty, and only 75 percent of undocumented migrants who were arrested were deported. Since in the past French administrations rarely succeeded in deporting more than 50 percent of arrested undocumented migrants, Sarkozy offered multiple statements underlining the great success of deportations. His strategy was helped by pro-immigrants activists who were reluctant to publicly declare that many immigrants were succeeding in escaping deportation.

In the same way, I found it revealing that, of all the critical articles I wrote about Sarkozy's immigration policy under his presidency, just two were really badly received by his ministry of the interior, which even wrote to *Le Monde*'s editor in chief to complain. In these articles, I had written that after 10 years at the head of France's migration policy (before being elected president in 2007 he was the minister of the interior), Sarkozy had never succeeded in controlling or reducing immigration. Before these articles, Sarkozy's press officer was always very kind to me. He gave me information every time I needed it, even on Sunday or late in the evening. In fact, during this period, Sarkozy seemed to have only one interest: that I write that his policy was a scandal and that it was harder and harder to enter France and that I interview activists saying this. Of course, the situation was not perfect. There were many things to denounce. I did it every time it was necessary. But it was also important to underline that the number of entries had remained more or less the same since 2002: around 200,000 per year.

In order not to fall prey to this successful media strategy—that appeared to feed on critical coverage to highlight an aggressive immigration control policy that was actually way less effective than the political debate indicated—I felt it necessary to start to escape the controversies altogether and provide articles focused on aspects of immigration that were not part of the popular discourse.

"Third Approach Articles": A Way to Change Immigrant Representations

In writing articles that told things differently from what was commonly said about immigration, I was motivated by the idea that this is a way to change representations about the immigrants in public discourse. The aim is not to absolutely give a "positive image" of immigration but to bring complexity to a debate that always represents immigrants as poor, discriminated against, jobless, and so on.

For instance, in June 2011, I decided to write about the relatively unknown Asian community in France. In that article, headlined "Thirst for Visibility," I showed how several community leaders, including a parliamentarian assistant born in Vietnam and a Cambodian working for the office of the Mayor of Paris, complained about racism and a lack of "visibility" in the public debate. The same month I decided to write about the Portuguese community, which is also relatively unknown but is one of the biggest and oldest diaspora groups in France. This time, I went to see them to ask them what they were thinking of the International Monetary Fund's intervention in their home country—and found little sympathy on the part of an aging and hardworking population for their "spendthrift" compatriots.

It was also fascinating, in January 2011, to investigate the Ivory Coast community, for an article headlined "Paris-Abidjan, the Mirror Effect." I did it because, one day, a small dispatch indicated that these immigrants were fighting with each other with knifes and machetes in the middle of Paris's streets. This was at the time when former president Laurent Gbagbo and the new president, Alassane Ouattara, were fighting over control of the country, and political activists were agitating the French community, too. Writing about the local unrest that was affecting immigrants, from those in "afro" hair salons to members of a private club for the African middle class, was a way for me to show how a diaspora is able to reproduce the internal divisions of its home country and how, for an African diaspora, Paris is where a big part of the power and money is.

Another example of my "third approach" was published in December 2011. It was a long article about the Tunisian diaspora in France, headlined "The Quiet Islamism of French Tunisians." In the first democratic elections after Ben Ali left power, Tunisians immigrants were allowed to vote from France. But 30 percent of them voted for the Islamic party Ennahdha, which shocked the French public, which had perceived this group as especially well integrated both socially and economically and, therefore, more progressive politically. Going to interview these immigrants, I gave visibility to their explanations—some felt bound to religious and social traditions, others wanted to speak for their poorest and least emancipated compatriots. Thus, it became clear that they were conservatives, but they did not agree to implement sharia law in their home country, as many clichés were showing them eager to do. A 27-year-old undocumented migrant, who had arrived in Paris through the Italian island of Lampedusa after Ben Ali's fall, said he had voted Ennahdha because it was a "safe" party, not a "political" one. His dream? That it could make Tunisia into a country where, once France regularizes him, he can travel with his wife and children, "by car, on holiday."

12 SOCIÉTÉ

Le Monde
Mardi 6 mars 2012

Yves Béguin et Lahcen Hakki, un passage de témoin en douceur dans la boucherie

A Pantin, le dernier boucher « traditionnel » a cédé son pas de porte à un artisan « halal »

Reportage

Il a pris sa retraite à 58 ans, le jour de l'ouverture de la chasse. Le temps n'était pas mauvais. L'un de ses derniers clients lui a fait la surprise de déboucher une bouteille de champagne à la boutique. Une autre lui est tombée dans les bras en pleurant. C'était il y a tout juste cinq mois, le 25 septembre 2011, après quarante-quatre années de boucherie, et Yves Béguin veut croire que c'est par attachement à sa bonne viande : *« Quand je suis parti, les gens ont congelé des paupiettes. »*

A Pantin (Seine-Saint-Denis), M. Béguin était le dernier de sa lignée. De celle qu'il appelle, avec son parler fort et son accent natal d'Etricourt (Somme), les *« traditionnels »*. Comprendre, les bouchers qui ne sont pas *« halal »*. Depuis son départ, cette commune de 52 000 habitants de la petite couronne parisienne n'a, pour la viande à la coupe, plus que des boucheries musulmanes. Et à commencer par le maire, Bertrand Kern (PS), qui l'a *« obligé à faire un an de plus »*, M. Béguin sait que ça en a chagriné plus d'un.

Du petit manoir de Picardie qu'il s'est offert en récompense de ses années de labeur, où il passe désormais la moitié de ses semaines, M. Béguin a pu entendre, samedi 18 février, les propos polémiques

> « Je lui ai donné ma recette des merguez et une astuce pour les côtes de veau »
> **Yves Béguin**

de la candidate du Front national à l'Elysée, Marine Le Pen, sur les abattages rituels. *« C'est archifaux que toute la viande d'Ile-de-France est halal ! »*, proteste-t-il. La disparition des bouchers *« traditionnels »* et l'essor des *« halal »*, par contre, *« ça... »*, souffle-t-il.

C'est qu'à Pantin, où plus de 20 % de la population est étrangère, beaucoup de vieux bouchers ont, ces dernières années, remisé leur taillanderie au profit de repreneurs musulmans. Comme dans d'autres communes qui accueillent une forte immigration, le passage de relais s'est fait au gré des départs en retraite et de la désaffection du métier.

Avec ses tempes blanches et ses rondeurs acquises au fil des matins à Rungis, M. Béguin en parle aujourd'hui de façon décontractée. Mais ça lui a pris un peu de temps. Car lui aussi a en fait cédé à *« un halal »* : un jeune homme d'origine marocaine, 33 ans, naturalisé, encore sans papiers au début des années 2000.

Lahcen Hakki (à gauche) a repris l'affaire d'Yves Béguin le 25 septembre 2011. GUILLAUME HERBAUT/INSTITUTE POUR LE MONDE

Lorsque M. Béguin a organisé son pot de départ, en novembre 2011, dans une école de Pantin où il avait convié plus de 200 personnes, c'était un non-dit omniprésent. A côté du buffet, il y avait là le maire, sa femme, la teinturière, toute la clientèle d'habitués de M. Béguin. *« Le métier n'existe plus, que voulez-vous ! »*, avait confié, Mme Brassac, centenaire de la ville, à la retraite depuis 1970.

Ses états d'âme sur l'évolution de la profession, M. Béguin les justifie, malgré lui, à travers le récit de ses débuts. Une carrière démarrée à *« 14 ans et un mois »* dans une campagne du Pas-de-Calais parce que *« l'odeur du sang ne le dérangeait pas »*. Un endroit où les *« rares Maghrébins »* étaient, au mieux, ceux qui *« vendaient les tapis sur les marchés »*. Au pire, ceux que *« détestaient les anciens d'Algérie »*.

Au fil de ses années à Pantin, comme résident d'abord, à partir des années 1980, puis comme boucher, dès l'an 2000, M. Béguin a bien vu sa ville *« changer »*. *« Six magasins »* sont devenus *« des taxiphones »* ou des *« boucheries halal »*, a compté son épouse, blonde fragile, assise à côté de lui. Mais M. Béguin a préféré miser sur les *« bourgeois bohèmes »* qui s'installaient, eux aussi, progressivement sur la commune. Pour eux, il ne vendait que produits *« bio »* et viande *« d'origine France »*.

Ce n'est qu'à l'heure de la quête d'un repreneur que M. Béguin a vraiment été confronté à l'évolution sociologique de son environnement. *« Pour le quartier »*, il tenait absolument à un *« traditionnel »*. Pour trouver un héritier digne de l'appellation, il est allé jusqu'à confier la tâche à une agence spécialisée. Mais après cinq mois de recherches, il a compris qu'elle n'y pourrait rien. Et de guerre lasse, il a déposé une annonce sur Lebon coin.fr.

Pointilleux, les Béguin ont tenu à recevoir, un à un, les postulants dans leur boutique, située près de l'église. Une dizaine en tout. *« Des Maghrébins »*, tous. *« Même si on savait que ça serait un halal, on voulait quelqu'un avec une certaine prestance »*, justifie Mme Béguin. Finalement, ils ont trouvé Lahcen Hakki et ont tout bradé : 65 000 euros le fond, sans même la prise en compte du chiffre d'affaires – *« le prix d'il y a dix ans »*.

Face à ce qui lui paraissait comme un grand chamboulement, M. Béguin a toutefois trouvé ses marques dans une sorte de trans-

> Il faut désormais compter trois stations de métro si l'on tient à des rillettes maison

mission douce de son savoir. Une ou deux fois par quinzaine, à chaque retour de ses virées campagnardes, il résiste mal à l'envie de saluer son successeur. Comme une excuse au dérangement, il dispense alors ses conseils : *« Je lui ai donné ma recette des merguez (...) et une astuce pour que les côtes de veau restent tendres »*, détaille-t-il.

Derrière la devanture qu'il a rehaussée d'un store rouge où claque désormais *« boucherie halal »* en lettres blanches, M. Hakki, carrure large, bouc brun, yeux rieurs, jure qu'il accueille avec *« plaisir »* les virées inspectrices de M. Béguin. *« J'ai toujours appris sur le tas avec les Français ! »*, assure-t-il. Avant la boucherie, au Maroc, il a été, tour à tour, tailleur pour femme, maçon et plâtrier.

M. Béguin aurait voulu le convaincre de constituer un petit rayon de bouteilles de vin, comme il l'avait créé pour ses *« bobos »*. Mais M. Hakki a refusé : *« On n'a pas le droit à l'alcool dans la religion musulmane, vous savez ? » « Je lui ai dit : "L'Arabe du coin, il en vend bien du vin !" »*, raconte le retraité. M. Hakki a fini par céder sur les produits bio : *« Mais ça ne se vend pas vraiment »*, glisse-t-il.

A l'ex-boutique des Béguin, M. Hakki a aussi ajouté sa touche personnelle. Sur la vitrine réfrigérée, il a placé deux plats à tajine et des dattes d'Algérie. Sur les étagères, il propose du couscous et des épices orientales. La viande, elle, vient maintenant des *« Pays-Bas, de Belgique, d'Irlande et d'Allemagne »*. Des produits moins chers qui lui ont attiré une clientèle *« plus jeune et plus regardante sur les prix »*.

L'inscription *« halal »* de la devanture a toutefois fait fuir les plus âgés : *« J'ai bien vu que les petites mamies avaient du mal à pousser la porte »*, admet M. Hakki. Certains clients ont aussi été déçus de ne plus trouver de porc. Il faut désormais compter trois stations de métro en direction de Paris si l'on tient à des rillettes faites maison. *« La plupart se sont rabattus sur d'autres viandes »*, assure M. Hakki. Dans la ruelle en pente douce bordée d'immeubles gris où la boucherie poursuit sa vie, le bistro voisin s'appelle L'Avenir. ■

ELISE VINCENT

« Une forme d'intégration locale assez réussie »

PATRICK SIMON est directeur de l'unité Migrations internationales et minorités à l'Institut national d'études démographiques (INED). Il a notamment travaillé, lors de sa thèse, en 1994, sur *« les relations interethniques et interclasses »*, dans le quartier de Belleville, à Paris.

Comment analyser cette transition entre boucheries « traditionnelles » et boucheries « halal » ?

Cela reflète une évolution plus générale des actives économiques des immigrés, avec une hausse du travail indépendant. Ces boucheries répondent à l'expansion d'un marché de consommation locale, mais aussi à une reconversion d'anciens salariés, principalement d'origine maghrébine, qui se mettent à leur compte. Ce n'est donc pas une conséquence d'une immigration récente mais au contraire les effets différés de l'installation des immigrés du Maghreb, de Turquie et d'Afrique subsaharienne dans les quartiers populaires. En ce sens, c'est une forme d'intégration locale assez réussie.

Ce phénomène est-il important ?

Il est difficile d'en fournir un panorama précis. Cela diffère selon l'importance de l'immigration maghrébine et subsaharienne et de la disponibilité des commerces à la reprise. Mais en se développant, les boucheries musulmanes dépassent le cadre de leur clientèle initiale et s'adressent finalement à une clientèle de quartier. En cela, elles deviennent des commerces de proximité, comme l'ont été avant elles les boucheries bretonnes ou corréziennes. Cette banalisation des commerces dits « ethniques » s'observe aussi en Allemagne, en Belgique, aux Pays-Bas, ou au Royaume-Uni.

Dans ce cas de figure, l'immigration comble-t-elle un besoin de l'économie française ?

Le petit commerce a toujours été un secteur d'installation pour les migrants. Mais encore plus aujourd'hui où les transmissions patrimoniales se font rarement dans la famille. Les conditions de travail exigeantes n'attirent plus, et c'est un secteur qui correspond bien à de petits entrepreneurs qui pratiquent des prix bas avec une grande disponibilité horaire. Les stratégies des immigrés coïncident avec cette transition et la fin de la génération des commerçants « traditionnels ». On peut observer la même chose pour les boulangeries. Les cessions se font désormais en faveur de ceux qui sont prêts à faire des sacrifices pour ce métier.

La conséquence de l'essor des boucheries musulmanes, du point de vue des consommateurs, n'est toutefois pas tant qu'elles vendent de la viande halal, mais qu'elles ne proposent pas de porc. Or, dans des quartiers comme Belleville, à Paris, ce sont les rayons boucherie des supermarchés asiatiques qui ont récupéré les clients qui cherchaient du porc.

Le thème de la France « multiculturelle » est relativement absent de la campagne électorale. Qu'en pensez-vous ?

Je ne suis pas sûr que cela soit un mal, car ce sujet est souvent abordé de façon caricaturale. Mais il est certain que les candidats se réfèrent à une France dématérialisée, où l'expression de la diversité est souvent présentée comme conflictuelle. Elle constitue pourtant le quotidien banal d'une majorité de Français. Il faudra bien un jour actualiser le logiciel multiculturel de la France du XXIe siècle. ■

PROPOS RECUEILLIS PAR E. V.

Enquête ouverte sur les emplois de deux figures du PS par un cabinet de conseil

Christophe Borgel et Razzy Hammadi ont été employés, il y a plusieurs années, par Maât

La justice s'interesse à une ancienne société de conseil immobilier qui aurait employé, il y a plusieurs années, dans des conditions jugées douteuses, deux figures connues du Parti socialiste (PS). Il s'agit de Christophe Borgel, aujourd'hui secrétaire national du PS chargé de la vie des fédérations et des élections, et de Razzy Hammadi, secrétaire national aux services publics.

Une enquête préliminaire a été ouverte, en août 2011, par le parquet de Paris sur le cabinet Maât. Les investigations visent avant tout à éclaircir les circonstances dans lesquelles cette SARL a été mise en liquidation en avril 2011, après avoir accumulé un passif important. La responsabilité de l'ex-gérant, Jean Naem, pourrait être engagée, d'après un rapport d'expertise judiciaire du 31 décembre 2011 révélé par Lepoint.fr.

La société Maât bénéficiait d'une bonne visibilité au sein du monde HLM et du « 1 % logement ». Elle proposait aux bailleurs sociaux des missions de conseil et intervenait auprès de collectivités territoriales afin de favoriser le lancement de programmes de construction. A partir du milieu des années 2000, son chiffre d'affaires avait fortement progressé, grâce aux contrats conclus avec l'Association foncière logement, une entité du « 1 % ».

A son zénith, Maât a employé 40 à 45 salariés, dont *« une dizaine qui avaient un affichage politique public »*, explique M. Naem. *« Il n'y avait pas d'élus »* parmi le personnel permanent de la SARL, soutient-il, mais quelques hommes de gauche, titulaires de mandats électifs locaux, ont effectué des missions ponctuelles pour Maât (par exemple un maire d'une commune de Seine-Maritime). Des prestations ont aussi été assurées par des personnalités marquées à droite.

Pour établir son rapport, l'expert judiciaire a entendu d'ex-cadres de Maât. Les déclarations sibyllines de l'un d'eux pourraient laisser supposer que plusieurs personnes ont été payées par le cabinet pour un travail dont la consistance serait incertaine. Ainsi, cet ancien responsable affirme à propos de M. Hammadi : *« Je n'ai pas pu constater de résultats commerciaux à mettre à son actif. »* Salarié de l'entreprise pendant environ un an et demi, de 2008 à 2009, M. Hammadi rétorque qu'il a partagé son bureau *« au quotidien avec une dizaine de consultants »*. *« Tous ont confirmé ma présence et mon travail »*, souligne-t-il. Deux anciens salariés de Maât, interrogés par *Le Monde*, abondent dans le même sens.

Dépenses somptuaires

Le rapport d'expertise judiciaire pointe également le versement en 2008 de 57 000 euros à M. Borgel – qui n'était pas salarié de la SARL mais *« partenaire »*. Les factures de ses prestations *« n'ont pas été retrouvées »*, selon l'expert. Celui-ci cite dans son rapport le témoignage d'un ex-cadre : *« Je n'ai jamais été informé des résultats commerciaux tangibles* [du] *partenariat* [entre Maât et M. Borgel]. *»* Ce dernier fait valoir qu'il n'aura aucun mal à prouver la réalité de ces interventions. *« D'anciens salariés peuvent en attester »*, dit-il – ce que deux d'entre eux ont fait lorsqu'ils ont été questionnés par *Le Monde*. M. Borgel assure que les émoluments octroyés par Maât pouvaient être cumulés avec la rémunération qu'il percevait à l'époque en tant que *« chargé de mission à l'Inspection générale de l'éducation nationale »*.

Autre personnalité épinglée dans le rapport d'expertise judiciaire : Etienne Guéna, un ancien patron du « 1 % logement », issu du patronat, qui fut l'un des responsables de l'Association foncière logement (AFL) lorsque celle-ci était la principale cliente de Maât. Débarqué du Medef, du « 1 % » et de l'AFL en 2008, M. Guéna a été embauché, peu de temps après, par Maât. Son salaire mensuel : environ 16 000 euros. L'expert conclut qu'*« on peut sérieusement »* se demander si M. Guéna n'occupait pas, *« de fait, un emploi fictif »*. Contre-vérité, objecte l'avocat de M. Guéna, Me Bernard Vatier : *« Mon client a eu un emploi réel et effectif, et la rémunération perçue correspondait au salaire contractuel. »*

Quant à M. Naem, l'ancien patron de Maât, il est accusé par l'expert d'avoir commis divers manquements : dépenses somptuaires, utilisation des fonds sociaux à des fins personnelles, spoliation d'une filiale de la société de conseil, etc. M. Naem récuse en bloc toutes ces allégations. Il a l'intention de porter plainte en diffamation contre l'expert. ■

BERTRAND BISSUEL

Enfance « Hypersexualisation » des mineurs : un phénomène marginal mais inquiétant, selon un rapport

L'*« hypersexualisation »* des enfants est un phénomène encore marginal en France mais qui inquiète les parents, souligne un rapport de la sénatrice UMP Chantal Jouanno, remis, lundi 5 mars, au ministère des solidarités. A l'origine de cette mission, des photos parues dans le magazine *Vogue* français de décembre 2010 mettant en scène une petite fille dans des postures suggestives. Mme Jouanno propose notamment d'interdire qu'un enfant puisse être l'égérie d'une marque avant l'âge de 16 ans et de supprimer les concours de mini-miss. – *(AFP.)*

Santé François Hollande favorable aux actions collectives en justice pour les patients

A l'occasion des dix ans de la loi Kouchner sur le droit des malades, le candidat PS à l'Elysée, François Hollande, s'est dit favorable, dimanche 4 mars, dans un communiqué, aux « actions collectives en justice » (class-actions) pour les patients. Il a aussi prôné l'indemnisation sur fonds publics des associations d'usagers pour leur participation à diverses instances de santé, condition nécessaire de leur indépendance.

Fait divers Une famille tuée dans un accident de la route à Romorantin

Quatre personnes d'une même famille recomposée – deux adolescents de 13 et 16 ans, leur père et leur belle-mère – ont trouvé la mort dans une collision, samedi 3 mars au soir, à Romorantin-Lanthenay (Loir-et-Cher). Légèrement blessé, le conducteur de l'autre véhicule, un jeune né en 1987, présentait un taux d'alcoolémie de 0,74 mg dans l'air (contre 0,25 mg autorisé) mais ne se souvient de rien. Il a été placé en garde à vue. – *(AFP.)*

Figure 9.3 Third Approach: A Way to Change Immigrant Representations (courtesy of *Le Monde*)

But perhaps one of the most interesting stories I published with the "third approach" is about an old traditional French butcher living close to Paris, whom I had met by chance.

Yves Beguin—that is his name—one day decided to retire, but he discovered that the only people who wanted to buy his former shop were immigrants coming from the Maghreb, which meant only people who were going to sell halal meat, meat butchered according to Islamic guidelines. One of the reasons for the situation, apparently, was that being a butcher is a hard job, and it is hard to find even one French guy to do it. Most poignantly, in the city of Pantin, where 20 percent of the population is immigrant, Beguin, as a butcher for 44 years, was greatly appreciated by many people because he was the "last traditional French butcher"—so much so that on his last day in the shop, one client popped a bottle of champagne and another fell into his arms, crying. So, at the beginning, he was clearly against the idea of selling his shop to one of these immigrants. But, after a while, he got to know a Moroccan man, Lahcen Hakki, and he finally sold him his butcher shop in what we called "a sweet passing of the torch"—and the older man has continued to mentor his successor (Figure 9.3).

I am especially fond of that story because it was a way to write about halal, which is a very sensitive issue in France, but from the uncommon point of view of French people. I published it right in the middle of the political campaign for the presidency, in March 2012, when the far right was rising and when there was a controversy about halal meat. I knew I was taking risks by doing it. But this article was asking several delicate questions, such as: "Is it a problem if, in a city, people who do not want to eat halal foods cannot do so?" The article points out that shoppers needed to travel to nearby villages if they wanted to get fresh cuts of pork, for example. And, at the same time, the article was forcing readers to look at how France was inexorably becoming a multicultural society, partly due to economic needs—as I concluded the article, the now-halal butcher shop stands near a bistro called "The Future."

CONCLUSION

Immigration is a normal and inescapable process, but it has to be explained to the general reader in order to inform public opinion. For a beat reporter, it is a hard job. It takes time. It was a particularly hard job in France under Nicolas Sarkozy's presidency with the National Front's ascension. But it is important to do it. And media have an essential responsibility in this work. For my part, the "three journalistic approaches" I tried to explain will continue to be my guideline.

Nevertheless, since the victory of François Hollande and the Socialist Party in May 2012 in the most recent presidential elections, immigration issues have become much less a topic of controversy. This does not mean public opinion is no longer concerned with the issue. But it means immigration is not in the headlines every day anymore. This new environment allows much more time to write deeply and peacefully about immigrants. It also offers more freedom to talk about "problems"– such as delinquency—immigrants may cause because there are fewer risks of systematic stigmatization.

So now, the "third journalistic approach" may take more and more space in my agenda, rather than the first two types of stories. A good thing.

10 Shooting Immigration for the World
International Photojournalism at Italy's Borders

Domenico Stinellis
The Associated Press, Rome

In the past two decades, Europe has experienced an epochal demographic redistribution, mostly because of radical political and economic changes or, in some countries, as a direct consequence of war. The most visible migratory flows were those that followed the disintegration of the Soviet empire with the collapse of the Communist regimes in Eastern Europe after 1989 and those related to the so-called Arab Spring, starting in Tunisia in 2010. Both exoduses impacted the Italian borders and, for different reasons, had a large echo in Italian and international media—media that themselves underwent radical, fundamental changes across this period. This chapter explores the different photojournalistic practices during the coverage of these two events, in which I participated as a photographer and photo editor for different international wire services—the vastly understudied backbones of international journalism, as noted in this book.

A historical perspective is necessary when comparing media practices related to facts separated by 20 years. The histories of both the countries making news and the media organizations' home countries evolve, so news about the Albanian exodus or the Arab Spring on Italian television reflects not just those events but also Italian public debates over them and ultimately Italian society as a whole. But the two decades under consideration, from 1991 to 2012, also witnessed the transformation of media practices because of the "digital revolution," probably the biggest innovation in the circulation of information since the invention of radio, so discussion begins with tracing those pivotal changes at the very heart of photojournalistic practices.

ACROSS THE DIGITAL MEDIA REVOLUTION: MOBILITY AND DEADLINES IN ANALOG TIMES

When covering spot news occurring over a wide—and often troubled—area, the ability to move quickly as the scenario changes is vital. Equipment portability and processing speed are fundamental influences on daily news coverage, so it bears remembering that laptop computers capable of handling large picture files emerged only around 1991, for example, when computing power was still just a fraction of today's standards and battery life was more of a dream than a feature. When photography was still analogic and the equipment was bulky and heavy (darkroom, drum transmitters, chemicals), it was impossible to bring it along all day, not to mention the difficulty of finding the electricity to power it. For these reasons, photojournalists, especially those working for wire services such as The Associated Press or United Press International, or Reuters from the late 1980s, had to set up their darkroom/office "behind the lines," typically in a safe place like their hotel that, depending on the event, was never too close to the action. Daily trips to the scene of action often allowed for only a few hours of shooting before the photographer had to come back to process and file the images over fixed landlines in time to meet international deadlines.

With such limitations, the coverage had to be planned every day very carefully, trying to anticipate the action or the absence of it. The roundtrip distance that could be covered daily would routinely and inevitably influence the choice about where to go and what to cover, and so did newspaper deadlines, when print journalism was the backbone of information and for a while later. Wire photographers have always known that even their strongest images, in order to have a sound chance of getting published the following day, would need to land in the newspapers' newsroom before their competitors', especially for events happening close to newspaper deadlines and in countries in a different time zone. A picture not chosen for the edition in print would fatally lack appeal—was "burned," in journalistic jargon—the next day and would probably be soon forgotten, also because the chemical coating of the paper used by Wirephoto® or Laserphoto® printers was very thin and tended to age poorly, if the photos were even archived. So, as late as in the 1980s, the requirements for a winning wire photo were essentially two: hit the wire first and obviously be able to tell the story.

Today we are used to seeing pictures piling up in the newspapers' servers at rates of hundreds per minute. In the 1980s, a newspaper would receive only a few hundred copies a day. A color picture would take around 35 minutes to transmit from one point to another. This means 35 minutes to reach the nearest wire photo hub from the origin and, in the easiest scenario, another 35 minutes to relay it to the newspapers from the wire photo hub. Because of the geographical distances involved and the way the network was designed, most of the time wire photos had to go through more than one hub before reaching the final recipients. The three color separations required to reproduce a color image in print (cyan, magenta, and yellow) were filed back to back independently, and the combined physical analog transfer time for a color photo from the location where the news was unfolding to the end user was slightly less than 50 minutes if relayed through only one hub between the photographer and the newspaper. Usually, the analog lines from the remote location had "noise" and were prone to glitches or failures, so one or more color separations had to be transmitted again in order to complete the process. With bad luck, a single color picture could take up to two hours to get through.

Until the early 1980s, every newspaper had a hardwired connection to the photo network, and every picture had to be routed through this physical network. The total of pictures moved worldwide from a wire photo agency like AP or UPI would never exceed a hundred copies on a typical day. On an average assignment, a wire photographer would file one color picture, if required by the importance of the event, and three or four black-and-white copies. Because of the long transmission times, every "second" black-and-white picture, transmitted at deadline by the wire photographer, would hit the network at least 10 minutes after the first one. The third picture would inevitably increase this delay up to 25 minutes and so on, with publication chances diminishing with every delay. Being able to choose the best picture and to file it first was a vital skill for a wire photographer, and we learned not only to choose pictures quickly but also to shoot photos that would incorporate the maximum possible number of news elements and thus make editing choices faster and possibly easier. The gift of visual synthesis would make for a talented wire photographer, able to wrap up the essential details of a story in the strong composition of a single image and thus to save wire and newspaper budgets transmission, ink, and paper costs.

The combination of synthesis and speed gave birth to most of the iconic images of the 20th century—though we do not know how many excellent pictures were lost in the game of print journalism deadlines, nor do we know if any of those pictures would have deserved the front page had they reached the newspapers earlier. In fact, print journalism had little time tolerance and in many areas adhered to a rigid one-edition-a-day scheme that made most of the late pictures unusable the next day. The importance of transmission speed was somewhat less significant for a global wire service distributing its content in different countries across time zones, so that, even in the 1980s, an AP picture that did not meet the deadlines in one country would probably still be usable in another country in an earlier time zone. However, given that an iconic picture is a social object, speaking to the common cultural background of a public, it often happened that if a prominent newspaper or group of news-papers in an influential country made large use of a photograph that told the story and arrived in time, the majority of the media in that country and those culturally close to it would tend to toe the line, unless peculiar domestic inter-ests would collide as a result of this choice. Deadlines in the 1980s imposed a rigid time frame reflecting wide geopolitical areas of the world and etched in the awareness of wire photographers, for whom transmission speed was even more urgent than for newspaper or magazine photographers, who were the last to convert their equipment from film to digital.

MOBILITY AND DEADLINES IN THE DIGITAL ERA

In the past twenty years, with news photos appearing online and updated 24/7, the concept of deadline has drastically changed. So has the audience: while a website's audience is still geo/language centered, visual content is always accessible across borders. Breaking news pictures that did not meet the local deadlines are still newsworthy online in different time zones. In addition, online news websites require a fast turnover and, through hyperlinks, constantly connect to an infinite variety of content—photos, which can move faster than traditional print and video, always have a chance to show in this new media carousel. Further, online archives proliferate, acting as a time buffer for the wire images that today can be retrieved at any time by new media, whose editorial structure is certainly more flexible than that of 1980s newspapers.

The increased speed and ubiquity of Internet connections, lighter equipment, and a substantial drop in cost have made photojournalistic reporting more flexible, too. That flexibility translated into evolving journalistic practices that influenced the photo coverage of the two migratory processes central to this chapter, the migration of Albanians to Italy at the cusp of the digital age and the so-called Arab Spring in the full swing of it.

THE ALBANIAN EXODUS

The collapse of the Communist regime in Albania in 1991 ignited the largest emigration process in Europe since the population movements at the end of World War II—and it produced some of the most iconic pictures of modern Europe. Around 800,000 people are estimated to have left Albania between 1989 and 2001. About half of them crossed the Adriatic Sea to reach Italy. To understand the combination of factors that led to such exodus, a brief review of the political and economic background that made one-fifth of the Albanian population flee their country in the span of a decade is necessary, and its roots date back to World War II, during which Italy briefly occupied Albania.

The Communist faction of the Resistance, under the leadership of Enver Hoxha, ousted the Nazis in November 1944. Hoxha, who maintained power until his death, in 1985, nationalized all industry and commercial properties, progressively plunging Albania into political and economic isolation after breaking relations with the Soviet bloc and later with China. The majority of the population lived in rural areas, and the weak domestic economy was almost solely based on socialized agriculture. Attempts to migrate were regarded as acts of treason and punished by death or imprisonment. A high-voltage fence lined the border with Yugoslavia and Greece, and even internal mobility was difficult, with some 600,000 concrete bunkers scattered around the country to control population movements.[1]

In the late 1980s, when Ramiz Alia succeeded Hoxha and, feeling the pressure of the changes occurring in the Soviet bloc, tried to launch a series of reforms, it was too late. The opening to the world market that he cautiously tried to start was not supported by an internal economy, whose poor-quality products were uncompetitive. Via the news broadcast by Italian television across the 100 miles of the Otranto strait separating the two countries, Albanians were also watching other Socialist countries struggling for freedom. In December 1985, the six Popa siblings took refuge in the Italian Embassy in Tirana asking for asylum, on the grounds that they were the children of a pharmacist who had been executed by Hoxha, and said that they would commit suicide if they were not sheltered. The Popas remained in the Italian Embassy for five years before they could leave for Italy in May 1990.[2]

The gates had opened for Albanians who sought to grab a chance at a different life for the first time in decades. On July 2, 1990, scores of Albanian men, women, and children assaulted the Western embassies in Tirana, asking for asylum. By July 13, through UN negotiations, some 4,800 refugees were evacuated to Italy and to other hosting countries; in less than six months, as authorities liberalized the issuing of passports, some 20,000 Albanians left the country. In early 1991, economic unrest and social turmoil exploded. On February 9, 1991, about 10,000 people who had converged on the Adriatic port town of Durres gathered at the harbor and hijacked any vessel available to cross the Adriatic Sea, arriving on the southern Italian shores in little groups.

From the beginning, local Italian authorities had difficulties handling the moderate but steady flow, and ordinary citizens from coastal towns across Apulia stepped up to feed and shelter the migrants. On March 7, however, the numbers changed dramatically, and so did the welcome. In the three towns of Bari, Otranto, and Brindisi, separated by a handful of miles, about 25,000 Albanians arrived in a few days, straining the weak emergency measures available beyond capacity. Using a new law requiring that asylum seekers prove they had been persecuted in their own countries for their religion or political creed, Italian authorities denied asylum to Albanians, whom they contended were escaping from poverty.[3] Some ships loaded with people, like the *Tirana* (3,500 people) and the *Lirija* (3,000 people), were kept off the shores of the town of Brindisi, while an Italian delegation flew to Tirana to negotiate a solution. The refugees were allowed to disembark only after two days at sea, pursuant to an agreement that the Italian government would grant a one-year visa to those who would agree to attend training courses, find a job, and be able to make a living.

A few days later, on March 31, the Labor Party, later called the Albanian Socialist Party, won the country's first free elections in 46 years, but many Albanians doubted it would usher in real change, and a second boat exodus started in August. The Italian government now held that, given the democratic elections just concluded in Albania, the new wave could not be treated as refugees fleeing a tense political situation. Most of the 20,000 new arrivals were repatriated. Despite the launch of an Italy-supervised, three-year international operation, "Pelican,"[4] with a military contingent in Albania to help rebuild social order and to distribute humanitarian aid, clandestine migration to Italy continued. From 1991 to 1993, some 300,000 migrants, one-tenth of the population, are believed to have left Albania for Italy and Greece. Later in the 1990s, new crises, including the Kosovo conflict, produced more flows of migrants to Italy, which fluctuated from welcoming refugees to following firm repulsion policies with sometimes tragic consequences, and human smuggling and fraud flourished.

Capturing the Exodus

The dramatic images of the first mass landings in 1991 have become the symbol of the Albanian diaspora, marking a turning point in the way migration was represented in the Italian media. What had been mild interest in the curious ways of "foreigners" became a strong reaction to the social pressure generated by the mass arrival of "immigrants." Immigration had become a problem. The very first media images and narratives were simplistic and contradictory: Albanians were leaving their country compelled by poverty and lack of freedom and would seamlessly integrate in Italian society. A day before the first wave of immigrants arrived in Brindisi, on March 6, 1991, for example, Milan's daily *Il Giorno* fronted a picture of an Albanian couple celebrating their son's first birthday in the southern town. In this picture, the trio appears just like any Italian family, smiling, well dressed, and posing for the photographer—starkly different from the half-naked, hungry Albanians photographed later. The headline warned, "The Albanian Wave Does Not Stop, as Thousands of Refugees Wait in the Ports of Durres and Vlore." But because there were no details about these refugees and the picture was an uncritical stereotype of normality, everything seemed to imply that the Albanian wave was under control and that future newcomers would seamlessly integrate into their new country as the couple shown in the picture had done.

Just two days later, on its March 8 front page, the same newspaper carried a picture taken by AP photographer Massimo Sambucetti that leaves nothing to the imagination about the size of what the headlines now defined an "invasion." The picture shows thousands of Albanians jumping ashore from a ship that reached Brindisi after running a blockade. Some 13,000 migrants had arrived in one day. The same picture was used on the front page of almost every Italian daily, as well as many international newspapers. It was the photo that launched a thousand pictures of ships, covered in immigrants, as the national discourse shifted to concerns about the inability of local and national authorities to handle the immigrants and about the humanitarian emergency and began to consider also what was happening at the other end of the strait.

On August 8, some 15,000 Albanians approached the port of Bari aboard the ship *Vlora*. Their arrival was anticipated by widespread concern generated by dramatic and contradictory news of deadly clashes in the ports of Durres and Vlore between Albanian policemen and would-be migrants.

Upon their arrival in Bari, families with children were accommodated in hotels or Red Cross camps, but Interior Minister Vincenzo Scotti ordered the majority of the new arrivals rounded up and held in the local soccer stadium. Clashes broke out between the migrants, barricaded inside the stadium and with weapons available, and the Italian policemen who were trying to deport them.

Once again, it was AP photographer Massimo Sambucetti who nailed the iconic image of an Italian policeman in riot gear, standing guard over an exhausted, half-naked Albanian lying at his feet (Figure 10.1).

Figure 10.1   "An Italian riot policeman stands over an injured Albanian refugee who tried to escape from Bari's soccer stadium, southern Italy, where he was held with some 8,000 compatriots before being sent home, Friday, August 9, 1991." Courtesy of The Associated Press, photograph by Massimo Sambucetti

The Italian media conveyed mixed sentiments—empathy for the humanitarian crisis and worries about the impact of these new poor on Italian society. But world media offered widespread criticism of the Italian government's use of force in the repatriation—one headline in the London newspaper *Independent,* for example, read "Incompetence and Brutality." Italy's president, Francesco Cossiga, rebuking media criticism during a press conference, criticized Sambucetti's picture, arguing that the photo misrepresented Italy as an unwelcoming country. The set of pictures the AP produced, first in Brindisi and then in Bari, were finalists for the 1991 Pulitzer Prize for spot news coverage—though the AP won its 36th Pulitzer and 19th for photography that year for coverage of the dramatic changes in the Soviet Union. Instead, Sambucetti won the 1992 Baia Chia Photojournalistic Award, which recognizes the best of Italian photojournalistic reporting, with his controversial picture showing the policeman and the Albanian refugee outside Bari's stadium.

The picture incorporated a comprehensive mixture of relevant news elements and strong visual composition. Many TV stations had videographers at the stadium, and their images of the clashes were aired almost at the same time or shortly before the wire photos reached the newsrooms. Sambucetti's photograph summarized exactly what everybody had seen on TV, and it did it in a very convincing way. The picture conveys the idea of the hopeless confrontation between the desperate and starving refugees and the antiriot policemen who were sent to snuff out the revolt. This disproportion is perceived at a visual level too, because most of the image is occupied by the towering policeman, while the worn-out figure of the succumbing Albanian immigrant is confined to the lower corner. Pictures of clashes between groups of people are often confusing because they often fail to reveal the story behind them. Sambucetti's picture is different because it makes immediately clear the disproportion between the forces involved and between the two different personal stories: the emaciated Albanian and the well-equipped policeman, a metaphor for the contrast between the exploited Third World and the developed West.

In 1991, at the AP, we had just started to use the Leafax II negative transmitters. While still analog, they eliminated the need for paper, and the color-film scanner could complete the acquisition of a 35mm negative in a few minutes. An incorporated keyboard and a word processor helped to write the captions, but, more important, the edited pictures could be saved and put in a transmission queue, thus freeing the photographer for other tasks. When I talked with him for this chapter, Sambucetti recalled how this affected his work on the day after the ship *Vlora* arrived in Bari:

> I was in my hotel room, transmitting the pictures of the Vlora, which had just been brought to me by our Bari stringer Luca Turi, and that showed thousands of refugees just disembarked and waiting on the quays of the harbor. All of a sudden, a rattle coming from upstairs

shook the building. I rushed out of my room to check what was causing all that noise and saw dozens, maybe hundreds, of policemen in anti-riot gear running down the stairs. "Where are you going?" I shout. "There is a revolt in the stadium!" A policeman answered me. I just had the time to grab my cameras, queue a couple of pictures in the Leafax and run to the stadium.

At the stadium, he later took the iconic picture of the policeman and the exhausted Albanian—a clear example of how the technology can influence journalistic practices. Before the Leafax II, the historic views of the *Vlora* in the harbor of Bari would have been delayed, with the consequence that they might not have created the international uproar that they did, or Sambucetti would have missed the revolt at the stadium and his iconic picture. In addition, while setting up or packing a Leafax II took just a few minutes, it used to be more difficult and time consuming to set up a traditional darkroom, with a photo enlarger and tanks for chemicals, especially if your hotel room's bathroom—the typical "darkroom on the go"—was not lightproof.

Nevertheless, Sambucetti, who retired from the AP in 2005, recalls transmitting no more than a dozen pictures on a busy day in Brindisi or Bari, still over analog telephone lines, so that a black-and-white image would still take some 10 minutes and a color one about 30 minutes to go through to the local AP bureau. In the 1990s coverage of the migrations from Albania to Italy, most of the pictures taken by AP photographers in Italy were still selected the old way, by looking at color negatives with a loupe.

As anybody who has tried would agree, there is a substantial difference between looking at a real-color image on a high-resolution monitor and looking at a 24-by-35-mm inverted image revealed through an orange-masked celluloid. When choosing a frame from a negative film, what photographers have experienced and seen and remember of the scene influences their choices to a high degree, because some details and especially colors are difficult to gauge looking at a negative film. Because there was generally no time to print or scan all the pictures taken on a single assignment, the selection of the right image from a negative film was a critical task that would distinguish good photojournalists and ultimately determine the success of their pictures, something that has dramatically changed in the digital era. Today, we can remotely edit one or multiple photographers' production from the newsroom or a defined editing position with minimal assistance on their part.

By way of comparison, one more illustration of the "old" photojournalism in covering the Albanian exodus, this time from Greece where about half of the migrants went. Dimitri Messinis, the AP's chief photographer for Greece who was then working for the European Pressphoto Agency, was one of the first to record the arrival of Albanians at the Greek border. On December 31, 1990, he drove about 600 kilometers from Athens to the border village of Sagiada: "It was about 4 a.m. when we reached Sagiada, and two people playing cards in a café were the only villagers awake. I asked them if they had seen any Albanians around. They went agape and laughed at me: 'What are you talking about?'" The Greek photographer decided to move a bit forward toward the border, but as he started the engine of his car, he realized that it would not be necessary. "They came out like ghosts from the dark," Messinis recalls. The Greek side of the border was not guarded, and the refugees came in easily—some of them Albanian soldiers themselves or ethnic Greeks living in Albania—and even after the Greek government set up camps near the border, they continued to move about freely. No jarring pictures here, even though the total numbers of immigrants were the same as in Italy.

While this chapter does not aim to explore the intricacies of the 1990s exodus or the entire dynamics of news coverage, the difference in media coverage of the Albanian migrations to Greece and to Italy illustrates how the visual impact of news can influence its dissemination and relevance. In 1991, the Albanian diaspora split into two streams, with the bigger one bound for Greece and the other for Italy. But news relevance was disproportionate to the numbers, and two factors seem to have played a decisive role. The flow bound to Italy across the sea –with its human pathos of half-wrecked ships braving rough seas to run Italian blockades—was more *visible* in the process, while Albanians fleeing to Greece became massively visible only when they had already settled in the camps. There was never a situation when 20,000 refugees would cross the Albanian-Greek border all at one time—and, as John Hooper's chapter in this book argues, the media tend to focus on visible migration and ignore the other, often larger, dynamics. As photojournalists, of course, we are largely responsible for what becomes literally visible.

The second factor links to the broader cultural background of the public. Unlike the images of Albanians escaping to Greece, the pictures of the boat exodus across the Adriatic Sea incorporated a strong and unprecedented allegoric value. In the medieval *Divine Comedy,* a journey through Hell, Purgatory, and Paradise that is the preeminent work of Italian literature and one of the world's greatest poems, Charon ferries souls in a boat across the river Acheron to Hell. The skeletal silhouettes of the tens of thousands of dehydrated and starving Albanians, framing the decks of ships like the *Vlora,* reminded Italians of the damnation scenes described by Dante Alighieri. Significantly, the Albanian exodus was also described by the Italian media as "biblical," referencing the departure of the Israelites from Egypt, the crossing of the Red Sea, and the Israelites' wandering in the desert on their way to the Promised Land.

What was seen happening along the coast of Italy—standing in for the borders of the Western world—was something that did not need to be excessively elaborated because it already resonated in the common cultural background. News photographers are always struggling to condense a story into a single strong picture. To achieve that, they need to balance composition and news elements, technical accuracy of the reproduction and spontaneity in the subject, and overall appropriateness of the form to the content. The pictures produced during the Albanian exodus—like Sambucetti's ships and policemen—incorporated most of these attributes and became iconic.

THE ARAB SPRING

Less than 20 years after the Albanian exodus, another wave of migrants dominated the news in Italy. This time, the migrants came from the Middle East and North Africa in the aftermath of the second Iraq war and the Arab Spring. Both photojournalism and the international context had dramatically changed, with the geopolitical polarization turning from East-West to North-South and the war on terror taking over from the Cold War. The demonstrations and protests that started in Tunisia in December 2010 shook the Arab world and rapidly expanded to Egypt and Libya, overturning the long-established political regimes in those countries.

A 26-year-old Tunisian street seller, Mohamed Bouazizi, set himself on fire on December 18, 2010, to protest police corruption. He died after 17 days, and a series of increasingly violent street demonstrations followed, ultimately leading to the ouster of longtime president Zine El Abidine Ben Ali in January 2011. In Egypt, Abdou Abdel-Moneim Jaafar, a 49-year-old restaurant owner, set himself alight in front of the Egyptian parliament. His act of protest helped instigate weeks of unrest and, in February 2011, the resignation of President Hosni Mubarak. In Libya, after 42 years of Muammar Gaddafi's tribal regime, an organized antigovernment protest in the form of guerrilla warfare began in February 2011 and quickly seized most of Benghazi, the country's second-largest city. As government forces failed to quell the protests, the rising death toll, numbering in the thousands, drew international condemnation. An international coalition led by France, the United Kingdom, and the United States intervened with a bombing campaign against the pro-Gaddafi forces. Tripoli fell in August, and Gaddafi was captured and killed two months later. Throughout this period, new waves of migrants escaping the violence landed on Italy's southern shores, again dominating the news—but this time, unlike the gripping images of Albanian ships overloaded with desperate refugees 20 years earlier, migrants arrived in small vessels and groups of 20 to 30 people, failing to inspire the kind of massive coverage that the high visual impact of the Albanian exodus had sustained.

The Role of Social Media

In the interval of time separating the two migrations, the development of the Internet and the birth of social media have revolutionized the way news is collected and distributed. In an interview on Al Jazeera, speaking of the self-immolation of Mohamed Bouazizi, political analyst Ali Al-Bouazizi recalled: "On 17 December 2010, a relative called me to say that a young man had set himself afire in front of the governor's office. Some of my family members, many activists and politicians gathered in front of the building. Almost all the residents of Sidi Bouzid were here to see what was going on. I just grabbed my mobile phone and started filming. . . . I edited the video with some of my friends and posted it on Facebook. The video was really touching. Everybody now knows what 17 December 2010 means."[5] The video was quickly broadcast by Al Jazeera and then by networks around the world, galvanizing Tunisians who realized the power of their personal media in a country with no press freedom.

Al-Bouazizi, speaking of the video he took with his mobile phone, argued that, "if it weren't for the video, nobody would have ever known about the fact. It had a decisive role in winning the sympathy of the public opinion." That was particularly true for the majority of the population living in remote areas of the country where domestic news was usually even scanter than in Tunis and where the unemployment rate was very high. The Ben Ali regime realized how devastating the impact of the videos could be and promptly tried to counter the power of the dramatic images taken spontaneously by residents in the streets with a last gasp of old-style paternalistic propaganda. Ben Ali was shown, in a picture released by his office, visiting Bouazizi at his bedside in a hospital.

It will certainly take some time before historians explain the complex dynamics that led to a quasi-continental upheaval in a peculiar historical and macroeconomic conjuncture that goes well beyond one person's tragic act captured on video.

Nevertheless, there is no doubt that the social networks had a key role in spreading the protest and showing it to the world. Habitual bloggers as well as ordinary citizens had their part in breaking the established monopoly of information in most of the countries involved. When these people saw the pictures and videos that they had shared being broadcasted worldwide by the major networks, they not only felt themselves in the limelight but also realized that they had a role in keeping the world's attention focused on their situation through social media such as Facebook and Twitter, which, although recent innovations, were already widely spread among the "people of Internet."

Twitter's breakthrough reporting moment had come with the picture of frightened passengers standing on the wings of a plane, uploaded by one of the passengers in the first ferry that approached US Airways flight 1549 after its emergency landing in the frigid waters of the Hudson River, in New York City, on January 15, 2009. After the presidential elections in Iran later in 2009, social media became the natural aggregator for pictures produced by the citizens during the ensuing riots. On May 1, 2011, the news of Osama bin Laden's death was tweeted from the White House before President Obama announced it to the public.[6] Mainstream media realized that from then on they needed to monitor social networks as a possible source of information.

Many of them decided to be part of it: today the AP is officially on YouTube and Facebook, and it has a Twitter account followed by 1.6 million people. Some 900 AP staffers have personal accounts and have their own followers, and Twitter had some impact on our photo operations in Italy, too, as the Arab Spring unfolded.

Covering the Arab Spring

During the international military operation in Libya, Italy contributed its air bases for the air strikes, so, as the AP's national photo editor for Italy, I was obviously involved in the coverage. Because of the tight security, very little information was available from the military. We sent photographers outside most of the bases requesting permission to photograph the activities related to the various missions; when they could not enter the base, photographers would shoot from a distance, with a telephoto lens, the planes coming and going. For someone like me, who is not an expert in military aviation, it was almost impossible to identify the type, nationality, and the ordnance of the different assets—but captions had to contain all these details. A big help came from Twitter, particularly from a couple of its users. David Cenciotti is an expert on military aviation and a renowned blogger who maintains the website "The Aviationist."[7] During the nearly eight months of war, his tweets helped us to cross-check many details that we included in the captions and in some cases enabled us, after achieving a better understanding of the development of the operations, to decide whether and how to assign photographers.

Although I had already ventured in the labyrinthine world of social media, it was only during the Arab Spring that I fully realized the potential that these new media have as a source. Obviously they need to be handled with extreme caution. We must not let the apparent spontaneous nature of the format beguile us about the truthfulness of the source, because, just as in real life, when a source's identity is concealed, there is room for all sorts of falsification. As a rule, we always try to verify by phone or in person, when possible, who is behind a tweet or a post on Facebook. Social media are tools that news organizations and freelancers regularly use together with traditional sources. A number of litigations, however, on issues like privacy, content property, and news manipulation have made it clear that, while most of the success and appeal of social media reside in the ease of access and freedom of expression they appear to incorporate, they are a double-edged sword in cases when their content is fraudulently rerouted into commercial networks, for example, or when somebody passes himself or herself off as somebody else to deceive the public or to harm commercial interests.

Recently, a judge in New York ruled that images made available to the public through social media could not be used for commercial purposes by third parties. The case concerned the pictures that a professional French photographer, Daniel Morel, had posted on Twitter in the aftermath of Haiti's earthquake and that were later disseminated by Agence France-Presse without permission.[8] But the value of social media for traditional media is not just in the possibility of reusing content. Twitter and Facebook are also a phenomenal resource for finding contacts that virtually spans horizontally across nations and continents and vertically across different social and cultural groups. And they are just one facet of the transformation of news media in the digital age.

In 1995, the AP introduced its online Photo Archive, the image container on which AP Images, the AP's commercial division, was built in 2004. Today almost all traditional newspapers have gone online with editions that are constantly updated and frequently enriched with the multiformat features that the Web offers. A wire photo today has good chances to survive its deadline. Online archives and websites act as a time buffer, making every wire photo available regardless of how fast it was delivered and rendering nearly obsolete the traditional deadlines of the early 1990s. Moreover, websites today tend to collect pictures into galleries that are updated in real time and, most of the time, kept available for a long time.

Smartphones are increasingly replacing personal computers in the business of news dissemination, and this new delivery platform is also having an effect on photojournalism. Almost all news providers have applications for smartphones that can deliver general news content or on-demand selections of it to the final reader. While the advent of ultrafast 4G phone networks will change delivery, for now the data speed of the mobile network is too slow and expensive in many countries to support the frequent update of pictures. The small size of the screen of these devices creates quite an interface design problem that reflects on their ability to keep pace with frequent updates of content and, significantly when compared to traditional Web pages, advertising. These structural limitations seem to have revived a rigid deadline system for news pictures delivered to the portable device platform. Nevertheless, digital technology has also changed photojournalism on the ground.

The Role of Technology in the Field

Twenty years after the Albanian exodus, when the Arab Spring broke, the diffusion of digital technology throughout the field had already changed the practices of photojournalism. Since the early years of the 21st century, almost all wire photo agencies had fully converted their cameras to digital. The era of film processing was definitively over. From the Leafax or similar machines, the editing had moved to personal computers, imposing a transformation of the professional profile of news photographers and photo editors.

The first digital camera aimed to photojournalists that successfully hit the professional market was the AP NC2000e, developed by the AP with Kodak in 1994 and based on a Nikon film camera. The camera, 1.3 megapixels for a cool US$18,000, seemed very advanced, but, by today's standards, it is difficult to understand how we got usable pictures out of it. If shooting black-and-white photos was problematic, color photography was just guesswork with the NC2000e, showing electronic noise the size of snowflakes. By the early 2000s, almost all wire photographers were shooting digital. With the dramatic improvement of the speed of data transmission over cellular phone lines and, later, data streams, photojournalists were eventually able to file their pictures before they got back to base at the end of the shooting. Transmission times dropped significantly, with a color image taking less than 10 minutes to move. Today, in spite of the fact that the resolution of digital pictures has doubled, a color picture takes not more than a minute to transmit over a 3G data connection and just a few seconds where 4G connectivity is available.

In picture resolution and color rendition, today's sensors equal, if not surpass, those of traditional film. The average professional camera has 16/24 megapixels, and the larger sensors make it possible to shoot with available light up to the equivalent of 6400 ISO without significant quality degradation—five times more than the NC2000e. Improved stabilization systems incorporated in the lenses stretch this limit by an additional two notches. In general terms, it is possible today to work in extremely poor light conditions but achieve an overall satisfactory picture quality.

Because a photojournalist can transmit pictures from the spot and as the action unfolds, it seems that news photography today has unleashed all the potential that the digital technology has infused into it. A clear example of that is represented by the work of AP photographer Emilio Morenatti, who was covering the Tunisia-Libya border in the spring of 2011. Morenatti was assigned to cover the refugees arriving from Libya, fleeing the war and the unrest in that country. His pictures of this exodus and of the refugee camps in Tunisia offer an insightful slice of life of the hundreds of thousands of foreigners who were living in Libya and who were displaced, mostly to nearby Tunisia and Egypt, when the war begun. The majority had sought work in Libya from their homelands in Ghana, Bangladesh, and Pakistan.

Such pictures would have been unavailable to a wire photographer of the early 1990s, who would have been entangled with the print deadlines and probably discouraged from venturing into fruitless working hours outside their rigid time frame. Instead, the type of pictures that Morenatti shot in March 2011 gave a phenomenal added value to the AP's report on the consequences of the war and ultimately contributed to provide readers with wider and deeper information.

This is the case, for example, for the picture of a lonely refugee walking along a road at moonrise. The picture was taken at 8:50 p.m. local time, in Tunisia, on March 19, 2011 (Figure 10.2).

Another image, this one of a boy selling eggs from a van near a refugee camp in Ras Ajdir, Tunisia, on Sunday, March 20, 2011, was taken at 10:31 p.m. Just a few years ago, it would have been unthinkable for a wire photographer to venture into such working schedule (Figure 10.3).

Figure 10.2 "A man from Ghana, who used to work in Libya and fled the unrest in the country, walks alongside a road after crossing from Libya at the Tunisia-Libyan border, in Ras Ajdir, Tunisia, Saturday, March 19, 2011." Courtesy of The Associated Press, photograph by Emilio Morenatti

Figure 10.3   "A boy sells eggs from a van near to a refugee camp set up for displaced people who recently crossed over the border into Tunisia, fleeing from the unrest in Libya, in Ras Ajdir, Tunisia, Sunday, March 20, 2011." Courtesy of The Associated Press, photograph by Emilio Morenatti

In fact, because of the better picture resolution and transmission speed, together with the improved print quality of newspapers and magazines and the peculiarity of Web formats, the visual narrative of today's wire photo services has changed greatly. Bold, direct images with a few strong, clear details have left room for a more inventive approach. Because coated papers and processed inks can reproduce finer details in vivid colors, a wire photographer today can indulge in fine textures and shades of color while composing pictures to illustrate a story. Freed from the need to process film, the contemporary wire photographer has more time to look for great shots and more time to shoot them, producing more pictures on every assignment. The postprocessing and filing of images are based on a portable device and can be remotely controlled by the newsroom. None of this translates into an easier life for photographers, however. Caption descriptions are increasingly complex and incorporate more details every day. Unlike the early 1990s, today when a photograph hits the wire it already incorporates all the metadata that would properly locate it in the online archives. The international-standard IPTC fields are used not only by the AP but also by any media that wish to easily retrieve the same image after some time or simply allow the photo editor at a newspaper to quickly and effectively search the daily photo stream.

So today's photojournalists are required to collect and type in a whole lot of additional information regarding the pictures they take, which can paradoxically take longer than it took in the analog era to develop the film and print hard copies. Computer skills are now required to handle a photo assignment, and this simple fact has made the photojournalist a new professional figure. Moreover, the use of industry-standard file formats and personal computers, instead of heavy electronic darkrooms based on proprietary systems, has obviously increased the occasional use of content from freelance photographers or even from ordinary citizens. Today to send a picture to the AP, Reuters, or AFP is as easy as attaching it to an e-mail. At the time of the Albanian exodus, no photo editor would even think of looking for images taken by anyone other than professional photographers. In fact, before the diffusion of digital cameras and, later, of camera-equipped portable phones, intentional citizen photography of news events was extremely rare, while today blurry, grainy cell phone stills seem to have nearly replaced iconic professional images.

Covering the Invasion That Never Happened

This new and complex interplay of digital media, public interest and professional photojournalism brings us to the coverage of the European migration aspect of the Arab Spring. For centuries, the Sicily Strait has been a corridor between Tunisia and Italy, bringing migrants, commerce, and occasionally war to both sides. From the end of the 19th century through the 1930s, an intense flow of migrants looking for a better life reached the Tunisian coast from Sicily. Census data from 1926 show that of the 173,281 Europeans living in Tunisia, 89,216 were Italians and only 71,020 were French—an anomaly that made a scholar call Tunisia "an Italian colony under French administrators."[9] The flow reversed in the last decade of the 20th century, with undocumented immigration to Italy from North Africa crossing the Sicily Strait regularly. Human trafficking from North Africa has never stopped, not even after the tragedy of the F174, an old, severely overloaded wooden ship that sank off the coast of Sicily the night of December 25, 1996, dragging to the bottom some 283 lives in what has been dubbed "the Christmas massacre" and that is described in detail in Hooper's chapter in this book.

Soon after the revolts in North Africa revealed their vast proportions, Italian politicians and opinion makers in favor of stricter immigration control tried to awaken in the public the specter of a mass invasion. Again, the use of metaphors like "biblical exodus" and "apocalypse" in the xenophobic propaganda fomented public concern, which was instrumental in seeking internal political support to solicit EU aid.

It is true that, over just a few months, the emigration flows from North Africa to southern Europe and especially to Italy—the principal terminal of what is called "Central Mediterranean Route"—increased sharply. About 11,000 arrivals were logged in 2009, 4,500 in 2010, and about 64,000 in 2011, double the 36,000 peak recorded in 2008, possibly because the financial crisis in Greece—another EU border—made that country much less attractive to migrants than Italy.[10]

With the exception of Tunisians, the majority of migrants landing in Sicily were not nationals of the countries where the Arab Spring had broken out; despite the alarmist declarations by both Italian and Libyan leaders, the majority of those fleeing the war there went to bordering Tunisia and Egypt instead of proceeding to the traditional routes of clandestine migration across the Sicily Strait. Of the 797,000 migrants who crossed Libyan borders, only 26,000, or about 3.4 percent, went to Italy, and among them very few were Libyan nationals; most were sub-Saharan Africans or Asians.[11] Nevertheless, the increased flow, which reached its peak in the first three months of 2011, placed Italy that year in fourth place (behind the United States, France, and Germany) among countries with the most requests for asylum.

With the collapse of the various dictatorial regimes in those northern African countries that were at the same time a destination and a starting point to Europe for migrants from the Horn of Africa and the sub-Saharan regions and that up to that time had more or less controlled clandestine migration, people saw the opportunity to reach Europe. Soon after the first boats landed in Sicily from Tunisia in February 2011, it was clear, once again, how inadequate the Italian laws on immigration were to manage a humanitarian emergency. Most of the procedures provided by the international agreements on repatriation between Italy and Libya (2009) and Tunisia (1998) were not applicable to people who were only temporarily displaced or working in Libya or Tunisia but were originally from third countries. Because of the power vacuum in both Libya and Tunisia, any collaboration with the authorities to resolve the different issues was impossible.

In this chaos, Italian media attention was attracted by a fierce polemic that erupted between the Italian government and the EU Commission, voiced by Italy's interior minister, Roberto Maroni. Italy contended that it was sustaining the whole cost of immigration pressure at Europe's southern borders. Forecasting mass migration from North Africa as a reaction to turmoil there, the Italian government asked the EU for 100 million euros to face the emergency. Speaking at the European Council for Justice and Internal Affairs in Brussels on February 24, 2011, Maroni said, "I'm asking Europe to adopt all the necessary measures to face a catastrophic humanitarian crisis . . . an invasion of a million, million and a half people that would bring any country to its knees."[12] Other European colleagues minimized the possibility of a crisis and ridiculed Italy's request, noting that the EU had already granted 25 million euros to Italy to deal with the emergency of the first landings, but what Italy was seeking was the recognition of long-term support. In the press conference after the meeting, Maroni bitterly remarked on the lack of "burden-sharing": "It's no news, however maybe I deceived myself into believing that this humanitarian emergency could convince [other countries] that Europe has to develop a system of European asylum."[13] This rhetorical battle was happening before any Western involvement began in Libya that might also address the mass exodus threat; the Secretary General of NATO had in the same days denied rumors of a possible military action.[14]

Maroni's concerns were widely reported by the Italian media, and the story of potential mass migration became the story of a feud between Italy and the EU after he reacted to the EU Council for Internal Affairs' dismissal of the aid request by saying, "I'm asking myself if our presence in the EU still makes any sense."[15]

Thus, interestingly, the story of millions of people in the process of being displaced by war from the country where they were living and working came out in the Italian media as a dispute between Italy and the EU over the distribution of funds provided by the Schengen treaty. Soon a series of squabbles emerged between the Italian minister and his political opposition and between him and his European colleagues.[16]

After days of this tug-of-war, journalists, photographers, and cameramen who had gathered in the tiny Sicilian island of Lampedusa, only 61 miles from Tunisia, were still waiting for the expected mass invasion. Lampedusa is a beautiful island that lives off its small fishery industry and boutique tourism. In winter, not much goes on in the island, and the connections with the mainland are less frequent, often interrupted by bad weather. Initially the increase of arrivals of would-be immigrants was sporadic, and, having to cope with ever-shrinking budgets, many news media were waiting for a clear sign that the announced catastrophe was really going to happen before setting up a large-scale operation in the island. Going there too early would mean a waste of resources, but not being there when the mass arrivals started would mean missing the story.

At AP, we first had a local stringer cover the modest increase in arrivals, with the plan of beefing up the coverage when the number of immigrants would escalate. I remember that the last thing I would do at night and the first thing I would do in the morning before deciding the type of coverage we would need every day was to check the weather bulletins. If there was no wind in the strait, the crossing would be easier and the coming day probably a busy one for our photographer in Lampedusa. From the start of the unrest in Tunisia in January to the middle of March 2011, about 8,700 migrants arrived on the island—a significant number but far from the six-figure flood dreaded by Minister Maroni.[17] The exodus situation worsened as the season for good weather approached. By the end of June, the United Nations estimated that 40,000 migrants[18] had transited through the detention center in Lampedusa, many of them Tunisians who wanted to go to France, where most of them had families.

On March 14, 2011, Marine Le Pen, the daughter of France's longtime far-right leader, who had taken over his National Front party in January, visited the island. The initiative caused some criticism because of her party's anti-immigration policy, but she insisted before her arrival that her visit was aimed at gathering information, not at provocation.[19] When in Lampedusa, she advocated turning migrants back to sea before they could reach European shores. Instead of patrolling European shores, she said Europe's navies "should go as close as possible to the coasts from where the clandestine boats departed to send them back."[20] In line with the Italian position, she warned that the migrants were arriving "in proportions that Italy can no longer handle. . . . In truth, we are about to witness a catastrophe."[21] At a press conference in Rome, she continued in an alarmist tone that Italy should prepare to "accept half of the world population" if it started taking in economic refugees.[22] Le Pen's visit to Lampedusa attracted most of the media attention the same day that at least five new boats, laden with migrants, were approaching the island—a stark reminder of how the story had become political instead of focusing on migration itself.

While the EU support requested by Italy was still under scrutiny, the detention center in Lampedusa started to get more and more crowded every day as the transfers to other immigration facilities slowed down and were finally halted on March 15. Designed for 800 people, the center contained some 2,700 immigrants on the day Le Pen arrived. In very little time, the number of migrants held in Lampedusa equaled and occasionally surpassed the number of island residents, about 5,000. Those who could not be sheltered in the detention center were allocated open spaces outside it, with little water and poor sanitation.[23] Tension between the immigrants and the islanders soon reached a boiling point, especially with the approach of the tourist season, the main source of income for the island. [24]

On March 30, Premier Silvio Berlusconi, who had been under fierce criticism for his handling of the emergency, flew to Lampedusa and promised to the angry residents that in 48 to 60 hours he would have all the immigrants evacuated on six chartered ferries that were already heading to the island. Among other things, he promised tax breaks in compensation, the support of his media empire in promoting tourism in Lampedusa, the creation of a resort, and the nomination of local residents for the Nobel Peace Prize. He also promised that he would buy a 2-million-euro waterfront villa in the island.[25] Opposition Democratic Party leader Pierluigi Bersani alleged that Berlusconi was trying to divert public attention from a measure being worked on in the parliament that would have trimmed the statute of limitations for first-time offenders and thus canceled Berlusconi's ongoing trial for allegedly bribing British lawyer David Mills.

The altercations between Italy and the EU and between Berlusconi and his opponents, fueled by the increasing migratory flows from North Africa, frequently prevailed in the Italian media over the narrative of the humanitarian implications. After Operation Odyssey Dawn started on March 19 to enforce a UN no-fly-zone resolution over Libya and later continued as Operation Unified Protector under NATO, the news of the war in Libya obscured that of the odyssey of millions of people moving across North Africa and to the border shores of southern Europe.

CONCLUSIONS

National and international media covering the Arab Spring and its consequences on Italy's shores followed different narratives and some new practices. At the AP, we were able to cover the refugee emergency at the Tunisian and Egyptian borders with Libya thoroughly as never before in such cases, thanks to the improved technology in communication, digital cameras' sensors, and news dissemination. In this regard, the difference with the coverage of the Albanian exodus in the 1990s is huge. Picture transmission speed passed from 30 minutes to a few seconds. The gap between the shoot and the transmission is virtually inexistent today, while in the 1990s it could take several hours before the film could be processed and the pictures transmitted. In the 1990s, the number of pictures that a photographer could shoot on a daily basis was limited, not only by circumstances such as light availability but also because the more rolls of film a photographer shot, the longer it would take to develop and choose among them. Today all photographers have to do is check their takes in the LCD real-color display of their camera.

The guesswork implied in choosing from negatives inevitably reflected on editorial decisions, and in many cases the photographer out shooting was the only one who could look at the entire production. Photo editors could see and edit only what they received from the photographer. Today, photographers transmit more pictures every time, and photo editors can choose from wider collections or even check remotely all the production that photographers downloaded to the computer they carry. The seamless deadlines of the Internet and social networks have replaced the day-by-day pace of print media. The temporal frame in which photojournalists operate today has changed. On one hand the multiplication of deadlines has imposed a phenomenal speed on the production process, while on the other hand the persistence of the online content, which different studies quantify in several days,[26] reduces the importance of the time factor for the fortune of wire photos.

This chapter analyzed how the Albanian exodus was depicted in some iconic images, whose strength resided in their profound visual link with some common cultural facts and in the fit with prevailing media narratives. Looking at the pictures emerging from the coverage of the Arab Spring, which took place over a much wider area, in a time of constant uproar and among a populace shaken by war, it is hard to find an equivalent. This is not unique to the Arab Spring, however. Other recent epochal events that have been widely represented in the media share the lack of a single defining image, perhaps because of the proliferation of images that prevent any photograph from becoming the collective memory of an event. The cultural icons of today are therefore the result of a visual accumulation upon which their evoking power is based.

In fact, the Arab Spring, while generating a myriad of images, is not remembered for any particular one of them. Significantly, the shot that everybody remembers is that of the fixed video camera broadcasting live,

24 hours a day, from Tahrir Square in Cairo. When we think of Tahrir as the icon of the Arab Spring, we are practically referring to a combination of images, evolving day after day. None of these images isolates a particular moment in time: quite the contrary. It is the continuity of the broadcast, showing the upheaval going on for days that was the peculiar characteristic of the revolt. There have been protests before in Egypt and elsewhere in northern Africa, but they have been only sporadic, although sometimes violent. In this case the fixed camera showed a protest, persisting through many days, as the background against which the reports on the fate of the Mubarak regime were played. The syntax of this narrative seems the same as that we have absorbed from TV's reality shows, a strong background that supports the unfolding of news, as the house is the backdrop for personal stories unfolding in a "domestic" environment like that of *Big Brother*.

These simple facts seem to suggest the death of the iconic image, as we knew it. From what we have seen in the two examples discussed in this chapter, the practices in covering immigration during 20 crucial years at the southern border of Europe have been modified by the progress of technology, by an ever-shrinking economy, and by the different ways news photos are disseminated today. In 1991, a single shot by a photojournalist became the center of the storm. Today, images shot by nonprofessionals and spread on social media are talked about as causes of revolutions. For better and for worse, traditional news media have a wider reach but perhaps a diminishing grip on the world's understanding of what literally moves it.

NOTES

1. Russell King and Julie Vullnetari, *Migration and Development in Albania* (Brighton, UK: Sussex Centre for Migration Research, 2003).
2. Edwin E. Jacques, *The Albanians: An Ethnic History from Prehistoric Times to the Present* (Jefferson, NC: McFarland, 1995).
3. Legge 28 febbraio 1990, n. 39, G.U. n. 49 del 28 febbraio 1990 [Law n.39, published in the *Gazzetta Ufficiale* n. 49 of Feb. 28, 1990].
4. http://www.esercito.difesa.it/Attivita/MissioniOltremare/MissioniconiReparti/MissioniNazionali/Pagine/PellicanoAlbania.aspx.
5. "Revolution through Arab Eyes," Al Jazeera English, February 14, 2012, http://www.aljazeera.com/programmes/revolutionthrougharabeyes/2012/02/201221125310989525.html.
6. Brian Stelter, "How the Bin Laden Announcement Leaked Out," *New York Times,* May 1, 2011, http://mediadecoder.blogs.nytimes.com/2011/05/01/how-the-osama-announcement-leaked-out/?src = mv.
7. http://theaviationist.com.
8. Agence France Presse v. Morel, US District Court for the Southern District of New York, No. 10–02730.
9. Moustapha Kraiem, *Le fascisme et les Italiens de Tunisie: 1918–1939* (Tunis: Cahiers du CERES, 1969); Laura Davi, "Memoires italiennes en Tunisie," Mémoire de maîtrise: Etudes italiennes, Tunis I, 1996.
10. Frontex Risk Analysis Unit, *Frontex Annual Risk Analysis 2012* (Warsaw: FRAU, 2012).

11. International Organization for Migration, Department of Operations and Emergencies, *Humanitarian Response to the Libyan Crisis. February-December 2011 Report* (Geneva: IOM, 2012).
12. "Maroni chiede aiuto su immigrati, ma l'Ue non condivide l'allarme," RAINews, February 24, 2011, http://www.rainews24.rai.it/it/news.php?newsid = 150402.
13. Ibid.
14. "Immigrati, ancora scontro Italia-UE," *la Repubblica*, February 24, 2011, http://www.repubblica.it/esteri/2011/02/24/news/libia_politico-12864700/.
15. "Immigrazione, Italia bocciata," *Quotidiano*, April 11, 2011, http://qn.quotidiano.net/politica/2011/04/11/488278-immigrazione_italia_bocciata.shtml.
16. Ibid.
17. "Far-right Leader Le Pen Arrives in Lampedusa," *The Guardian*, March 14, 2011, http://www.guardian.co.uk/world/feedarticle/9545007.
18. "Angelina Jolie and UNHCR Chief Guterres Visit Boat People on Italian Island," *United Nations High Commissioner for Refugees News Stories*, June 19, 2011, http://www.unhcr.org/4dfe05879.html.
19. Patricia Thomas, "Far-right leader says Europe can't handle migrants," The Associated Press, March 14,2011, retrieved from: http://www.washingtonpost.com/wp-dyn/content/article/2011/03/14/AR2011031401724.html.
20. Ibid.
21. Ibid.
22. Ibid.
23. "Lampedusa, MSF denuncia condizioni igienico-sanitarie peggiori dei campi rifugiati," *Medici Senza Frontiere* press release, April 1, 2011, http://www.medicisenzafrontiere.it/msfinforma/comunicati_stampa.asp?id = 2582.
24. "Lampedusa, chiuso il Cpt per sovraffollamento," *Peace Reporter*, March 15, 2011, http://it.peacereporter.net/articolo/27416/Lampedusa,+chiuso+il+Cpt+per+sovraffollamento.
25. Tom Kington, "Berlusconi Claims He Will Empty Italian Island of Lampedusa of Migrants," *The Guardian*, March 30, 2011, http://www.guardian.co.uk/world/2011/mar/30/berlusconi-empty-island-lampedusa-migrants.
26. Junghoo Cho and Hector Garcia-Molina, "The Evolution of the Web and Implications for an Incremental Crawler," *Proceedings of the 26th International Conference on Very Large Data Bases*, 2000, 200–209; Brian E. Brewington and George Cybenko, "How Dynamic Is the Web? Estimating the Information Highway Speed Limit," *Computer Network* 33 (2000): 257–76; Dennis Fetterly, Mark Manasse, Mark Najork, and Janet Wiener, "A Large-Scale Study of the Evolution of Web Pages," *Software Practice and Experience* 34, no. 2 (2004): 213–37; Alexandros Ntoulas, Junghoo Cho, and Christopher Olston, "What's New on the Web? The Evolution of the Web from a Search Engine Perspective," *Proceedings of the 13th International Conference on World Wide Web*, 2004, 1–12.

11 Now You See Them, Now You Don't
Italy's Visible and Invisible Immigrants

John Hooper
The Guardian and *The Observer*

CHRISTMAS DAY, 1996

In the early hours of the morning, people in Italy, as on the Mediterranean island of Malta, were fast asleep, dreaming perhaps of the presents and feasts that awaited them in the hours that lay ahead. But in the stretch of sea between their two countries, hundreds of Indians, Pakistanis, and Sri Lankans were being loaded onto a former RAF patrol boat, the F174—it was never given any other name—which had slipped out of a Maltese port the night before. The job of the F174 was to carry the Asians—clandestine migrants—from a freighter, the Honduras-registered *Yiohan,* into the shallower waters around the Sicilian port of Portopalo.

The F174 could carry only about 100 people. But eventually there were more than 300 people aboard. Somehow in the confusion, the patrol boat collided with its mother ship. The F174 began to sink with at least 283 people aboard. Those still on the *Yiohan* watched in horror. "People were desperately screaming for help," said a Pakistani survivor, Ahmad Shahab. "I saw my brother go down. I yelled 'Please, please. He can't swim.'" Some later said they could see people they knew through the portholes screaming but not making any sound. They could not have known it at the time, but what they were witnessing was the biggest maritime disaster in the Mediterranean since the Second World War.

Ten days later, I was on duty in Rome, where I was the correspondent for the British Sunday newspaper *The Observer.* It was the first Saturday of the New Year, and nothing much was happening. I decided it would be safe to slip out with my wife to do some shopping. I say "safe," because in those days—only 15 years ago—cell phones were still rare and costly. I had asked my employers to give me one and was brusquely told they could see no reason for spending the company's money that way. So the next time I would be contactable was when I returned home.

I had already closed the front door and was turning the key in the lock when I heard the telephone ring inside. With reluctance, I unlocked the door and answered the phone. The foreign editor had seen a Reuters news agency dispatch that puzzled him. It said large numbers of clandestine migrants had come ashore in Greece and told police of a disaster on Christmas Day in which many more drowned. Could I make some checks?

Over the next couple of hours I managed to raise the search and rescue services in Italy and Malta. Both said they had been informed by the Greek authorities of the claims. But for a newspaper, there were at least three problems with the story:

- First, it was hard to understand how such an enormous disaster could have remained unnoticed and unreported for a week and a half.
- Second, neither the Italians nor the Maltese had found either debris or bodies.
- Third, and this is well known to anyone who has dealt with clandestine migrants, they often lie. They frequently give a false nationality to avoid repatriation. And sometimes they exaggerate the hazards and discomforts of their journeys to garner sympathy.

That said, the second objection counted for little. According to the migrants in Greece, the boat had gone down with its human cargo trapped inside and, as the air-sea rescue people stressed to me, the debris might easily have been missed. The alleged survivors had given only the vaguest indication of where they were, and the Sicily-Malta channel covers well over 3,000 square miles. As for the truthfulness of the alleged survivors, the police in Greece said their accounts coincided, and some of the Muslims among them had called for Korans on which to swear that what they said was true.

In the first edition of *The Observer* that day, we played safe. The headline read: "280 May Have Died in 'Phantom Sinking.'" Note the "may" and the single inverted commas. The story ran on page four, next to one about a boy killed while being towed on his roller blades behind a moped in Bognor Regis.

I was convinced we were underplaying the story. I managed to talk round the deputy editor, who in turn convinced the editor at the midevening news conference. By then, his hand had been strengthened by a statement from the Greek Marine Ministry—later, in fact, retracted—that accepted the stranded migrants' account as true. It made clear that, after the disaster, the traffickers had brought the survivors to a remote spot on the Greek coast, where they were released ashore. An extended version of my story was moved to the top of page one, and I was asked by the deputy editor to write a long piece for an inside page on the perils of migration in the Mediterranean.

By the time we all finished work that night, we felt rather pleased with ourselves. My dispatch was not a scoop. But *The Observer*, alone among British newspapers, had given the story the prominence it deserved. And we all thought that, the next day, the daily newspapers would follow it up. In the event, only *The Observer*'s sister newspaper, *The Guardian*, published a story. And that was probably because, at the time, I was the correspondent in Southern Europe for *The Guardian* as well. Such was the silence from the rest of the press that the editor of *The Observer* decided to send one of his best reporters to Greece and assigned me, along with other correspondents, to dig up more facts on what had happened.

Together, we managed to establish the history of the ship, the names of the crew, and even the routes taken by the various groups of migrants and the amounts they had paid for the journey. By then, calls were pouring into the embassies of India and Pakistan in Greece and elsewhere from people in Europe and America whose relatives had not arrived as they had expected. My colleague in Greece wrote that it was "disconcerting to arrive to cover a disaster that did not, apparently, happen. It numbs the soul to realise that it did."

But in that he was alone—or almost. Not one other leading British or even Italian newspaper followed up on our report. And a new doubt was added: If all these migrants had been landed from the *Yiohan,* where was it? Surely, a large vessel like that could not just vanish off the face of the sea.

Now more angry than irritated, *The Observer*'s editor decided to put another reporter on an aircraft out of Britain, this time bound for Pakistan. There, he found the stricken families of the victims and yet more detail about the background to the disaster. At this point, newspapers throughout the Mediterranean accepted that hundreds of people had died and put the story on their front pages. No?

No. They continued to ignore it.

Scroll forward six weeks. It is a Friday, and I am listening to the news on Italian radio. The last item is about a freighter that has run aground near the southern port of Reggio Calabria while landing clandestine migrants ashore. The news reader says the ship was flying the Honduran flag. I ring *The Observer* and tell the foreign editor it could be the *Yiohan.* I doubt whether, in these cash-strapped days, any British newspaper would let me book an airfare, hotel, and photographer all on a hunch. But 15 years ago things were very different in the newspaper industry, and *The Observer* did. I flew that night to the tip of the Italian "toe," and shortly after dawn the next day the photographer and I stole aboard the ship.

Within minutes, I was convinced it was the *Yiohan.* The name of the ship had been carved into a strut in one of the cabins where the desperate migrants had left other records of their terror and misery. "Pray to God. Only God," ran one partly obliterated inscription. "Help you to God . . . from this jail." After being detained by the Italian revenue guard and released after having given a statement, I went to the photographer's studio. Whatever my suspicions, we still lacked conclusive proof that this was what *The Observer* had termed the Ship of Death.

The name of the vessel on the bows had been crudely whitewashed over. But, remarkably, the photographer owned sophisticated image-enhancing software, which he used on his pictures. Before our eyes, as he ran the pictures again and again through the program, out of the white emerged first one letter, then another, spelling out O . . . H . . . A and part of an N.

This time, we really *did* have a scoop (one that later brought us a press award from the BBC, whose *Newsnight* current affairs program was the only one to take the story seriously). Yet, once again, the Western media just shrugged. The mainstream Italian media continued to ignore the story altogether. And yet another objection was found. Yes, I had discovered the *Yiohan*. But where was the F174?

The whole sorry story indicated that the European media were instinctively reluctant to face up to the appalling cost of attempted migration across the Mediterranean. It was and is a perilous undertaking. The Council of Europe reckons that in 2011, which was admittedly a particularly bad year because of the conflict in Libya, more than 1,500 migrants lost their lives. When the *Titanic* sank, in 1912, 1,514 people died. Compare the thousands—probably millions—of words still being written about that disaster 100 years later with the publicity being given (or not given) to what is happening right now in the seas between Africa and Europe; the contrast is striking. Perhaps "disturbing" is a better word.

A disinclination on the part of editors not to confront—or make their readers, viewers, and listeners confront—the ugly realities of clandestine migration is part of the story. But it is not the whole story. Values intrinsic to the media have also played an important role.

One of these values might be termed *concentration*. The media do a good job of reporting *events,* but they cannot be relied upon to reflect with the same degree of accuracy *developments* (in the sense of changes—including dramatic and otherwise newsworthy changes—spread out over time or space). If hundreds of people die in their homes during a heat wave (as sometimes happens in southern Europe), it is—as I know from personal experience—impossible to "sell" the story to a news desk outside the country in which the heat wave took place. But if the same number of people were to die in, say, a hotel fire, it would be seen as a huge story. The number of deaths may be the same, but it is their concentration into a single news event that makes the difference.

The same process can be seen at work in the coverage of traffic accidents, and not only in southern Europe. Six people die on the roads in separate accidents in different parts of the country? "No story." Six people die in a single accident? "Front-page story."

The second news value that comes into play in dealing with clandestine migration is *visibility*. As we have seen in the story of the *Yiohan* and the F174, where the tragedy is invisible and an excuse, however implausible, can be found for believing that it has not happened, that excuse will be used. But—and this is a remarkable paradox—when there *is* visible evidence of the danger and horrors, the media often react with great compassion.

This is undoubtedly the case with the coverage of landings on Italy's southern islands. Sometimes the boats reach the coast or territorial waters with dead bodies aboard, migrants having died after days adrift because the engine broke down or because there was no navigational equipment aboard. Even if no one actually dies, the migrants often arrive hungry, thirsty, and exhausted. They make a pitiful sight. But they also make for very good television—and not just for the Italian networks, which is where the first of two distortions specific to the reporting of this story creeps in.

It is probably fair to say that more than 95 percent of the media coverage in recent years of irregular immigration into Italy has concentrated on the arrival of people—mostly North and sub-Saharan Africans—on Italy's southern islands: Lampedusa, Pantelleria, and—occasionally—Sicily and Sardinia. That proportion is probably even higher for the international media, including the papers that I work for, though on October 1, 2012, Guardian News Media gave me a new role as Southern Europe editor of its two national papers, *The Guardian* and *The Observer*, which should allow me to take a more integrated approach to immigration issues that are common to all the countries on the northern shores of the Mediterranean.

That is especially crucial because, by concentrating on the trans-Mediterranean "boat people," we give an inaccurate impression of the real situation, because the bulk of irregular immigration into Italy takes place in a much less dramatic fashion. People from the Balkans, Eastern Europe, and Central Asia filter in through Italy's northeastern frontiers, having already entered the European Union through Slovenia or countries further east. Even more just fly into Italy on a tourist visa and overstay. The latest official figures I have been able to locate refer to 2006, and they appear in an Interior Ministry report in a table headed "Foreigners Irregularly Present in Italy according to Means of Entry." The text does not really make clear what the figures refer to. I presume from the context, however, that they represent the number of people in each category identified by the authorities, perhaps when they applied at a subsequent date for the regularization of their situation. At all events, the figures are startling: overstayers, 64 percent; entries by way of the frontier, 23 percent; and landings on the Italian coast, 13 percent.

This brings us to a paradox, because Italians can see this with their own eyes—much like the French public, as noted in Vincent's chapter. Anyone who travels on a tram or on the metro in any of Italy's big cities will see large numbers of Chinese, Filipinos, and Latin Americans. Such travelers will also see—though they may not notice them because of the lack of visible physical differences—considerable numbers of people from the Balkans and countries in Eastern Europe outside the EU. You can be pretty sure that none of these people arrived on rickety boats that had set off from Tunisia or Libya. It would seem, however, that when people have to choose between the evidence of their own eyes and what they see on television, they choose to credit the latter.

The second of the distortions I referred to earlier is the product not of inherent—and perhaps unalterable—media values but of sloppy reporting, in particular sloppy language that can and should be corrected. The intention is well meaning: in their attempts to generate sympathy among their readers, listeners, and viewers, the reporters who cover the landings on Italy's southern shores routinely describe the migrants as "seeking a better life." But that gives an impression that the people who arrive by boat on the northern shores of the Mediterranean are mostly economic migrants—an impression with possibly enduring consequences for public reactions to them, as noted in Popkova's chapter—and, as anyone who has covered the story knows, that is not true.

Until 2010,[1] according to the office of the United Nations High Commissioner for Refugees (UNHCR), roughly three-quarters of the migrants who crossed the Mediterranean to Italy were asylum seekers—and of those, approximately half were subsequently recognized as being in need of humanitarian assistance. So almost 40 percent of the sea-borne migrants reaching Italy were *not* trying to give themselves a better life but trying to escape a worse one that, in some cases, involved a threat of death, torture, or persecution. In trying to engender sympathy in the public, then, the media unwittingly perhaps divert attention from the very people who deserve it most.

It is only recently that the Italian media have begun to introduce into their vocabulary the term "asylum seeker." Its use should be encouraged and promoted.

In theory, the media contain an in-built mechanism with which to compensate for all the distortions to which reference has been made. Newspapers have pages for features as well as for news. TV and radio channels broadcast current affairs programs as well as news bulletins. And, to be fair, many of the feature articles and current affairs programs on irregular migration into Southern Europe have highlighted the fact that most of it does not take place across the Mediterranean and that a high proportion of those who do arrive by sea are seeking asylum and not opportunity or wealth.

But until very recently the relative weight of feature writing and current affairs program making within the Italian media has been slight. It is only in the last few years that mainstream newspapers and their websites have shown an enthusiasm for *approfondimenti,* while—partly for reasons of cost—the principal Italian TV networks have traditionally been much keener to deal with the issues of the day in talk shows rather than by means of in-depth reporting. At all events, it would seem that it is the *news* reporting of immigration that has had the greatest impact on public and political opinion.

That, at least, is the logical conclusion to be drawn from the policy debate in Italy in recent years. During the center-left Prodi government, which was in office from 2006 to 2008, there was growing alarm over the link between clandestine immigration and rising crime. This alarm was particularly noticeable in the TV network belonging to Silvio Berlusconi, who was at that time the leader of the conservative opposition. Alarm turned to something close to hysteria following the brutal murder of a naval officer's wife in a Rome suburb. But her alleged killer was a Romanian. And a large part of the rise in mainly petty crime resulted from a sudden and dramatic influx of people into Italy from Romania after Romania joined the EU, on January

1, 2007. According to the interior minister at the time, a half million people flooded in, and many of them ended up in shantytowns on the outskirts of the big cities, like the one in which the alleged murderer of the naval officer's wife was living at the time she was killed.

The fact that Romanians, as fellow members of the European Union, were fully entitled to enter Italy did not prevent Berlusconi and his party from launching a crusade to stop clandestine immigration. And since clandestine immigration was associated in the public mind almost entirely with the arrival of Africans on Italy's southern shores, they were able to portray a halt to this traffic as representing an end to *all* clandestine immigration (which, following the victory of the right in the 2008 election, became illegal immigration).

One of Berlusconi's first moves was to declare a rise in landings to be a national state of emergency. Soon after, he signed an intensely controversial deal with the then Libyan leader, Colonel Muammar Gaddafi. Under its terms, Italian patrol vessel could intercept boats carrying migrants and return them to the country from which they had set off. It is the same policy used by the United States in the Caribbean, and there, as in the Mediterranean, its legality is debatable.

The real problem with this push-back policy is that it denied asylum seekers the chance to seek asylum. The Italian government said they could apply in Libya. But, in practice, that was impossible. There was not even a UNHCR office in Libya, because Colonel Gaddafi would not allow the organization to operate there. Those who were turned back to Libya met with a hostile and, in some cases, brutal reception. But, once again, visibility was a key issue. Libya at that time was difficult, if not impossible, for journalists to enter, and so the suffering of the frustrated migrants went largely unreported.

The effect of the Berlusconi-Gaddafi deal was to block tens of thousands of would-be migrants in Libya, and it is ironic that the war that led to the Libyan leader's downfall and death (to which Italy contributed, albeit hesitantly and reluctantly) in 2011 should have also destroyed Berlusconi's immigration policy.

In the chaos, and even more desperate to escape from Libya than before, migrants were prepared to take hair-raising risks in their attempts to reach Europe. On the way, some of them once more became tragically invisible. In May 2011, my *Guardian* colleague in Cairo Jack Shenker brought to light the story of a vessel with 72 people aboard that ran into trouble on the crossing and that floated with the currents for two weeks before being washed back onto Libyan territory. All but nine of those on board died of thirst or starvation or were washed overboard. At the time, NATO was enforcing an arms embargo on Libya, and several of its ships were in the area. France, Britain, Italy, Spain, the United States, and Canada all had warships patrolling the so-called Maritime Surveillance Area.

The survivors said that a military helicopter flew over their boat and that the crew offered them food and water and motioned to them to remain in place. It then flew away and was never seen again. Eventually, after 10 days adrift, the vessel bumped up against a large naval ship. The survivors claim they held up the bodies of two babies who had died to try to get a response from those on board. But, again, nothing was done.

In March 2012, the Council of Europe published its official report on the affair, which said that distress calls relating to the boat were put out by the Maritime Rescue Coordination Center in Rome but that NATO's high command in Naples failed to relay them to its ships. The report pointed out, nevertheless, that at least one of the NATO vessels, a Spanish frigate, should have received subsequent emergency calls that were broadcast on different satellite networks by the coordination center in Rome. The nationalities of the helicopter and the ship that encountered the migrants' boat remain unknown.

Fifteen years have passed since the sinking of the F174. But it seems that the West has lost none of its readiness to turn a blind eye to evidence of appalling suffering in the sea that forms Europe's southern flank.

As for the F174, it too—you will remember—had become invisible. But, in 2001, an Italian reporter took an interest in the story after being contacted by a Sicilian fisherman who had brought up in his net some clothing and the ID card of a young Tamil. The reporter, Giovanni Maria Bellu of *la Repubblica,* managed to get together the funding to send an ROV— a remotely operated underwater vehicle—down to the seabed, where it filmed the wreck and the skeletons of the victims. But when a team from the History Channel returned to the spot, they could find no trace of the F174. Like so many migrants in the Mediterranean, it had vanished from sight.

NOTE

1. Figures up to 2010 have been used because 2010 and to an even greater extent 2011 were atypical, owing to the upheavals first in Tunisia and then in Libya.

12 This Is Not a Country for Immigrants
Journalists and Political Discourse in Italy

Riccardo Stagliànò
la Repubblica

INTRODUCTION: DEMONIZING IMMIGRANTS

This is not a good time to be an immigrant in Italy. Immigrants are the first to pay the price of the economic crisis, told to stay home from their jobs randomly one day without bothering with any formal procedure. And even when they work, they earn on average one-third less than we Italians do. And then they are obsessed by the "permesso di soggiorno," the document required to legally remain in Italy, which, even when all the papers are in order, takes such unforeseeable time to be obtained that it borders on the arbitrary—not to mention that, when the permit expires, the immigrants become *clandestini,* clandestine people, a condition that Italians have turned into with a felony, which turns immigrants into pariahs who can be blackmailed in any number of ways.

Since they are in the wrong by definition, they do not ask to be paid decently, nor do they seek medical care when they are ill, and they renounce any minimal humane labor protection. In a nutshell, things are going downhill, and there are no signs of improvement to be seen.

The most obtuse ideology poisons public discourse. And we, the journalists, have a share of responsibility, because a reporter is not just someone who holds a microphone or jots down on a notepad what politicians say. Reporters should be able to enter the conversation, on the basis of their knowledge and their professional dignity, perhaps highlighting the major incongruities in both the rhetoric and the proposed actions. Unfortunately, out of ignorance or laziness, reporters are not always capable of fulfilling this watchdog role, and they let grotesque pronouncements and actions go unchallenged.

A particularly revealing example of this toxic atmosphere concerns the "Ambrogino d'Oro," Milan's most prestigious award for citizens who have distinguished themselves for bravery and civic spirit, of a couple of years ago. In 2009 it was awarded, among others, to the public safety personnel of ATM, Milan's public transit authority—those teams of uber-conductors with license to detain who, for a short period, rounded up and arrested in a sort of prison bus the alleged "*clandestini*" who had been caught without paid fares. "So that they were exposed to the curiosity of passersby like animals in the zoo," to use the astonishing words of a city council member, Aldo Brandirali, who belongs to the center-right PdL (Popolo della Libertà, people of freedom) party.[1]

Here we go, I told myself—if we have gotten to the point that, instead of being horrified, we award with great pomp and circumstance a case of such useless meanness, the situation is really serious. It means that the factory of fear has been working at full speed and that the massive confusion of public discourse has gotten to a boiling point—a point, to sum up, at which it becomes imperative to line up the actual facts, because the inability to communicate that afflicts those on the Left and those on the Right on this topic of immigration derives precisely from the use of incompatible reasoning. Those on the left usually appeal to our sense of empathy, to the ability to "not do unto others," while the right talks about dangers to national identity, about stolen jobs, about imported criminality. But empathy, like the courage of the legendary coward Don Abbondio in Italian literature, is something you either have or cannot acquire, while fear comes standard in every human being and does not spare even the more progressive, especially when the going gets rough. And when the going is roughest, such as now, with the shipwreck of the middle class, the disappearance of permanent jobs, and the endless turn to precariousness that characterizes our "society of risk," the upgrade from fear to terror should not surprise us. When you are panicking, you lose your bearings and everything becomes blurred—to the point that Milan's bus shaming does not stand revealed as the disgrace that it is but rather is an idea worthy of medals.

A ROLE FOR JOURNALISTS: DISPELLING MYTHS

It is because of all this that, in 2010, I wrote a book of reportage, *Grazie: Ecco Perché Senza gli Immigrati Saremmo Perduti* (Thanks: This Is Why without Immigrants We Would Be Lost), with the grand purpose of contributing to getting past the dire straits in which Italian politics is stuck on the issue of immigration. I began by reading all that I could find on the topic of employment and immigrants, setting up Google alerts to be notified of all stories in Italian on it. For months, I rather mercilessly auditioned the best stories that would show a reader how many sections of our national economy would literally shut down without immigrants. At that point, I started making the first phone calls, setting up the first appointments, and booked the first plane and train tickets.

I was not even trying to persuade someone who did not already innately believe that black- or yellow- or olive-skinned people should be treated well because they are human beings. I was aiming not for readers' hearts but for their wallets. And in order to do that, very prosaically, I described how and how much immigrants contribute to our current lifestyle—what jobs they fill that we are no longer willing to take—and asked readers to imagine how we would fare if all of the sudden the immigrants were gone or even simply if they stopped working in a general strike.

First Argument: Invaded by Migrants?
Actually, There Are Too Few of Them

So let us start with some facts. The first rationale is demographic. In summer 2007, economists and experts from around the world met at the Munich Economic Summit and reiterated, without mincing words, that Europe is running on fumes when it comes to youth. Either it allows more immigrants to come in (in addition to setting a higher pension age and reduced welfare) or its population, which continues to live longer and reproduce less, will short-circuit the social security system and public funds in 2050 at the latest. Among all EU members, Italy was and remains the worst off, because the difference between the working population and the number of retirees is the biggest. While all member states need foreign workers, Italy's need is the most acute.

This same alarm is given at this point regularly, with increasingly dramatic tones as time goes by. In 1994, it was the alert issued by Italy's CNR (National Research Council) about an "extinction risk" if we did not open the gates for immigrants, going from the 50,000 who arrived at the time each year to at least 300,000. Even on this specific point, the crucial debate is not between the Right and the Left but between the deniers and those whose eyes are open. Listen to what former interior minister Giuseppe Pisanu, of the Berlusconi government, said to a financial daily: "We are in full demographic decline and consequently economic and political decline. Only immigrants can save us. The numbers tell us that the future well-being of Italians will depend on the ability to attract and integrate 300,000 workers per year."[2] But the regulations determining flows, which establish the numbers of foreign low-skilled workers we need, foresaw a meager 170,000 documented immigrants for 2008—to whom of course we should add undocumented workers. As of January 1, 2009, according to the report on migration by the Ismu Foundation, the undocumented numbered 422,000, less than a third the number who immigrated the year before (the total of regular migrants would reach 4.8 million).

"Clandestine" is a definition that does not exist naturally but rather results from faulty laws that make immigrants so, thereby dooming them to black-market jobs that are the essence of that "clandestine" brand. These laws and regulations should be changed to transform immigrants into regular workers who pay taxes. Nonetheless, and ignoring all the calls for help, we invented in quick succession the expulsions and the crime of being an illegal immigrant.

Second Rationale: They Cost Us Too Much?
No, They Give Us More

The second rationale is a fiscal one. "We cannot afford all these people who are a burden on public expenditures" is one of the most popular refrains in political conversations over coffee at the corner bar. The reality is quite different. According to estimates by the relief association Caritas Migrantes, when the number of documented migrants was 4 million, they paid 5.8 billion euros in taxes and used up approximately 700 million euros' worth of taxpayer-funded services. What is certain is that local governments in 2005 spent 136 million euros in services dedicated to migrants. As for the rest, as explained by the lead writer of the report, Franco Pittau, "immigrants are slightly more than 6 percent of the population and they generate about 10 percent of the GDP. Even assuming, to go big and avoid criticism, that they are triple that number, the amount of resources the State spends for them would get to the number we have hypothesized." According to these calculations, then—and for a while they have been the most authoritative source on immigration issues—with immigrants' giving 5.8 and taking 0.7, our country made a gain of a little over 5 billion euros.

To get down from the abstract level of numbers to the reality of politics, we need only to think about the abolition of the notorious "Ici" property tax, which to some commentators was the real magic factor in the center-right electoral victory and which cost "only" 2 billion euros. So, in essence, immigrants pay for "our" pensions. They pay for all of us, including those 60-year-olds, characteristically xenophobic, who grumble in the coziness of their living rooms that immigrants are younger (31 years old on average, compared to Italians' 45). Of those same 2 million foreign workers who pay into the national pension fund (Inps), only 6,000 get a pension, because many of them will return to their homelands at some point, at which time, thanks to a punitive law, they will lose a large part of those pension funds. In 2011, the figures were recalculated, both by Andrea Stuppini, manager of the Emilia Romagna region, who has a penchant for the economic aspects of migration, and by Caritas Migrantes, which revised its methodology and numbers. The disparity decreased significantly, with a gain of 11 billion euros and expenses of about 10 billion. Even if the numbers and the studies might be revised again, what remains the same is the basic point: they give us more than they take. And that is true without even looking at immigrants' crucial contribution to our national productivity.

Third Argument: They Steal Our Jobs? Not at All; They Leave Us with the Better Ones

The third argument revolves around employment. "They come to steal our jobs" is the standard refrain. I leave the answer to those notorious Communist sympathizers and development fanatics who work in the research branch of the Banca d'Italia, Italy's Fed. In its 2008 report on regional economies, the researchers explained that there is no overlap between the jobs taken by Italians and those held by immigrants.[3] It is not, in other words, a zero-sum game. On the contrary, the more immigrants fill out the base of the professional pyramid (the blue-collar jobs), the more opportunities open up for Italians to graduate to managerial and administrative jobs, which are less burdensome and better paid. Not to mention the change for Italian women—finally freed from domestic duties by the availability of migrant caretakers and domestic workers, they can finally aspire to a career on par with those of men. "Bullshit," was the response by Mario Borghezio, a European Parliament member from the Lega Nord party, with little courtesy and less proof.[4] The head of PdL, Maurizio Gasparri—one does not quite know on the basis of which superior academic credentials—disposed of the report as having "little credibility."[5]

He must not have known that, more or less around the same time, in that other "Bolshevist refuge" that is the United States, a similar study had been published to calculate the same impact. The well-known economists Maureen Rimmer and Peter Dixon concluded that "increased enforcement and reduced low-skilled immigration have a significant negative impact on the income of US households."[6] The two researchers, who explained how even the lowest-skilled workers contributed to the overall economy and opened up more skilled positions for native workers, quantified at $250 billion the economic differential between the most open and the most closed-door policies to migrants. And yet, it did not occur even to the most shoot-from-the-hip Republican to ridicule the study, especially since it was funded by the Cato Institute, a celebrated conservative think tank. In November 2012, a paper coauthored by Francesco D'Amuri, a researcher at the Bank of Italy, and Giovanni Peri, of the University of California, Davis, not only confirmed the absence of the mythical "theft of jobs" but also verified the effects over the past 15 years—and found that migrant labor moved Italians toward better jobs.[7]

Now, as a journalist, I know that these arguments have the advantage of being scientific and the disadvantage of being abstract. They deal with general categories (population, taxation, employment) that we might get with our brains but leave us no gut feeling. And I believe it is important to aim for the gut, too, because it is there that understanding becomes full and memory undeletable. Macroeconomic concepts need to become micro, history must become stories—like the stories that I covered, following migrants at their jobs across Italy, in the most disparate occupations and around the clock, literally, to show that in fact many sectors of the economy would stop without migrant labor. That too is sheer math: in some sectors, like caretaking for the elderly or pumping gas at service stations, foreigners are 50, 70, or even 90 percent of workers. And even where they account for a smaller percentage, their presence is so overwhelming in certain jobs that without them the whole sector would fail.

Following this story, in Trentino, the region of Italy that borders Austria and is framed by the Dolomites, I met the Senegalese who pick apples in Val di Non and, with their touching dedication, moisten with pride the eyes of mountain folks who have worked on these prize harvests for generations. In Veneto, the region around Venice, I talked with giant Nigerians who rip animal skins off mountains of meat to turn them into leather jackets popular from Rome to Hollywood. In Emilia Romagna, I interviewed migrants from the Maghreb who take miserly pay and reduced hours to clean offices and schools. Down the boot of Italy, in Campania, I met Sikh Indians who work overnight handling "bufale" cows and then spend the day cleaning up their manure so that their milk can become mozzarella di bufala, one of Italy's world-celebrated exports. And in Sicily, I recorded the experiences of Tunisian fishermen without whom the fishing fleet in Mazara del Vallo, which alone accounts for one-fourth of all seafood fished in the country, would not be able to sail.

This was undoubtedly the most energizing part of writing the book—to try out what it really means to live with buffalo cows or to work in Veneto's leather manufacturers is an experience that everyone should have. But nearly nobody does it, in part because to travel on assignment is expensive and newspapers have increasingly fewer resources and save them for stories they might consider more shocking. But perhaps the deeper reason is that the curiosity of wanting to know what it is like to be an immigrant is a kind of exotic experience for experts only. A sizable percentage of Italians feels that they are themselves so badly off that they do not need the additional sadness of discovering those who are in even worse shape. And yet I believe that it is very important to tell these stories, because they reveal the reality underneath the rhetoric of immigration that often stays at a theoretical level. And if it is easy to go after caricatures, it is much harder to do so with real people, people with a first and last name, who try to earn a hard living together with us.

THE REALITY: WORKING UNDER THE THREAT OF BLACKMAIL AND ACCIDENTS FOR LITTLE PAY

See what a nice list of jobs I found immigrants filling throughout Italy? Go ahead and apply; there is plenty of need. I doubt, however, that would occur to anyone the next time they hear a young man anxiously debating what job to get for a guaranteed income. And that is because, with a couple of exceptions, they are all jobs where the disparity between effort and pay is big—and Italians today, understandably, aspire to something better. But the ability to freely pursue those aspirations should elicit gratitude toward those who fill those less desirable jobs—not out of kindness but out of sheer self-interest. And yet, our national reaction is entirely different.

In 2009, we were formally reprimanded—the only country among EU members—by the International Labour Organization for having violated, in our treatment of immigrants, international labor norms that prohibit discrimination, mandate access to public jobs, and guarantee various other rights that we apparently neglect.[8] Not long before, another report by Inps-Caritas had found that, on average and given equal tasks, a non-EU immigrant took home a salary that was less than two-thirds their Italian coworkers' stipends. And that non-EU immigrant's annual salary, again on average, amounted to 10,042 euros, or 837 euros, gross per month, which can hardly justify the higher risks that immigrant workers are often bullied into accepting. In fact, on-the-job accident lists are quite telling: they have been decreasing for everyone except for immigrants, where the numbers went from 129,303 in 2006, to 140,785 the following year, to 143,600 the year after that, in a bloodied chart that keeps going up.

On the other hand, being starved is incompatible with being picky, and blackmail and odd jobs are not the ideal partners of safety. And when it comes to the economic crisis, it is almost as if immigrants had been for a long while our bulletproof vests, keeping us from feeling it too deeply. They were the first to be sent home, without an explanation or even an apology, the very moment that business started slowing down, because black market workers deserve no mercy. In Lombardia, one of Italy's wealthiest regions, 17 percent of those whose names appear in special lists for the summarily fired are immigrants—and that figure does not account for the invisible victims, the *clandestini,* estimated at a half million in Italy, who were fired with a nod or a grunt. In other words, this "21st" of Italy's regions—with nearly 5 million regular workers it has fewer inhabitants than only three Italian regions, Lombardia, Campania, and Lazio—does a lot for the welfare of the other 20, but often all it gets in exchange is a kick in the face.

THE MOST IMPRESSIVE MODERN EXODUS?
ITALIAN EMIGRATION

And yet, it should not be too hard for Italians to understand what it feels like to be an immigrant—all we need to do is look into the mirror. The most impressive exodus in modern history is the Italian one. Starting in 1861, the year when modern Italy became one nation, and for a century afterward, nearly 30 million Italians left to try their luck abroad—more than the entire population inside Italy's first national borders. Proportionately, that is as if today 33 million people left Morocco, or 22 million left Romania, or 3.5 million left Albania. We are everywhere. We were laborers in Sydney and millionaires in Brooklyn, we opened restaurants in Berlin and engaged in financial speculation in Malindi. And tomorrow, if the crisis does not get better, maybe we will be busboys in Beijing or New Delhi. Our most relevant contributions to globalization, for better or for worse, were pizza and the mafia. We know in our bones the enormous burden of starting from scratch in an entirely unknown country whose very language is a mystery. We know it is a toil that starts well before arriving in a new country. This is what Francesco Costantin, from Treviso, wrote when he finally landed in South America in 1889:

> I cannot find adequate words to describe for you the devastation on the
> boat, the weeping, the prayers and the curses of those who did not start

on this voyage voluntarily, in the middle of a storm. The fearsome waves rise up to heaven, and then form deep valleys, the steam is fought from aft to bow, and beats up against the sides. I will not describe the spasms, the retching, and the contortions of those poor passengers who are not accustomed to these circumstances. I will skip over the deaths, which average 5 or 6 in 100, and I pray to God Almighty that we will be spared contagious diseases, because with those there is no telling what could happen.

This is what Italians felt like when we were the Albanians, the Tunisians, the Libyans, on rickety boats that today we push back indiscriminately, against international norms, without even ascertaining who is on board and why. "You can feel all the terror that a farmer from Val Padana or from the mountains in Abruzzo and Lucania felt braving that Atlantic Ocean that separated the fearsome Italian misery from the great American dream," writes Gian Antonio Stella, presenting *Merica Merica,* by Emilio Franzina, the anthology from which I excerpted the quotation from a migrant's letter. Al Capone was the son of Gabriele Caponi from Castellammare di Stabia, just outside Naples, but among the bricklayers who mixed cement in France there was also Sandro Pertini, a future president of Italy. We should therefore still have in our collective memory how the last to arrive is always the first to be slapped when something breaks and there is no clear culprit. On the contrary, what is happening is that the very great grandsons, grandsons, and sons of men and women who went to embrace the unknown armed only with their cardboard suitcases now have a form of social Alzheimer's in reverse, which fixes the most recent past and forgets everything else.

A Catalog of Ungratefulness

The symptoms of this neurodegenerative disease are varied. To begin with, those who succumb to it develop a generalized anxiety regarding everything that has to do with immigrants, which is set off every day by the very news stories we publish in the press. For example, Milan's public transit authority refused to hire Mohamed Hailoua, an 18-year-old Moroccan who had come to Italy legally years before and had all the requisites to become a driver, on the basis of a royal decree of 1931 that required Italian citizenship for the job. Apparently there was a concern that, as an "Arab," he would be a natural-born killer bent on terror attacks in the subway (for the record, the young man sued and the judge ruled in his favor).[9]

Another media example: the Lega Nord senator Sergio Divina raised the alarm against a potential Islamist "fifth column" working at Iveco, a major manufacturer of commercial trucks owned by the auto giant Fiat. Given that 60 percent of the laborers who built the "Lince" armored vehicle are foreigners, the senator wanted to know their family histories to evaluate whether they might become spies for the Taliban. Recently, another member of the

Lega Nord party, Matteo Salvini, got his 15 minutes of fame by proposing that some subway cars be reserved for the Milanese, terrifying all those who on the contrary had learned something from *Mississippi Burning*. In Parma, in Italy's fertile Val Padana, his fellow party members recommended that City Hall forbid caretakers and other foreigners to sit on the benches in Ducale Park—one of the few places where they can gather for free—so that the places could be reserved for the elderly and women with infants. When a reporter went to check, at various times of day, whether there really was such an intolerable crowding that aging and pregnant citizens were left standing, he found the vast majority of the benches empty.[10]

Other proposed restrictions that created media sensations concerned kebab restaurants in historical city centers, ethnic menus for school lunches, and the like—as if the real and serious problem of native and immigrant living together could be resolved by pretending immigrants are not there, making them magically disappear.

Beyond easy political platforms, there are even reputedly serious academics who fall for this rhetoric, which makes it even more absurd because it purports to rest on sophisticated intellectual arguments. I will cite only Ida Magli, an anthropologist and a (former) feminist who a dozen years ago was writing about the violence innate in male sexuality and who today calls Italians to arms against the "foreign hordes." "As soon as other men arrive, bringing another base personality, another culture, the invaded one weakens and dies," she wrote in an editorial in the major national newspaper *Giornale,* going on to attack the lack of response by the Church as well as by the Left.[11] Speaking of the Left, she writes, "Why does it hate us? Why does it not do for immigrants the only right thing, which it could do much better than other parties, that is to help would-be immigrants stay in their own country? It is not by registering as Italian residents that foreigners will create the melodies of Monteverdi or of Puccini, will paint the Madonnas of Raphael or of Mantegna, will write the verses of Petrarca or Leopardi. And it should not be said that foreigners help with the demographic slump." As if the Kantian imperative to treat others as people were subordinate to their ability to create memorable masterpieces in the arts—as if their work caring for our children and washing our elders were not already work good enough to deserve some help. We can imagine what would happen if we were to grant Italian citizenship on the basis of those same prerequisites of artistic production: Would there be 60 million Italians or 60?

And so we continue to complicate immigrants' lives. There are more than 700,000 immigrants, according to the business newspaper *Sole 24 Ore,* who are awaiting the renewal of their residence permits. In theory, article 5 of Italy's immigration law mandates that the permit be "issued, renewed or exchanged within 20 days from the request." In practice, today they have to wait between 7 and 15 months, according to Radical Party activist Gaoussou Ouattarà, so that when it is issued, it either is about to expire or already has. It would make more sense to speed up the process than to harden the penalties for those without permits. Ouattarà, who is originally from Ivory Coast and has lived in Italy for 29 years, wrote:

> Without a permit we cannot move within Europe, we have a hard time going back to the home country as well as to simply perform daily tasks such as signing a rental agreement or work contract, getting a driver's license, registering our children in kindergarten. In a nutshell, the life of an immigrant who is waiting for the residence permit is comparable to that of someone incarcerated in an open-sky prison.[12]

I am quoting him not to move readers but to further the reasoning. Those who feel trapped at a certain point will do anything to escape.

"We Don't Like Being Mean, We Are Happy with Being Hypocritical"

"The United States, Switzerland, France, Germany, Sweden, let us say all the advanced countries, recognize the right to asylum, even though they might have high requirements that make life impossible for refugees; in Italy, we officially grant nobody asylum, except to those from Communist Eastern Europe, and then, hidden behind the police and bureaucratic routines, sometime we are more permissive and hospitable. We don't like being mean, we are happy with being hypocritical," wrote Giorgio Bocca in the newspaper for which I work, *la Repubblica,* on June 9, 1988. It was a memorable article that painted the national character and continued: "The world of the poor is moving toward the land of the wealthy. Someone calls it 'the sixth continent,' and it is a continent in constant, crisscrossing, heterogeneous movement, that nobody can check because no power in the world seems able to stop this mechanism of life."

More than 20 years have passed since this article was published, but, if we change the numbers, the rationales are current—Bocca even added: "To reduce the whole phenomenon to measurable data, prosaic and yet dramatic, we are not going to be able to pay pensions unless immigrants will fill in the void." I find especially poignant the mention of hypocrisy. There is an abundance of examples. Just to mention one: the news spread that the Indian group Tata would save MV Augusta, a historic brand of motorcycles based in the northern city Varese, a Lega Nord stronghold. At the time, downtown, you could still see the electoral posters for Lega Nord that featured a Native American and a block-printed, threatening warning: "If we do not stop immigration, we will end up like them." And yet the mayor, Attilio Fontana, despite belonging to the same party, unblushingly commented in *Corriere della Sera:* "If the Indians' arrival will help in saving a business and its jobs, I have nothing to object." There is Indian and Indian, one might say.

The first to beg for help when it comes to immigration are in fact Italian entrepreneurs. Fearful of losing foreign workers, they pleaded for the government to act smartly because their businesses risked collapse, threatening that they could not keep going with such an "amputation." And how did the government respond? It turned clandestine immigrants into felons—with the exception of domestic workers and caretakers, however, because ideology is all very well, but otherwise who would take care for the children and aging parents of Lega Nord parliamentarians?

It is not a secret that the black market for "regularizations" has flourished just as much as the medieval church market for "indulgences" from sin. The Chinese case is illustrative. The data show that 21,000 Chinese came under the amnesty for domestic workers and caregivers, or 6.7 percent of all requests. But these are clearly fictional data because no Chinese actually take jobs in Italians' homes; in fact there are plenty of Neapolitan babysitters for Chinese families, not the other way around. But there are many stories suggesting that for amounts between 4,000 and 10,000 euros, an immigrant can pretend to be a maid to obtain the permit. In fact, Roberto Menichetti, of the human rights association Arci in Florence, told the local newspaper *Il Corriere Fiorentino* that, just at the end of the period during which requests for regularization could be made, "many employers showed up at our association and declared that they wanted to get permits for their workers by falsely registering them as domestic workers—even though they might really be working in manufacturing or construction. There was even a sympathizer of the Lega Nord who, despite his political orientation, wanted to register as caretaker his precious laborer."[13] So we can be tough on the outside and very permissive inside—with the result that we have terrorized many workers who, scared that even doctors might tell on them, no longer seek treatment even if their lives are at risk.

And they are not being paranoid. A 21-year-old bricklayer from Bolivia stayed away from doctors for a dozen days despite strong abdominal pains. He tried some over-the-counter drugs. When he finally relented and showed up at the San Matteo hospital in Pavia, he was in such grave condition that he was immediately operated on five times. His appendicitis had become peritonitis, and he was in the ICU for a long time. Maccan Ba, a 32-year-old from Senegal, had better medical luck but no legal reprieve. For four days, he tried to ignore a shooting toothache. Then he gave up and went to the Spedali Civici clinic in Brescia, where he barely managed to pay his fees before the police came to detain him and give him deportation orders. Apparently it was a security officer, not a doctor, who gave him away—but to him it probably matters very little. Now he lives in the shadows and swears that if he ever goes into a hospital again it will be as a corpse. Even pretending that ethics are optional, are we Italians really sure that it is a wise idea to force people to live outside the law?

I do not believe so. And I am afraid that if we continue to chase people into the shadows, we will create the very problem that is at the basis of such politics. I can already hear immigrants, in the countryside near Rosarno where they pick our tomato crops or in the construction sites in Milan: "We are not animals, but you are making us ferocious."

NOTES

1. Franco Vanni, "Milano, polemica per l'Ambrogino: premiati i 'cacciatori' di immigrati," *la Repubblica,* November 20, 2009.
2. Fabrizio Forquet, "Così si alimenta la violenza," *Il Sole 24 Ore,* May 12, 2009.
3. Banca d'Italia, *Rapporto sulle economie regionali,* August 18, 2009.
4. "Bankitalia: Immigrati non tolgono lavoro. Favoriscono i più istruiti e le donne," *Il Messaggero,* August 18, 2009.
5. Ibid.
6. Peter B. Dixon and Maureen T. Rimmer, "Restriction or Legalization? Measuring the Economic Benefits of Immigration Reform," Cato Institute Trade Policy Analysis no. 40, August 13, 2009.
7. Francesco D'Amuri and Giovanni Peri, "Immigration, Jobs and Employment Protection: Evidence from Europe before and during the Great Recession," Working Papers 2012–15, University of California at Davis, Department of Economics.
8. Vittorio Longhi, "Agenzia Onu: L'Italia viola i diritti umani," *la Repubblica,* March 19, 2009.
9. Massimo Pisa, "Milano, Atm non assume stranieri, 'C'è il rischio di attentati sul metrò,'" *la Repubblica,* June 9, 2009.
10. "Via le badanti, panchine per soli anziani," *Parma Oltretorrente* blog, April 22 2009, http://oltretorrente-parma.blogautore.repubblica.it/2009/04/22/via-le-badanti-panchine-per-soli-anziani/.
11. Ida Magli, "Le società multietniche? Non esistono," *Il Giornale,* May 20, 2009.
12. Gaoussou Ouattarà, "Noi immigrati in sciopero della fame contro la 'prigione' dei Cie," *L'Unità,* December 22, 2009.
13. Jacopo Storni, "Se l'operaio passa per colf: 'Imprenditori pronti al trucco,'" *Il Corriere Fiorentino,* September 1, 2009.

Part IV

Fences and the Far West: Covering Immigration in the United States

13 The Border Beat in Battleground Arizona

Daniel González
Arizona Republic

Writing about immigration, which I have been doing for more than eight years, is among the most important and challenging beats at *The Arizona Republic*, the largest newspaper in Arizona and one of the largest in the United States. Since the late 1990s, Arizona has been ground zero for illegal immigration. There are several reasons the state has gained this "distinction."

First, Arizona remains the main gateway for illegal immigration along the 2,000-mile US-Mexico border. For more than a decade, roughly half of all apprehensions of illegal border crossers by the US Border Patrol have taken place in Arizona. Simultaneously, the number of annual migrant deaths along the border in Arizona has soared. Since 2000, thousands of people have died crossing the border illegally. Of those, most have perished in Arizona. The state began to see an influx of illegal border crossers in the late 1990s, spurred by an increase in border enforcement by the US government in California and Texas, which had the unintended consequence of funneling illegal immigration along the US-Mexico border through the rugged and desolate desert of southern Arizona. At the same time, a boom in the US economy and the lack of well-paying jobs in Mexico and other countries in Latin America, combined with the lack of favorable immigration laws for low-skilled workers, attracted record numbers of Mexicans and other Latino immigrants to cross the border illegally, further increasing the flow through Arizona. Moreover, the September 11, 2001, terrorist attacks turned illegal immigration into a national security issue.

In addition to being a gateway, Arizona, especially the Phoenix metropolitan area, has also become a major destination for illegal immigrants. Illegal immigrants tend to work in labor-intensive industries, primarily in housing construction, landscaping, hospitality, restaurants, and agriculture. Proportionately, Arizona now has one of the largest undocumented populations in the country. Also, Arizona is at the forefront of a movement by several states to crack down on illegal immigration. The protracted flow of illegal immigrants crossing the Arizona border, the rapid rise of the state's mostly Latino undocumented population, violence related to the human and drug smuggling trade, and Congress's failure to enact effective legislation to solve the problem have fueled intense public frustration in Arizona over the issue of illegal immigration. In response, some politicians have pushed for laws and policies to crack down on illegal immigration through a strategy known as Attrition Through Enforcement, a series of increasingly severe laws intended to make life so hard for undocumented immigrants that they will eventually "self-deport" either because of the threat of being arrested by local police and turned over to federal immigration authorities or because their access to jobs and public services has been cut off.

Over the past decade, the state has passed a series of immigration enforcement laws, capped in 2010 by the passage of Senate Bill 1070, a sweeping law that at its core attempts to turn local police into immigration enforcement agents and that, considered at the time to be the toughest immigration enforcement law in the nation, drew national and international attention. Critics believe it will lead to rampant racial profiling by police of Latinos, including US citizens and legal immigrants. Most of the law was put on hold after the US Justice Department filed a federal lawsuit contending the law is unconstitutional on the grounds that immigration enforcement is the federal government's responsibility, not that of states like Arizona.

In June 2012, the US Supreme Court threw out three provisions of the law but found no reason to continue a lower court's injunction on the most controversial part. That section requires local police to make a reasonable attempt to check the immigration status of people they encounter during traffic stops and other police encounters if they suspect that person might be in the country illegally. In September 2012, a US district court judge cleared the way for the provision, dubbed "Show me your papers" by critics, to take effect.

The collapse of Arizona's housing boom, a sharp decline in tourism tied to the "The Great Recession," and the enactment of SB 1070 and other immigration enforcement laws have spurred thousands of illegal immigrants to leave Arizona in the past couple of years. A 2012 study by the Department of Homeland Security based on 2010 census data estimated that there were about 360,000 undocumented immigrants in Arizona as of January 2011. An earlier DHS report based on 2000 census data estimated there were 560,000 undocumented immigrants in Arizona at the peak in 2008. Not all have returned to Mexico as supporters of immigration enforcement had hoped. Anecdotal evidence suggests the majority of them have moved to other states. In the meantime, several other states have passed similar laws aimed at cracking down on illegal immigrants.

At the same time that these major shifts have made immigration a crucial story for Arizona and the country in general, covering the issue has become significantly more challenging. *The Republic*'s commitment to covering immigration and border issues remains strong, but the immigration reporter has far fewer resources to work with than in the past. For most of the 2000s, the newspaper, which serves more than 300,000 print subscribers, employed a full-time immigration reporter, a full-time border reporter based in Tucson in southern Arizona, a full-time Mexico City bureau chief and research assistant, and a part-time immigration reporter based in Washington. By mid-2012, almost all of those positions were no longer staffed except for mine, the full-time immigration reporter. For nearly a year, I also doubled as the border reporter. In July 2012, *The Republic* assigned another reporter to cover the border full time, but from Phoenix, not Tucson, and thus much farther away from the border.

The decline in immigration reporting positions is part of an overall reduction in reporting positions to offset declining advertising revenues affecting all newspapers. The decline in revenues also means fewer reporting trips to the border, to Mexico, and other parts of the state.

However, *The Republic* has continued to invest resources to cover major immigration stories, especially in the aftermath of SB 1070. To assess its impact on the immigrant population, in June 2010, *The Republic* sent me, as the immigration reporter, and a photographer on a week-long trip to record the move of an undocumented family from Arizona to Pennsylvania because of the law. The resulting project was published as a series of front-page stories beginning with an A1 centerpiece story on a Sunday that included multiple photos and an online companion slide show and timeline.[1] The project then continued over the next three days, covering various angles of the story. One piece showed how the family's move, along with the exodus of other families, had left their apartment complex a ghost town. The same thing was happening at apartment complexes in other Mexican immigrant neighborhoods.

The crowning jewel of the coverage came at the end of the year. In mid-December, *The Republic* published a 16-page special section that appeared both in print and online, featuring a special project aimed at showing how illegal immigration had become a global phenomenon, not an issue unique to Arizona or the United States. For the project, I traveled to Germany, Italy, and Spain, while the paper's national political reporter wrote several analysis stories, a *Republic* photographer traveled to India, and the Mexico City reporter traveled to Costa Rica.

The rest of this chapter details these two major reporting projects tied to SB 1070 to illustrate the responsibilities and challenges in covering this extraordinarily complex issue for the publication of record in a frontline US border state at a time of turmoil in the journalism industry and the field of immigration policy.

A FAMILY ON THE MOVE

After Governor Brewer signed SB 1070, in April 2010, my *Republic* colleagues and I went out and started interviewing people "on the street" to see what effect the law was having. While the law still had not been implemented—that would not happen until late July, and not for all provisions—the possibility of police questioning people on the basis of their appearance or accent to see whether they were in the country legally created much fear in Arizona, where one-third of the population is Latino and there are about 524,000 Mexican-born residents. I started noticing yard sales popping up in neighborhoods with large concentrations of immigrants—you could drive down certain streets and see yard sales lining entire blocks, one after another. Clearly a lot of people were preparing to leave. In May, my editor, Kristen DelGuzzi, asked me to try to find a family leaving the state because of the new law. Sometimes it can take weeks or months to find the right subject for an immigration story. Undocumented immigrants are often reluctant to talk to reporters, because they do not want to call attention to themselves in newspaper articles. Finding a family for this story, however, turned out to be surprisingly easy.

My first thought was to head out to one of the many immigrant neighborhoods in the Phoenix area and start talking to people at supermarkets and shopping centers. This approach had worked in the past. But, before getting in my car, I remembered that, several weeks earlier, a landlord had called me to suggest a story. He wanted the public to know that the law was affecting not just immigrants but Anglos like him. He owned an apartment complex out in Surprise, a suburb west of Phoenix, where many families of renters were in the country illegally. One by one, they had started to move out. And, worse for him, there were no new families to replace the ones leaving. At the time, I had written his phone number on a piece of paper and told him I would get back to him. I decided to try giving him a call.

The landlord turned out to be very willing to help. I drove out about 45 minutes to see him that afternoon. I explained my assignment to him, and he called his wife and asked her to meet us at the apartment complex. A Latina, who spoke Spanish, she turned out to be the one who managed the units for him. She agreed to take me around the complex and introduce me to some of the tenants in the dozen apartments in the complex. It was not a very nice place. It was May, and already the temperature was reaching into the upper 90s, so not very many people were outside. She introduced me to one woman, and I told her who I was and that I was writing a story about the law and how it was affecting people. Right away she told me that she was planning to leave as soon as possible but that she had no definitive plans. She said her neighbor, however, was planning to leave immediately. I asked her if she could introduce me to her. She took me over to her apartment. I think she may have been outside because I do not remember knocking on her door.

The woman's name was Marlen, and she told me that she and her husband were moving to Pennsylvania in three weeks. She said she had three children, all born in the United States, and that they were selling as much of their stuff as possible before they left. I asked her whether she would be willing to let me follow her. She said she would have to wait until her husband came home. He worked for a landscaping company and would be home later that afternoon. I decided to wait for him, two hours in the courtyard under the shade of the tree, with a cold can of Coke Marlen brought me.

It was around 3:30 that afternoon when a white Ford pickup pulled into the parking space. A heavyset man with a braided ponytail that hung down to the middle of his back got out and started walking through the courtyard. Marlen went over and greeted him and then introduced me. He seemed a little taken aback to see this stranger hanging around in the courtyard waiting for him. I repeated my little spiel to him. He really did not look too happy about the whole idea. He said he wanted to talk it over with his wife. They walked away and sat down talking for a while on some white plastic chairs. By the look on his face, I was sure he was going to say no. After a while, he stood up and walked over. I cannot remember exactly what he said, but the answer was yes. I remember thinking, "Oh my God, this is going to be such a fantastic story." They were going to allow me to document everything about their move all the way to Pennsylvania. Before I even left the parking lot, I called my editor back. When she answered the phone, I remember exactly what I said: "I found someone."

The Republic assigned Pat Shannahan, a young and highly talented photographer, to work with me on the story. I was thrilled, because not only is Pat a really good photographer, he is easy to work with and very personable. I knew the family would like him, too. Pat and I started to visit Marlen and Luis and their family every other day or so. We hung out at their yard sales. We photographed Luis at his landscaping job trimming bushes outside an upscale office building as office workers passed by, seeming not even to notice him.

We went to their house the Sunday before they left, when they held a barbecue in the courtyard to say goodbye to all their neighbors. In the meantime, Pat and I were also planning out the logistics of our trip, as usual under pressure to keep costs as low as possible. We decided the most effective use of our time would be to rent our own car and follow them on the trip and then fly back to Phoenix from Philadelphia. The one-way car rental alone, as I recall, was upward of $1,500, but we did not want to spend another three or four days driving back to Phoenix. We knew that when we returned, we would have about four days to write the story, edit the photos, and get the whole project completed and into the paper. To save what little money they had, the family was planning to drive straight through to Philadelphia, sleeping at rest areas along the way. This would save us money, too.

Two other undocumented neighbors decided to join Marlen and Luis on their trip, to get out of Arizona and to see whether they could find jobs in Pennsylvania, too. One was the same woman I had talked to first, who would be traveling with her husband and their toddler daughter. The other neighbor was a young man who lived with his father, who had decided to give up and had returned home to Mexico. The son, however, decided to try his luck in Philadelphia. One day, Marlen and the woman were having a yard sale. The woman, always very friendly, approached me with a proposition. Their car was an old Jeep Cherokee with more than 200,000 miles. Her husband did not think it would make it all the way across the country without breaking down. She wanted to know whether I would be willing to split the cost of renting a car with them, saving money all around. Initially, I thought riding in the same car would give us hours to talk and get to know them. But of course it was out of the question. We could not be part of the story in any way, I explained to her. We were only observers. There was another issue I did not tell her. If we were to be pulled over by the police during the trip, we could be accused of aiding and abetting illegal immigrants. For days after that, she was no longer very friendly toward me.

That was not the only ethical dilemma we encountered during our trip. We left on Tuesday, June 8. We were a little caravan: Luis and Marlen and their kids in the white pickup, the other family in the red Jeep Cherokee, along with the single fellow, and then Pat and I bringing up the rear in our rental car. Lots happened along the way. But we had one really big scare. In Iowa, we were driving on the highway, midafternoon on a gorgeous summer day. I think Pat was driving. All of a sudden, a car zoomed up alongside us. Pat yelled out, "It's a cop." I looked over, and I could see it was a highway patrol officer in an unmarked car, talking on his cell phone. Obviously he had spotted our caravan. Three cars with Arizona plates. Traveling together. Filled with Mexicans. I am sure to him we looked suspicious. Perhaps he thought we were running drugs. He stayed alongside us for several minutes. Then he zoomed up to the Jeep in front of us. Pat and I started to panic. Especially Pat. A million questions started popping into our heads. What if he pulls them over? Do we keep driving? Do we stop, too? Do we take pictures? Would that make the police officer suspicious of them? What would we tell the officer—"We are following a group of illegal immigrants moving from Arizona to Pennsylvania"? We could not do that. Would we get them arrested?

The police officer stayed with us. He's running our plates, Pat said. Then he zoomed up to the next car. I remember my heart pounding in my chest. I could hardly breathe or think. This was going to be really bad. After what seemed like hours, the police officer zoomed ahead. In the end, he did not pull any of us over. The plates must have all checked out. I remember Pat and I breathing a huge sigh of relief. At the next rest area, we all pulled off the highway. When we got out of the car, we all laughed nervously and talked about what had just happened and how scared we had been. We felt like we had dodged a bullet. We stayed there for a while collecting ourselves and then hopped back in our vehicles and continued on.

The entire trip was fraught with tense moments. We had left Phoenix at about 5 p.m. Marlen and Luis wanted to travel through Arizona at night. They thought they would have their best chance of not getting pulled over by the police when there were fewer cops on the road. We crossed the state line into Utah about 1:30 a.m. I remember we pulled over on the side of the road. It was pitch black. The stars were like a ceiling over our heads. There was not a town for miles. We were in one of the most desolate places in the United States. Marlen and Luis were relieved to be out of Arizona.

Their kids were inside the pickup sleeping. The family in the other vehicle had also pulled over. I took out my notebook to write down some notes and quotes from Luis and Marlen. That is when I noticed a funny smell. After a couple more whiffs, I recognized the odor: radiator fluid. I remember thinking that it must just be my imagination.

We got back into our cars and continued driving through the darkness north into Utah. Giant rock formations passed by our windows like the shadows of ships in the night. We kept driving, but I kept smelling that odor. Then I noticed something that made my heart stop. There was smoke trailing behind the red Jeep. The more we drove, the thicker the smoke got. By then the driver was noticing it, too. We all pulled over and popped the hood. A thick cloud of steam poured out. I lent Luis my headlamp, and he crawled under the Jeep. He scooted out with the bad news. The water pump was busted. The first thought I had was that this was going to ruin my story. Our trip had barely started. These people would never make it to Pennsylvania. Luis was also getting frustrated. These people were tagging along. Luis's pickup was in good shape. Without them he could have kept right on driving. Now we were stuck on a desolate road in Utah with 2,000 miles to go.

Tempers started to flare. Luis thought the Jeep was overloaded with too much stuff. They started tossing suitcases full of clothing and belongings onto the side of the road. But there was still the busted water pump to deal with. There was no way they were going to fix it there. And they certainly did not want to stick around and wait for the police. They might start asking questions. The families decided they would try to keep driving. To cool the engine, they opened up their coolers. They did not have any gallons of water. They would have to use their drinking water. Luis and the other driver started twisting off the caps of plastic bottles of Dasani drinking water and pouring the water into the radiator one by one. After that, we got back into the vehicles and started driving. They drove until the engine got too hot, pulled over and waited for it to cool down and then poured in more Dasani. After about 45 minutes or so, we made it to a small town without seizing up the engine. It was the middle of the night. The town was totally still. We pulled into a gas station with a convenience store and turned off the cars. We would have to wait till morning to find a mechanic. Pat got some compelling pictures of the men sleeping on the hard cement sidewalk. After some hunting around, they were able to find a mechanic willing to fix the Jeep right away, for about $250. The driver of the Jeep had to borrow some cash from Luis to cover the bill. By about 10:30 a.m., we were back on the road.

We arrived in Pennsylvania utterly exhausted. Except for sleeping about six hours at a motel in Colorado and sleeping an hour or two here and there at rest stops, we had driven straight through for more than three days. In Pennsylvania I even fell asleep at the wheel. Pat noticed I was drifting into the other lane. He looked over and saw that my eyes were closed. He started yelling, "Dan, Dan!," and I snapped awake. With about an hour and a half to go, Luis also started falling asleep at the wheel. He pulled into a rest area.

It was night, and he did not think he could safely go on. We waited about 45 minutes and finally decided to keep going. We got to Luis's brother's house about 12:30 in the morning on a Saturday. His family was up waiting for us in their apartment. They fed us bowls of pozole with limes. Pat got some emotional pictures of them hugging and eating. They had made it. The next morning, Pat and I slept in and then went out for a big lunch. We expected Luis and Marlen to be doing the same. But when we called Luis, he was already out working with his brother, who had his own landscaping business. We drove over to a leafy neighborhood with large green lawns and big brick houses and found Luis in the backyard raking leaves and mowing the lawn. More great pictures.

Pat and I stuck around in Pennsylvania for two days photographing and interviewing Luis and Marlen in their new home. For now they would stay crammed into the same apartment with Luis's brother and his family. That Monday, we caught a noon flight back to Phoenix, and by Tuesday we were back in the office working on the story and photos. When they were published a week later, hundreds of readers posted comments online or wrote letters to the editor. Some of the comments were from readers who thought the story and photo portrayed "lawbreakers" in a sympathetic light. But most of the comments, as I recall, were positive and praised the paper's commitment to high-quality journalism. Some readers even wrote to offer their help to the families.

MOVING ACROSS THE SEA

Shortly after returning from the trip to Pennsylvania, we started thinking about how to broaden our coverage of SB 1070. For years we had been contemplating a major project examining the growing phenomenon of illegal immigration around the world. With the nation focused on Arizona's new immigration law, the timing seemed perfect. In late July, we got the green light from the publisher to do the project. Our budget was $6,000 to cover airfare, lodging, food, and payments to "fixers" to help me arrange and translate interviews and to serve as guides in Europe.

I spent most of August researching the issue of global migration. The first decision we had to make was what countries to visit. After deciding on Europe, I started calling immigration experts to pick their brains. The Migration Policy Institute in Washington, DC, put me in contact with its expert in Europe. At first, I was thinking of visiting Italy, Spain, and Greece. All three countries were experiencing problems with illegal immigration. But the European contact explained that, while a lot of media attention had already been placed on those countries, little attention had been paid to the countries where immigrants headed after entering Europe. She explained that Italy and Spain had a lot of unauthorized immigrants and problems with border security similar to Arizona's. But, also like Arizona, these were pass-through countries. She suggested I also visit a destination country, perhaps going to London, Paris, or Berlin.

Berlin seemed the most interesting. For one, Berlin has a large population of Turkish guest workers, many of whom came to Germany after World War II to help rebuild the country. Integration is a major issue in Germany, especially in Berlin. Political leaders have accused Turkish immigrants of not doing enough to integrate, while Turkish immigrants complain that they have not been accepted by German society and therefore do not feel German, even after several generations. For decades, under German immigration policy, while Turkish guest workers were allowed to live and work in the country legally, they could not become citizens. That is different from the United States, where anyone born in the country is a US citizen and where legal immigrants can apply for citizenship after a certain number of years. Berlin is also a magnet for immigrants from all over the world, both legal and illegal immigrants, many from Eastern Europe or Latin America. There was another, more personal reason I wanted to go to Berlin. I have been to London several times and visited Paris with my family when I was younger. But I had never been to Berlin. It seemed like it would be a fascinating city to visit, and that turned out to be true.

I also decided to visit Italy and Spain. Both countries are at the southern edges of the European Union, so immigrants who manage to enter legally or illegally can then move onto other EU countries without border controls. Italy's southern tip is less than 50 miles from Libya, which thousands of migrants from Africa were using as a launching point from which to travel by boat across the sea to the tiny Italian island of Lampedusa. Once they reached the island, the migrants had to be processed under European Union law and allowed into the country. Italy also has experienced a significant amount of human smuggling from Eastern Europe through Albania, as Stinellis's chapter details.

Spain has a similar situation along its southern border, which at the narrowest point is only 12 miles from Morocco across the Strait of Gibraltar. Africans from other countries make their way to Morocco and then are smuggled across the strait to Spain. Spain also has large numbers of immigrants from South America, many of whom come legally as tourists and then remain in the country to work as caretakers.

After deciding which countries to visit and setting up the trip, we started mapping out themes for the story: "integration" for Germany, an issue that also resonates in the United States; "enforcement" for Italy, since the country had begun cracking down on illegal immigrants and Roma; and "amnesty" for Spain. To deal with its large undocumented population, Spain had passed several amnesty programs allowing illegal immigrants to gain legal status and remain in the country.

In Arizona, I have written about immigration for more than 10 years, eight as an immigration reporter and before that as a Latino affairs reporter. I have a lot of experience finding immigrants to interview—not an easy task, as noted earlier. On deadline, the easiest way is to get in my car and drive to supermarkets in neighborhoods with large numbers of immigrants and try to interview people in the parking lot. I have also driven to the US Citizenship and Immigration Services building on Central Avenue near downtown Phoenix, where there are usually immigrants coming in and out of the building to apply for various immigration benefits, and to churches, parks, and festivals. Another way is to call the various immigrant advocacy groups in Phoenix. I have a wide network of contacts, and they can usually find me someone within a matter of hours, sometimes minutes. But I knew finding immigrants to interview in Europe would be my biggest challenge by far. I did not know my way around, I did not have any immigration contacts there, and I would be spending only about three days in each country. In this amount of time, I would have to find immigrants, gain their trust, and interview them, even though I do not speak Italian or German or any African language. The whole idea kept me up in the middle of the night filled with anxiety.

I decided the first thing I needed to do was to find people to help me on the ground in each country. For Germany, I first tried a German journalist from Berlin, Mario Kaiser, who had spent several months on a fellowship working at *The Arizona Republic,* but he was in the process of moving to New York City. He put me in contact with a Spanish woman, Ana Revuelta, who had lived in Berlin for years, spoke German, and had a lot of experience with immigrants. We began having conversations on Skype; we negotiated a fee, and she agreed to help me. I did not have any contacts in Italy, but the foreign editors at *USA Today,* a paper with which we had a relationship since at the time we shared the Mexico City bureau, sent me the e-mail address for their stringer in Rome. He gave me a lot of great background about Italy's immigration issues and suggested I visit Rome for a few days and then fly to the island of Lampedusa. He also said he would put me in contact with an Italian woman, Raffaella Pontarelli, who had set up interviews and translated for other *USA Today* reporters, and she agreed to help me out.

I still needed a contact in Spain. *The Arizona Republic* and Gannett also own a weekly Spanish-language newspaper in Phoenix called *La Voz,* which has its offices in our building, on the other side of a wall from me on the ninth floor. I was friendly with several of the *La Voz* staffers, partly because my immigration stories were sometimes translated into Spanish and published in their paper. *La Voz* had a relationship with the Spanish government to let young reporters work at *La Voz.* I had met one of the Spanish journalists one day at a café, and I remember chatting to him about my grandparents, who were originally from Asturias, in northern Spain. He had returned to Spain after his internship, but he popped into my memory. I talked to the officer manger at *La Voz,* which is like one big family, and fortunately for me, she had his contact information. His name was Francisco Sanchez, but he preferred to be called Javi, short for Javier, his middle name. He turned out to be perfect. He lived in Sevilla, in southern Spain, less than two hours from the Mediterranean. He also had not been able to find work as a journalist in Spain and was eager to help out. He even offered me a free place to stay at his aunt's apartment and access to his father's car. I could not believe how well everything was falling into place, all in about a month.

I left for Europe on Labor Day. I got up at 5 a.m. to catch my early morning flight. I remember sitting on the bed for several moments before jumping in the shower, wondering what lay ahead, filled with anxiety. The trip would either be a great success or a complete disaster. Everything depended on the groundwork I had done and my fixers' ability to help me find immigrants.

My flight from Phoenix to Berlin had a four-hour stopover in Minneapolis. Walking around the airport, I sneezed. I sneezed again. And again and again. Allergies? By the time I boarded my plane later that afternoon, I was in the throes of a full-blown cold. When I landed in Amsterdam the following morning, I was miserably sick. And I still had to catch a flight to Berlin. It was cloudy and cold when I arrived. The excitement of being in a city I had always wanted to visit made me feel less miserable. Plus I had no time to feel bad. Ana Revuelta was meeting me at my hotel at 1:30 p.m. I had enough time to drop my bags in my room, rinse my face, and get going.

Ana turned out to be a terrific guide and translator. She lived in the heart of Kreuzberg, a former East German enclave known for its large Turkish and immigrant population. Just a few doors away from her apartment, there was even a Mexican restaurant owned by an immigrant married to a German woman. In Berlin, with Ana's help, I interviewed an acrobat from Poland, a screen printer from Uruguay, a third-generation Turkish woman, an undocumented woman from Argentina, a restaurant owner from Nepal, and many other immigrants. I also interviewed a German public official who was an expert on immigration in Berlin and visited a community center that served immigrants from all over the world.

To keep my expenses down, Ana suggested I rent a bike. I felt kind of silly at first getting on my rental bike. Here I was, a 50-year-old man working for a major American newspaper, getting around on a bike. But riding a bike proved to be a great way to get around the city and save money on transportation. We rode our bikes everywhere, even in the rain and late at night. I remember one night finishing up an interview after midnight and then riding for miles through Berlin with Ana to get back to my hotel. I ended up not using a taxi during my three days in Berlin. It was quite an adventure.

From Berlin I flew to Rome. Again I had a lot to do in a little amount of time. I had to hit the ground running. I met Pontarelli in the lobby a half hour after arriving at my hotel. She was an aspiring actress who had just finished performing in a play. Raffaella told me we had an appointment to meet an architecture and urban studies professor from one of the universities who was studying shantytowns in Rome. The driver of our hired car took us to meet the professor, and then we all headed to an abandoned factory on the outskirts of Rome, which turned out to be a journalistic goldmine. The two buildings were covered with graffiti. Living inside were illegal immigrants from Africa, Latin America, and Eastern Europe. I also met a large colony of Roma, as gypsies in Europe are known. We spent the afternoon there walking around and interviewing people. By the time I left that evening, I was feeling really great about my story. Things only got better from there.

The next day, Raffaella took me to the outskirts of Rome, where she had heard there was a shanty built by immigrants. All she knew was that it was near one of the train stops. We took the train there and then started walking around the neighborhood. It took us a while to find it. The shanty was at the edge of a middle-class neighborhood surrounded by high-rise apartment buildings. The immigrants had taken over a small open area and completely filled it with homes constructed from scrap pieces of metal, cardboard, and wood boards. We walked around the edge trying to decide whether it was safe to enter. We could not see anyone walking around inside. The entrance was like the opening to a maze. Finally, we gathered our courage and slowly walked in, calling out hello to let anyone who was around know we were coming. Black immigrants from Africa started coming out of the makeshift doorways. They greeted us with smiles and friendly faces. Any fear we had quickly evaporated. Several invited us inside their humble structures and offered us food. We spent the rest of the morning interviewing, in Italian, immigrants from Eritrea, Sudan, and other sub-Saharan countries.

On my third day in Rome, Raffaella took me to another part of the city, also near a train station. It was a Sunday, and Raffaella had heard that immigrants from Ukraine gathered in the parking lot on Sundays to send money, food, and merchandise back to their families with couriers. The parking lot was filled with delivery vans with signs posted to their windshields listing the cities in Ukraine they serviced. Hundreds of Ukrainian immigrants were walking around with packages to send home. It was an amazing scene. The Ukrainians worked as what are known as *badanti* in Italy, immigrants who care for the elderly. They had amazing stories to tell, and we spent the morning and the early part of the afternoon walking around interviewing as many as possible. That afternoon, heading back to the center of Rome, we walked past a door with the word "phone" printed on a simple sign nailed to the wall. Raffaella told me these were little businesses that catered to immigrants who wanted to call home. Inside there were phone booths and computers the immigrants could rent to send e-mail. We met a group of teenage boys from Afghanistan. They had spent weeks hopping trains and hiding inside trucks to sneak into Italy. They told us they were on their way to Sweden to look for work. I took pictures and interviewed them for more than an hour. By then I had plenty of great material for my stories. In Rome, Raffaella also introduced me to several Italian experts on immigration. I interviewed them at their offices in between interviewing immigrants.

After three days in Rome, it was time to fly to Sevilla, in southern Spain, for the third and final leg of my trip to Europe. I arrived about 4 p.m., and

Javi came to meet me at the airport. He drove me to his parents' apartment in an affluent high-rise building near the old center of Sevilla. On the way, Javi broke some news. I would not have his aunt's apartment to myself, because some "couch surfers" from Croatia had shown up earlier in the day. Unbeknownst to Javi's aunt, Javi was using her apartment to let couch surfers spend a night or two in Sevilla for free. It was a good way to meet interesting people from other countries, he told me. He also thought it might be a good way to meet girls. But so far all his couch surfers had been guys. On the way to the apartment, Javi told me that a "couch surfer" from Germany had also arrived. He would be sharing the apartment with us as well, meaning there would be no privacy. I thought about checking into a hotel, but I did not want to make Javi think I was being rude by not accepting his hospitality. I decided to stick it out, and in the end I was glad I did.

We arrived at Javi's apartment complex right around time for *la comida,* the main meal of the day. I ate with him and his entire family—his mom, dad, aunt, little sister, and younger brother. I remember they prepared a delicious Spanish meal of baked fish over a bed of potatoes. After dinner, Javi and his dad left me in the living room, and I dozed off while his mother and aunt watched a telenovela on TV. It was the first down time I had had in a week. Later that evening, Javi and I took the elevator down to the parking garage and took a pair of bikes out of their storage compartment. We rode out into the streets to see whether we could find some African immigrants to interview. It was not hard. At almost every busy traffic intersection we found African immigrants wading into traffic when the light turned red to sell pocket-sized packages of tissues and air fresheners for cars. It was really a form of begging that was tolerated by the authorities. We spent several hours pedaling from one intersection to the next, interviewing African immigrants who had crossed the Strait of Gibraltar in rickety boats, often risking their lives, to seek work in Spain. At first they had an easy time finding jobs in Spain's booming construction industry, but now the housing market had crashed, and there were no more jobs. Hawking tissues and air fresheners was how they survived.

The next day, Javi and I spent mostly on the computer lining up interviews for the rest of the week. Javi made arrangements to meet with members of the Guardia Civil, Spain's version of the federal police, at their outpost in Algeciras, a port city that sits just 12 miles from Morocco across the Strait of Gibraltar. The next morning we left in the dark at 6 a.m. to make the two-hour drive in Javi's parents' car and arrived in Algeciras in time for our 8:30 a.m. appointment. We interviewed several members of the Guardia Civil. We watched a patrol boat arrive from a night out patrolling the shores off the coast of Spain, looking for drug smugglers and illegal immigrants arriving by boat from Morocco. We visited a surveillance room where men and women in uniforms monitored computer screens looking for signs of illegal trafficking. The whole scene was eerily reminiscent of my visits to the

Border Patrol's station in Nogales, Arizona. The only thing different was that instead of desert, there was water.

After the visit to the Guardia Civil, we drove to a Red Cross shelter in town. The two-story shelter, its stucco façade painted white and red, was filled with illegal immigrants from Morocco and Africa who had been caught by the Guardia Civil. Instead of returning them to Africa, the Guardia Civil had released them to the Red Cross so that they could receive medical treatment. Most had claimed asylum, which meant they would not be sent back anytime soon. We drove about two hours along the beautiful coast after leaving Algeciras to the coast city of Cadiz. It was late afternoon by then, and the streets were filled with people strolling. That is when I noticed something interesting.

Many of the elderly Spanish people I saw sitting on benches along the sidewalk or in parks were accompanied by people who looked much like the Latin Americans I see in Arizona and other places I have lived in the United States. In a park, I approached an elderly Spanish couple sitting on a pair of park benches. Next to them was a woman with brown skin, dark hair, and other Indian/Native American features. I asked the woman where she was from. I was right. The woman was from Ecuador. She was the elderly couple's caretaker. The couple's daughter was there, also. She explained that she worked as a nurse and could not care for her parents and her young daughter, so she had hired the woman from Ecuador. This was perfect for my story. Spain had passed numerous amnesties in recent years aimed at turning illegal immigrants into taxpayers. One of the amnesties was aimed at people like the woman from Ecuador, an illegal immigrant who had arrived in Spain on a tourist visa but remained after her visa had expired to work as a caretaker. It was yet another example of the incredible good reporting fortune I had during my entire trip.

The following day, Javi and I borrowed his parents' car again to drive to Huelva, a city where a college friend of Javi's was working at a prison. On the side, he had done some work advocating for migrants' rights for Amnesty International, including swimming 12 miles across the Strait of Gibraltar to call attention to the hundreds of migrants who had died trying to reach Spain. He took us to Moguer, a farming town with white stucco houses, where he had heard that African immigrants were living in shanties. We found the little shanty village on the outskirts of town behind a fruit warehouse. The conditions were deplorable, the worst of any of the shanties I had seen so far in Europe. There was no running water. No toilets. No electricity. The men were cooking what little food they had on open fires like camping. The houses were constructed out of cardboard and scraps of wood from fruit crates. To keep the water out when it rained, the men had covered the flimsy roofs with sheets of plastic. The immigrants we met there were from Morocco or from any of several sub-Saharan countries. Most of them seemed eager to tell their stories, and we spent several hours interviewing people and taking pictures. I even shot a video of one migrant from Senegal.

That afternoon, we returned to Javi's apartment building in Sevilla. We celebrated the end of my two weeks of reporting in Europe by meeting some of his friends at a local bar and then bicycling over to the apartment of the German couch surfer we had met earlier that week, who was starting graduate school. We drank from a large bottle of beer passed around from person to person until about 2 in the morning. I remember feeling kind of old among the group of students and young people from France, Germany, Spain and Mexico. Javi even started calling me Grandpa. Under a light drizzle, we pedaled our way back to his apartment building. I remember feeling pretty exhausted but happy with all that I had experienced and accomplished in such a short time. Before catching my plane the following day, I had time to track down my father's cousin, who lives in Sevilla with her husband. They made me a traditional Spanish lunch before driving me to the airport. To save money, I had bought a round trip ticket from Phoenix to Berlin. That meant I had to first fly from Spain back to Germany. My flight landed in Berlin just before midnight. I had enough time to sleep for about three hours at a nearby hotel and then get back to the airport for my 6 a.m. flight. After stops in Brussels and Atlanta, I finally made it back to Phoenix 20 some hours later. It was around 7 p.m. when my wife and three kids picked me up at the airport.

I took off a few days after returning from Europe to get over my cold and unwind after almost two weeks of working nonstop from breakfast until midnight on most days. When I returned to work, I had about a month to finish reporting and writing a half dozen stories so that I could turn them over to my editors and the copy desk. I wrote nonstop for the final three weeks. Since this was going to be a major 16-page special section, the top editors of the project also went through the entire project line by line. In the meantime, I worked with the photo desk to edit the photos I had brought back and with a videographer to add dialog and narrative to the video I had shot. I also worked with the graphics and online editors to produce a separate package that could be posted online, where the entire 16-page project could be downloaded as a PDF and viewers could click on various interactive graphics. The entire package was published in mid-December, about three months after I returned from my trip.[2] It was a fast turnaround for such a major project.

The response was terrific. Many readers wrote to congratulate and thank the newspaper for putting the immigration debate that had been raging in Arizona for years in a global perspective. Now, several years later, the online version of the project continues to draw readers from all over the country.

The series of front-page stories documenting one undocumented family's move to Pennsylvania and the major 16-page special section and online package about the rise of global migration show that *The Republic* continues to have a strong commitment to pursue ambitious journalism endeavors that serve and inform our readers despite declining revenues, economic uncertainty, and a rapidly changing media landscape. This type of journalism, however, is done much more judiciously than in the past. Careful consideration is given to the cost and to the potential impact of a story before it receives a green light. And the expectation that reporters will produce top-notch work with limited budgets and resources has become the norm.

NOTES

1. http://www.azcentral.com/news/articles/2010/06/27/20100627arizona-immigration-law-leaving-state.html
2. http://www.azcentral.com/news/global-immigration/index.php#intro.

14 Violence, Drugs, and Migration in the Border of Ciudad Juárez-El Paso

The Challenges Facing Journalists

Lourdes Cárdenas

El Paso Times

At the beginning of 2008, the war between two powerful Mexican drug cartels generated an incredible wave of violence in some cities along the US-Mexican border. In Ciudad Juárez, located in the northern state of Chihuahua and to the west of the Texas-Mexico border, the feud over control of drug-trafficking routes between the Cartel de Sinaloa and the Cartel de Juárez has claimed the lives of more than 10,000 people since the war began. Figures from the Chihuahua's State Attorney Office offer a clear picture of the escalation of violence: in 2007, 307 people were killed in cases related to drug trafficking; in 2008, the number rose to 1,607; in 2009, it was 2,601; and by 2010, the most violent year in the period, assassinations escalated to 3,156.[1]

At the height of the drug war, killings became so randomized that anyone could fall victim, including journalists, as the next chapter details. An entire society was affected by an increase in kidnappings, extortion, robberies, and a vast array of crimes, with youth often becoming favorite targets. The massacre of 15 teenagers and football players during a birthday party the night of January 31, 2010, was an indicator of the level of deterioration of the city. In July, a car bomb exploded in the middle of a busy avenue in downtown Juárez. It was the first time that drug cartels used a car bomb to attack civilians and police. The explosion of the vehicle, packed with 22 pounds of a powerful water gel explosive, left three people dead and a dozen civilians wounded. The violence was reaching an unprecedented level, particularly on the weekends. Reports of slaughtered scores were the top stories in local newspapers every Monday morning. During one weekend in February 2010, 53 people were massacred in different incidents. The violence had yet to reach its peak.

For journalists like me, covering the border from both sides in such a flashpoint as Juárez-El Paso, the challenges and dangers are omnipresent and range all the way from difficulty in finding correct figures on migration to risking one's own life. In this chapter, I detail some of the tasks that reporters face when covering this porous border during a violent international drug war.

MIGRATING TO FLEE THE VIOLENCE

As an immediate and visible consequence of the rampant violence, hundreds of people fled the city. Juárez lost a core part of its population due to internal and external migration. Data from the Instituto Nacional de Geografía Estadística e Informática—the equivalent of the US Census Bureau—shows that by 2010 the number of unoccupied dwellings in the city had reached 111,103, and more than 10,000 businesses were shut down because of the violence and the economic crisis.

In August 2010, an official representing the Mexican government described the feud between the two cartels as the bloodiest drug war thus far. The killings had escalated to more than 8,000 at the time of the official's comments. Juárez was labeled the most dangerous city in the world—a remarkable contrast with its sister city, El Paso, Texas, where I am based, known as one of the safest cities in America, with a homicide rate of 16 people per year on average throughout the past decade.

Violence and the migration associated with it have always been present in the history of the Ciudad Juárez-El Paso border region—but it is an increasingly difficult and dangerous story for journalists to tell. It is believed that almost half a million people fled the city during the Mexican Revolution at the beginning of the 20th century to establish themselves across the river or farther into the United States. Several historians, including Mario T. Garcia, have documented the exodus of people fleeing the violence of either the rebel troops or the Mexican Army.[2] In 1912, for example, El Paso welcomed a group of 4,500 train passengers, most of them Mormon refugees, fleeing the violence of the Mexican Revolution. According to historians and academics, the five-year-old George W. Romney, father of the 2012 Republican presidential candidate Mitt Romney, was among the passengers.[3]

A NEW KIND OF ECONOMIC MIGRATION

Economic conditions have been always behind waves of immigrants. As Garcia states, it is believed that between 1880 and the Great Depression, almost 1 million Mexicans entered the United States, thousands arriving first in El Paso. The El Paso-Juárez region is situated midway along the 2,000 miles of the United States and Mexico international border. Both cities have a combined population of more than 2 million, making it the largest community on the border. The cities call themselves "sister cities" in allusion to their mutual dependence, which has its most visible expression in the daily crossing of more than 250,000 people across the four international bridges. People from both sides usually cross to study, to work, to shop, or just to have fun.

In the urban space of this border region, most of the people make a living from the manufacturing industry, trade, and services. According to the El

Paso Regional Economic Development Corporation (Redco), an El Paso–based consultant firm, the El Paso-Juárez area is ranked fifth in land trade among the top US foreign-trade gateways. In 2011, 18 percent of all trade between the United States and Mexico ($80.1 billion) crossed through the El Paso-Juárez border. In addition, the Dallas Federal Reserve estimates that in 2010, Mexicans spent about $1.4 billion in retail in El Paso. The same institution estimates that for every job created by the *maquiladora* industry in Juárez, another job is created in El Paso.[4]

These figures were the reasoning behind remarks made by former El Paso city council member Beto O'Rourke in 2009 about the cities' mutual dependence. He warned that the violence in Juárez would have long-term effects in the region. "If Juárez dies, El Paso will die, too," he said.[5] The dynamics of the two cities are so intertwined that any significant event on one side of the border has the potential to affect the other in almost predictable ways. In that sense, when the drug-trafficking violence escalated in 2008, the migration of people from Juárez to El Paso seemed to be an expected phenomenon.

Abundant stories published in the media were descriptive about something that was evident for most of the people in El Paso: A growing number of Mexican businesses—mostly restaurants and bars with a long tradition and reputation in Juárez—were closing down their doors because of the violence and establishing new branches in El Paso. The new businesses were dramatically changing the entertainment scene in the city.

By the beginning of 2010, the chief of the El Paso police, Greg Allen, launched the first estimate of the magnitude of this migration, saying that 30,000 Mexican nationals had moved to El Paso after fleeing the violence in Juárez. However, he did not explain how he came up with that figure or what kind of research was behind his estimate. After the chief of police's estimates, researchers from the Ciudad Juárez Autonomous University (UACJ) released a study concluding that approximately 250,000 people fled Juárez from 2008 to 2010 and that, of those, around 124,000 went to El Paso. In a much more conservative estimate, the mayor of El Paso, John Cook, calculated that just 10,000 people moved to the city as a result of the violence.

With so many discrepancies in the figures, the challenge for most journalists became how we could measure in some way the magnitude of the exodus, to establish who were these migrant transplants, how were they adjusting in their new homes, and what kind of impact they were having on their arrival city.

When analyzing the historical migration flows from Mexico to the United States, it is easy to identify some unchanging factors, such as poverty levels and social condition of the migrants—they usually come from impoverished regions—as well as other factors such as economic cycles. Within that historical migration flow, the Juárez region was traditionally considered more of a crossing point than a migrant-expelling place. In other words, people coming from the south and central states headed to the border of Juárez to attempt to cross to the United States, especially to the northern and central states of the country.

But the violence seemed to change that trend.

The 2008–2010 newcomers were not precisely the typical undocumented immigrant crossing in the middle of the night or helped by *coyotes* (human smugglers). On the contrary, it became easy to identify the two kinds of immigrants fleeing the violence. Some were middle- or upper-class people who, after being victims of kidnappings, extortion, or threats, were transferring their businesses to El Paso, buying houses, and fueling the local economy in several ways. Others were (and still are) crossing the border seeking political asylum because their lives had been threatened and the Mexican government had not been able to protect them.

In the spring of 2011, I led an investigative reporting class at the University of Texas at El Paso. The class was part of a project named "Mexodus," which was founded by the Ethics and Excellence Journalism Foundation. The students enrolled in my Special Topics class were assigned to report and document in all possible ways the exodus of people from Ciudad Juárez to El Paso as a result of violence related to the drug war.

It was not an easy task for them, considering the lack of formal studies or analysis about the ongoing phenomena. With the exception of the UACJ study, none of the estimates of the magnitude of this new migration were based on a clear source or methodology that could explain where those numbers came from. For the students enrolled in my class, finding those figures and sources to measure the exodus became their main assignment. But, given the daily dynamics of this border region and its interdependency, it was a daunting task.

In any other city far away from the border, one of the first places a reporter would look to find traces of the impact of a new wave of immigrants would be the school system. The logic would be simple: if thousands of people are fleeing the violence and moving to the city across the bridge, public schools would immediately feel the impact, not just because of an increase in enrollment numbers but also because of the problems typically associated with newcomers from other countries, particularly lack of language proficiency. Thus, the first direction I gave to my students was to look at those specific numbers.

However, a detailed analysis of the enrollment number for a period of five academic years (from 2005–2006 to 2010–2011) in the three most important school districts in the area did not show a significant increase either in enrollment numbers or in the number of students classified as Limited English Proficient (LEP), English as Second Language (ESL), or Economically Disadvantaged Students.[6]

As a whole, the El Paso Independent School District had an enrollment increase of no more than 600 students in the period analyzed, which was the first relevant indication that the newcomers were not impacting the school system significantly. The other important school districts, Ysleta Independent

School District and Socorro Independent School District, showed a similar trend, although the latter had a bigger increase in its student population—around 3,000—which authorities attributed to several factors, including the impact of Fort Bliss's expansion, internal migrations within the country, and, to a lesser extent, the arrival of children coming from Juárez.

Were these numbers an indication that the number of people experiencing the drug cartel violence was not as big as the most extreme analysis suggested? Most likely yes, but, at the same time, it did not mean that the migration of Juarenses fleeing the violence was not happening. It was just a question of the magnitude of the phenomenon.

One of the major difficulties in trying to document the migration in this border area is paradoxically the constant movement of people that characterizes borders. In the particular case of schools, it is well known—but poorly documented with hard data—that hundreds if not thousands of children cross every day from Mexico to the United States to attend school. Many of these children live in Juárez but come to school in El Paso. It has been this way for many years. It is likely that many of their families moved to El Paso when the violence got worse but that, because the children were already enrolled in school, there was no visible impact in the whole system when the families moved to live on the American side of the border. That could explain why the enrollment numbers did not show significant increases.

However, if the general numbers did not give us a whole picture, we found some particular data helpful. For example, looking at the ESL and LEP figures helped us to identify which specific schools in what particular areas of the county were dealing with the largest incoming flow of Mexican immigrants. These numbers made it possible for the journalism students to develop more human-interest stories on how teachers and students were dealing with the problems of language, trauma, and the permanent adaptation to a new political and cultural system.

As I previously noted, the particular dynamics of the border make it difficult to get conclusive data with which to analyze the flow of migration and its impact on specific situations. The same also applies to the problems in finding conclusive data on the number of businesses originally from Ciudad Juárez that moved to El Paso.

Considering that restaurants and bars were the most visible indicator of the migration of Juarenses to El Paso, a reporter would usually track the numbers of new licenses granted by the local commission for alcoholic beverage businesses, as well as the databases of the local secretary of state containing the names of new companies establishing a presence in the area. Those records usually contain the name of the company, owner or representative, type of business, and contact information. However, none of these records provide specific information about the nationality of the owner or his or her immigration status. In other words, if the owner of a furniture company shut down his business in Juárez and decided to reopen it in El Paso, there would not be a public record to document that transition.

Making matters even more complicated is the high percentage of people with dual citizenship in the border area. A good example is that of Mexican-American businessman Jose "Pepe" Yanar, a well-known entrepreneur in Ciudad Juárez, whom I interviewed for the Mexican business magazine *Expansion* in 2010. Yanar moved the main operations of his furniture factory to El Paso after escaping his kidnappers in 2009. Yanar was born in the United States, but he grew up, married, and raised a family in Ciudad Juárez. He is fully bilingual and gets around easily in either of the two countries. He is part of a group of people, usually middle or upper middle class, who maintain strong links with the cities on both sides of the border. When Yanar was able to escape from his kidnappers, he did not hesitate for a second. He took very few things from his house and crossed the border with his family, using his US passport. He then opened an office in El Paso and changed his management style mainly by using video cameras to follow the production process of his furniture factory in Juárez step by step. He registered his business in El Paso as an American citizen.

Other Juárez businessmen might have permanent resident status, which allows them to open businesses in El Paso. Some have US-born children who help them transfer their businesses across the border. A few of them were likely to apply for special visas such as the E1 or E2 (usually granted to investors) or for the visa Nafta, which is granted to citizens of North American Free Trade Agreement countries. A review of the US Citizenship and Immigration Service numbers regarding these kinds of visas shows that between 2001 and 2005, the United States granted 7,603 business and investor visas to Mexicans. That number soared to 31,068 between 2005 and 2010.

Looking at those figures, however, does not necessarily provide a good indicator of migration patterns because, as explained, many of the businesses that opened in El Paso were owned by people who already lived on both sides of the border. Many were American citizens with family ties both to Juárez and to the United States. Many others had properties on both sides, and many more had children born in the United States who were petitioning for their parents and trying to arrange their legal residence. So, when the violence increased and they moved to El Paso, these families entered the country as citizens or green-card holders, and, again, there was no official record of that movement, making it another story that was hard for journalists to report.

JOURNALISTS AMONG ASYLUM SEEKERS

In November 2008, Mexican journalist Jorge Luis Aguirre, director of the online news site La Polaka, fled Juárez hours after the assassination of Armando Rodriguez, a reporter from *El Diario de Ciudad Juárez,* who had written hundreds of stories related to drug trafficking and corruption in the city. Aguirre argued that his life was in imminent danger and that he had received death threats within minutes of Rodriguez's killing. He fled to El Paso seeking political asylum.

Aguirre was only the best-known case in a group of journalists who came to El Paso in 2009 and 2010 seeking political asylum. The reporters, mostly from Juárez, argued that the Mexican government was not able to guarantee their safety, and some of them even blamed the government, particularly the army, for the threats against them. Their cases were the tipping point of the other side of the migration caused by the violence in Mexico's border cities. Their cases were considered "high profile," and therefore they were widely documented by the press, but many other cases were emerging and showing the real drama behind the asylum seekers.

In June 2012, the last two members of the Reyes-Salazar family, known in Juárez and in the small town of Villa Ahumada (a few miles from Juárez) for their social and political activism, fled Mexico to join their 20 relatives who were already seeking asylum in the United States. The story of the Reyes-Salazar family clearly shows the fear and terror in which many people were living in the area: since November 2008, six members of the family had been brutally assassinated and their tortured bodies dumped in the streets. Some of the family members were granted asylum in early January 2012, and others are still waiting for it. The Reyes-Salazar family story is not unique. In the El Paso area, several activists, ordinary citizens as well as policemen, have been seeking asylum since the drug war started in 2008. Few cases have been solved positively, and many others are still awaiting resolution. Carlos Spector, a local immigration lawyer, is handling most of the asylum cases in El Paso, and, by October 2012, his office had 195 pending cases, most of them from families coming from Ciudad Juárez and Chihuahua.

The Executive Office of Immigration Review reported that more than 3,200 Mexicans filed for asylum in 2010 and 1,671 applications were withdrawn. Only 49 were granted. In the El Paso area, the immigration courts received a total of 147 asylum petitions, but just two petitions were granted. Needless to say, the people involved in these types of cases are usually traumatized, and, although they feel relatively safe in the United States, they are still afraid for their lives and tend to keep a low profile. When they talk to the press, they usually ask to remain anonymous, and, sometimes, many details of their story cannot be told without endangering their lives even more. As a reporter, one must then deal with ethical and moral issues before reporting and writing their stories.

DRUGS AND THE BORDER: THE US CONNECTION

The drug-trafficking war has produced more news stories than ever along the Juárez-El Paso border. Most of those stories have to do with the violence and its general impact in society. However, an issue not yet thoroughly explored is the role of the United States in the explosion of the problem and particularly the role that border cities play in its continuation.

When Representative O'Rourke warned, "If Juárez dies, El Paso will die too," he was trying to bring attention to the need to get the United States more involved in the solution of the drug violence problem. In January of 2009, O'Rourke, a liberal El Pasoan, made headlines when he proposed a city council resolution asking Congress to start an "open and honest debate" about ending the prohibition of illegal drugs such as marijuana. This, he argued, was a way to support Juárez and to enforce legislation against money laundering and human and weapons trafficking. He also emphasized that part of the violence in Mexico, and particularly in Ciudad Juárez, was a direct cause of the insatiable US appetite for drugs. All city council members approved the resolution, but Mayor John Cook vetoed it days later, arguing that the city would lose federal money if the controversial discussion continued.

The United States is the prime consumer of illicit drugs in the world. A report from the Congressional Research Services indicated that Mexico is America's largest supplier of marijuana and methamphetamines.[7] The 2011 National Drug Threat Assessment (NDTA) found that the overall demand for drugs in the United States is increasing, particularly among young people, who are consuming more marijuana, heroin, and methamphetamines than ever before.[8] It is estimated that 90 percent of the cocaine consumed in the United States gets into the country through Mexico, and a large percentage of that crosses through various southwestern ports of entry.

Along the US-Mexico border there are 43 ports of entry, 18 of them in Texas. Through Ciudad Juárez-El Paso's four ports of entry, huge amounts of illicit drugs are trafficked every day. According to an Immigration and Customs Enforcement report, 2.7 million pounds of drugs (including cocaine, heroin, marijuana and methamphetamines) were seized in 2010 through the Texas ports of entry, mainly in El Paso. However, authorities believe that amount is just a small percentage of the total amount of drugs that goes through the US ports of entry yearly. In fact, El Paso is one of the cities mentioned in the NDTA as a storage and initial distribution center: "More illicit drugs are seized along the Southwest Border than in any other arrival zone. Mexican DTOs (drug trafficking organizations) have developed sophisticated and expansive drug transportation networks extending from the Southwest Border to all regions of the United States. They smuggle significant quantities of illicit drugs through and between ports of entry (POEs) along the Southwest Border and store them in communities throughout the region. Most of the region's principal metropolitan areas, including Dallas, El Paso, Houston, Los Angeles, Phoenix, San Antonio, and San Diego, are significant storage locations as well as regional and national distribution centers."[9]

Mexican drug cartels have built networks and alliances with US street gangs to work together, not only in the retail-level distribution of drugs but also in other specific tasks such as smuggling cash and weapons to Mexico and the killing or disappearance of rivals. In the El Paso-Juárez area, *Barrio Azteca,* a violent gang, originated inside an El Paso prison in 1986 and became the armed muscle of the Cartel de Juárez in fighting the Cartel de Sinaloa.

In a congressional hearing on May 2011, Gomecindo Lopez, commander of the El Paso County Sheriff's Special Operations Bureau, said that drug traffickers and Mexican hit men lived on the American side of the border and crossed regularly to the other side to perform their illegal activities. "We know that we have drug cartels members, we know we have hit men living in the American side. Typically they do their 'business' in Mexico and then they cross again," Lopez said.[10]

One of the most notorious cases showing this elaborate collaboration scheme was the killing of three Americans in Ciudad Juárez in March 2010. A US Consulate employee, Lesley Enriquez Redelfs; her husband, Arthur Redelfs, an El Paso County sheriff's detention officer; and Jorge Alberto Salcido Ceniceros, whose wife also worked at the US Consulate in Juárez, were fatally shot during an attack after leaving a children's party in Juárez. According to court documents, one leader of the Juárez Cartel, who later was arrested and extradited to the United States, ordered the killing. The reason behind the crime was never clear, but a member of the cartel said the Americans were killed because some within the cartel had information that the consulate employees were issuing visas to members of the rival cartel. Another person who was arrested said the real target was the El Paso sheriff employee. US authorities indicted 35 alleged Barrio Azteca gang leaders, members, and associates in connection with the slayings.[11] The only explanation US officials have given for the slayings is that gang members mistook the victims for other targets.

The killings made national headlines in the United States and Mexico, and the pressure to find the killers was felt on both sides of the border. The perpetrators were arrested and brought to justice in less than a year, something unusual in a country like Mexico, where more than 90 percent of criminal cases are never resolved. Because it involved American officials, this became a high-profile case, relatively easy to report. But other cases of kidnappings, killings, and other crimes related to drug trafficking on the American side of the border have been difficult to document or to report, mainly because of the lack of investigation and concrete data.

According to sources from the US State Department, a total of 37 US citizens were killed in Juárez in 2010, and 39 were killed the year before.[12] There are no data to indicate how many of those killings were solved or what was the reason behind the murders. Documenting and investigating these criminal events and establishing the possible connections between Mexican drug cartels and their multiple branches in the United States is one of the pending assignments for reporters in the border.

The proximity of the two cities has been also crucial for the trafficking of weapons. It is often said that drugs flow to the north and money and weapons flow to the south. In September 2011, the *Los Angeles Times* documented that a number of lost weapons from the US government's "Fast and Furious" operation were in storage in El Paso and were eventually going to be sent to Mexico.

"Fast and Furious" was an undercover operation by the Bureau of Alcohol, Tobacco, Firearms, and Explosives (ATF) that aimed to stem the flow of firearms into Mexico by interdicting straw purchasers and gun traffickers within the United States. The main purpose of the operation was to track the guns to Mexican drug cartel leaders. But the operation became a complete disaster because the majority of the 2,000 weapons were lost after they entered Mexico. Some of the firearms trafficked by smugglers were later found at several crime scenes in Mexico, including the killing of US Border Patrol agent Brian Terry. Former officials from the Drugs Enforcement Administration have also said that criminal organizations, such as Los Zetas, are using El Paso as a central operations point to smuggle weapons to Mexico. The number of weapons smuggled to Mexico is unknown, but the Mexican government has said that 85 percent of the firearms used by drug cartels come from the United States.

CONCLUSIONS

The proximity, interdependence, and geographical location of Ciudad Juárez and El Paso explain the uniqueness of this area and the complexity of its problems. For any journalist, a border like this one offers an exceptional opportunity to explore the intricacy of the US-Mexico relationship in extreme situations, such as the ones posed by the war on drugs, and the political and social implications of any decision taken on either side of the border.

It is a tremendous challenge to report on both sides of the border for different but similar reasons. On the Mexican side, the dangers are as clear as a death threat can be. More than 65 journalists have been killed in Mexico since 2006, when President Felipe Calderon launched a crackdown on drug trafficking. Two of those journalists, Armando Rodríguez, an investigative reporter, and Luis Carlos Santiago, a photographer, were killed in Ciudad Juárez. Both worked for *El Diario de Juárez*. Many other journalists in the city have been threatened and work under extreme stress and pressure. Because access to public information, such as indictments or affidavits, is practically nonexistent in Mexico, reporters have to do their own basic research, putting their lives in constant risk. However, they have never stopped reporting and continue researching, having learned to traverse and survive in a war zone. On the other side of the border, journalists often feel safer, but that does not mean they are immune to threats. Journalist Diana Washington Valdez, who extensively investigates the murder of women in Juárez, received several death threats when reporting for the *El Paso Times*. She continues reporting on issues related to women, violence, and drug trafficking, but mainly from the US side. Because of the availability of information, most of the reporting on drug cartel activities and connections on the US side of the border is based on US court documents, affidavits, or indictments. Those documents offer a glance at how the drug cartels operate in the United States. However, a few El Paso reporters dare to venture to Juárez to do reporting. One reporter who does constantly cross into Juárez is Angela Kocherga, Border Bureau Chief for Belo TV, a Texas media company, whose stories usually offer a comprehensive view of the complexities of the drug war and its cost on both sides of the border.

As the editor of SomosFrontera.com, the Spanish website of the *El Paso Times,* I am always concerned with the security of our photographer, who is based in Juárez, and our reporters, as well as my own. We cover stories in Juárez that deal with violence, trauma, neglected urban areas, and many other issues that imply some kind of risk. In a situation like that, it is important to implement some type of safety protocol to reduce the possibility of incidents.

Unfortunately, the idea of implementing safety protocols has not been adopted in many newsrooms in the border area. At the *El Paso Times,* for example, we care for ourselves by letting friends or colleagues know that we are going to Juárez—no more. As the editor of SomosFrontera, I always ask the reporters to inform me whom are they going to interview, where and at what time, and which other places they will go to complete the story. We try to be extremely careful when dealing with stories that involve killings and drug-trafficking issues. Precautions include the evaluation of the risks associated with the story, as well as discussion of access to and the accuracy of the sources. For me, no one story is worth a reporter's life, so the big challenge becomes to continue writing about this important issue, but without putting at risk our lives.

The National Drug Intelligence Center has predicted that Mexican transnational criminal organizations will maintain their reign over the drug trade for the foreseeable future. As those organizations solidify their dominance on the US wholesale drug trade, the challenges journalists face in covering the implications of that criminal system will be exacerbated every day. The complications that stem from thoroughly and accurately covering a border region, its nuances and its far-reaching effects, are inescapable.

NOTES

1. By 2011 the violence started decreasing, an ongoing trend. This chapter was written in September 2012, when violence showed a significant and remarkable decrease from the years before. In 2011, the number of drug related homicides in the city reached 1,910; by June 2012, the number of homicides was 653. These figures are from the Chihuahua's State Attorney Office and may differ from independent and media accounts.

2. In *Desert Immigrants: The Mexicans of El Paso, 1880–1920* (Yale University Press, 1981), Mario T. Garcia offers a detailed and powerful description of the exodus of people fleeing the Revolution and the conditions they faced when crossing the bridges and entering the United States

3. Steven Olsen, curator for the Church of Jesus Christ of Latter-day Saints in Salt Lake City, Utah, told a story about the 100th anniversary of the Mormon exodus to the *El Paso Times* on July 30, 2012.

4. Roberto Coronado, "Impact of Cross-Border Retail Activity on El Paso's Economy," presentation to the International Council of Shopping Centers Hispanic Market—El Paso Program, June 1, 2011, http://www.icsc.org/2011S08/Dallas%20Fed%20EP%20Economy%20%206-1-2011.pdf.

5. Around the time this article was written, in fall 2012, O'Rourke was elected US Representative for Texas's 16th congressional district after defeating incumbent Silvestre Reyes in the Democratic primary election.

6. The three most important school districts in the El Paso area are El Paso Independent School District (EPISD), Ysleta Independent School District (YISD), and Socorro Independent School District (SISD).

7. Kristin M. Finklea, William J. Krouse, and Marc R. Rosenblum, "Southwest Border Violence: Issues in Identifying and Measuring Spillover Violence," Congressional Research Service, August 2010, http://fpc.state.gov/documents/organization/148803.pdf.

8. National Drug Threat Assessment 2011, US Department of Justice, National Drug Intelligence Center, http://www.justice.gov/archive/ndic/pubs44/44849/44849p.pdf.

9. Kristin M. Finklea et al., "Southwest Border Violence: Issues in Identifying and Measuring Spillover Violence," Congressional Research Service, June 2011, http://fpc.state.gov/documents/organization/166836.pdf.

10. José Díaz Briseño, "Reportan que sicarios mexicanos viven en Estados Unidos," *Terra*, May 4, 2011, http://www.terra.com.mx/gobierno_obama/articulo/1103074.

11. "Thirty-five Members and Associates of Barrio Azteca Gang Charged with Racketeering and Other Offenses, including 10 Charged in U.S. Consulate Murders in Juarez, Mexico," Department of Justice press release, http://www.justice.gov/opa/pr/2011/March/11-ag-299.html.

12. Diana Washington Valdez, "US Citizens Dying in Mexico: American Deaths Expected to Increase in 2011," *El Paso Times,* November 5, 2011, http://www.elpasotimes.com/juarez/ci_19264315.

15 Investigative Reporting at Risk

The Heroes and the Horrors behind Attacks on Journalists in Mexico

Lise Olsen
Houston Chronicle

Nearly 200 investigative journalists converged from all corners of the US-Mexico border at the salmon-colored Hotel Lucerna in Ciudad Juárez to discuss their targets: corrupt politicians, contaminators, criminals, rogues and wrong-doers of all stripes.[1] The gathering came in late 1997—a high point in the halcyon days of border journalism. After seven decades, the ruling PRI party had loosened its iron grip on the Mexican media, and muckraking border reporters had won backing from powerful media moguls in both the United States and Mexico. Some of us quaffing Coronas around tables covered with white linen in the reception room that night believed we might finally be about to break some of the biggest untold stories of binational crime and corruption without facing much—if any—threat of retaliation.

We sat together, swapping tips in Spanish and mingling over drinks and hors d'oeuvres when the police radio squawked on Angel Otero's hip. A bohemian long-haired former seminary student, Otero served back then as city editor for the local *El Diario* newspaper, part of a local chain that remains one of northern Mexico's most powerful and gutsy media companies.

A murder victim had been gunned down over dinner and was lying face down in a plate of sushi in a glitzy restaurant only blocks away. A large group of reporters rose from the table and rushed out. It was a clear case of cartel-on-cartel crime—entertainment Juárez style. No one worried that journalists who examined or photographed a crime scene faced any real danger.

These days, it is the journalists in Mexico who have become targets. More than 40 journalists have been killed or have disappeared since 2000, according to a horrifying but conservative count from the New York–based nonprofit Committee to Protect Journalists (CPJ). Mexico's own Commission Nacional de Derechos Humanos (National Human Rights Commission) counted 82 deaths as of July 2012. That is about twice the tally of fatal attacks carried out against journalists in Mexico during the previous decade.

After a decade of serving as an investigative reporter for the *Houston Chronicle*, Texas's largest newspaper, I am among many who have seen good friends slain or silenced in this senseless and seemingly endless violence. Attackers repeatedly have targeted important border truth tellers and investigative reporters and impaired the ability of both the Mexican and US press to cover these stories, including the drug wars and the resulting migrations and the exchange of licit and illicit business between our countries.

Coverage on the US side of the border, though safer, has grown skeletal. The ranks of reporters focusing on both Mexico and the border have been weakened by a lethal combination of budget cuts and bureau eliminations by national media and major metro newspapers in Texas, Arizona, and California. Facing a seemingly endless barrage of threats, shootings, and even grenade attacks, some Mexican media stopped covering crime, and many American media have reduced or ceased covering or crossing the border (Figure 15.1).

That has left gaping holes in the published accounts of what has happened in Mexico and along the border in the past eight years. Though permanent immigration to the United States from Mexico has slowed to a trickle, movement within the border zones of the many binational residents has been dramatic, and border businesses of all kinds have continued to boom (as noted in the previous chapter).

Alarmingly few experienced border journalists who are able and willing to undertake investigative work on complex issues, such as immigration, organized crime, corruption, or the environment, remain in these conflict zones in 2013. Brave individuals in major cities and even tiny towns continue to try to cover these important themes. But the risks they face and the terrifying isolation within which they often work make me want to scream: "Backup. We need backup."

This decline in resources and manpower for investigative reporting in both Mexico and the United States has come at a time when the need for border investigations is perhaps greater than ever. Consider this single underreported fact: in addition to the 100,000 homicides that occurred under the cartel wars during the administration of President Felipe Calderon, there are 25,000 stories of unexplained disappearances collected by the Mexican attorney general's office.[2] Scores of young men have simply been exterminated in cartel turf wars and cartel-government gun battles in every US-Mexican border state. Innocents have lost their lives, many witnesses and survivors carry emotional or physical scars, and thousands of children have been orphaned.

No one has seriously attempted to analyze this apocalypse, track disappearances, or tally movements of border residents—described as Mexodus as Cárdenas explains in the previous chapter—that appear in Mexico's own census statistics in the form of many abandoned houses in border cities and towns.

As a national correspondent for the investigative magazine *Proceso*, reporter Marcela Turati is one of the journalists who repeatedly risks her life to criss-cross conflict zones, often working alone and arriving to interview witnesses and grieving families when blood and tears have not yet dried.

Individual investigative reporters like Turati and news organizations have published searing accounts that strip away myths and misinformation about some of the worst atrocities, such as mass graves found in a Michoacan mining

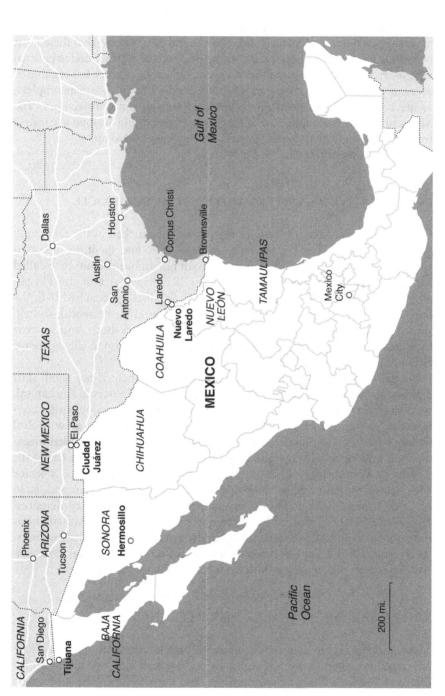

Figure 15.1 Map of the US-Mexican border (courtesy of the *Houston Chronicle*)

pit, houses of death in Ciudad Juárez, evidence of massacres of immigrants in remote ranchos in Tamaulipas, and vats of acid used to conceal a psychotic hit man's serial homicides in Tijuana. But she and others know that these most notorious incidents are only pieces of the evidence of a larger underreported war. Journalists feel frustrated that no agency in either country has reliable or accurate data. The kidnapping stats kept by border FBI offices are incomplete, as are the records on murders tracked by Mexican state prosecutors. The Mexican census tracks the towns that have emptied, but no one accurately tracks where these abandoned towns' residents have ended up.

Who can investigate this? Who will?

INVESTIGATIVE REPORTERS AND EDITORS IN MEXICO

I drove down to Mexico City with my possessions tucked in the tiny trunk of a white Honda Civic Del Sol convertible in 1996 and spent the next two years there as the founding director of a small but ambitious initiative called Investigative Reporters and Editors–Mexico (IRE–Mexico). Our effort began after several leading Mexican investigative journalists approached IRE, the largest nonprofit investigative reporting organization in the world, to help start a membership group to provide conferences, workshops, and support in Spanish. The Robert R. McCormick Tribune Foundation in Chicago gave IRE a grant to launch the project.

As the only American working on IRE–Mexico, I helped our small staff and fast-growing army of volunteers to organize conferences in the capital, workshops in newsroom all over Latin America, and two major border conferences, in Juárez in 1997 and in Tijuana in 1999. We soon grew to 200 members. Later, Periodistas de Investigacion became an independent organization and eventually merged with another Mexican nonprofit called the Centro de Periodismo y Etica Publica (CEPET). Leonarda Reyes, a senior Mexican investigative editor who was a founder of IRE–Mexico and, later, of CEPET, initially kept running investigative workshops and conferences. However, she has felt forced by the frequency of attacks and assassinations to focus on responding to violence against journalists and fighting impunity. As a result, CEPET has not offered regular national or binational investigative reporting conferences in Mexico for years. Sadly, no one does.

WHERE ARE THE '97 JUÁREZ REPORTERS NOW?

Most conferences are lifeless meetings with little long-term impact, but IRE–Mexico's investigative conference in Juárez inspired many people and produced or reinforced lasting relationships and partnerships. The subsequent stories and struggles of those who gathered there reflect the pressures on investigative reporters as a whole. Some continue to investigate crime and corruption in Mexico, on the US side of the border, or in seemingly constant transit. Other senior journalists were laid off, transferred, or left what journalists call "the business." One young reporter I remember as especially friendly was outed as a mole for a drug cartel. Others have continued to do their jobs ethically and been threatened or shot for it.

A few have been killed.

In one memorable session, *El Diario* veteran crime reporters Martin Orquiz, with a kindly face and oversized eyes, and his best friend, Armando Rodriguez, a mesmerizing storyteller nicknamed El Choco for his chocolate-colored skin, kept the crowd riveted with an account of their ongoing investigation into the suspected serial killings of young women. Their work had begun years before the "Juárez femicides" gained international attention. Rodriguez punctuated his grisly eyewitness crime-scene accounts with an occasional joke and a broad smile, holding spellbound even the most hard-boiled beat reporters and foreign correspondents in the crowd.

The brutalized bodies of women and girls—sometimes just bones—were often found dumped in remote industrial areas in the desert on the burgeoning city's dusty edges. In his reporting and via a related database analysis, Rodriguez had discovered what he described as two distinct serial killers' signatures—one strangled women and another favored a knife—though he had also become convinced that other opportunistic killers and cartel members were using the spree to cover their own crimes. He told how cartel thugs sometimes snatched women for rough rape parties, disposing of them dead or barely alive.

Clearly, Rodriguez, like Orquiz, had cultivated sources among cops and within the cartels (some sources likely represented both groups). Yet he obviously enjoyed enough freedom to be able to pursue such cutting-edge research. Even in the late 1990s, this seemed surprising, since Juárez had long been headquarters for the hugely powerful Juárez Cartel, also known as La Linea. Cartel-ordered killings were common there, as they were in Tijuana (in Baja California Norte) and Culiacan (in Sinaloa), other cities known as power bases for Mexican organized crime. Still, all three states hosted important and independent newspapers, such as *El Debate* and *Noroeste* in Sinaloa, *Norte* and *El Diario* in Chihuahua, and *Zeta* in Tijuana, that regularly published investigative stories. Rodriguez and other reporters believed themselves safe—if they were not too aggressive. There seemed to be rules to the madness. Violence was generally cartel-on-cartel. One cartel generally dominated each state or crossing—so it was easier to know the players, establish truces, or at least learn the local limits and stay safe. Corrupt or compromised journalists or even "PR" people for cartels served as messengers, letting others know what could or could not be covered.

Ciudad Juárez, the largest Mexican border city, with a booming industrial zone of prosperous *maquiladoras,* seemed safe for ordinary people. Its annual homicide rate was similar to that for Dallas or Houston, with about 300 murders a year for most of the 1990s and 2000s. Juarenses felt comfortable strolling at midnight along the Paseo Triunfo de la Republica, lined by massive brightly lit restaurants with world-class menus and over-the-top nightlife. The city's never-ending street-party atmosphere changed only after a massive cartel killing spree broke out in 2008.

That year, Rodriguez continued to cover crime at *El Diario*. A married father of three, he still mined sources and used documents and analytical skills to describe the scenes as a major homicide wave struck Juárez, pushing it past Baghdad and making it one of the world's most dangerous cities. In only the first few months of 2008, the city surpassed the prior year's homicide tally as a massive conflict broke out between La Linea and the invading Sinaloa cartel, which sought control of the "plaza." Gun battles began to break out with frequency in broad daylight on busy city streets. Women, schoolchildren, obviously innocent bystanders, and even US government officials were killed in shootouts or ordered hits.

Rodriguez visited many murder scenes, interviewed witnesses, explored patterns, and kept a careful tally as the death toll skyrocketed. Most crimes remained unsolved. It was largely his reporting that prompted stories to get picked up by national and finally international journalists, who all began to sound an alarm. Simultaneously, he delved into tips about alleged ties between state government officials and the underworld, publishing a story about the criminal activities of the relative of a prominent prosecutor and judge. Rodriguez received pointed threats. Still, he refused his editor's pleas to go work, even for a while, at the office his company maintained in sleepier El Paso, Texas.

On November 13, 2008, an unidentified gunman shot and killed Rodriguez as he prepared to drive to work in his company car. His eight-year old daughter sat beside him as a hit man opened fire with an AK-47. In minutes, his appalled and grieving friends arrived to cover the crime scene. Some cried as they took notes, snapped photos, or later edited copy. Rodriguez had become part of his story.

As his friend Jorge Luis Aguirre, who ran a website called La Polaka, drove to the funeral home, his cell phone rang. The husky voice delivered a chilling warning: "You're next." "I left Ciudad Juárez in panic the same day," said Aguirre, who fled to El Paso and eventually obtained asylum from the US government.[3]

Journalists in Juárez organized protests, published calls for justice, and urged international groups to raise Rodriguez's case with the Mexican government. And they kept covering the story. More than four years later, his homicide remains unsolved.[4]

VIOLENCE INCREASINGLY FOCUSES ON SILENCING THE PRESS

Along with Colombia, Mexico has long ranked as among the most dangerous Latin American countries to work in as a reporter. Many Mexican journalists, particularly in border zones, narcopueblos, and cartel stronghold states, have never felt particularly safe writing about organized crime.

A surprising number of US journalists have tried to convince themselves that the recent increase in border violence is a purely Mexican problem, though many Americans have been killed or been identified as the killers, the violence has affected border migration and tourism, and the exchanges of drugs and of dirty money enrich and corrupt both countries. The violence, particularly from 2007 to 2012, led to diminished coverage of all of these topics and of the border itself, a rich region with many stories to tell.

Nine Mexican journalists were murdered for their work between 1992 and 2001, according to CPJ's conservative count. In those years, most fatal attacks targeted reporters, editors, photographers or columnists at small or medium-sized news organizations who worked alone or in isolated offices. Big-city reporters felt fairly safe and investigative reporting had continued to boom partly because of investigative teams at newspapers like *Siglo 21* in Guadalajara, *Norte* and *Milenio* in Monterrey, and *Reforma* and *El Universal* in Mexico City. Even in large border cities like Mexicali and Laredo, reporters and photographers felt secure covering crime and digging up dirt. It was mainly in smaller towns and in the sprawling border metropolis of Tijuana that journalists spoke of the potentially lethal risks of provoking the local cartel.

Legendary Tijuana editor Jesus Blancornelas, an eloquent bearded man with a piercing gaze, specialized in doing just that. Blancornelas had in the 1970s been driven out of a series of Baja California newspapers after receiving threats for his aggressive coverage of the activities of the ruthless and politically connected Arrellano Felix brothers' organization. He unsuccessfully applied for asylum in the United States before returning to Tijuana in 1980 and founding his own weekly alternative newspaper, *Zeta,* with his friend Hector Felix Miranda. After Miranda was murdered, in 1988, Blancornelas dedicated himself to bringing the killers to justice. He traveled everywhere with a bodyguard but continued to publish and report aggressively despite decades of almost constant threats. In middle age, Blancornelas had evolved into an internationally recognized icon for freedom of the press and for the importance of denouncing corruption through reporting. He was the keynote speaker at the IRE–Mexico conference, delivering stirring words even as his body guard, Luis Valero, watched.

Only a year later, Blancornelas was attacked on his way to work in an SUV by cartel gunmen whose bullets struck him four times and killed Valero, who died attempting to shield him. Blancornelas kept on working. "Thanks to God, my faithful friend Luis Valero, and the marvels of medical science, I am alive," Blancornelas wrote from his hospital bed in a column *Zeta* published not long after the attack.[5]

TWO BORDER EDITORS FALL IN ONE YEAR OF THE CARTEL WARS

The sense of security and of excitement that many border journalists had felt in northern Mexico diminished dramatically in 2004 with a particularly vicious pair of fatal attacks against the managing editors of two of the region's largest and feistiest newspapers.

Roberto Mora, a talented and idealistic editor with dark hair, who had risen through the ranks in the competitive newsroom of *El Norte,* had arrived in Nuevo Laredo from Monterrey, Mexico's third largest city, just three years before his murder. Nuevo Laredo was a cartel conflict zone, but Mora had jumped at the opportunity to run his own show in the newspaper chain that covered all Tamaulipas. The feisty, smaller family-owned *El Mañana* newspaper aggressively covered two border cities, Nuevo Laredo and nearby Reynosa, and was overseen by a colorful publisher named Ninfa Deandar Cantu, an outspoken journalist known to dabble in politics, and, later, by her two sons. Mora, however, had not felt safe enough to take his own wife and child when he moved to Nuevo Laredo, and he lived alone in an apartment. He was attacked in the street as he walked home after work on March 19, 2004. He fell bleeding and died of 26 knife wounds.

His death came as Nuevo Laredo, a colonial city intimately connected to Laredo, Texas, became ground zero of a vicious cartel war when the Sinaloa Cartel sent gunmen to wrest control of the city's prime smuggling routes from the resident Gulf Cartel and its brutal hired guns, the Zetas. Murders, kidnapping, and a new brand of cartel viciousness proliferated. The Zetas appeared particularly eager to silence journalists, and for a time most in town were afraid to say aloud the name of plaza boss Miguel Trevino, better known by the number "40." *El Mañana,* working with Mexican journalists, nonprofits, and the Interamerican Press Association, insisted that state prosecutors attempt to solve Mora's murder. Under pressure, Mexican police claimed Mora's murder had nothing to do with his job and arrested two of his neighbors, an openly gay couple, one of whom was a US citizen.

Meanwhile, in Tijuana, a hit man employed by a different cartel executed a top *Zeta* editor named Francisco Ortiz Franco. Ortiz was shot dead in front of his children after leaving a physical therapy appointment. A swarthy tough-talking reporter with bristly hair and a thick beard, he had long been a top manager under Blancornelas, and in the weeks before his murder Ortiz's byline had topped hard-hitting stories. For years, Ortiz and other *Zeta* staff members had helped Blancornelas unearth clues on cartel activities and the still unresolved 1988 contract killing of *Zeta*'s cofounder, Felix Miranda. Now Ortiz's colleagues would be forced to investigate his murder, too. "Since the traffickers cannot buy us, they always seek to eliminate us," said Blancornelas in a typically bold response that was repeated by news organizations all over the world.[6]

Two murders of managing editors at different well-respected border papers in Mexico in the same year sent shock waves through the loosely knit community of journalists who closely cover the two countries' nearly 2000-mile-long border—an unconventional bunch who often subsist on meager wages and adventures as freelancers, correspondents, Web editors, bloggers, and members of small news teams. This tribe kept in touch with far-flung friends via e-mail (and, later, via Skype, Twitter, and Facebook) and in occasional but all-important encounters during reporting trips, conferences, and drinks at border watering holes, like the Cadillac Bar in Nuevo Laredo (until 2010, when even the Cadillac closed).

Imagine the reverberations in the United States if in a single year organized crime groups had taken out the editors of the *San Diego Union* and the *San Antonio Express-News,* two of the largest US border region newspapers. *Zeta* and *El Mañana* were smaller in circulation, but each had clout and served as a major media voice for its state. Journalists and nonprofit organizations in both nations rallied, sending messages of support and launching independent investigations.

Shortly before Mora's murder, I had moved to Texas to work as an investigative reporter for the *Houston Chronicle* and had begun talking to Mora about organizing an IRE border conference in Nuevo Laredo along with Reyes, a good friend, to boost synergy and morale among border journalists the way we had done back in Juárez. As conditions worsened in Tamaulipas, we all agreed it seemed vitally important to maintain old ties and forge new ones.

Even after Mora's murder, journalists at *El Mañana* and Reyes, who had worked with Mora, one of her best friends, in Monterrey, refused to give up the idea. We held the conference that November and attracted 100 journalists from the United States and Mexico even as the American consul in Nuevo Laredo was issuing bulletins on disappearances, kidnappings, and murders and receiving reports of bodies of murder victims being dissolved in barrels of acid. Pretty much everyone who attended the 2004 conference, from California to Texas to Tamaulipas, remembers the presentation given by *El Mañana* editor Daniel Rosas, a relentlessly positive and tech-savvy journalist, who spoke frankly about how dangerous reporting on anything in his town had become. We dedicated the event to Mora. And we hoped that by standing together we might help make things better for border journalists.

Reyes and CEPET assisted *El Mañana* in conducting an independent investigation of Mora's murder, known as the In Memoriam Commission, which concluded that Mora was beaten before being stabbed and that a kitchen knife seized by police from Mora's accused neighbors could not have been the real murder weapon. The findings were published and presented as a complaint to the Human Rights Commission in the state of Tamaulipas and subsequently to other national and international groups. "Crimes in Mexico achieve prominence only when they involve famous people. Many go unnoticed," Reyes said in an interview that the Knight Center for Journalism in the Americas published about the effort. "The objective of the commission is to ensure that this crime does not go unpunished. . . . We're not asking for special favors. We are asking for sound work on the part of the authorities."[7]

Years later, questions persist about Mora's murder. The case remains on CPJ's list of murders of Mexican journalists with murky motives. One of the two men arrested for his murder, the US citizen neighbor, was killed in prison.

Meanwhile, in Tijuana, *Zeta,* the alternative weekly, similarly never stopped pushing for justice in the homicides of Ortiz Franco, Miranda, and Blancornelas's bodyguard. Though Blancornelas died of cancer in 2006, *Zeta*'s current managing editor, Adela Navarro Bello, a Tijuana native, and her small news team continue to report and investigate crime and corruption. Thanks to their work, a break in the 1997 murder of Blancornelas' bodyguard came in 2008—a full 11 years after the crime—with the arrest of a cartel henchman who almost certainly planned the ambush in which Blancornelas himself also was badly wounded.

A NEW LAW BRINGS NEW OPPORTUNITIES FOR INVESTIGATIONS

Despite the double executions of border editors in 2004, investigative journalists remained optimistic in Mexico. The country's first federal open-records law was approved in 2002, partly thanks to the efforts of investigative Mexican journalists like Rossana Fuentes-Berain, a cofounder of the IRE–Mexico project. The law was better designed than the US Freedom of Information Act, complete with an oversight body able to crack the whip if bureaucrats balked. Similar state-records laws, approved by legislators in Baja California Norte, Chihuahua, and other states, opened up avenues for reporters to publish stories about contractor corruption, bridges and highways to nowhere, and other boondoggles: overpriced towels and the high cost of redecorating the presidential mansion, secret budgets, salary and bonus data. All that information had previously been almost impossible to obtain.

Yet Nuevo Laredo and the entire state of Tamaulipas remained stuck in an intensely repressive era. Tamaulipas lacked any state version of the open-records law. No challenger had ever defeated the gubernatorial candidates presented by the PRI, which controlled the governor's office and the state attorney general's office, responsible for prosecuting crimes like homicide. Over-the-top violence had drawn international attention to the Zetas, who broke away violently from the Gulf Cartel and seemingly were using the state to create a new model of narcoterrorism.

Conditions worsened for reporters in Tamaulipas, which borders Texas and the Gulf of Mexico and contains major drug and migrant smuggling routes. Journalists who attempted to do any real reporting were threatened and attacked and had cameras, film, and notebooks seized. Zetas, state officials, or both—it became hard to tell them apart—sought to control most news content. Bodies of murder victims were sometimes carted away from the crime scenes, even as journalists or families watched and were warned never to report what they had seen. Some journalists were shot, kidnapped, or bought off. It became more and more difficult to figure out exactly what had happened or why. Many people feared to talk or felt forced to lie. Some turned to anonymous Internet posts and Twitter for news.

In 2006, *El Mañana*'s newsroom was subjected to a grenade attack carried out by a crew of invaders wielding automatic weapons whose barrage of bullets sent everyone diving under desks and left one reporter paralyzed. In the aftermath, *El Mañana* journalists admitted to extensive self-censorship in the name of attempting to preserve lives. Their experiences later became part of a disturbing CPJ report issued in 2010, "Silence or Death in Mexico's Press."[8]

It was after two more bombing attacks in 2012 that *El Mañana* formally announced that it would cease doing any enterprise reporting on organized crime at all. This statement was in itself a kind of protest. *El Mañana* was announcing that terrorists had forced the state's largest newspaper chain to give up covering the ongoing drug war, arguably the biggest story in the region and in all of Mexico. The newspaper, still published daily, spoke through its silence.

ATTACKS ON MEXICAN JOURNALISTS—AND HOW THEY SPREAD FROM 2004–2012

The assassinations of top editors in 2004 were followed in 2005 by the murder of a photographer at *El Debate* in Sinaloa—a crime scene to which police took an inexplicably long time to arrive—and then by the unexplained disappearance of the chief investigative reporter for the newspaper *El Imparcial* in Sonora. These incidents, all targeting newspapers considered leaders in investigative reporting in their states, ushered in a new era of fear among journalists in northern Mexico and in other cartel conflict zones. Unfortunately, after President Felipe Calderon took office and declared war on the cartels in December 2006, deploying the military in response to the unprecedented violence occurring in states like Tamaulipas, attacks on journalist only increased and spread.

The worsening situation prompted the legendary editor Blancornelas, long used to working under death threats, to declare, "Today there are cities where journalists work as if walking through a minefield," in a speech he gave in accepting his second National Prize, Mexico's highest journalism honor.[9]

Despite the many military deployments and an unprecedented binational effort under Calderon to deport the worst criminals to the United States, armed attacks increased both on individual reporters and on media companies throughout northern Mexico and in other states suddenly plagued by cartel conflicts. Many media companies that were targeted had maintained active investigative teams or supported investigative reporters.

As awful as the situation had become by this decade, Mexico City–based journalists, foreign correspondents, and field correspondents who lived in conflict zones but worked for major national publications still took few precautions and traveled alone. Many felt that press credentials and their media companies' status served as a kind of shield. But that last shell of security has been falling away as national correspondents too became the subject of threats and attacks in the last years of Calderon's presidency.

Quietly, some simply fled. A *Proceso* reporter sought asylum in Spain. A *Reforma* border correspondent went to Canada. Others who wrote for national newspapers moved to different states after getting threats. Then, in 2010, two staff members covering a prison riot for the Mexican broadcasting behemoth Televisa were kidnapped in an incident that made national news. Another Televisa journalist was shot and killed in the beach resort city of Acapulco.

All of these events underscored a horrifying new reality. No journalist in Mexico was safe.

SHATTERING THE MYTH OF UNTOUCHABLE BIG MEDIA

Proceso magazine has for nearly four decades served as a megaphone for dissident and aggressive Mexican investigative journalists. Once a week, the magazine has published critical, sometimes incredibly opinionated and in-your-face reports on military, government, and cartel activity and corruption. Over time, *Proceso*'s sometimes controversial reports seemingly left no taboo untouched, though the fearless voice for democracy and press freedom is based in a small office on a nondescript side street of the Mexico City suburb of Del Valle, with surprisingly little security. While in the past two decades Mexican newspapers created investigative teams and upstart magazines and TV programs began to compete, *Proceso* remained an iconic leader.

To cover the militarization and proliferation of the millennium's drug wars, *Proceso* methodically deployed experts to cover all aspects of the story—the military response and human rights abuses, victims' stories, state government corruption, cartels, and criminal justice. Its skilled staff includes the drug-trafficking specialist Ricardo Ravelo, whose contacts in the secretive Mexican criminal justice system are seemingly unsurpassed, as well as fresh voices like Turati, who writes extensively and on the side cofounded a group called Periodistas de a Pie, which assists journalists who fall victim to attacks and organizes protests and press-freedom events.

So a shock wave went through journalists across Mexico when, in April 2012, a *Proceso* staff member was murdered. Days after publishing a report on police corruption, Regina Martinez, a 10-year correspondent based in the state of Veracruz, was beaten and strangled at her home in the colonial city of Jalapa. "She was among the journalists that you see looking for news: walking and talking with the people, denouncing and as in the case of many women, opening doors in her profession," wrote Martinez's *Proceso* colleague Eileen Truax.[10] "Regina [was] 49 years old, short, thin and discreet and although she appeared fragile she possessed both strength of character and professional integrity. . . . She was not a big fish or aligned with the powerful or owed favors. . . . Her error was attempting to work under a government in which impunity has become the norm."

Hers was the third murder of journalists in less than a year in Veracruz, an oil- and orange-producing coastal state in central Mexico long home to many thriving news organizations and a respected journalism school. Only five days later, the dismembered bodies of two other Veracruz-based photojournalists and their friends, including a former photographer who had only recently left the profession, were found stuffed in sacks and floating in a canal. Such gruesome mutilations had become familiar in Tamaulipas but shocked Veracruz. *Proceso*'s response was defiant—it would fight on and seek justice. But Veracruzanos from smaller media companies quickly left the profession or the state. The son of one of the 2012 murder victims, also a journalist, crossed the border and sought asylum in Texas.

In the 2010s, Mexican and US journalists who continue their work in states ravaged by the cartel war say they now worry most about reporting on government corruption or politicians' collusion with cartels. Some have gone underground, passing information that is published anonymously on websites or by publications in faraway cities in what Maria Idalia Gomez, a long-term investigator for the Inter-American Press Association and author, calls "the journalism of resistance." Manuel Clouthier, a congressman from Sinaloa and a former newspaper publisher, is among those who affirm that the worst threats come from "those in power, not from organized crime," as he told NPR's John Burnett in 2012.[11] The Mexican Congress recently approved a new law that supposedly will create additional protections for journalists and human rights activists. However, many remain skeptical of the Mexican federal government's continuing pledges to investigate crimes against journalists, noting that the special prosecutor's office created for this vitally important and extremely difficult job under Calderon perennially lacked funding, resources, or clout. Many doubt that this will improve under his successor, a PRI president.

As 2012 ended, no major border newspaper had been left untouched on the Mexican side by killings, threats, or kidnappings. *El Debate* in Sinaloa has been bombed. So has *Norte* in Ciudad Juárez. Three bombings have been carried out at the offices of *El Mañana*—and grenades have been repeatedly launched at offices of the *El Norte* newspaper, the mother ship of the Reforma newspaper chain based in Monterrey. Reporters and editors have been murdered at *El Imparcial* in Hermosillo, at *Zeta,* at *El Mañana,* and at many other companies. In July 2012, a young freelance photojournalist from San Antonio with dual US and Mexican citizenship disappeared in Nuevo Laredo after leaving his hotel to snap a photo of a crime scene. Apparently, he did not know he could be killed for carrying a camera.

BORDER REPORTING HAS GROWN DANGEROUSLY THIN ON THE AMERICAN SIDE

On the US side, the ranks of informed and experienced Mexico and border reporters have thinned in all border states, largely for economic reasons, though the violence has had an impact, too. Every major newspaper in the region eliminated bureaus and cut coverage. In California, the largest border region newspaper, the *San Diego Union,* had a five-person border team in the late 1990s. One person remained to cover Tijuana in 2012. The *Los Angeles Times* has a single border reporter, though he works with a team of two in Mexico City. *The Arizona Republic* has lost border staff, too, as González describes. In Texas, the *Dallas Morning News* formerly deployed five to Mexico City; one remains. The *Houston Chronicle* and the *Express-News,* both Hearst newspapers located only 150 to 300 miles from Mexico by car, once had three border reporters and two in Mexico City. One of those jobs remained in 2013.

Many large and small US newspapers no longer allow reporters on any story to cross the border or allow it only under limited circumstances and conditions. Both national US and Mexico City-based media companies have reduced binational coverage, too. Smaller papers on or close to the line generally lack the resources to carry out tough or long-term investigations, and many discourage or bar their staffs from crossing the border. Continuing cuts have left fewer roaming US reporters with experience to cover the complex stories in Mexico—and fewer still who understand both languages and the complex cultural context of binational stories. This results in more mistakes and in stories that perpetuate myths, rather than reveal truths. Many common assumptions about the nature of immigration, the nature of organized crime, and the relationships of our two countries are changing fast or are flat-out wrong. Mexican net migration to the United States recently dropped to zero. An estimated 500,000 to 1 million US citizens live in Mexico, and 14.4 million visit. Many border residents are truly bilingual and binational, defying definitions.

Criminals and cartels are binational, too—even some top cartel bosses are American, like the broad-faced blond Edgar Valdez Villarreal, who is best known as "La Barbie," the moniker bestowed for his doll-like appearance by his Laredo, Texas, high school football coach. Many of Mexico's worst criminals—those arrested, at least—have been exported to US prisons.

Luckily, outstanding journalists remain committed to telling complex stories—NPR's John Burnett, the *Dallas Morning News*'s Alfredo Corchado, and, until the bureau was closed in December 2012, the *Houston Chronicle*'s Dudley Althaus—each of whom has decades of experience and often mentors less experienced reporters and networks with Mexican colleagues. Bloggers and young reporters, often working for tiny websites or as freelancers, help to fill voids.

But it is not enough. As the PRI resumes presidential power after the Mexican elections of 2012, fewer American journalists are in place to report important stories—or to provide reinforcements for Mexican reporters who believe the new government intends to use official advertising and other forms of pressure to force them to "habla bien" (speak well) of Mexico. It has long been a mantra that it is safer to publish a sensitive story in two cities or in two countries. As fewer news outlets report or publish sensitive information, it is increasingly likely individuals and news organizations will be targeted.

US BORDER REPORTING CUTS SHIFT MORE BURDEN TO VULNERABLE MEXICAN JOURNALISTS

I was an elected IRE board member from 2007 through 2011 and again pushed hard to respond more to the threats to border journalists, including by organizing a series of border meetings. Logistics were complex since fewer border reporters got company support for travel or training expenses; some journalists were denied visas, and others feared land journeys in northern Mexico. We offered smaller gatherings in El Paso, Tucson, San Diego, and Laredo and reached out in each region to journalists known as leaders, regardless of whether they were still able to publish. Some agreed to attend but refused to speak. Others asked that their sessions not be recorded. We took as many precautions as possible. We tried to invite only those we trusted. At the first event, in El Paso, we held a dinner to honor the work of slain reporter Armando Rodriguez and invited his widow and children. There was still hope in these gatherings—but it was mixed with fear and with tears.

What remained clear to me was that many Mexican and US border journalists continue to feel compelled to investigate despite increasingly difficult conditions. We exchanged information. We talked about how to cope, to adapt, and to survive. We grieved our losses and celebrated the good work that continues. Impressive acts of courage are often overlooked in the many reports published by nonprofit journalism and human rights groups that tend to focus on violence and self-censorship in the Mexican press.

Both US and Mexican media companies have adopted survival strategies to protect reporters and preserve their integrity. Among other things, they have stripped names from sensitive stories, banned publication or photos of inflammatory narco threats posted on bridges or on corpses, emphasized the use of only official and verified information posted on social media, and embraced encryption software and Skype and other technologies for exchanging sensitive information. Individuals, media, and nonprofits alike are finding ways to work together, too, though more support is needed, especially for those who regularly deal with on-the-job stress, whether from constant threats or from viewing unspeakable scenes of horror.

Though fewer reporters remain to report the stories, the Internet and social media have amplified their voices and their impact. Some have launched independent websites so that they can write whatever they choose from a virtual office with or without bylines or major financial backing. In every region of the Mexico-US border, journalists remain dedicated to the idea that their reporting is an important part of democracy. A core group of expert reporters and master storytellers remains that knows the nuances, the characters, and the ground rules. They can get the records, and they can tell the toughest stories, though they often lack resources and backup.

On both sides of the border, relatively new independent Web outlets play increasing roles in keeping press freedom alive: the Blog del Narco, La Polaka, frontera.com, and enlinea directa are a few examples from the Mexican side. On the US side: Narconews, the *El Paso Times* Somos Frontera website, the University of Texas–El Paso Borderzine (and its student-produced Mexodus project), Borderreporter.org, Molly Molly's Frontera mailing list, and NPR's Fronteras: The Changing Americas desk all contribute.

Some in-depth investigative stories on organized crime in Mexico in recent years have originated from small companies with talented investigative staff. *El Faro* in El Salvador, a website, produced a detailed investigation of how the Zetas seized control of human trafficking routes all the way from the US border to Central America. *EmeEquis* magazine in Mexico City has chronicled La Familia Cartel's operations in Michoacán and dissected the illicit business of kidnapping and the activities of the DEA in Mexico. The impact of such stories explodes via blogs, listservs, Twitter, and Facebook and through international reporting awards. Fortunately, most of the investigative reporters behind these reports were able to return after risky trips and to sleep in homes hundreds of miles away from those they interviewed.

However, many local border journalists continue to investigate, though they live, eat, and sleep in the communities they cover. Their neighbors and school chums work for cartels. They recognize murder victims' faces— Sandra Rodriguez, a veteran investigative reporter based in Ciudad Juárez, has talked publicly of having waking nightmares about repeatedly envisioning her face on one of the mutilated corpses she has so often seen dumped in the street.[12] They see trails of blood, burned, mutilated, beheaded bodies, and victims scarred by torture and interview bleeding survivors and screaming, grieving families. They have invented new words to cope with the carnage: *encobijados* for murder victims wrapped in blankets; *encajuelados* for those stuffed in trunks; *levantados* for those taken away.

When I ask friends how they manage, some go quiet. Some spin a long tale about something stupid they did late one night after they had pushed too hard or seen too much. They cry, laugh, get drunk, or talk about quitting or moving away.

And then they go back to work. These journalists—the crazy ones who refuse to give up—they are my heroes.

¿QUÉ QUIEREN DE NOSOSTROS? WHAT DO YOU WANT FROM US?

In 2010, two young photographers for *El Diario* newspaper were shot and one killed in an attack in Ciudad Juárez that might have been meant for a well-known human rights activist, whose car the victims had borrowed. The largest Mexican newspaper on the border, *El Diario de Juárez* subsequently published a front-page editorial that got worldwide attention. Only two days after Mexican Independence Day, the paper issued a "grito"—a cry— an act considered the hallmark of the first Mexican revolution.

"¿Qué quieren de nosotros?"—what do you want from us?—was its evocative title.[13] Some less informed commentators immediately opined that *El Diario* was giving up and asking the cartel for orders, but when I read the editorial online that morning I realized the message was deeper and defiant. Journalists, the editorial insisted, have an important role in society and in protecting democracy that is valuable to all, one that even criminals should recognize and respect:

> We do not want more deaths. We do not want more wounded nor more intimidation. It's impossible to perform our role in society in these conditions so tell us, therefore, of your expectations of a media company. This is not a surrender. Nor does it mean that we will cease the work that we have been developing. This is a proposed truce with those who have imposed the force of their law on this city in order that they respect the lives of those of us who dedicate ourselves to the task of informing society.

Those who misinterpreted these words perhaps failed to notice that *El Diario* had never ceased investigating corruption and crime, despite Rodriguez's 2008 brutal assassination. The paper has maintained a small, close-knit team of investigative reporters who kept filing records requests and producing substantive stories. Despite their own grief and threats, reporters like Sandra Rodriguez, Martin Orquiz, Lucy Sosa, and Rocio Gallegos have continued to produce hard-hitting signed and unsigned reports about questionable land grabs in industrial zones by corrupt city officials and the absolute innocence of a group of soccer-playing teens whose mass murder shocked the nation. Relentlessly, they probed the utter failure of the Chihuahua state government to prosecute even the high-profile criminals, exploring human rights abuses and how cases against the culprits who had been trotted out for TV cameras in national press conferences on particularly notorious crimes repeatedly fell apart. After the national cameras' attention flagged, *El Diario* kept on following up.

In its editorial, *El Diario* boldly asked that its journalists be left alone to do these jobs. The provocative request eventually garnered international coverage—and ultimately Mexico's national journalism prize in 2011, for the audacity and bravery of the message. In an acceptance speech, editor Raul Gomez Franco laid bare the logic behind the editorial signed "De la Redaccion"—from the newsroom:

> The question that El Diario de Juárez issued in 2010, What do you want from us?, never was intended to seek a response nor to establish a

dialogue with organized crime groups, nor to subject ourselves to their orders as some mistakenly believed at the time. In reality, our text was a cry of desperation—a sort of protest against the powerlessness we all felt after the second of our journalists died riddled by bullets in less than two years.

This editorial was meant to be a call for attention to awaken the collective consciousness both inside and outside our country, in particular among our elected leaders and our justice system to the barbarity that was being committed in Ciudad Juárez and the absolute defenselessness in which journalists do their jobs in such perilous times.[14]

The dream of investigative reporting on the border—free from fear—lives on.

EPILOGUE: SNAPSHOT FROM HERMOSILLO

Investigative efforts continue all along the border despite all of the attacks and all of the lives needlessly lost. But each death leaves scars—among them the unsolved disappearance of Alfredo Jimenez Mota in Sonora.

By 2005, Jimenez, a fun-loving, thick-set, and intensely curious Sinaloa native, emerged as a leader among those who dared to probe organized crime in western Mexico. At 24, he was already an expert on the mammoth Sinaloa organized crime group, led by Joaquín "Chapo" Guzman, listed by Forbes as one of the world's richest men. His parents felt relief when Jimenez accepted a job as an investigative reporter outside his native Sinaloa in Sonora, a state that they considered safer. Jimenez continued to work late, develop new contacts, and probe for the larger *El Imparcial* newspaper, part of a Hermosillo-based, family-owned chain. *El Imparcial* had a long tradition of investigative reporting, and its editor had played a prominent role in fighting for press freedom as a member of the Inter-American Press Association.

Jimenez published several hard-hitting reports—perhaps none as sensitive as a piece on the murder of a state prosecutor believed linked to a prominent trafficker who lived in a gaudy megamansion topped with cupolas that shimmered like a mirage in the desert just outside Hermosillo. According to research by border reporter Michel Marizco and other journalists, on April 2, 2005, Jimenez got a tip, canceled dinner plans with a friend, and went off to meet a nervous source. Then he disappeared. Though he is presumed dead, his body has never been found.

Journalists and nonprofits responded strongly to what seemed like another clear-cut case of deliberate retribution against an investigative reporter. From all over Mexico, they converged on Hermosillo to launch the so-called Phoenix Project, inspired by a group of American journalists who decades before had gathered in 1976 in Phoenix, Arizona—the US state bordering Sonora—to continue an organized-crime investigation interrupted when reporter Don Bolles, an Arizona reporter and cofounder of IRE, was killed in a car bombing after meeting a source at a hotel. On March 31, 2006, the first results of the Phoenix Project were published in more than 100 newspapers in an attempt to continue Jimenez Mota's investigation—and uncover his fate.

Yet Jimenez's presumed murder remains unpunished and his gravesite unknown.

Border journalist Michel Marizco, an unorthodox and fearless Tucson-based blogger who is now part of the NPR Fronteras team, is among those who believe that the murder profoundly changed Sonoran press coverage. On May 17, 2007, Marizco responded quickly to the scene after hearing reports that 11 people had been kidnapped by a drug trafficker and that a running gun battle had broken out in the colonial town of Cananea, only an hour from the Arizona border. He arrived to find a "manhunt by state police and then the Army, [with] riflemen in a helicopter . . . stalking the band of killers who tried to escape down the banks of the Rio Sonora. The list of the dead grew by the hour. Seventeen. Then 20. Twenty-two. Maybe more. I lost count," he wrote in an article in the *Mexico City News* and on his blog, borderreporter.org.

> The only element missing was the media. . . . I am certain that if you asked the publishers and editors they would give you very rational answers to why they avoided sending reporters to the scene of one of the bloodiest days in Mexico's narco war. Travel logistics, deadlines, budgets you name it.
>
> But I suspect that a darker secret was at work here, reluctance by the press to report, to question. . . . What happened in Cananea proved one thing: As the narcos grow stronger, the press retreats in silence.[15]

For seven years now, Marizco has, between other assignments, conducted an independent and risky investigation into Jimenez's disappearance. He plans to write a book—but refuses to finish. He wants to find the killers and the patch of ground in the desert where Jimenez's bones lie.

Just as elusive are answers about the future of investigative reporting along the US-Mexican border. Many of us are just too stubborn to give up hope.

NOTES

1. Thanks to journalists Dudley Althaus and Lourdes Cárdenas and other friends in Mexico who provided context and feedback; any errors are my own. All translations from Spanish are mine.
2. William Booth, "Mexico's Crime Wave Has Left about 25,000 Missing, Government Documents Show," *Washington Post*, November 29, 2012.
3. Patricia Giovine, "More Mexicans Fleeing the Drug War Seek U.S. Asylum," *Reuters,* July 14, 2011.

4. Lise Olsen, "Violence Silences Journalists," *Express-News*, November 30, 2008.
5. This comment appeared in *Zeta*, January 9–15, 1998, the first edition published after the attack.
6. "Valentia Periodistica," undated blog entry from the Libreta de Apuntes RMC # 102 by Omar Raul Martinez, director de Revista Mexicana de Comunicación, http://omarraulm.com/?page_id = 477.
7. "After a Year, Mexican Editor's Death Goes Unpunished," Knight Center News, March 16, 2005, http://knightcenter.utexas.edu/knightcenternews_article.php?page = 4271.
8. Carlos Lauría and Mike O'Connor, "Silence or Death in Mexico's Press," Committee to Protect Journalists, September 8, 2010, http://cpj.org/reports/2010/09/silence-or-death-in-mexicos-press.php.
9. Jesus Blancornelas, full acceptance speech of Mexico's Premio Nacional de Periodismo on May 3, 2006, http://www.periodistasenlinea.org/modules.php?op = modload&name = News&file = article&sid = 20.
10. Eileen Truax, "Regina Martinez: Impunidad y Silencio," *Proceso*, May 3, 2012.
11. John Burnett, "Mexican Crime Reporters Risk Becoming the Story," *NPR*, May 9, 2012.
12. Drawn from an interview Sandra Rodriguez gave to the L.A. Press Club after being chosen as the 2013 receipient of the Daniel Pearl Award for Courage and Integrity in Journalism. http://lapressclub.org/uncategorized/courageous-mexican-journalist-to-receive-the-daniel-pearl-award/.
13. "Qué quieren de nosostros?," *El Diario de Juarez*, September 20, 2010, 1. As this book goes to press, the newspaper carries a banner at the bottom of its online front page with the names of its murdered journalists and the note "We require justice for our colleagues," http://diario.mx/.
14. An account of the speech given by Raul Gomez Franco on Nov. 30, 2011 is translated from "Gana El Diario de Juarez Premio Nacional de Periodismo," published Dec. 1, 2011 and available on the Terra Noticias web site at http://noticias.terra.com.mx/mexico/estados/gana-el-diario-de-juarez-premio-nacional-de-periodismo,6116216e0caf3310VgnVCM3000009af154d0RCRD.html
15. Michel Marizco, "Secreto a Voces," Borderreporter.org, December 29, 2007.

16 Beyond the Far West
Translating the American Border for Italians

Guido Olimpio
Corriere della Sera

Italy, in recent years, has been a veritable *border* country. In fact, it has become the border of the European Union, with an alternate influx of legal and illegal immigrants, who challenged the natural wall and the dangers of the Mediterranean Sea. Hundreds of people—men, women, and children, sometimes babies—lost their lives trying to reach the Italian coast, the first step on the continent in their long journey of hope.

Immigration has known many stages. In Italy, the first wave was represented by the sudden influx of thousands of individuals crossing the Adriatic Sea from Albania to Puglia, the southeastern heel of the Italian peninsula, in the early 1990s, as Stinellis's chapter discussed. Then came the wave of Middle Eastern and Turkish refugees. The latest wave sees the influx of Africans fleeing war, starvation, and persecution—a human tragedy. The situation involves multiple aspects, with an impact on Italian society, economy, politics, and national security. Therefore, the interest of the Italian media is focused mainly on the closest flow of immigration, the one happening in our country.

COVERING THE US BORDER FOR THE ITALIAN PRESS

As a special correspondent for a leading Italian newspaper, based in Washington, DC, I find it difficult to drive my readers' attention to the issue of immigration along the border between the United States and Mexico, which presents Italians with different and faraway problems, with few implications for Italy, tragedies competing with other similar tragedies, if you will allow me to use what seems a cynical expression. I must give credit, anyway, to my newspaper, *Corriere della Sera,* for listening to the message I convey and publishing my reports and stories. It has been hard, but after working in this position for five years, I can say I have succeeded in giving my readers the whole framework of events on the US-Mexican border and beyond. My interest in border stories has been motivated by different elements, beginning with the fact that the link among violence, drugs, and immigration provides strong news. Other striking features are the effectiveness and the sophistication of the smugglers' techniques and the sheer geography of a border connecting two giants like the United States and Mexico. Most recently, I have been struck by the possibility of doing a comparative analysis with the same phenomenon in Europe, especially in these years of economic crisis, which is increasing the cross-border influx of people and products.

News stories, features, pictures, tweets, social media—I use all the wide range of media branded *Corriere della Sera* and also my own Facebook page. Starting from the articles in the newspaper, reporting mainly features, to reportage and photojournalism in the weekly magazine, which is offered for free to the readers of the newspaper, I admit that the channel for my regular updates on the issue is the online edition of the paper. I also post a greater volume of news, images, video, and comments on both the newspaper's and my personal Facebook pages, on my Twitter feed, and sometimes on Storify. Most frequently, I analyze and compare illegal immigration issues that intersect the traffic of drugs and the narco wars in Mexico. Apparently, the problems stem from different causes at the origin, but they often end up interconnected, as Olsen's and Cárdenas's chapters show.

I have traveled many times along the border, and if you walk, as I did, on the hills around Sasabe or Douglas (both in Arizona), you know that there are connections and sometimes a dramatic reality. The hard and steep path of the immigrants to "El Norte" of their dreams is the same as the narcos', who take advantage of them by exploiting the illegal immigrant "market," directly or indirectly. The cartels impose a toll on all who want to cross the border illegally, and sometimes armed men oblige the poor people to smuggle drugs into the American territory, while in other circumstances they are used as human shields in the gang conflicts. The San Fernando and Tamaulipas massacres, in the frontier area with Texas, demonstrate that the migrants are the first victims of the narco war. In many of my stories, the "violence" factor is at the core of the events—such as the migrants robbed by the *bajaderos,* the bandits of the border, a few miles from American villages, or their odyssey of death from thirst in the Arizona desert.

Hooking Readers with the Old West

In the readers' view, sometime human tragedies can cast a shadow on other aspects related to the immigration phenomenon, while other times the focus is mostly on the militarization of a region, like the Nogales wall, the helicopters, the sensors in the prairie, or the drones. If we balance the information on both sides, the combination can draw the readers' attention and help them better understand why the issue can be interesting—even in Italy, where the average Italian reader usually wonders: "Why bother about what happens on the Rio Grande, when we have the canal of Sicily?"

Nowadays, speaking without hypocrisy, the media world is facing the highest level of news competition at the core of the information system. The speed of news is ultrasonic, and the multiple platforms to launch it increase the volume offered to the public. Therefore, we need to "hook" the audience with news stories that are extremely interesting. A curious or unusual aspect of the story can be attractive and become the first line of an article debating a topic already known by the newspaper desk selecting the news of the day. We can call the hooks "Trojan horses," made to break through the wall of the desk, after which we introduce the regular army of the news. I do not mean to encourage an attitude of looking for the sensational, but it is a pragmatic solution. The alternative can be no story at all.

I found out that the fascination that emerges from the "frontier" as a metaphor in the Italian public imagination helps my daily routine of proposing stories. Landscapes and lifestyles that evoke the "Old West" of the movies— it was said with a reason that the names in the West refer not just to geography but also to stories and events in recent or past history. When a journalist tells that a path followed by the illegal immigrants is a corridor near Apache Junction or crosses Skeleton Canyon, where Geronimo surrendered, immediately in many readers' minds an image surfaces from their childhood, even though they might have never been to Arizona. When I see the places, it is emotional even for me, as happened in Tombstone, which reminded me of the challenge at the "shootout at the OK Corral." That was an historical site that allowed me to describe the anti-Chicano vigilantes. This is an example of a "Trojan horse." All it takes is three lines with a picture in an article, maybe a map showing current events that take place on the hills where the pioneers camped during their journey. It is hard to escape the parallel lines of the present and the past when you describe a sheriff who founded his "posse" of volunteers obsessed by the fear of immigrants or when you talk about militias patrolling the border. Some academics may disagree with my recommendations, but, in my opinion, highlighting these links between familiar images for the readers—stereotypical as they might be—in order to draw their attention to momentous news stories is the right choice for a journalist in our times.

STRATEGIES FOR BORDER COVERAGE: BUILDING AN ARCHIVE

I started traveling throughout the United States in the 1980s, for work and leisure, concentrating my visits on the West, including the border areas. Since 2007, when I was posted as correspondent in Washington, my research project has expanded and acquired greater depth. My daily routine is devoted to reading the national as well as the international press, as well as the regional and local press as far as the Southwest and the border states are concerned. Then I create a database, building an archive that is ready to use whenever I need to write an article. I do not know yet if I will ever need my contact in Arivaca, Arizona, to write a story; however, if anything happens down there, I will be immediately ready.

I have been using such rigorous methodology during my 30 years of research and archiving materials to use as I write news and features about international terrorism, the Middle East, weapons and drug trafficking, and other illegal activities. An example can explain how it works. During the 1980s, I was covering Middle Eastern as well as European terrorism, and it was extremely hard. The newspaper had no Internet to handle research, and the written sources were limited. The foreign press was on my desk only the day after publication, and the satellite channels did not exist. Even with those basic means, I was able to create the foundation for a monumental archive on international terrorism. My database allowed me to analyze the jihadist fundamentalist groups starting in 1992–1993. In 1996, I had already a file profiling a still-unknown jihadist: his name was Osama bin Laden. At that time, newspapers had no big interest in this kind of information. It was a topic that used to be in the news only in the aftermath of a terrorist attack. I was making a mid- to long-term investment, without any immediate profit, but my choice did pay off. In fact, that same year, in July, I was invited to testify at a hearing of the counterterrorism and nonconventional weapons task force of the US Congress. The topic was the proliferation of Islamic fundamentalism by the Afghan conflict, its first cells in Europe, and the covert operations of the Iranian intelligence service. Therefore, when I was posted to the United States, I decided to apply the same methodology in my research on illegal immigration and the narco challenge.

The Network

My working day is defined by reading and analyzing the media. It is a system of "circles" that I repeat every day, weekends included. My research extends beyond the US Mexican border to reach out to the Middle East as well as the issue of international terrorism. The first circle is composed of a wide range of newspapers—the list includes the leading American papers (*New York Times, Washington Post, Miami Herald, Los Angeles Times, Wall Street Journal, USA Today*), the British *Telegraph* and *Guardian,* and the French *Le Figaro* and *Le Monde*—from which I select news for my database. The second circle includes the regional newspapers in Arizona, California, and Texas, followed by a number of Mexican papers. The third circle is made up by the frontier blogs, especially the Mexican chat pages, which represent a precious source of details, names, numbers, maps, and situations to explore. The fourth circle is the most direct: sources on the border, members of humanitarian associations, researchers, not to mention, of course, my contacts with the Border Patrol, Immigration and Customs Enforcement (ICE), local police departments, and institutes or academic centers.

It is precisely from such a "net" that you can fish out the most interesting topics to develop in a story. A little event in Rio Rico (south of Tucson), not far from the US-Mexican border, could be put in a "to do" file. Then I find my contact on the spot; I look into the possibility of meeting him in the future; we exchange e-mails. It is obvious that it is going to be the kind of article that requires traveling to the location. I usually put together two or three ideas to develop during my trips, in order to save money. In the past two years, I have had to reduce my travels for budget reasons, and this trend is likely to last for a long time. The next generation of reporters will need to cover most features from their desk rather than on location to cut expenses. I can only hope that they will be allowed shorter trips, even though countries as large as the United States require long-distance flights. Undoubtedly, the economic crisis is reshaping the job of journalists, though, on the positive side, the Internet and social media can keep us connected with our sources and help us get special information, as well.

This "network" for researching and archiving news allows me to get a record of episodes that may demonstrate a trend that deserves to be discussed in the news in the near future. An example can better explain this process. In *Nogales International,* a biweekly newspaper covering both cities of Nogales (in Arizona and, directly across the border, in Mexico), you can often find short news articles reporting attacks against illegal immigrants. Just a few lines, but that is not important. I mark a map I have in my office, check the location on Google Earth, trying to find out whether it is an area of dense population and how far the highway is. I know Arizona well, but I prefer to double-check the area through Internet sources. The same procedure is used to get a record of illegal immigrants found dead in the desert. Some humanitarian organizations, such as No More Deaths, Humane Border, and Samaritans of Green Valley, are really helpful as I track down and map this information. Occasionally, I follow the findings about tunnels in Nogales and the San Diego area, built for drug trafficking, as such activity is an indicator of the presence of criminal organizations at some specific points of the border. Finally, the Border Patrol official bulletins provide information about the kind of drugs, the smugglers' techniques, and the illegal aliens' profiles.

All of this information goes into my archive, where I also collect files with pictures, videos, graphics, and maps. When I propose a story to my newspaper, I must provide photos or get the desk in touch with a photographer or agency that sells them. Generally speaking, this research process is expensive, as well as time and energy consuming, and requires a lot of resources. I end up publishing only some 10 percent of my documentation, but it is exactly the surplus that allows me to make a selection and to dig deeper in a story. An example: I worked on the issue of the mini submarines used by the narcos from Colombia to transfer cocaine and the little airplanes that reach Mexico from South America with their load of drugs. I examined the routes, analyzing the shoreline and the depth of the sea, searching the illegal routes on Google Earth. It was a long research that produced short but frequently updated news stories on a critical, underexplored topic.

I need to add that, employing an approach I used to follow as *Corriere*'s correspondent in Israel, at times I update stories I have already published. It is a way to point out trends, understand the choices of the actors, and analyze their changes in judgment on such sensitive issues as immigration.

Therefore, for example, several times I interviewed and went along with the volunteers who bring water in the desert to prevent illegal immigrants from dying of thirst, and on one occasion this spring, we assisted a man who had gotten lost in the remote area north of Nogales.[1] I have been constantly in touch with the volunteers over the years, and it has been an incredible professional as well as human experience for me, one that has a lot of important meaning for a journalist who wants to study the phenomenon of the influx of immigrants from the southern border of the United States.

Getting to Know the Territory

Walking along the border or through the desert or following the tracks of the immigrants' paths gives you a perspective that you cannot find in the statistics.

You can feel the tiredness, the strain, and understand the risks and the severe weather conditions they suffer day and night. You can also estimate their movements by following the trails and checking water consumption. The number of empty bottles can be an empirical but useful piece of evidence, since the water containers are marked with a number and a date, which makes it possible to track the migrants' routes. The volunteers are an

Figure 16.1   The US-Mexico border wall at Jacumba, California. Courtesy of Guido Olimpio

unofficial but well-informed source. You can interview them and compare
their statements with the official data released by the authorities. If the government reports a decreased influx of migrants, you can check it out with
your sources. Obviously, the knowledge of the humanitarian associations
is territorial and limited to a specific geographic region, but that area is
the most important for your research, and the volunteers are generous and
available. They show you the real meaning of solidarity.

Shura Wallin volunteers for the Green Valley Samaritans, an association
that brings water to migrants in the Arizona desert. She crosses the border every week to bring aid to "El Comedor," a shelter for the deported
in Nogales, Mexico, where I collect dramatic interviews with people who
attempted unsuccessfully to sneak into US territory and whose dream of
a better life was broken. You understand by their words that they will try
again because they have nothing left back in Guatemala or El Salvador.
Among the volunteers is Ricardo (this is his nickname), a retired pilot and
very special gentleman who always surprises me every time I meet him. He
is the best informed person about the trails in the desert and on the hills. Ed
McCullough, a retired professor from the University of Arizona, is committed to keeping track of illegal immigration scientifically by mapping the area
with a GPS. The Samaritans use the maps to find points for the water delivery aimed at preventing deaths from thirst. Just a look at Ed's maps gives
you an idea of the concentration of trails in the southwestern region around
Tucson. They all converge in the direction of the towns and highways, where
the human smugglers wait for immigrants.

The trails are especially interesting because illegal immigrants must aban-
don their belongings on the way. These items are generally taken for rub-
bish, but not by artist Valerie James. She has been collecting what she finds
around her house in Amado, Arizona, for years, and her little "museum"
offers great knowledge. Here is a quotation from the article I wrote for
Corriere della Sera in December 2009 about James's museum of "what they
leave behind":

> A baby bottle, a birth certificate for Jeronimo Castro, farmer. Hundreds
> of shoes. Children backpacks with printed cartoon characters like Tweety.
> A handbag with the image of Marilyn Monroe. Canteens covered in fab-
> ric to keep the water cooler. Letters. Bibles. Books of literature. Children
> textbooks. Phone cards. Human rights pamphlets. Belts. Family pictures
> with pathetic words, like "I will take care of your children, we will
> never forget you." "Bordados," embroidered handkerchiefs for sons
> or fiancés. Everyday objects with a dramatic story, fragments of a life.
> They belong to the illegal immigrants attempting every day to reach
> the United States from Mexico. Once they cross the border, they have
> to endure a dangerous journey through the desert. Three or four days
> hiking in a land where water is really a mirage. . . . When the "polleros"
> are approaching the meeting point with the smugglers, they are forced

to get rid of their little luggage. There is no room for luggage on the van and the criminal organizations don't want their clients to be identified as OTAN (other than Mexican). Those objects become like signals of a wreck. Objects that talk, like the pages written by a child on a notebook, they tell a fragment of the story of their owner.[2]

James's mission is to give a voice to the people in despair sneaking into this territory. A few lines written with uncertainty on the back of a sacred image or a photo can revive those people, while the "bordados" are a symbol of love that the immigrants adapt for a practical use, by using them to wrap some food for the hike in the desert. The colored blankets may reveal the migrant's country of origin. An expulsion decree means that, as often happens, this was a repeated and ultimately unsuccessful effort.

Interviews across the Border

I have crossed the Mexican border to interview the deported—the individuals arrested, then expelled. The assistance center in Nogales, Mexico, where many volunteers work, is an unlimited source of personal tales of real life. There, numbers turn into names and stories. I have used the same system on the other side of the frontier to interview the people who oppose immigration. The owner of a ranch in an American border state has often been subjected to violations and thefts on his property. Not all of them are carried out by illegal immigrants, but it is obvious that their passage is the main reason for such criminal activity, which has a strong impact on the daily life of a ranchero. Other Americans are against immigration just for ideological reasons. In recent years, I have met many ranchers, listening to their complaints, their accusations, and their requests for stronger intervention by the federal authorities.

An interview with a cattle farmer offers a different perspective on the illegal immigration issue. It made me realize that, during 2011 and 2012, the criminal operations of the drug cartels were increasing. The ranchers tell you about the crossing of the marijuana smugglers and show you the tracks and the notorious lookout posts created by narcos on the top of hills to monitor the movements of the Border Patrol. This kind of direct experience gives you a deeper knowledge than you can get from the official reports. If we imagine the border protected by a "wall," the rancheros show you how large portions are protected only by a thin iron wire that anyone can bypass. As a result, the drug cartels concentrate their activity in some strategic areas of Arizona that are unprotected by any "wall," and use these to smuggle drugs for the US market. My meetings with the ranch owners and the residents of the Arivaca-Douglas area, who really live on the frontline, led me to group them, even if not in scientific terms, into three categories:

1. People who feel the insecurity of the frontier as a constant threat to their lives and property. In this case, their perception of the immigration

issue is connected to the criminal activity of the drug dealers. If you roam around the deserted areas south of Arivaca, a remote Arizona town west of Nogales, you realize that they are linked by the same geography and the same business, since the *coyotes* and the "narcos" arrange the passage of people as well as drugs. The consequences are burglaries, thefts, and damage to infrastructure and cattle. After the much-publicized 2010 killing of a rancher, Robert Krentz, by an unknown man, probably a narco scout, also in southern Arizona, I made several trips to witness the hard living conditions. I visited many ranches south of Tucson and met people of great humanity, like Jim Chilton, whose family has owned the land for generations.

2. People who firmly oppose any form of immigration for ideological reasons. This position can be manifested in either verbal expressions of concern or by action. While some people just have an opinion, others decide to "do something, since the government is not doing enough." I wanted to interview one of them, the controversial engineer Glenn Spencer. When he retired, Spencer bought a house a few yards from the border and founded the American Border Patrol. With a team of a few men, he controls the "wall" with CCTV and sensors. In the past, he used to fly on little planes on long missions to film the border. His footage is of great interest for journalists, showing the lookouts of the narcos and the camouflage posts hidden in the desert and revealing the insolence of the smugglers. Spencer's story is a wonderful feature for a journalist—even more so because you have his dry words, as hard as stones, but you also have "action," as exemplified by the hangar with planes and drones, the video-computer set in his bedroom, the kennel of German shepherds that follow him during his inspections. He has set up a high-tech microstructure a few miles from the Homeland Security station with its official drones.

3. Vigilantes, small groups of people who assume that the residents of the border area need extra protection. They exploit the feelings of insecurity and the populist rhetoric that is widespread in the area. The vigilantes are key characters because of the Western passion for firearms, possession of which is a right granted by the Second Amendment to the US Constitution but raises concern in Italy and Europe. In Arizona and Texas, many households claim the right to keep and bear arms for self-defence. The spillover, as many sheriffs call the immigration stream toward to the North, causes fear and anxiety. In other words, if I lived in one of those remote areas, I would buy a gun. In the eyes of a European, though, buying weapons without a specific license is too easy, and the ostentatious use of guns draws attention. I would also realize how many assault rifles and pistols and what a great deal of ammunitions end up in Mexico, in the hands of the cartels. You

have plenty of documentation thanks to the images and pictures of the narco arsenal, the statistics, and the political inquiries into the botched gun-trafficking federal operation "Fast and Furious."

Finally, parallel to the civilian initiative is the institutional action of the police authority. The officers are available for interviews—it is just up to you to understand what is a public relations statement. There are some circumstances in which the authorities are interested in offering information and research material, so it is essential to have a screening process with a follow-up later on. I often went back to official sources after studying my data, with a new perspective and with a target in mind. The information is so detailed in this digital era that a scoop is really unusual. Nonetheless, in these years, I have developed a 3D knowledge of the security situation along the US-Mexico border, greater than that required by my profession.

A Special Correspondent on the Ground

I was able to learn a lot about the geography of the most sensitive segments of the frontier with my boots on the ground. My concentration areas were San Diego-Otay Mesa (California); Yuma-El Centro (Arizona); Tohono O'odham reservation-Nogales-Douglas (Arizona); El Paso (Texas); and Laredo (Texas). In these regions, I compared the different techniques used by the Border Patrol, ICE, and Customs and Border Protection agents by following them on their jobs, embedded with them. I have found that getting in contact with US federal authorities is easy for a foreign reporter. The State Department Press Center in Washington facilitates requests to interview members of the administration and Congress and to find the right channels to develop an investigation. In my years of reporting from Washington, the answers from various agencies have almost always been positive. My only remark is that the standardized format tends to offer a general overview, not detailed information. I spent days on the border with the agents engaged in the effort to crack down on illegal immigration and smuggling. Even when I was not embedded, I was allowed to observe the work of the officers. My goal was to find new topics of journalistic interest, so I visited the stations several times and was able to research the *coyotes'* tricks.

A very nice feature I found during my trips was a report about the Shadow Wolves, a special team recruited by ICE and composed exclusively of Native Americans. It was a great opportunity to link present and past in the narrative of my article.[3] The unit works on the territory of the Tohono O'odham Reservation, considered one of the most important channels of illegal smuggling. The Native American officers are able to find tracks in the sand, the dust, or the ground in every kind of terrain, and their mission is vital, since they can see the passing of people as well as motor vehicles. They inherited the art of reading tracks from their ancestors, and this is knowledge that every child learns from his father. What is fascinating is the combination of a legacy from the past and the most advanced technology that enables Homeland Security to enforce the law with a wide range of resources.

There is a formidable human factor in the Shadow Wolves team, since members belong to one of the most famous Native American nations. A story about their difficult work, including the angle of this unusual fight against crime, is extremely attractive to readers in my country who loved the western movies in their childhood and still have a passion for the Old West. This is a perfect example of a "hook." It is a mixture, unusual and alive, of the possibilities of life on the border, painted in shocking colors. At the same time, by roaming the Tohono O'odham Reservation, I could clearly see that, while the area is an often lethal obstacle for the migrants crossing the desert, it can be a formidable ally for the smugglers. I would define it as the perfect synthesis of all the events happening along the US-Mexico frontier.

In a news story like the one on the Shadow Wolves, four factors have particular relevance and make the subject appealing to readers in Italy: the human factor, the role played by men of different cultures (Native Americans, illegal immigrants, smugglers, outlaws); the geographical and meteorological conditions, with extreme heat, temperature drops at night, water deprivation, difficult desert trails, and dangerous animals representing the dramatic background of the narrative; the crime, with this area representing a perfect "case study," since it is the site of multiple aspects of illegal activities, intertwined with the immigration issue; and the historical component, the Native-American tradition, the symbolism of the border. The reactions from my readers to stories such as this one are not homogeneous. Readers with a specific interest follow the tricks of the criminal activities, while the general audience is more fascinated by the landscape and the setting of the stories I report, since Arizona and California always conjure up the images we can see in the movies. A reader who was studying the trackers' technique in Italy asked me very specific questions. Some are critical, mainly wondering why an Italian reader should care about the Mexican border, while several other readers show interest in Mexico (not only about immigration) and about the tragic events along the border. Finding a "hook" for all of them becomes all the more important.

A Special Correspondent under and above Ground

Another startling story I have been monitoring over the years is the use of tunnels by criminal and terrorist organizations, guerrillas, and governments. Sophisticated tunnels or bunkers and camouflaged underground shelters are a constant at crisis points. North Korea, Burma, Gaza, southern Lebanon, Iran, and obviously the American-Mexican border are political regions where tunnels are massively present, for different reasons. All the data, images, and videos that I have been systematically collecting since the year 2000 highlight three elements: the tunnels are built with a smart technique; it is very hard to neutralize them; and they can be used for multiple purposes.

Three of my border trips were focused on covering the issue of tunnels along the Mexican-American border, particularly in San Diego-Otay Mesa (California) and in Nogales (Arizona). Each time my tour was guided by Border Patrol agents. They were showing me improvements in the construction of these underground structures. I constantly file in my archive the new tunnels found, their locations, and the innovations that I find through the newspapers mailing lists, and the Google alerts, and then I make a comparative analysis with illegal tunnels in other areas of the world in crisis.

The same format works in the sky—for example, the ultralight planes the smugglers use to ship the drugs. Apparently, in 2012, there was some evidence that the Piper aircrafts shipped illegal immigrants, too. My studies of the aerial dimension of the matter led me to the region of Douglas and El Centro-Yuma, in Arizona. My interest is not driven by specific events or current circumstances but reflects ideas about future trends. Even in limited cases, the illegal use of ultralight aircraft to cross the border offers a good story to write, with the adventure on the flying machine over the border and the pilots corrupted by the smugglers. US Representative Gabrielle Giffords of Arizona, who was shot by a mentally ill man in Tucson in 2011 during a public debate outside a mall, wanted Congress to pass the bill she proposed before resigning because of the health consequences of the attack, a law to strengthen the fight against the ultralight planes of the narcos.

Finally, there is the ocean. The "American ocean" has two coasts, the Atlantic with the Caribbean and the Pacific. The sea opens great opportunities for immigration and smuggling, so it is worthwhile to research maritime routes. In the San Diego area, smugglers often succeed in overcoming the strict controls set up by customs officials. The smugglers take a risk; they can have access to information and can predict what might happen. The US coast is at a close range. I had the chance to work on the maritime dimension on the California shores, but the same thing is happening in Cuba and in Haiti. The numbers of refugees has dropped over the past decade, but people still die while fleeing despair. I research with interest the narcos' "minisubs," the semi-submarines that are made in Colombia and Ecuador and then used to transfer cocaine to the coast of Mexico, Honduras and Nicaragua. I have included in my archive a huge file on "minisubs," with photos released during the investigation of the Key West Task Force in Miami and Colombia.

CONCLUSION

In conclusion, I would like to share a reflection about the tools of my job as a special, Washington-based correspondent for one of Europe's leading newspapers. A good combination of my archive and daily events is the key. A great many files and an always-growing database on the issue of the border allow me to cover any topic at any required moment, especially if the information available is scarce. Time is even more of the essence since I am writing for an Italian newspaper, nine hours ahead of the Arizona time zone, so I need to work in a great hurry. My archive helps me find the most detailed news in case of emergency. In times of budget restrictions, my archive can also save me a long-haul trip.

The border is hard, fascinating, and mysterious because of its contradictions. It represents a crossing point of hope, endurance, pain, atrocities. A few miles on a dry land can mean either life or death. Politics and individual stories melt and influence each other in the same dimension. Every time I travel to the frontier, I always learn more and find something new about the immigrants trying to escape from misery, facing a new and unknown world on the other side of the fence, and about the organizations inventing new sophisticated techniques to exploit and manipulate this gigantic movement of people.

This is the reason why a journalist must be there to tell the truth.

NOTES

1. Guido Olimpio, "Viaggio con i samaritani", *Corriere della Sera*, May 21, 2013, 15.
2. Guido Olimpio, "Il museo dei clandestini," *Corriere della Sera*, December 12, 2009, 15.
3. Guido Olimpio, "Le tracce dei narcos," *Magazine del Corriere della Sera*, February 20, 2012, 34–35.

17 Immigration
A Minefield for Journalists

Laure Mandeville
Le Figaro[1]

Immigration has become one of the central political debates of our time. That is true in the United States and maybe even more so in Europe. The massive flows of immigrants, both legal and illegal, are rapidly changing the face of both America and Europe—a reality that calls for serious journalistic and academic work. In that sense, this book, which attempts a reflection of how journalists are dealing with the issue, is very timely. Reporting on immigration issues is needed. But it is certainly one of the most difficult exercises a journalist might have to deal with. Why is it so? Because the topic of immigration is a very politically charged issue, which carries very emotional reactions and beliefs.

Whether we are talking about the United States, France, the Netherlands, Norway, Britain, or other European countries, the subject of immigration immediately brings forth many ideological prejudices and suspicions. It triggers very polarized visions of its consequences for the country of immigration.[2] Many observers see it as an exclusively positive phenomenon that enriches the fabric of the nation, is economically unavoidable, and should be supported whatever the social costs. In France, the formula used is that "immigration is a chance for the country." A common approach is to portray those who question the positive benefits of massive immigration as racist and xenophobic. The opponents to immigration tend to stress the dangers of uncontrolled immigration and the political, cultural, economic, and social challenges of a multicultural society.

Immigration is such a hot topic—a minefield, I would even say—that very often the persons a journalist is going to talk to in order to get information will be defending a cause or pursuing a mission, rather than providing an objective picture, making attempts at "honest journalism" (objectivity does not exist!) a daily challenge.

In fact, the debate on immigration is particularly sensitive because it is unavoidably associated with the question of racism, as discussed in Popkova's chapter. Where is the frontier between thinking of uncontrolled immigration as a potential threat and being xenophobic? Is it journalistically and politically acceptable to even raise this question? The worry is always in the background, and it should be. But should it prevent us from even raising questions and attempting to see the whole picture?

In Europe, the old wounds of the colonial past nurture the suspicion and poison the debate—particularly in France and Great Britain, two former empires. In France, many associate anti-immigration parties with the anti-Semitic ultraright parties of the 1930s. Because its historical leader Jean Marie Le Pen indulged infamously in anti-Semitic remarks for many years, the National Front in France, an ultraright party that remains the only party in France to advocate strong limitations on immigration, has continued to be presented and perceived by the mainstream political parties as neofascist, despite its partial evolution, leaving out the reason why this organization has become so popular.

Other parties have cautiously avoided the question of immigration—even though France's current socialist foreign minister, Laurent Fabius, once acknowledged that the National Front's immigration approach offered bad answers to real questions—letting Le Pen (and now his daughter Marine) literally hijack the debate, as Vincent's chapter notes. Raising the question of illegal immigration has for a long time been a taboo, both in the press and in politics, a reality mirrored in many European countries. It has driven journalists to cover immigration mainly through the lens of the humanitarian catastrophe that is occurring in the Mediterranean Sea every day, when thousands of desperate Africans embark on frail boats to reach the "promised land of Europe." These are dramatic and important stories, but should they be the quasi-exclusive way to cover immigration? These questions have been bothering some journalists covering immigration, if silently.

As the worries of the European core population have grown and the difficulties of integrating an ever-growing immigrant population have become more obvious, things have gradually changed.[3] Some intellectuals and politicians (like Sarkozy on the right) have entered the debate, albeit with reluctance and with risks. In the Netherlands, for instance, there was an abrupt change of mood and coverage, both on the right and on the left of the political spectrum, after the death of the libertarian politician Pim Fortuyn, who was pointing to the dangers of keeping open the gates of uncontrolled immigration.[4] Articles started appearing about the failure of multiculturalism and about the immigrants of the second generation who preferred to marry a wife from very rural and conservative areas of Morocco rather than a modern Dutch Muslim girl, raising the spectrum of an endless immigration process through family unification that was bound to change the face of Dutch culture in the long term. These trends led to the voting into law of tight immigration legislation, designed to limit family reunion and to avoid an abusive interpretation of the concept (the very loose interpretation of family reunion accelerated the flow of immigrants, making it the largest source of immigration, even though it was originally designed as a guest worker program). In the case of France, the Left, which is dominant both in the press and in academia, has basically continued to present immigration as a nondebate, avoiding the question of tensions created by immigration and the question of the transformation of French society, which is on the minds of so many. It has created a big vacuum, which is dangerous because it is filled with hearsay, extremist Internet content, and false journalism, creating a huge gap between segments of the population directly confronted with immigration and the elite.

There is an elephant in the room, but no one wants to discuss it.

Interestingly, some of the ones who have made the attempt to start this discussion in France are Jewish intellectuals, like Alain Finkelkraut and Eric Zemmour. Their evolution is linked to the debate on the place of Islam in French society—although Muslims are not the only new immigrants. Because he is Jewish, Finkelkraut, an intellectual, who was always on the left, was at first unlikely to be accused of being racist. But since he jumped into the debate about France's capacity to retain its stability under the pressure of multiple identity groups, he has come under very strong attack—thinking against the mainstream on immigration condemns you to be intellectually "excommunicated," he noted during a conference on the topic at Georgetown University in 2010.

One of the many problems facing the journalists who cover immigration concerns statistics, which are at minimum imprecise but are used by the Right, the Left, and the ultraright for their own political purposes, a problem noted by both Chauzy and Grobet in this volume. How many immigrants are entering the country legally and illegally each year? The data remain extremely blurry and are open to deliberate manipulation. Michèle Tribalat, a well-respected demographer, who has criticized what she sees as a biased and ideological treatment of data by some of her fellow demographers, got into a tough dispute with the newspaper *Le Monde* over an article it published about "France's new face."[5] The paper was arguing that immigration had stabilized over the years. She said that the starting and ending dates used to demonstrate this assertion were a deliberate attempt to mask the 25 percent increase in the number of immigrants that had in fact occurred between 1987 and 2002. In a piece published in the journal *Marianne* a few days after *Le Monde*'s article, with many figures and data supporting her argument, the demographer accused the journalist Anne Chemin "of having deliberately truncated data," leading "to total nonsense."[6] "That *Le Monde,* usually presented as the paper of reference, engaged in such a montage is disheartening," wrote Tribalat. "This article of the 4th of December shows that good feelings and the pedagogical intent to straighten out public opinion that does not think correctly lead to catastrophe. They lead to trampling on the basic deontology of any self-respecting journalist, whose duty it is to inform, not to console or reassure. *Le Monde* has just demonstrated that data can be manipulated and, in a result that it most probably never wanted, comforts those who think that the media do not tell the truth on the question of immigration."

In her book, *Les yeux grands fermés*,[7] Tribalat, who defines herself as politically on the left and has also written a book against the ideology of the National Front, delivers a critical vision of the way immigration is generally perceived and presented, stressing the massive flows of immigrants linked to family reunification and questioning the idea according to which immigration boosts the economic development of the receiving countries. She also warns that the demographics of territories are hardly studied and views the quasi shutting down of this field of investigation as way to avoid a discussion that would give credence to the pessimists, by revealing the increasing concentration of immigrants and their ensuing difficulties to integrate.

ARE THE CHALLENGES IN THE UNITED STATES DIFFERENT?

The American context is obviously different from that in France and in the rest of Europe. America is a new nation, made of immigrants, that thinks of itself as such. There is still a deeply rooted faith in the virtues of immigration as a way to regenerate society and to bring new energy and ideas to the fabric of the nation. The worries are related more to the question of the border, with economic and national security issues like drug trafficking linked with massive immigration. Moreover, the identity argument appears less important, because the flow of immigrants comes from Latin America, mainly a Christian region. The question of the capacity of Islam to be congruent with democracy, which has become so important in Europe in the discussion of immigration (notably in places like Denmark during the debate of the Mohammed cartoons or in France during the debate on the veil or the burqa), is marginal in the United States, where Muslims represent only 0.8 percent of the population, rather than close to 10 percent, as they do in France, Belgium, and the Netherlands.

But we still have the same fog that seems to surround the discussion of data, the same tendency to cover immigration mainly from the point of individual immigrants' stories—the same reluctance to tell the story from the point of view of the people who speak in favor of a tightening of immigration laws.

THE CASE OF SB 1070

I was able to observe some of these processes during the discussion of Arizona's SB 1070 law, a law approved, according to local elected officials, to fill the vacuum left by federal authorities in terms of addressing illegal immigration (Figure 17.1).[8]

When going to Arizona, I was able to observe the political circumstances under which the Republican leadership decided on a tightening of the controls of potential immigrants—apparently to boost its political image, which was rating very low with the public.[9] The law, giving the police leeway to check on the identity of people if they have reasonable doubt concerning their immigration status, generated a very heated debate in America because

Figure 17.1 Arizona, a Border of Dangers and Passions (Courtesy of *Le Figaro*)

of the potential for racial profiling. It was very interesting to observe, because the French have a different political culture—the French are more in favor of government controls and prerogatives, what we call the "regalian" powers, and the practice of checking on the identity of people is very common. I accompanied a police officer on a ride at night, in Tucson, to get a better sense of his understanding of the law and its consequences. His approach was very pragmatic, far from the heated political debate that was taking place at the time. On one hand, he was shocked by the accusations of potential racial profiling, saying that police officers were trained not to racially profile and would not do so even under SB 1070. But he was also expressing very strong doubts about the efficiency of the legislation, saying that it would create less trust in the Latino community toward police officers and therefore would destroy the capacity of law enforcement to prevent crime. The story, however, was never published because of lack of space.

As all reporters covering the border do, I went to the other side of the border, in Mexico, to meet some illegal immigrants who had just been deported by border patrols. It was very interesting and moving to talk to them about their past, their desperate longing to cross again despite risks of getting caught or even dying in the desert. But I also went to meet with some Arizona ranchers, who live on the border and see hundreds of illegals crossing their property in the desert. The ones I met were not racist or extreme in their views but expressed a mix of pity for the clandestine travelers and worries for their daily safety. They were angry at the federal government for "pretending," according to them, to solve the problem, and they questioned the efficiency of border patrols, walls, and electronic surveillance. They pointed to the special status of Tucson, the city nearby, as a magnet attracting ever more migrants, because the firms there were happy to use low-paid labor. They expressed views that are not often published in American papers, although a majority of Americans supported SB 1070, according to most polls.[10]

Most newspapers, probably out of fear of appearing unsupportive of immigrants, tend to avoid features on the mood of the general public. When they cover opposition to illegal immigration, they tend to create portraits of more caricatural figures like Maricopa County Sheriff Joe Arpaio—and I did that as well! (Figure 17.2)—or even racist "minutemen" chasing illegals on the border.[11]

These extremists exist, and it is right to write about them because they nurture a potentially dangerous narrative of "us and them." But is it right to avoid covering the "in-between majority" that is spontaneously and historically favorable to immigration but also has serious reservations about and criticisms of the way the issue is handled at the political and economic level? Again, as in the case of Europe, a more diversified journalistic approach would certainly inform us better about what is going on.

What is sure is that the mission of journalists is not easy given the way political leaders tend to stick to a very careful script when expressing their views. Democrats need the Latino voices, and that likely conditions their

jeudi 8 juillet 2010 LE FIGARO

16 | trait & PORTRAIT

Joe Arpaïo, shérif version Far West

Ce flic de l'Ouest, provocateur et populaire, n'a pas attendu la loi anticlandestins adoptée en Arizona pour appliquer ses méthodes musclées.

PAR LAURE MANDEVILLE
ENVOYÉE SPÉCIALE À PHOENIX (ARIZONA)

Avec son bagou et son côté cow-boy paternaliste, Joe Arpaïo n'a peur ni du mauvais goût ni des idées simples : « Les autres s'indignent, moi j'agis », aime-t-il répéter. ALESS. FRANK/A. AP

Il est 7 h 30 ce matin-là quand le shérif Joe Arpaïo déboule toutes voiles dehors avec quelques voitures de police dans une banlieue nord de Phoenix en Arizona, pour l'une de ces chasses aux immigrants illégaux qui lui ont tissé une réputation de « flic le plus impitoyable d'Amérique ». Tandis qu'une vingtaine de « ses gars », guns (pistolets) à la ceinture, investissent la petite entreprise de construction d'emballages plastiques dont ils surveillent les activités « depuis plusieurs mois », Joe, 78 ans, large visage, cheveux gris tissés sur le côté et bedaine en avant, fait son numéro médiatique du jour, planté devant les micros des journalistes qu'il a convoqués. « Les autres s'indignent, moi j'agis », lance-t-il, ravi d'avoir du public, malgré l'heure matinale et le soleil de plomb qui écrase déjà la ville. « J'espère que vous n'allez pas vous laisser gagner par le poison politiquement correct de vos confrères », glisse-t-il en aparté à une jolie stagiaire envoyée par l'*Arizona Daily Star*.

Arpaïo explique que ses hommes ont arrêté cinq ouvriers en situation irrégulière sur les onze présents dans l'entreprise ce jour-là, « soit presque la moitié de l'effectif ! ». Il souligne que ces hommes ont été appréhendés pour avoir volé des cartes de sécurité sociale, qui leur ont permis de bénéficier d'avantages sociaux dont ils étaient privés en tant que clandestins. « Usurpation d'identité, c'est un délit grave, insiste-t-il. On devrait me donner une décoration pour libérer des places au profit des travailleurs américains, au lieu de m'accuser de racisme, ajoute le shérif, goguenard. Je ne fais qu'appliquer la loi ! Et je ne crois pas une seconde aux contes de nos politiciens quand ils affirment que les Américains ne prendront pas les boulots des illégaux malgré la crise économique. Simplement, les entreprises devront les payer plus cher au lieu d'exploiter de malheureux étrangers. »

Il explique que la nouvelle loi contre l'immigration illégale, que le Parlement d'Arizona vient de faire passer, suscitant une vaste polémique à travers les États-Unis et, hier, la réaction judiciaire de Washington (lire page 5), va l'aider dans son combat. « Jusqu'ici, quand je pénétrais dans une entreprise, je ne pouvais contrôler que les gens dont j'étais sûr qu'ils avaient enfreint la loi. Désormais, je pourrai demander un contrôle d'identité de tous les autres et les emmener en prison si leur statut n'est pas en règle. Ce n'est pas une question de racisme, c'est une question de respect de la loi ! »

Un fils d'immigrés italiens

Il balaie d'un revers de main l'argument d'un risque de « chasse au faciès » que mettent en avant les adversaires de la nouvelle législation, censée entrer en vigueur le 29 juillet si elle n'est pas remise en cause par la justice. « Pourquoi serions-nous moins compétents que les *garde-frontières* ? J'ai cent officiers de police qui travaillent sur ces dossiers et ils sont très professionnels. Ils ne vont pas se mettre à arrêter n'importe qui dans la rue sous prétexte qu'il a la peau foncée, c'est interdit par la loi. » Beaucoup d'autres officiers de police, comme par exemple le shérif du comté voisin de Tucson, Clarence Dupnik, pensent au contraire que ce risque de chasse au faciès existe et que cette nouvelle loi va les couper de la communauté hispanique, rendant leur travail plus délicat.

Arpaïo réplique qu'il n'a jamais été pris en défaut de racisme, même si ses ennemis ont tenté plusieurs fois de le faire tomber. Une enquête fédérale lancée par l'Administration Obama est pourtant en cours. « Ils cherchent mais ils ne trouvent rien ! », rigole-t-il, sûr d'être inébranlonnable parce que « la population me soutient ».

Joe Arpaïo n'a pas toujours été la bête noire des organisations de droits de l'homme et des libéraux. « Il est sans aucun doute l'homme le plus puissant de l'État, plus puissant que le gouverneur », dit-il. Il a longtemps été un simple fonctionnaire fédéral, passé par les services d'immigration et l'agence de lutte contre les drogues. C'est en 1992 qu'il s'est installé en Arizona, où il s'est porté candidat au poste électif de shérif du puissant comté de Maricopa. Son bagou, son côté cow-boy paternaliste prêt à protéger de sa forte stature les honnêtes gens, a séduit un électorat qui, dans ces terres de l'Ouest, continue à apprécier la force et le muscle. Arpaïo, qui n'a peur ni du mauvais goût ni des idées simples, a été élu avec près de 80 % des suffrages, et réélu cinq fois de suite avec des scores écrasants. Loin de lui aliéner l'électorat, ses méthodes provocatrices, ses coups de gueule contre Washington et ses barrettes de cravate en forme de colt sont justifiés, notamment par les retraités en quête du soleil qui viennent s'installer en Arizona et s'habituent mal à la présence massive des hispaniques (30 % de la population). Pas étonnant, dans ces conditions, qu'il ait fini par se prendre pour John Wayne.

Caleçons roses pour les détenus

Provocateur et de plus en plus mégalo, Arpaïo a créé un concept de « prison de tentes » à ciel ouvert, sur lequel il n'a cessé de communiquer pour peaufiner son image de fer. Installée en plein désert, dans une banlieue de Phoenix, la cité de tentes du shérif aligne des rangées de lits en fer, protégés que de simples bâches. La température montant à 45-50°C pendant l'été, y séjourner pendant la saison chaude est redoutable pour les prisonniers, mais Arpaïo a placé des partout ceux qui expliquent que « les soldats qui risquent leur vie en Irak n'ont pas de meilleures conditions, alors qu'eux n'ont pas enfreint la loi », dit-il.

Il est aussi très fier de « caleçons roses » et des draps et serviettes de la même couleur imposés aux détenus, même si ce détail humiliant a suscité une levée de boucliers dans l'opinion. « Je suis qu'ils détestent cette couleur, c'est pour cela que je l'ai choisie. Je ne suis pas là pour leur faire plaisir. Mon but est de tout faire pour qu'ils n'aient pas envie de se retrouver à nouveau en taule », dit-il.

C'est en partant du même principe qu'il a réduit le coût des rations alimentaires, passé de 2,50 dollars (la moyenne américaine) à 39 cents. Oscar, un Mexicain de 43 ans, rencontré sous une tente où il purge une peine pour conduite en état d'ivresse, dit que la nourriture est tellement mauvaise qu'il est constamment pris de coliques. « Arpaïo est un méchant homme, il déteste les Mexicains », lâche-t-il, allongé sur son lit, en épongeant son front. Le gardien de prison Dan Campbell précise que le shérif a supprimé toutes les chaînes de cinéma et de sport que les prisonniers peuvent habituellement regarder dans les autres prisons américaines, sauf une chaîne de cuisine, une chaîne météo et la chaîne parlementaire C-SPAN. Enchanté de l'humour noir du shérif, pour lequel il ne cache pas son admiration, le gardien pointe du doigt le mirador qui domine la prison de tentes, où une enseigne clignotante indique qu'« il y a des places », la nuit venue. « Si vous n'aimez pas votre peine, ne commettez pas de crime », dit aussi un poster affiché sur un mur de son bureau.

Toutes ces provocations valent à Arpaïo de solides ennemis dans les rangs du Parti démocrate, de la presse et des organisations de droits de l'homme. Mais le journaliste local Stephen Lemons le compare à une « sorte de roi », omniprésent et difficile à déstabiliser. « C'est sans aucun doute l'homme le plus puissant de l'État, plus puissant que le gouverneur », dit-il, invoquant la formidable base de pouvoir que représentent les structures de maintien de l'ordre sous son autorité. Arpaïo compte d'ailleurs se représenter en 2012. « J'aurai 80 ans, et alors ? Je me sens en pleine forme », lance-t-il.

Il est régulièrement réélu avec 80 % des voix. Pas étonnant qu'il ait fini par se prendre pour John Wayne

Figure 17.2   A Far West Sheriff (Courtesy of *Le Figaro*)

vision of the topic of immigration. Republicans respond to the worries of their electorate, which has been asking for reinforcement of the border, but have been under pressure from the corporate world, which was until recently unwilling to tackle illegal immigration because it provided cheap labor. The attitudes of the Republican Party are bound to change as it tries to engage the Latino community and to find new approaches to immigration reform, looking ahead to the 2016 election. But it is not certain to create a franker discussion of the issue; quite the contrary, in fact.

What is clear is that there is a real internal debate going on inside journalists' heads and their guts about what they should write about. Covering immigration and integration stories in the United States has been from that point of view extremely interesting for me, because of the parallels and differences that exist between our models. The United States is a multicultural society, and, in that regard, it is interesting to French society, which is rapidly becoming one. There are lessons to be drawn from the exceptionally successful American collective experience of different ethnic groups living together, bonded by a minimal definition of integration: a patriotic consensus and economic opportunity. But I have also been struck by the raw racial or religious conflicts that can arise between communities in the United States. The persistence of racial tensions and discrimination in America that I was able to perceive when covering, for instance, the murder of the young black teenager Trayvon Martin and the tense racial situation in the little town of Sanford, Florida, was quite an eye opener to the challenges of multiculturalism and therefore immigration, even in a country like the United States.[12] America is by no means a multiracial Eden—neither is France! One more reason for an honest and thorough coverage of immigration and integration challenges.

NOTES

1. The point of view expressed is the responsibility of the author and does not reflect the view of *Le Figaro*. It is the point of view of a "generalist"—I am the bureau chief for *Le Figaro* in Washington—who is by no means a specialist on immigration.
2. See articles cited in this chapter for coverage of the United States, France, and the Netherlands; for an example of my reporting from Great Britain, see Laure Mandeville, "Londres s'interroge sur le multiculturalisme," *Le Figaro*, September 6, 2004, 6.
3. Laure Mandeville, "Les Européens se demandent comment intégrer l'islam," *Le Figaro*, July 11, 2002, 4.
4. See the following, all by Laure Mandeville and in *Le Figaro*: "Les Néerlandais bousculent le débat sur l'islam," November 27, 2005, 6; "Banlieues: les Pays-Bas redoutent la contagion," November 23, 2005, 6; "L'islamisme brise le modèle hollandais," November 10, 2004, 6; "Les lézardes béantes du modèle hollandais," June 20, 2002, 5; "Ayaan, candidate musulmane éprise de Voltaire," January 21, 2003, 4; "L'héritage populiste de Fortuyn plane sur les législatives," January 22, 2003, 3.

5. Anne Chemin, "Le nouveau visage de la France, terre d'immigration," *Le Monde*, December 3, 2009.

6. "Michèle Tribalat au Monde : 'Vérifiez vos chiffres sur l'immigration,'" *Marianne*, December 9, 2009.

7. Michèle Tribalat, *Les yeux grands fermés* (Paris: Denoël, 2010).

8. Laure Mandeville, "Arizona, frontière de tous les dangers et de toutes les passions," *Le Figaro*, May 27, 2010, 8.

9. Laure Mandeville, "L'immigration au coeur de la primaire en Arizona," *Le Figaro*, February 28, 2012, 2.

10. A Rasmussen poll administered at the moment of the signing of the law showed support at 60 percent, an Angus Reid Report at 71 percent, a *New York Times*-CBS report at 60 percent of support, and a Fox News report at 61 percent. In 2012, according to a new poll quoted by the Arizona Central, 65 percent of Americans still supported SB 1070.

11. Laure Mandeville, "Joe Arpaïo, shérif version Far West," *Le Figaro*, July 8, 2010, 16.

12. Laure Mandeville, "L'Amérique d'Obama renoue avec les tensions raciales," *Le Figaro*, April 13, 2012, 2.

Conclusion
Understanding Border Journalism and Its Sociopolitical Impact

Giovanna Dell'Orto and Vicki L. Birchfield

With immigration continuing to make headline news both in the United States and in the European Union in the 2010s, raising critical issues for Western democracies and global movements, this book sought to bring scholars and practitioners into dialogue to shed new light on the role of the media in immigration debates, with the goal of illuminating *why* news stories about immigration are what they are in the transatlantic space. Using a multiple-stakeholder approach, this book did not seek to pit one set of "experts" against the other or provide either a how-to manual for immigration journalism or an advocacy political argument. On the contrary, it created a conversation so that journalists, human rights advocates, and scholars could explore original research and, crucially, experience firsthand some of the complexities and structural constraints on the ground, providing the conceptual and methodological benefits of synergetic, reflective work.

Many studies have usefully researched how news media tend to distort and caricature immigration coverage and how polarizing media discourse tends to impede workable solutions to an international challenge of urgent human, political, social, and economic gravity. The first two parts of this book strengthen and update this scholarship by providing a focused, comparative perspective on these challenges at the southern borders of the United States and of the European Union. The original research explores links among immigration, multicultural policies, and national identity; successes and failures of entry and integration policies; challenges to human rights protection; genre differences in US and European migration coverage; the foundations of international newswire reporting on immigration; and the new influence of audiences and non-Western media on immigration journalism.

Parts III and IV of the book then substantially advance and refine our understanding of these phenomena through exceptionally honest and in-depth assessments of the structural, economic, ethical, and logistical constraints that do so much to shape how journalists cover immigration—described by the journalists themselves on the front lines. The candid portraits of daily life under deadline reveal just how news narratives emerge from sets of challenges that range from the mundane—tight car rental and train travel budgets, bulky and tech-heavy photographic equipment, tricks to draw readers' attention—to the literally vital—the increasing number of assassinations of border reporters. Our ultimate mutually reinforcing goal is to encourage more realistic understanding of journalism in the academy and more critical reflection on practice in professional journalism—and both in converging but still different environments on either side of the Atlantic.

It is certainly our hope that readers across disciplines and practices might derive from these analyses normative conclusions about the challenges and opportunities for reporting about immigration on two continents today and that reporters on these endangered beats might benefit from sharing their experiences with colleagues across the ocean. The main purpose of our effort, however, is to create a valuable and rare tool to overcome the major challenges in studying practitioners and their texts, trying to go beyond what might be taken for granted (and therefore be unexpressed in both content and interviews) by journalists. Practitioners and scholars worked together to reflectively analyze the creation and negotiation of meaning in immigration news and did so in two specific comparative contexts, the southern borders of the United States and of the European Union.

Ultimately, this model could apply to all investigations of the role of the news media in policy and public debates informed by the assumption that the world as portrayed in the mass media helps shape the contours of public perceptions of major political and social issues and therefore of proposed and implemented policies. But immigration in the second decade of the 21st century is an especially critical question because the decision of who belongs "in the circle of we" assumes new relevance in multicultural democracies in an era of unprecedented economic and communicative interconnectedness—and of crisis for watchdog journalism. In the United States, the unavoidable realities of the changing electoral demographics (particularly the proved strength of Latino voters) and the economic unease (with the subsequent plummeting in border apprehensions) have created a realistic chance for a much-delayed overhaul of federal immigration legislation in 2013. In Europe, the eurozone's meltdown and political unrest and the ferment on the Mediterranean's southern shores will likely continue to create both populist and humanitarian pressures on migration and integration management strategies. And all of this is happening under the decreasingly watchful guard of mass media that often lack the financial, time, and human resources to do more than cover the latest boat arrivals, desert deaths, and politicians' inflammatory pronouncements.

Despite historical, political, and professional differences, the similarities in the journalism of immigration in Lampedusa and Nogales, in Paris and Phoenix, in Calabria and Tamaulipas are the most surprising and significant contribution of this research. Our journalist contributors provide empirical evidence about the various aspects and levels of the decision-making process that shapes news stories, which in turn influence public discourse, often with consequences that scholars and human rights practitioners critique. Their experiences and self-reflections go a long way to offer fresh explanations of some of the consistent scholarly findings in the literature and in the first two parts of this book. Together, scientific investigations and professional analyses suggest that the impact of media coverage of migration at the US and EU southern borders revolves around three major conceptualizations: the interplay of national identity and integration; the visibility of migratory phenomena; and the crucial, fraught choice of news sources.

THE NATION AND THE IMMIGRANT

The book's first chapter delves straight into a controversial fact that news media, as many journalists explain, are reluctant to tackle because it represents what Mandeville bluntly calls the ultimate minefield: immigration is forcing host societies to reimagine their national identity, an exercise fraught with natural discomfort that can be easily manipulated by dangerous populist extremism. Citrin's analysis of public opinion data from Europe and North America shows a lurking fear of immigrants "not like us" who come through the southern borders and an association between patriotism and anti-immigrant sentiment, with backlash following non-assimilationist multicultural policies. This fear—which comes standard in all human beings, as Stagliano mercilessly argues—could explain why the question of who belongs in the nation looms so large in public and media discourse. The very visibility of ethnic, racial, and religious difference becomes central, pushing the numerically much more relevant legal, high-skilled, Western internal migration off the front pages and often even the back ones. As Vincent narrates, the French, without the reference point of a real frontier such as exists in the United States and Italy, point fingers at Muslim North Africans as the "different ones," and it is the journalist's task to show how diverse layers peacefully exist across French society—or point out when they do not, a story that Mandeville suggests is even harder to publish.

The transatlantic comparison is especially stark here. Because of history and policy, immigrants to the United States merge comparatively seamlessly into the country's self-understanding as a haven for tired, poor, and huddled masses, as well as into the American economy, where the foreign born are employed at a much higher percentage than in European economies. In Al Jazeera's broadcasts or in *The Arizona Republic,* the typical US immigrant featured is like González's SB 1070 refugee, who is hard at work hours after a grueling cross-country relocation. Stagliano's 24-hour portrait of Italy's immigrant labor force could be a parallel—if it were part of the popular media discourse instead of a pointed critique to it. Perhaps most critical, immigrants in the United States are something else that they never seem to be in Europe—future voters. As Schain argues, there is a direct link between the more welcoming US policies and US politicians' courting of the "minority vote," while European political parties seem to increasingly thrive on restrictionist rhetoric that rejects cultural diversity. It is fascinating to note the cavil that anti-immigration advocates use in the United States—the focus on legality, which of course is another way to draw a very plausible though uselessly simplistic distinction between the immigrants who belong in the nation and those who do not. (Just how similar in practice Europe's blatantly racial and religious discontent and America's more impersonal illegality disapproval are becomes clear in legislation, such as Arizona's SB1070, that asks law enforcement to make inquiries based on "suspicion of illegal status," a hardly visible characteristic.)

These political and policy links between national identity and attitudes toward immigration, which form the philosophical basis to entry policies and the factual basis to integration ones, appear reinforced and reflected in media coverage because, as virtually all journalists somewhat despondently argue, they do need to cover major political pronouncements. Again, the transatlantic contrast is evident: as Zamith and Popkova found, mainstream media and their online-engaged readers privilege discourses of cultural and national identity in Europe and of border and law enforcement in North America. The word choice of readers posting comments to immigration articles in *The Guardian* as opposed to the *New York Times* is revealing: the first argued that the majority of Europeans opposed "unwanted" immigrants who came to live off welfare though they despised the host societies, while the latter felt that most Americans resented "illegal" immigrants who engaged in criminal activities. Bennett and Zamith found that even Al Jazeera, which prides itself on providing a more "humanitarian" approach to news, reflected the cultural debate in Italy and the security and border issues in the United States, though it is remarkable that the Arabic-language network ignored the advocacy of its English-language counterpart, perhaps a reflection of Qatar's own less-than-ideal treatment of foreign workers.

Indeed, humanitarian advocates such as Chauzy and Appave of the International Organization for Migration and Grobet of the United Nations Alliance of Civilizations argue that more "positive" media coverage, with an emphasis less on differences and more on the richness of diversity, is essential to fair management of migration, social cohesion, and, in Grobet's striking words, "conflict prevention." Some of their recommendations echo the journalists' own frustrations at being played by politicians whose rhetoric about national identity and immigration can be destabilizing and yet makes news. Vincent's and Mandeville's lament at the inability of the French Left to effectively counter Sarkozy's strategy—and therefore their difficulty in providing a balanced perspective without editorializing in straight reporting—raises a critical question: What can media do? How can they break through the political agenda while remaining neutral observers?

VISIBLE AND INVISIBLE IMMIGRANTS

One answer that this book's findings and reflections suggest is paradoxically to observe better and to look out for the invisible, for what is rhetorically or literally out of sight—with the recognition that this is an increasingly unpopular and, along the US-Mexican border, lethal task. The visual simplification of the immigration discourse is linked to the questioning of national identity. Zamith's analysis of newswire copy—the backbone and agenda-setter of international journalism—found that the issue of immigration was treated almost exclusively by The Associated Press and Agence France-Presse as a Latino matter in the United States and as a Muslim or North African matter in France. In Italy, Hooper and Staglianò found the public riveted on the boat arrivals in Lampedusa and all too willing to ignore not only the vessels that never made it ashore but also the immigrant presence easily observable on public transportation, in public parks, and at family tables, among apple orchards in the Dolomites and at tuna fisheries in Sicily. Hooper's denunciation of the silence shrouding the disappearance of migrant-laden vessels in the Mediterranean in the mid-1990s and today is disturbingly similar to Olsen's chilling description of dogged border reporters searching for their buddies' bones in the rugged southwestern deserts as Mexican cartels kidnap and murder journalists who dare pry into their affairs.

The price for bearing witness, for shining a spotlight on the inconvenient truths of migration, can be their own lives for reporters or dollars and euros for media managers who are increasingly reluctant to spend them on investigative stories with little popular value. Olimpio reminds us that journalists cannot even stop at making migration visible—they also have to make their audience look. There is a remarkable incongruity between the monumental research that this senior newspaper correspondent carries out to follow the minutest developments along the US-Mexican border and what he calls the "tricks" he has to use to draw his Italian readers' attention to critically important stories. Leading articles with eye-catching, pop-culture references to cowboys, pioneers, and "Apaches" can be a "pragmatic solution," as Olimpio puts it, to break through the indifference of editors and readers. Mandeville, another senior correspondent who traveled to Arizona, also reported on Phoenix's "Far West sheriff," while remaining critical of such "caricatures." Similarly, Stinellis argues that images of massive migrant exodus, with their strong biblical undertones, easily resonate with the public and thus with photojournalists.

More routinely, institutional and professional constraints serve as blinders to most media. As Hooper argues, highly visible, "concentrated" events—such as boatloads of people cramming a tiny, barren island—have all the elements of newsworthiness that ongoing, massive sociopolitical, economic, and demographic changes do not. With a revenue crisis affecting even the most prestigious news media, budgets shrink the most revealing, eyewitness coverage—so that Olimpio can make fewer trips to the Southwest,

González rents a bike and sleeps on a couch to report from Europe, and Stinellis studies weather bulletins in the Sicily Strait to figure out how to best deploy his lone island photographer. And then, of course, there are the logistical and technological constraints that affect in the most literal sense what the media can *show* us—seemingly trivial technical issues, like equipment portability and processing speed for photos, that have dramatic political and social consequences.

Stinellis vividly illustrates this point by showing how the digital revolution transformed the AP's visual coverage of two major migration flows to Italy, the Albanian exodus in 1991 and the ongoing "Arab Spring" movements. When transmission was laborious and photographers could grab only a few frames at the scene, the best photojournalists produced iconic pictures that synthesized an era and became its symbol, like the shot of an Italian policeman towering over an exhausted Albanian at his feet that provoked the ire of Italy's president. Today, digital equipment, remote connections, and 24/7 deadlines leave newswire photographers freer to shoot more and differently, capturing nuances and escaping some of the strictures of breaking news. The increased competition from and reliance on social media, however, also means that established journalistic institutions are losing their grip on public narratives and public debates, a disturbing development in light of this book's premise of the importance of media narratives. The technology and budget-driven retrenchment of big media can have devastating consequences in dangerous assignments—as Olsen explains, US border reporting cuts shift the burden of covering one of the world's most violent areas to much more vulnerable Mexican journalists, whose murders have steadily increased in recent years but who continue to investigate.

GETTING TO THE SOURCE AND BEYOND IT

Perhaps no aspect of journalism is more routine and yet more fraught with consequences than the choice of where to go and to whom to talk. As the two preceding sections illustrate, popular and political sentiment invoking simplistic definitions of national identity as well as the mere visibility of some facets of immigration can drive news coverage. The biggest challenge is to break through that straitjacket by reaching previously unheard voices and going beyond the microphone-ready glib statements by public officials. Benson argues that French media are better equipped to do so because of their "multigenre" formats, while the US narrative style tends to obscure structural complexities and ultimately limit the public's understanding. Our two French journalists, however, detail their own challenges, with Mandeville emphasizing the particular difficulty of quoting immigration opponents without falling into racism and xenophobia.

González's detailed and frank account of his search for real voices in Arizona and three European countries spotlights the importance of experiential journalism, of preparedness, and, crucially, of an unflinchingly ethical demeanor that protects the story's integrity and the sources involved. González's panic as his car and the caravan of undocumented migrants are approached by law enforcement is a dramatic example of the split-second decisions journalists have to make between chasing the story and minimizing harm.

Cárdenas describes similar difficulties in writing about "Mexodus" and the refugees from the Mexican cartel wars without further traumatizing or endangering them. Her challenges in investigating the multiple ramifications of the cartels' activities on both sides of the border point to the basic problem of finding reliable data, even from government sources. Adamant political pronouncements are another kind of challenge, particularly in Europe, because, as Vincent puts it, they do not leave a reporter a lot of choice in angles or perspectives. Paradoxically, she welcomed the receding of immigration news from the headlines in post-Sarkozy France as an opportunity to delve deeper into stories without immediate politicization. Both she and Stagliano argue that journalists should "enter the conversation" on immigration that roils politics in the transatlantic space. The consensus of all the journalists who wrote for this book seems to be that it was their role to challenge caricatures by persistent reporting, by digging through the inflamed rhetoric to show the reality of the immigrant experience, for both migrants and natives, in a way that audiences can and want to pay attention to.

CONCLUSIONS

In closing, it is worth remembering the touching *El Diario de Juárez* editorial that Olsen quotes: "What do you want from us?" What do we—scholars, advocates, reporters, citizens of democracies—want from journalism covering immigration at the southern borders of the United States and of the European Union?

This book has provided detailed analyses and candid self-reflections of journalistic practices in France, Italy, and the United States to help readers begin to answer that question. The challenges, ranging from the mundane to the existential, are profound and should not be dismissed with facile simplifications. Immigration does impact a nation's sense of identity and its subsequent enrichment or polarization, which in turn shape entry and integration policies. The more visibly different the "other" is, the more the spotlight will shine there, skewing media and public discourse, as well as policymaking, to the detriment of sophisticated and realistic reasoning. Decreasing resources, flagging public interest in nonspectacular news, and growing dangers conspire to reduce the import of public affairs journalism. The practitioners' observations are sobering reminders that constraints on the media make them fragile watchdogs—but their resolute attempts to continue to investigate one of the most difficult phenomena of our era also give hope for the possibility of more enlightened public discourse.

Index